This
band
has
no
past.

THIS BAND HAS NO PAST
HOW CHEAP TRICK BECAME CHEAP TRICK
BRIAN J. KRAMP

A Jawbone book
First edition 2022
Published in the UK and the USA by
Jawbone Press
Office G1
141–157 Acre Lane
London SW2 5UA
England
www.jawbonepress.com

ISBN 978-1-911036-87-6

Printed by Short Run Press, Exeter, Devon

1 2 3 4 5 26 25 24 23 22

Contents...

Foreword...

BY JEFF AMENT

In the summer of 1977, I heard some older kids talking about going
up to see KISS in Lethbridge, Alberta, which was ONLY 200 miles
to the north of the swimming pool parking lot in Big Sandy, MT,
where I was currently standing.

How was I going to see this show? Could I ride with the high school
seniors who were going? (If you can't imagine this scene, watch DAZED
AND CONFUSED.) Did Wilfred Knottnerus (real name) say that Cheap
Trick is opening? Holy shit! I had just heard a Cheap Trick tune called
HE'S A WHORE that sounded like the heaviest BEATLES song ever.
How do I talk my parents into seeing this ultimate event of a
lifetime? After many schemes and lies, my dream show was not to be.
I would be driving a tractor that afternoon west of town while the
older kids drove north to Lethbridge on Thursday, July 1977.
Missing that show made me love KISS and Cheap Trick that much
more. Soon after I grew out of the cartoon characters of KISS and
focused on what CREEM, CIRCUS, and ROCK SCENE magazines were
telling us about, which included Cheap Trick, Aerosmith, Nugent,
Zep, Queen, Alice Cooper, the Sex Pistols and the early punk records.
By 1978, Cheap Trick was my favorite band, bridging the punk rock
of Ramones, Clash, Devo, and Sex Pistols with the heavy rock of
Aerosmith, Zeppelin, and AC/DC and referencing the music of my
youth, the Beatles and the Kinks.

HEAVEN TONIGHT was playing all summer with the first DEVO
record and ROAD TO RUIN while we skated the skateboard ramp
next to our house.

This music connected us to the exciting world that existed far
away from the isolation of our little farm town. The world in the
magazines and record covers.

One day.

Some day.

SERIOUSLY.

That one day my band would play shows with Cheap Trick?

Write up a setlist for them?

I'd own a twelve string bass, built by Jol Dantzig at Hamer, the
same guy who built Tom Petersson's classic basses?

Would I see them play in my childhood backyard of Great Falls,
MT, with the Great Falls Symphony, 36 years after missing that
Lethbridge show?

Who says I wouldn't play Rick's checkerboard Hamer Explorer on
SURRENDER with the band in Spokane?

HA HA HA HA. Impossible.

I've had a ten year text thread with a few friends, all music
fanatics, about who is the greatest American band of all time?
Much discussion about criteria and what constitutes a band (Bruce
and Petty are not bands in my very strict criteria). Three classic
albums? Hit songs? Influence? Originality? Longevity? Great album
covers? Classic logo?

My friends all claim some solid choices with their own criteria. E
Street Band. Heartbreakers. Aerosmith. Grateful Dead. Black Flag.
Metallica. Beach Boys. CCR. The Doors. Ramones.

My own choice occasionally fluctuates, but barely. I always come back
to the one band that meets all of MY criteria.

Cheap Trick.

Three classic albums? Yes. More than three. Dream Police, Heaven
Tonight, first, In Color, and Budokan if you're counting live albums.

Hit Songs?

I Want You To Want Me

Surrender

Dream Police

The Flame

Influence?

Nirvana, Guns N Roses, Green Day, Smashing Pumpkins, and yes, Pearl Jam.

Originality?

The CT mash up is all time. The Beatles, the Move, Yardbirds, AC/DC with some pop sweetness and a tinge of heavy classical tone. The whole rock n roll package thru the lens of a small midwestern city. The juxtaposition. Black and white versus in color. The goofy carnival band members versus the heartthrobs.

Longevity?

They are still killing it. I saw them just before this COVID madness and I swear Robin's singing better than ever and the band is swinging harder.

Album covers?

They took the heartthrobs/nerds imagery into the peak covers of the circus nightmares of Dream Police and All Shook Up.

Logo?

The best.

Rick, Tom, Bun E., and Robin created a furious and hopeful soundtrack for (especially) those of us in small town America (and fans all over the world). That there was hope, a chance to make real life from our dreams . . . with a little help from the DREAM POLICE. After all, they live inside of our head.

Jeff aMP

Introduction...

Rockford.

A city in Illinois named for the point in the river shallow enough to traverse on foot: just shuffle across the limestone. What river, you ask?

The Rock River.

Where else would Cheap Trick be from? Rick Nielsen, Tom Petersson, and Bun E. Carlos all grew up in Rockford and attended the same high school, Guilford. Robin Zander was born twenty miles to the north in Beloit and grew up in nearby Loves Park. Robin would appear to be the odd man out in terms of his 'Rock' roots, but wait: the Rock River flows through Beloit, and Beloit happens to be located in ...

Rock County.

'This band has no past' is the first line of the farcical biography penned by Eric Van Lustbader, future heir to the Jason Bourne saga, and printed on the inner sleeve of Cheap Trick's self-titled debut album. Cheap Trick, of course, does have a past, a past steeped in history. The history of the Midwest—specifically, Rockford, Illinois. The history of the Baby Boom generation, from post-war prosperity to the uncertainty of the Vietnam era. The history of the electric guitar and its unruly progeny, rock'n'roll. The Beatles hit stateside just as the Baby Boomers hit puberty.

The Cheap Trick origin story straddles two very different decades, from the tumult of the sixties, when hope clashed with hate and fear, to the anticlimax of the seventies and the subsequent cynicism, a regression perfectly encapsulated by author Bruce J. Schulman in his book *The Seventies*. 'The peace sign gave way to the finger,' he writes, 'the single upturned middle digit. That obscene gesture lacked the hopefulness of the Sixties but still expressed a clear point of view.'

From 1974 to 1976, as the CBGB punk scene developed on the East Coast and the Sunset Strip glam scene developed on the West Coast, on the Third Coast, Midcoast, or Last Coast (three different names longtime manager of Cheap Trick Ken Adamany has applied to his companies) a dedicated bar band built a following, slowly but surely, over the course of innumerable long nights at the various watering holes scattered about the Midwest. Cheap Trick might have stormed either coast and successfully joined the fray, be it punk or glam. Instead, they braved blizzards and brawls to forge a unique style and sound that defied scenes or genres. When Cheap Trick invaded Max's Kansas City in 1976 or the Whisky A Go-Go in 1977, they conquered both. Trendsetters on both coasts loved them, in part because Cheap Trick bucked trends. They were 'Midwest artsy,' as Rick Nielsen once put it.

On March 14, 1976—the night Aerosmith producer Jack Douglas 'discovered' Cheap Trick at the Sunset Bowl on Sunset Drive in Waukesha, Wisconsin—I was very close by, barely two years old and living with my parents in a ranch style duplex on Freeman Street. Stand in our front yard that night and you would have heard (or felt) the rumble and thud of Cheap Trick reverberating from the bowling alley across the street. I actually DJ'ed my parents' twenty-fifth wedding anniversary party from the very same stage. The room looks quite different today—the L-shaped bar and rickety stage are long gone—but in 1997 it remained much as it was in 1976, with its wood grain paneling and rough, stained carpeting. I remember it well. My parents' wedding reception was held in that same room in 1972.

Who am I? Just a huge fan of rock'n'roll and its many subgenres: seventies rock, proto-metal, glam rock, hard rock, punk rock, power pop, heavy metal, AOR, hair metal, sleaze rock, shoegaze, alternative rock, indie rock, pop punk … you name it. Only one band is all of them. What makes Cheap Trick great is the incredible songs and how well those songs are performed. What makes Cheap Trick really great, and my favorite band of all time, is the genre-bending variety, the over-the-top presentation, the quixotic sense of humor: the subtly satirical, comically mysterious tongue-in-cheekiness of it all.

Cheap Trick are the best of both worlds: music made by huge rock fans for huge rock fans. They love doing it and are really good at it. Unlike anything else because, like everything else, but better. A cornucopia of dichotomies: cool and dorky, smart and dumb, mainstream and underground. Low-brow/high concept. Either you get it … or you don't. I wrote this book because I get it.

1

Like in a storybook...

The Rock River is a three-hundred-mile-long tributary of the Mississippi that flows south from Wisconsin and cuts diagonally across northern Illinois. Over time, numerous cities and towns sprung up along it, including Rockford and, forty miles to the southwest, Dixon. It was in Dixon that Ralph Nielsen and Marilyn Kahler were born, raised, met, and finally married, in 1942. Ralph enlisted in the army that April, just a few months after the Japanese attacked Pearl Harbor, and soon found himself dropped into the middle of the only battle of the war to be waged on North American soil, on the Aleutian Islands off the coast of Alaska, where a wave of American troops fought to expel a Japanese incursion. Much of the combat was hand-to-hand in thick fog and high winds. Luckily, Ralph survived. He was transferred to Roswell, New Mexico, where Marilyn joined him for the duration of his almost four-year enlistment.

Ralph was honorably discharged in November of 1945, just five months after Little Boy and Fat Man flattened Hiroshima and Nagasaki, and two years before an unidentified flying object crashed near where he was stationed in New Mexico. The couple returned to Illinois and settled in Elmhurst, a suburban city west of Chicago. Ralph studied Music and Voice at the American Conservatory and performed for audiences when he could, making regular appearances on Chicago radio. On December 22, 1948, a Wednesday, Marilyn gave birth to a son they named Richard Alan (born with one neck, not five). It was at about this time that Richard's Uncle George, tired of the rat race, went into business for himself, as reported by the *Rockford Register-Republic* in February of 1949:

George Nielsen today disclosed that he has purchased the Record Shop at 318 North Main Street from Mrs. Ethel Fisher and assumed the management

Monday. For a number of years Nielsen represented Cluett-Peabody & Company in this territory and for the last four years has made his home in Rockford. He is a member of the Rockford Men Singers and Tebala Chanters.

A brother, Ralph Nielsen, is a well-known oratorio tenor and will be tenor soloist with the Rockford Men Singers when that organization gives the Messiah at the Shrine temple April 7.

It is reasonable to assume that Ralph visited his brother George's shop in July of 1951 when he traveled to Rockford to perform at Sinnissippi Park, as reported in the *Rockford Morning Star* beneath the amusing headline, 'Tenor Competes With Puppy, Mosquitoes During Concert.'

Ralph Nielsen, lyric tenor from Chicago, had competition from two sources Thursday night in Sinnissippi Park as he sang in the third outdoor concert presented by the Rockford Civic Symphony orchestra. A puppy, found in the park by two youngsters, diverted several people and the mosquitoes claimed the unwilling attention of most of the spectators. Nielsen sang music ranging from a current hit tune to an aria from Cavalleria Rusticana. The hit tune was 'The Loveliest Night Of The Year,' set to the melody of 'Over The Waves,' popularized by Mario Lanza. Listening to Nielsen, few people in the large audience would have thought that when he was a child 'he couldn't carry a tune in a bucket,' which is the description given by his brother, George Nielsen, owner of the Record Shop here. Ralph Nielsen was the only one of his five brothers and sisters not to get music lessons during his childhood, and now he's the only one who is a musician. He also did a fine job singing 'Ever So Pure,' from Martha, by Friedrich von Flotow; 'Pale Hands I Loved' by Woodward-Finden; 'La Donna e mobile' by Verdi; 'Bird Songs At Eventide'; 'Yours Is My Heart Alone'; and the well-known 'Donkey Serenade' by Friml. But, back to that puppy. Found in Sinnissippi Park around seven o'clock Thursday night by Mary Younger and Nancy Steen, the puppy seemed completely healthy and happy. He weighed no more than five pounds and probably was about four weeks old.

Ralph eventually earned a master's degree from the American Conservatory. A 1956 article from the *Arlington Heights Herald* listed his many accomplishments to that point:

A distinguished tenor has been named as one of the principal soloists in Arlington high school's production of The Messiah next month. He is Ralph Nielsen, member of Chicago's Lyric Opera company and a soloist twenty times with the Chicago Symphony orchestra. He has appeared seven times with the Grant Park symphony, two seasons with the Kansas City Philharmonic, and many other orchestras. In addition to more than eight hundred solo TV and radio broadcasts, Nielsen has sung two hundred times in oratorio, with most leading choral societies of the central West. Last season this minister's son made ninety more appearances in opera, symphony, concert, and oratorio, in addition to producing and directing the world-wide 'Temple Time' radio broadcast. Commenting on Ralph Nielsen's talent, the Aurora Beacon News said: 'The kind of tenor whose voice just rises and soars and makes you want wings to keep up with it.'

Earlier that year—the same year that Elvis Presley appeared on *The Ed Sullivan Show* from the waist up while Lonnie Donegan's rollicking version of folk standard 'Rock Island Line' sparked the skiffle craze across the pond—George prevailed upon Ralph to follow his lead and secure for himself and his family a more stable existence in Rockford. Rick Nielsen remembered his uncle telling his father, 'You need to do something else besides singing for your supper. There's a music store here in town, do you wanna get involved?'

'He talked my Dad into going into retail,' Rick told *Guitar Aficionado*. 'So we moved out here in 1956, and we lived at a place called the Flying Saucer Motel.' The motel (shades of Roswell?) was only temporary.

* * *

In the mid-twentieth century, the city of Rockford pulsed as a ventricle of the 'Heartland,' a term of European origin that came to be applied to the Midwestern region of the United States after World War II, perhaps in reference to the Midwest's location on an anthropomorphized map of the nation; the lifeblood of raw materials and finished goods that flowed from the region; a healthy economy's dependence upon the region; or even in reference to the region's role as a font of human ingenuity and creativity (the emotive 'heart'). Luminaries of invention and the arts like Thomas Edison, Henry Ford, Orville and Wilbur Wright, Frank Lloyd Wright, Harry Houdini, Laura Ingalls Wilder, Mark Twain, Walt Disney, Ernest Hemingway, F. Scott

Fitzgerald, Charles Lindbergh, Amelia Earhart, Ray Bradbury, Orson Welles, Langston Hughes, T.S. Eliot, Charles M. Schultz, Judy Garland, Benny Goodman, James Dean, John Wayne, Jack Benny, Bob Newhart, Chuck Berry, Les Paul: all hailed from the Midwest.

The state of Illinois, given its reputation as the nation's crossroads, developed as a sort of microcosm thereof, hence the marketing idiom, 'Does it play in Peoria?' Shaped by glaciers, Illinois was all prairie, flat and fertile— the 'Prairie State.' For a time, the Illinois Central Railroad was the longest in the world. Illinois's neighbor to the north, Wisconsin, was first opened to white settlers in 1833 after the second Treaty of Chicago was ratified, at which point thousands of natives were displaced. Immigrants from Europe soon comprised ninety-five percent of the population. The spot that became Rockford was almost part of Wisconsin, as the northern boundary of Illinois was originally drawn at the southern tip of Lake Michigan. The land mass containing Rockford was ceded to the United States by the Sauk tribe in a treaty that was never ratified—a dispute that culminated in the fifteen week Blackhawk War and nine hundred native casualties. Soon after, a speculator named Germanicus Kent arrived in the area along with his twenty-one-year-old slave, Lewis Lemon. Kent established a settlement on the west bank of the Rock River, eighteen miles south of, eventually, Wisconsin.

The settlement rapidly expanded; within a year a dam, a blacksmithery, a sawmill, and a cluster of cabins had been constructed. Meanwhile, across the river, another aspirant named Daniel Shaw Haight staked a competing claim, the advantage being that travelers arriving from the east might settle there in lieu of crossing the river. An inevitable rivalry ensued, but the competing settlements managed to co-exist enough to eventually merge as 'Midway,' named in reference to the community's proximity to Galena (a booming mine town at the time) and Chicago. Winnebago County was established in 1836 with Daniel Shaw Haight as sheriff. Two years later, Germanicus Kent was elected to the Illinois General Assembly. In 1839, when Midway was about to be incorporated as a village, Haight balked at the name, which he credited to Kent. A compromise was reached when a doctor from Chicago found inspiration in the limestone ford that made the Rock River passable to settlers.

The ensuing decade was a harrowing one for the village of Rockford, and saw both Haight and Kent strike out for greener pastures. Their departures were premature, as by 1851 the Rockford Water Power Company had begun to generate electricity, and a year later the railroad arrived at the newly chartered city. Rockford became an industrial hub, its population tripling over the course of the 1860s, making Rockford second only to Chicago, in terms of size, in Illinois. Hailed at various points as the 'Reaper City,' 'Furniture City,' 'Machine City,' 'Screw City,' and 'Forest City,' Rockford weathered the Great Depression and two World Wars, after which the economy boomed. Tammy Webber described this robust era in an *Associated Press* article in 2009:

> People here used to joke that they could lose a job in the morning and get another by the afternoon. There were auto parts makers, aerospace companies, machine shops and gadget manufacturers. Almost half of workers took home a factory paycheck—often holding the same job for forty years—making this northern Illinois city among the most prosperous in the country.

* * *

In the spring of 1956, Ralph and Marilyn Nielsen, with help from her parents, purchased a music store on the 400 block of 7th Street in downtown Rockford. The American Beauty Music House was originally founded by the Pierson Furniture Company in 1921. The store was a mile away and on the other side of the river from George Nielsen's Record Shop. Now a business owner, Ralph still maintained a rigorous performance schedule, as an October article in the *Rockford Morning Star* made clear:

> On less than two hours' notice, Rockford tenor Ralph Nielsen Monday night sang in Cedar Rapids, IA, 175 miles from home, after a hectic dash by commercial and chartered airplane. Two hours before concert time, Nielsen was on his way home from Chicago, unaware of his assignment. At 6:15pm he walked into American Beauty Music House, 404 7th St., which he operates with his wife, Marilyn. She was waiting for him with a suit of formal clothes, and instructions. Nielsen dressed hurriedly, and at 6:44pm caught a plane to Moline, where a chartered plane was waiting to take him to Cedar Rapids.

The article concluded thusly: 'The Nielsens and Mrs. Nielsen's parents purchased the American Beauty Music House about six months ago. While Ralph Nielsen's musical chores keep him busy and away from the store, Mrs.

Nielsen, secretary-treasurer of the store corporation, and her parents, vice presidents, operate the business.'

Ralph saw his regular absences referenced again a year later, this time by the *Rockford Morning Star*: 'From October through May he is away from Rockford 80 percent of his time. Nielsen in the eleven years he has been singing professionally has appeared in over two thousand radio broadcasts, over all the networks and Chicago stations and some television stations.'

Not long after taking over the store, Ralph and Marilyn changed its name to the Ralph Nielsen Music House and purchased a home eight miles to the east on Spring Creek Road. Rockford presented an idyllic place for their son Richard to grow up, but business operations loomed large. Rick called it 'feast or famine' and bemoaned the 'long, long hours,' which made him 'realize being in retail is not the greatest thing on earth.' Home-cooked meals were rare: 'Maybe five times in my life,' Rick once said. More often than not, downtown restaurants provided sustenance.

Rick Nielsen was seven years old when his parents entered the music business and told *Guitar World* he started working when he was eight—in on the ground floor. Rock'n'roll was not yet the cultural behemoth it would become, but soon ...

Rick spent his formative years immersed in music, surrounded by instruments. Then, when he was a teenager, the British Invasion hit. As the sixties unfolded, the family's store became a sort of home base—a hub for Rockford's young rockers. Nielsen was perfectly placed to become a central figure in that community.

* * *

Sixty-five million babies were born in America between 1944 and 1961, many to parents whose upward mobility promised them a bright future. Personal incomes nearly tripled, and postwar prosperity yielded a thriving middle class. The Baby Boom generation came of age in the midst of the Johnson administration's vision for a 'Great Society.' Causes like Civil Rights and the War on Poverty were championed, consumer and environmental protections were implemented, and organizations like the National Endowment for the Arts and Corporation for Public Broadcasting were founded. Education was prioritized, and by 1965—the first year that the nation's high schools came to be filled entirely with Baby Boomers—ninety-five percent of American children were enrolled in public schools, and seventy-five percent would graduate.

FM radio was on the rise, and the Baby Boom was the first generation to come of age with television as an influence. The result: a swollen mass of savvy young Americans primed and ready for the arrival of The Beatles and the British Invasion. A world away in England, things were decidedly different. Piles of rubble and lingering trauma meant Europe was a far less inspirational place in which to grow up. Pete Townshend was deadly serious when he called it a 'teenage wasteland.' Andrew Werner described the dreary outlook for *Creem* in 1973, lamenting 'casual street-fighting and mind-numbing boredom and schools that are day internment camps and above all, the prospect of dead-end factory jobs.'

British youth had little choice but to look afar for entertainment and developed an obsession with all things American. As former Rolling Stones manager Andrew Loog Oldham put it, 'You sucked up America as energy, to get you out of the cold, gray, drab streets of London.' Americans enjoyed the world's highest standard of living, which fueled a thriving pop culture that was duly exported. Young Brits went wild for American rockers like Bill Haley, Elvis Presley, and Gene Vincent. 'Rock Around The Clock' was the no.1 song in the UK for three weeks in 1955 and two more in 1956. Then came skiffle.

Skiffle came out of New Orleans in the early twentieth century, when musicians used rudimentary, often homemade instruments to entertain each other with music that was fast and rhythmical, requiring minimal expertise. The style made its way to London in the early fifties, and jazz musicians started playing skiffle on the side for fun. When Lonnie Donegan hit the Top 10 with his take on a decades-old Leadbelly song, critical mass was achieved, prompting thousands of youngsters to form skiffle groups. Guitar sales skyrocketed in the UK, from around five thousand in the early fifties to more than two hundred and fifty thousand by 1957. Fourteen-year-old Paul McCartney witnessed Lonnie Donegan perform at the Empire Theatre in Liverpool in November of 1956, and by July of 1957 he had joined a skiffle group called the Quarrymen, fronted by an acquaintance named John Lennon. Mick Jagger, Graham Nash, Ron Wood, Jimmy Page, Ritchie Blackmore, and countless others got their start in skiffle groups.

The skiffle craze fizzled fast but lit the fuse for the likes of Buddy Holly, Chuck Berry, and Eddie Cochran, all of whom became arguably more influential in the UK than the US. Paul McCartney auditioned for the

Quarrymen with 'Twenty Flight Rock' after seeing Eddie Cochran perform the song in the film *The Girl Can't Help It*. Cochran's 'Three Steps To Heaven' went to no.1 in the UK in 1960. Chuck Berry had Top 10 hits in 1959 and 1960 with songs that failed to even chart in the United States. It is important to note that Holly, Berry, and Cochran wrote their own songs, unlike their predecessors Haley, Presley, and Donegan.

Meanwhile, in America, rock'n'roll was yesterday's news. Buddy Holly died, Elvis enlisted, Little Richard converted, and Jerry Lee Lewis married his thirteen-year-old cousin. TV heartthrob Ricky Nelson found widespread popularity as a watered-down, family-friendly version of Elvis. Non-threatening folkies like Peter, Paul & Mary and The Kingston Trio dominated the charts ('Some of my best friends are trios'—Rick Nielsen). At the same time, purveyors of an upstart genre called surf-rock repurposed and popularized a relatively recent invention: the solid-body electric guitar. Dick Dale urged his pal Leo Fender to build bigger, louder amplifiers capable of more reverb, and with them he helped launch the surf craze with the singles 'Let's Go Trippin'' and 'Misirlou' in 1961 and 1962. By the end of 1963, novelty hits like 'Wipeout' and 'Surfin' Bird' had elevated surf rock to Top 10 status.

The first electrically amplified guitar, the 'frying pan,' was assembled by George Beauchamp in 1931. Four years later, Walter Fuller created the first 'pickup,' copper wire coiled around a plastic spool. That same year, Gibson went to market with a Spanish electric guitar, the E-150, which Charlie Christian made famous with the Benny Goodman Orchestra. In 1940, Les Paul built a prototype instrument he called 'The Log.' The next year he pitched the concept of a solid-body electric guitar to Gibson, who passed, enabling Fender to be the first to bring one to market with the Esquire in 1950, followed soon after by the dual-pickup Broadcaster, later renamed the Telecaster. Recognizing they'd dropped the ball, Gibson named its first solid-body electric after Les Paul in 1952—the same year Fender partnered with Freddie Tavares to create the Stratocaster. The electric guitar was ready and waiting for someone, anyone, to come along and optimize its potential.

The Beatles first played the Cavern Club in Liverpool on February 9, 1961, and the phenomenon of 'Beat Music' soon eclipsed the popularity of skiffle. Thousands of beat groups formed across the UK, hundreds in Liverpool alone. Beat paired electric guitars with sweet harmonies, fusing elements of rock'n'roll, R&B, and doo wop, all driven by a steady beat. Merseybeat, a subgenre spearheaded by The Beatles, married the party atmosphere of pop and soul with the characteristic anarchy of rock'n'roll. The Beatles maintained a relentless performance schedule and became a tight, efficient machine.

Beatlemania, which Lonnie Donegan described as a 'strange bedlam,' swamped Britain in 1963. The Beatles' first album, *Please Please Me*, seized the no.1 spot for thirty weeks, only to be replaced by their second album. The Beatles were strikingly different: self-sufficient writers and performers with a distinct vision, and timing was everything. With Britain back on its feet, rising affluence meant a plentitude of young people flush with discretionary income. American media caught wind, and by the fall of 1963, articles about 'Beatlemania' turned up in *Time, Newsweek*, and the *New York Times*. On December 10, 1963, Walter Cronkite anchored a four-minute segment about the phenomenon for the CBS Evening News, and a week later 'I Want To Hold Your Hand' broke the record for pre-orders.

When The Beatles landed at the recently rechristened John F. Kennedy International Airport on February 7, 1964, 'I Want To Hold Your Hand' was the no.1 song in America. The country was little more than two months removed from the assassination of the President. Footage of three thousand screaming teenagers greeting the Fab Four's 1:20pm arrival was broadcast on the CBS and ABC Evening News. Walter Cronkite remarked, 'The British Invasion this time goes by the code name Beatlemania.' *The Ed Sullivan Show* was deluged with fifty thousand requests for the 728 available seats in the studio audience. At 8:04pm, more than one third of the United States' 192 million residents dialed bulky black-and-white television consoles to the CBS network to watch The Beatles permanently alter the culture. The Beatles sold twenty-five million records to Americans over the course of 1964 and 1965. The 'Can't Buy Me Love' single moved a million copies on its first day of release.

England's biggest pop star up to that point, Cliff Richard, never successfully crossed over. He had more than twenty Top 10 hits and seven number ones in the UK but only cracked the American Top 40 once. The Beatles broke the States wide open and ushered in, as Cronkite predicted: The British Invasion. In 1963, only three British artists hit the Top 40. By May of 1965, nine of the top ten songs in the country were from British invaders. Twenty-two million American teenagers, half of whom owned a phonograph, spent $100 million on records in 1964 alone. Guitar sales peaked during the same period (Fender was producing 1,500 per week). It has been estimated that by the end of 1966, nearly two thirds of all American males under the age of twenty-three had joined a rock'n'roll band. This rings true, as in 1967:

Rick Nielsen (19) was in a group called The Grim Reapers.

Tom Petersson (17) was in a group called The Bol Weevils.

Brad Carlson (16) was in a group called The Paegans.

Robin Zander (14) was in a group called The Destinations.

* * *

Rick Nielsen first experienced the exhilaration of eliciting laughter from an audience at age three, when he wandered out onstage during a performance of *The Barber Of Seville*. His father was The Barber. 'People started laughing and clapping and I went, That's what I like,' Nielsen remembered. His path to the stage became music. 'I played drums until I found out that there was too much junk to carry and it was easier to find somebody else that could count to four,' Rick told *Rock Scene*. He also played the flute in the middle-school marching band until being ejected from the program for calling the instructor a drunken fool. 'I'd never have admitted I was the class clown, but I was,' he told *Planet Rock*. (In 2012, Rick had his band privileges officially reinstated during the Burpee Museum's grand opening celebration for the *Rick's Picks: A Lifelong Affair With Guitars & Music* exhibit.)

Rick told Ira Robbins about 'pictures of me with a ukulele when I was about four.' He eventually picked up a guitar, at first his mother's Goya with nylon strings, but he soon graduated to a Gretsch electric with a single pickup and flatwound strings. After one lesson he decided to teach himself, at first by playing along with the television, mimicking the themes for shows like *Peter Gunn* or *Have Gun—Will Travel* ('The Ballad Of Paladin'). 'I'd play the melody, I knew what melody was,' he told *Rock Scene*. Nielsen had perfect pitch. 'And that's how I kind of taught myself how to play guitar, just by TV shows, because that was kind of the hippest music around.' He had other influences as well: for example, 'I'd say the sax player for Spike Jones influenced me. He had heavy baritone sax bass runs, and good feel.' Learning in an unconventional way, Nielsen developed his own style.

Tom Petersson's parents bought him his first guitar when he was fourteen, even though they could barely afford it. 'It was on a payment plan,' he told *Gretsch News*. 'It was a lot of money at the time, and it was a lot of money for them. I can't believe they did that, but it was great. They were supportive even though they didn't approve of or understand that kind of music I was interested in.' He told Ira Robbins that the first guitar was a Gibson archtop with one pickup and no cutaways. Probably an entry-level ES-125.

Brad Carlson (hereafter referred to as Bun E. Carlos) grew up in a very strict household, but music was an important feature, as both of his parents were musicians. 'I plunked around and taught myself how to play the piano but when The Beatles came out it was time for drums,' he remembered. In 1964, his mother bought him a set of Sonor drums from Ralph Nielsen's Music: a blue marble four-piece kit. 'I'm a fourth-generation drummer, cross my heart, all the way back to the Civil War. My folks didn't tell me that until after I'd gotten a drum set. They didn't want to encourage me,' he told Robin Tolleson.

Robin Zander also started with the drums. 'My mother went to Sears and bought me a set of drums when I was eight years old, nine years old,' he told Dan Rather. 'My dad was a musician in a weekend warrior band that played in our basement. So I just sort of walked around the house and said, Hell, I wanna try that.'

Duane Huoy, a childhood friend and Robin's bandmate in The Destinations, recalls Robin's father playing piano at Rockford airport and organ at the roller-skating rink. 'He played all by ear,' Huoy told me. 'That was just amazing to me, that he could do it that well from memory.' Zander remembered there being instruments all over his house growing up. 'My dad got me a saxophone,' he told Ira Robbins. 'But the first instrument I learned how to play on was a piano. After the Beatles and the British Invasion, I immediately wanted to play guitar.'

The boys' initial influences ran the gamut: Duane Eddy, Sandy Nelson, Gene Pitney, Johnny Cash, Roy Orbison, Sam Cooke, The Orlons, Tommy Roe, The Ventures, and, of course, Elvis Presley. Then came The Beatles and the next wave. 'When The Beatles and The Kinks came out, that was it,' Nielsen told *Planet Rock*. Tom Petersson agreed. 'When I first heard The Who and The Kinks, I thought I was gonna have a heart attack,' he told the *Chicago Daily News*.

'I remember driving home from camping and my father turned on the radio. Beaker Street in Little Rock Arkansas had a huge radio station that covered a lot of ground. "I Want To Hold Your Hand" came on the radio and I was stunned by it. It was like the sun shined; it was something special,' Robin Zander told Mick Burgess for *Metal Express Radio*. 'So, from that, I really started listening to Beaker Street because they played a lot of British Invasion music. I really got into The Animals who were a Newcastle band. I also loved The Kinks and The Rolling Stones, The Beatles, of course, as well as The Yardbirds and Fleetwood Mac. All these bands from the UK became my favorite bands, and I formed a band because of it.'

'That was our whole life. You know, bands like The Small Faces, the Stones, The Who, and The Kinks, and, of course, The Beatles,' Tom Petersson told Ken Sharp. The unprecedented popularity of The Beatles became a trojan horse for even more seductive gurus—trendy insurgents whose influence carved a cult from a hobby. The incrementally more incendiary British Invasion groups. 'The whole British Invasion and all the English groups by far were our biggest influences,' Tom told *Gretsch News*. 'We were just dumbstruck, honestly.'

'I was more of a fan of The Rolling Stones and the early Small Faces and The Idle Race and The Move and bands like that than The Beatles,' Rick Nielsen told Redbeard. 'I had a ticket to the Beatles at Shea Stadium and I didn't go.' As Robin Zander explained, 'It was that sort of secondary blues influence that turned me on. It was energetic, louder and more exciting than the kind of blues we had over here. I was really truly influenced by The British Invasion … it gave me that feeling of, *That's what I want to do.*'

2

So you missed some school...

On August 2, 1965, a week before the second feature film from The Beatles, *Help*, premiered in US theaters, a photo appeared in the *Register-Republic* of Rockford's own answer to the Fab Four: a smartly dressed combo called The Phaetons. Sadly, layout limitations resulted in two of the group's six members being cropped from the image for space, thus Ken Bagus, Grant Johnson, Gary Schuder, and Terry Sullivan secured bragging rights while bandmates Willie Walsh and Rick Nielsen did not. The photo's caption promoted an upcoming benefit concert that was mentioned again two days later in the *Rockford Morning Star*:

> In order to assist in sending the United States Maccabiah Team to Tel Aviv, Israel, for international competition Aug. 23 to 31, Rockford Jewish Community Center and Rockford Committee for the Sports for Israel, Inc., will co-sponsor a dance tonight at the center. Mrs. William Laven is acting chairman for the Rockford Committee. The dance will be held from eight to eleven o'clock this evening, and the music will be furnished by The Phaetons, who are donating their services for the benefit.

Rick Nielsen has dismissed The Phaetons as 'rinky-dink.' The youngsters borrowed the name from the classic open-air automobile design, but the moniker was short-lived: little more than a month later, an ensemble calling themselves The Grim Reapers were pictured in the *Rockford Morning Star* within an advertisement for the Ralph Nielsen Music House, now an 'exclusive dealer' of Vox amplifiers (thanks to Rick cajoling his father into making the leap). This time, all six band members were pictured, and they were: Ken Bagus, Grant Johnson, Gary Schuder, Bill Morris, Willie Walsh, and Rick Nielsen. Drummer Terry Sullivan had been replaced and the band re-christened since August, but Bill Morris's tenure with The Grim Reapers would not be long either, because a skilled and confident drummer named Jim Zubiena had recently relocated with his family from St. Louis to Rockford.

JIM ZUBIENA *During the first dance held at the school that year, I approached the drummer of the band and asked him if I could play his drums in order to introduce my skills to the school, in the hope of getting together with a band. To my surprise, he said, 'Go ahead.' So I went up onstage and played a drum solo comprised of very fast bass drum work and very fast hands. The next morning at school I was approached by Rick.*

Back in St. Louis, Zubiena had been in a band called The Nomads. Coincidentally, there was another band in Rockford with the very same name, its members being Kim Bowers, Bill Bremner, and drummer Mike Myers, along with a recent addition, Mike's thirteen-year-old brother Craig, a budding guitar prodigy. 'After two years of piano, starting age seven and eight, my parents gave me a plastic Roy Rogers toy guitar with nylon strings,' Craig told *It's Psychedelic Baby* magazine. 'I quickly learned to tune it to a chord, and that day I could play three-chord songs by laying just one finger across the fretboard.'

CRAIG MYERS *Mike made up a little homemade drum kit out of boxes and tambourines and stuff… he had sticks and he would drum, and I would play a nylon-string guitar. He would sing backup harmony to me, and we'd go down in the basement and try to do Beatles songs, the two of us just loving music.*

The Myers brothers' passion for rock'n'roll swiftly developed from child's play to a more serious endeavor.

CRAIG MYERS *I spent five to six hours a day when I was twelve and thirteen, teaching myself.*

Once Mike joined The Nomads, his brother soon followed.

CRAIG MYERS *He brought me to the practice because I knew the words to the songs.*

So I was practicing with them as lead singer. But I was thirteen and these guys were like sixteen, seventeen, eighteen. We only did a couple of jobs. The first one I couldn't even go to, I was too nervous. I'd never performed, I had stage fright, I was home with a headache. There was a church called Gloria Day where we performed.

The Nomads failed to gel, and the Myers brothers soon defected to form a new band called The Rogues with an ambitious young bass player named Denny Orsinger. Craig just wanted to play guitar, but he was still singing, at first.

DENNY ORSINGER *Craig used to try to sing when we were in The Rogues, but he kind of sounded like Alfalfa at the time.*

To liberate Craig from vocal duties, the trio recruited a singer named Bob Langenberg, who was actually a founding member of The Phaetons.

BOB LANGENBERG *Gary [Schuder] lived two doors down from me, and Rick [Nielsen] lived a couple of blocks away. We just started as just a regular old garage band.*

The Phaetons had moved on without Bob, to the benefit of Craig, who was now free to concentrate on his guitar playing.

CRAIG MYERS *I thought,* Well, I better take guitar a little more seriously. *I learned how to tune it the right way and within about three weeks I was doing a lot more stuff than our guitarist had been, so I noticed,* Okay, I've got natural ability here.

At some point, The Rogues added a second guitarist, an acquaintance of Bob's named Tom Petersson.

DENNY ORSINGER *I can't remember the name of his group, but Tom was the lead singer and lead guitar player. I know he was playing at Fairview Bowling Alley.*

MIKE MYERS *He had a real electric guitar and an amplifier, so he was in.*

Petersson by then owned a Gibson model ES-335, the semi-hollow-body most famous for its association with B.B. King. The expansion of the lineup merited a new name, therefore The Rogues became The Bol Weevils—fitting, as a boll weevil is a type of beetle. 'Boll Weevil' was also the name of a traditional blues number made famous by Leadbelly in the thirties. Brook Benton scored a top ten hit with his version in 1960. There was also the *Secret Order Of The Boll Weevils*, a mock secret society out of Memphis whose members wore green capes.

BOB LANGENBERG *Tom's Mom made these green fuzzy vests for us, to go with the 'Bol Weevils' theme.*

One of their first paying gigs took place in the ballroom at the historic Faust Hotel in Rockford on November 15, 1965, the same week as the first major battle between the US Army and the People's Army of Vietnam, the Battle of Ia Drang. Less than a month later, the Ralph Nielsen Music House advertised a 'Beatles Fan Special,' which included a solid-body electric guitar (brand unspecified), a 'powerful' Fireball amp cable, a strap and picks for just $88.88. Rock'n'roll was a cultural juggernaut. The Bol Weevils even recorded an advertising jingle for Beloit-based Dell Food Specialties.

DENNY ORSINGER *I think we recorded in this guy's house—he had an advertising agency, he was a neighbor of Tom Petersson's. All Bob had to say was, 'Dell potato chips are dell-licious,' and it took him about ten takes to say it.*

Another memorable Bol Weevils appearance took place at an all-girls Catholic high school called Bishop Muldoon, which operated in Rockford from 1929 to 1970. The Bol Weevils experienced a microcosm of Beatlemania (or, in this case, Beetlemania) that day, with the exuberance of the schoolgirls disconcerting the nuns and clergy. It might have gone to the boys' heads.

DENNY ORSINGER *Bob was always smoking, and he was a little bit of a wiseass at the time, and a nun came up to him and said, 'Son, you can't smoke back here.' With the curtains on the stage, it was a fire hazard, and he looks at the nun—and I'm a good Catholic boy—and he said, 'Kiss my ass.' He really said that, and I thought we were gonna go to Hell!*

Langenberg's days with The Bol Weevils were numbered.

* * *

December 11, 1965, was a big day for budding musos in Rockford. The Yardbirds featuring Jeff Beck paid an afternoon visit to the local roller rink, the Rock River Roller Palace. Among the approximately two hundred in attendance were three dedicated (but as of yet unacquainted) rock fans: Rick Nielsen, Tom Petersson, and Bun E. Carlos. Carlos remembered, 'They did two sets. Needless to say, it was pretty cool. I snuck into the dressing room between sets and talked with the band. They were really nice to put up with a fourteen-year-old kid like me. Jeff Beck even explained feedback to me! They were using the opening act's Vox amps. Except Beck, he had an AC30 Vox with a blown up speaker.'

Jeff Beck was Rick Nielsen's favorite guitar player. 'Because he came up with things no one else played,' Rick explained. 'He was always the most animated guitar player. His mistakes were tasty.' (Rick might as well have been describing his eventual self). Less than two years later, Nielsen unwittingly performed on a Yardbirds session, even though by then the only remaining original member was vocalist Keith Relf. Nielsen's keyboard track, recorded at Chess Studios in Chicago, was used for The Yardbirds version of Manfred Mann's 'Ha Ha Said The Clown,' produced by Mickie Most. The basic track was recorded at Columbia Studios in New York and the tapes then shipped to Chicago for Nielsen's overdubs. Relf's vocals were recorded later, in England. According to Rick, 'I've played on stuff that I don't even know I played on.'

* * *

On June 16, 1966, a startling image appeared in the *Rockford Register-Republic*: a VW Bug upside down in the middle of the road. A frightening accident had occurred, but it could have been much worse.

> Rick Nielsen, 17, told police he applied the brakes and swerved but could not avoid hitting the girl. The east bound car rolled over on its top coming to rest on a median strip. Two companions riding with him were unhurt. The girl, who was walking around following the accident, was taken to Rockford Memorial Hospital for examination.

It was a crazy summer. In July, the entire nation was stunned when a disheveled ex-con named Richard Speck murdered eight student nurses in Chicago. Speck had been crashing with his sister ever since he caught a bus from Dallas to the Chicago suburbs, fleeing from an arrest warrant. He made some halfhearted attempts to find work as a deckhand on one of the ships docked in Lake Michigan, but when nothing landed in his lap Speck soon wore out his welcome at his sister's place. On July 11, his brother-in-law handed him twenty-five bucks as he dropped him off at the National Maritime Union Hall at 2315 E. 100th Street in a southeast Chicago neighborhood called Jeffrey Manor.

Speck haunted the neighborhood for three days, roving from bar to bar, and took note of the student nurses coming and going from the row of townhouses that occupied the same block as the Union Hall. On July 13, by happenstance, he pilfered a pistol from the purse of a woman he'd accosted and, no doubt buoyed by the random acquisition of the weapon, that night walked a mile and a half to 2319 E. 100th Street, where he pried open a rear window through which he reached to unlock the back door. Speck crept upstairs, gun in hand, and corralled six disoriented student nurses in a bedroom. When three additional young women arrived at the residence soon after, they unwittingly delivered themselves to Speck.

Speck cut a bedsheet into strips and bound the young women, then murdered them one by one, at some point losing count and leaving Corazon Amurao, who had wedged herself beneath one of the bunk beds, alive. Cora provided a description of the brute that matched that of the strange man reported to have been lurking in the area over the past few days. The career criminal (he had been arrested more than forty times) was swiftly identified using fingerprints left at the scene. The hunt was on, and in addition to Speck's pockmarked face, the media publicized another identifying characteristic, the obnoxious phrase tattooed on his arm: *Born to Raise Hell.*

Speck, drunk in a flophouse, clumsily slashed his wrists and was identified at the hospital when an alert doctor wiped away the dried blood to expose the tattoo. Two weeks later, Charles Whitman climbed to the top of the UT Tower and assassinated fourteen strangers with a rifle. Meanwhile, the US troop count in Vietnam was elevated to four hundred thousand.

The Baby Boomers faced a harsh reality, but how cognizant were they? Consider a letter from Rockford resident Jody Gadwell, published by the *Rockford Morning Star* on August 6, 1966:

To the Editor:
Recently I noticed the time teen-agers in Rockford spend 'doing nothing' or just 'hangin' around.' Why, six out of every ten teen-agers are idle during the

day while the other four are working or having a good time. There's nothing extra special about these four, except they're smart enough to want to be a part of things so they look for things to do instead of acting as if they hadn't a care in the world. A few days ago I made a survey on the things there are for teen-agers to do in Rockford. It's very surprising that most of the 'kids' haven't thought of them. There is a place out on Forest Hills Road called the Rockford Speedway. Every week or so they have a special feature for the whole family. Some of the teen-ager who go there say it's a pretty 'swinging' place. Then there are always the dances if one can't make it to the Speedway. Friday night there was a dance at the YWCA. There were quite a few kids there, and I'll bet if you would ask any of them if they had a good time the answer would be 'Yes.' There is always a dance in some part of town. The Hotel Faust always has a dance and some of the best groups play there, like the Seeds, Bol Weevils, and the Grim Reapers. But if one doesn't like to dance, there is always something else to do.

At the end of July the *Rockford Register-Republic* reported on 'Frontier Days' at the Highcrest Shopping Center, where 'the biggest crowds Highcrest has ever had,' made up of 'screaming, stomping teen-agers,' enjoyed the sounds of a 'local folk-rock-noise combo' called The Grim Reapers. Rick Nielsen was pictured, alongside shots of the youthful horde. Not long after, on August 20, 1966, the *Rockford Morning Star* reported on a rather raucous appearance by The Bol Weevils:

About three hundred uninvited enthusiasts crowded into a private party for seventy Neighborhood Youth Corps members Friday night in Sinnissippi Park. The gatecrashers were invited to join the party, and all had a good time dancing to the sounds produced by a band called The Bol Weevils. The only casualty was a dance contest planned for the Youth Corps men. In the overcrowded park shelter no contest was possible. The problems started when a radio station said the band was to appear, and many teen-agers took it as an invitation.

An August 25 article in the *Rockford Morning Star* described the same event. 'After the short speeches ended, the Bol Weevils begin to set up their equipment. Many adults fled the center as the band tuned guitars. Outside, small groups were talking, laughing, shaking hands. Blackhawk Islanders were proud of the new center. It was a still night. You could hear the band a block away.'

On August 29, The Beatles performed in front of a concert crowd for the final time, at Candlestick Park in San Francisco. That same month, the landmark *Revolver* album was released. The significance of these events were overshadowed by resurfaced (and technically accurate) comments from John Lennon about his band being 'more popular than Jesus.' Rock'n'roll was a magnet for controversy, as evidenced by an article about The Bol Weevils published by the *Rockford Register-Republic* on August 30, the very controversial topic being: a haircut. A photo was included, taken at Custer Collura's barbershop, with new singer Joe Sundberg in the hot seat, surrounded by his grinning bandmates.

Rock'n'roller Joe Sundberg, 14, a freshman at Lincoln Junior High School, presented a problem to the barber. As Sundberg phrased it, 'I need my hair cut to get back into school—but don't cut much off.' The problem seemed a delicate balance between school regulations and the demands of rock'n'roll. Sundberg and four friends compose the Bol Weevils, a long-hair group making rock'n'roll sounds in Rockford. Denny Orsinger, 16, 3206 Corbridge Lane, is the leader. The others are Tom Peterson, 16, 1419 Rebecca Drive; Mike Myers, 18, and Craig Myers, 14, both of 2608 Hampden Court; and Sundberg, 1333 Casper Lane.

Orsinger, a senior at Guilford High, defends the Bol Weevils hair styles. 'At least the band provides an excuse for our long hair,' he said. 'We all get static from our parents over our hair,' Orsinger said. Peterson, a junior at Guilford High, added 'My parents don't like it, but my mother says it's okay for the band.' One Bol Weevil was sent home from class last year and two were ordered to barber shops. Mike Myers, a freshman at Rock Valley College, said, 'We wouldn't wear it long if we didn't have the band!' The boys admit the complaints are wearing on the nerves, but Sundberg said 'Long hair will be popular as long as the Beatles and other famous groups set the style.' Sundberg emerged from the barber chair with most of his locks intact.

Joe Sundberg had replaced Bob Langenberg.

BOB LANGENBERG *My mom wanted me to go to college, so I had a choice to make— play music or go to college—and it wasn't really a choice, they didn't give me much of a choice then. So I left.*

Bob wound up in New Mexico, where he attended the University of Vera Cruz. It beat being drafted. Meanwhile, Joe Sundberg proved a valuable asset to The Bol Weevils.

DENNY ORSINGER *Joe could sing anywhere from James Brown to Robert Goulet. I mean, the guy actually could sing. He was phenomenal.*

JOE SUNDBERG *I wanted to be a drummer but ended up singing by a fluke. My first band, The Six Pack, had a drummer but needed a singer, so I was in.*

At some point, The Bol Weevils drove to Janesville, Wisconsin, for a recording session at the Leaf Records studio (actually a barn). They recorded an original song called 'Return,' written by Craig, and versions of 'Wild About My Lovin'' by The Lovin' Spoonful (originally recorded by blues legend Jim Jackson), 'La La La Lies' by The Who, and 'And Your Bird Can Sing' by The Beatles.

CRAIG MYERS *That's double-tracked with two guitars, and I somehow came up with a version on one guitar. That was kind of one of our, Wow, we're getting there, moments, when we learned that song.*

DENNY ORSINGER *Craig was a genius. Craig could listen to anything and give everybody their parts to play.*

The Grim Reapers and The Bol Weevils represented just two examples of the innumerable clusters of young boys from across the country (and around the world) who joined forces to emulate their heroes. *Life* magazine published an article about the rising popularity of the electric guitar in 1966, pointing out that 'with an electric guitar today, a teen-ager can make not only a big noise but he can also make money. ... Teen combos are fast becoming the country's most popular form of musical entertainment.' Case in point: on September 10, 1966, an article with the headline 'Roscoe's Rockin' To Quartet's Festival Music' appeared on page 3A of the *Rockford Morning Star*:

Activities at the 57th annual Roscoe Fall Festival continue today with one of the youngest, loudest rock'n'roll groups in the Rockford area. The group, which calls itself the Destinations, consists of three thirteen-year-old guitar players and a ten-year-old drummer. 'One day they were playing on our porch, and a guy drove by and asked if they were a group. They said yes and he said, "How would you like to play the Roscoe festival?" "Sure," they said,' explained Mrs. Elaine Zander, whose son Robin plays a guitar in the group. The four practice in the garage of Duane Keller at 425 Fitch Road. Police once visited the garage to see what all the noise was about, but they left when they observed that neighborhood youngsters were dancing in their yards and the adults were clapping in time with the music, Mrs. Keller said. The Destinations, whose musical experience ranges from three months to four years, are playing at the Roscoe Festival for fun, not profit—'unless someone gives them a donation,' Mrs. Keller said. The guitar players, Duane Huoy, Robin, and Art Brazel, all attend Alexander Hamilton Junior High School in Loves Park. Kevin Keller, who started playing the drums four years ago when he was six, attends Riverdahl Grade School in Rockford.

DUANE HUOY *Art Brazel, Robin, and myself were just three guys taking lessons at the Williams School Of Music.*

Located on North 2nd Street in Rockford, the Williams School Of Music also sold instruments.

DUANE HUOY *Art's dad used to take Art, myself, and Robin out to Kevin Keller's house. He lived down off of Kishwaukee, south—near Harrison, actually. That's where his parents lived, and we used to go out there and do all our practicing in their basement.*

The Roscoe Fall Festival was The Destinations' very first show. When asked if he remembered his debut performance by Eddie Trunk, Zander's recollection was that he was fourteen and played at a park in Beloit (in fact, he was thirteen, and it was at Leland Park in Roscoe, just eight miles from Beloit). Robin remembered that his group played for half an hour to 'about three people in the audience.' The one song he remembered singing was 'I'm A Man' by the Spencer Davis Group. Again, he was thirteen. They also played 'We Gotta Get Out Of This Place' by The Animals.

DUANE HUOY *We really didn't play that many gigs before everything went away but*

I think probably the biggest one for us would have been playing at the Harmony Grange on Harlem Road. It's now a church, I guess it's trying to redeem itself because that was the rock'n'roll place that nobody's parents wanted them to go to, or I should say responsible parents. We played songs of the day like 'Gloria' and songs by Mitch Ryder & The Detroit Wheels. Just mostly the standard stuff that you were gonna get off the radio. Stones music, Beatles music for sure, The Monkees—we played a few of their tunes, not necessarily at the Harmony Grange. That place was a little more hardcore.

After The Destinations, Zander put together a psychedelic rock combo with a friend from the neighborhood, Fred Brace. They called themselves The Purple Haze, but soon switched to Butterscotch Sunday. On October 21, 1966, an article by Isabel Culhane about the widespread phenomenon of teen rock bands appeared in the *Rockford Register-Republic*. 'Almost any neighborhood has a boy in a rock'n'roll band,' she noted. 'And the rock'n'roller has to take his turn having practice at his home. Rock'n'roll music has really taken hold with the teenagers. It is their music. If you have a beat, you're in business.'

The article mentioned The Bol Weevils and The Grim Reapers and included an illuminating quote from Rick Nielsen's father, Ralph: 'I used to think it was a lot of noise, but over the last few months it has gained my respect.' Ralph's conversion presumably resulted from prolonged exposure, as described by wife Marilyn to *Rolling Stone* in 1979: 'We always had them in our garage. I can remember the noise. It rattled the glasses in the kitchen. ... I used to sit in the kitchen and think, Oh dear, will I ever live through this!' Marilyn also told the *Rockford Register Star* that 'they were playing almost day and night. We got a letter from the district attorney that they would have to cease and desist at dusk.'

In October of 1966, The Bol Weevils competed in a battle of the bands at the Rumpus Room in Belvidere, their rival being a group called The Paegans, featuring Bun E. Carlos on drums. According to the newspaper, 'more than 1,000 youngsters to age twenty attended the ball and cast votes.' The Paegans probably defeated The Bol Weevils, as five months later the *Rockford Register Republic* reported that The Grim Reapers had defeated a band called The Cave Men, and now 'fans are anticipating a battle of the undefeated bands, those being The Grim Reapers and Paegans.' The paper was wrong on both counts: it was actually a rematch, and The Grim Reapers were not undefeated, having fallen to The Paegans at the Boone County Fair (according to Carlos).

The Paegans also had a single out, released by a regional promoter named Ken Adamany on his Rampro record imprint. In March, the single was mentioned by the *Rockford Morning Star*:

> To the Paegans, Rockford teen-age group, goes the distinction of originating the only recording ever to 'beat' the Beatles on Chicago radio station WCFL's Joe Sebastian Show. Last Tuesday The Paegans' 'Good Day Sunshine,' their first and only recording to date, was played back-to-back with the Beatles' version of the same song. Tally of the telephone vote afterwards was in The Paegans' favor. Personnel of the group includes Brad Carlson, drums; Steve Carlson, lead guitar; Jerry Parlapiano, rhythm guitar; Rick Schneider, organ; and John Furland, bass guitar.

'We had a local hit in Rockford,' Bun E. Carlos remembered. 'My mom was real upset. People will grab you and do terrible things to you, she said. So my sister would drive us to all the gigs in the next town.' According to fellow Paegan John Furland, 'All of the Dads drove us to and from our gigs and pulled the equipment trailer when we were too young to drive. Don Furland dragged The Paegans all over the Midwest!'

RUSS FREIMAN *They struck me always as highly professional, always wearing the suits, had the Beatles Vox amplifiers, the equipment, everything about them was polished.*

Freiman played in a band called Crystal with Carlos's brother Mark. He frequently hung out at the Ralph Nielsen Music House, and was also very familiar with The Grim Reapers.

RUSS FREIMAN *The Reapers were a little bit looser in their approach—they weren't so scrubbed—I guess it would be something like The Beatles being The Paegans and The Rolling Stones being The Grim Reapers, scrubbed and unscrubbed.*

The *Belvidere Daily Republican* published an article about The Paegans on April 13, 1967. Bun E. Carlos bragged about how many copies of the single they had sold—'Five-hundred copies in one week!'—and writer Bonny Kaski eventually found time to comment on the band's music:

They wear matching outfits, usually Mod styled clothes, like yellow shirts and paisley pants. Off-stage, they run around in Navy Blue peacoats. Brad brags about having the only genuine 1927 chauffeurs' license in Rockford pinned on his. They also feature plaid pants, various colored turtleneck shirts, or suits. … The group gets their songs from many albums, including those by the Who, Them, Rolling Stones, Beatles, Animals, and Dave Clark Five.

BUN E. CARLOS *We sold about fifteen hundred singles and would get played on WCFL and WROK.*

JOHN FURLAND *Some weeks we made more than our teachers. They knew it, too. My counselor told me!*

In January, *Time* declared the entire 'Under 25 Generation' 'Man of the Year.'

* * *

On March 1, 1967, Rick Nielsen filled out a questionnaire for Ken Adamany's RAM Productions, a booking agency and management company headquartered in Janesville, Wisconsin. The purpose of the questionnaire: 'It will be a great help to me in the promotion of you, your group and your recordings.'

Under 'Likes and Dislikes,' Nielsen answered:

Favorite …
color: BLACK
group: STONES, BEATLES, BYRDS
actor or actress: LAUREL + HARDY
song: JEFF'S BOGIE (sic)
movie: HELP!
area of country: CALIFORNIA

Likes …
clothes: NEW—BRIGHT COLORS
hobbies: COLLECT GUITARS
sports: SWIMMING
cars: BIG

What do you like in girls? GOOD LOOKS, FRIENDLY, NOT PRUDISH
What do you dislike? SNOBBY, WON'T TALK, RATTED HAIR
What are your pet peeves? PACKING UP EQUIPMENT, GETTING UP
IN MORNING
What are your shortcomings? ACT STUPID
What is your social life like? HAVE FEW DATES, NOT MUCH WHEN
PLAYING
Is being a performer a help or not? NO—BUT I DON'T CARE
What magazines do you read? TIME, LIFE, PLAYBOY, MAD, ERRIE (sic)
Have you a favorite book/author? KAUFMAN + HART
What do you want that you haven't got? LONG HAIR, LOTS OF MONEY
If you are just starting your career, how will you react to success; or, if you
are established already, what difference has success made in your life and the
lives of those close to you? I DON'T THINK IT WOULD CHANGE ME
MUCH AT ALL.

He made good use of that shortcoming.

* * *

On March 25, Cream and The Who made their US debuts at a concert in
New York City sponsored by Murray The K. The crowd went wild when
Pete Townshend inexplicably smashed his Telecaster. On May 11, a *Rockford
Register-Republic* article with the headline 'Small Bands Play It Big' highlighted
both The Paegans and The Grim Reapers. The Paegans were pictured, and
their victory over The Beatles in the radio contest was mentioned. Rick
Nielsen, described as the leader of The Grim Reapers, explained that his group
'got started about two years ago' and called themselves The Phaetons. 'We
started with three people,' he explained, 'then added a couple more. It just
kind of happened.'

Those 'three people' were Rick, Gary Schuder, and Bob Langenberg. The
Grim Reapers played 'many out of town dates' using a rental truck, as did The
Paegans, 'one of Rockford's youngest but biggest successes.' Bun E. Carlos
explained that The Paegans had 'a master plan on how to pack everything' in
the truck.

The article also revealed that The Grim Reapers had experienced another
lineup change: 'Currently the personnel includes Rick, Gary Schuder, Bill

Walsh, Jim Zubiena, Ross Anderson, and Joe Sundberg, ranging in age from fifteen to nineteen.'

With the enlistment of former Bol Weevils frontman Joe Sundberg alongside Gary Schuder, The Grim Reapers now had two singers—an embarrassment of riches.

JOE SUNDBERG *Gary was the singer in The Phaetons, which was Rick's very first band, and then when we formed The Grim Reapers, Gary was a backup singer and he played a lot of percussion stuff and did the Stones songs because he did those well.*

JIM ZUBIENA *He pimped Mick Jagger. He looked like Mick Jagger. He had Mick Jagger hair. He had Mick Jagger physical affectations when he was onstage … we were doing The Kinks and The Rolling Stones and Ten Years After, and when Joe came into the band all of a sudden we're doing Sam & Dave and all that kind of soul stuff because Joe had a very raspy, Otis Redding–type voice. Gary would do the rock'n'roll, Joe would do the soul. So that's how the music changed—it just brought in a whole different genre to the sets.*

The departure of Ken Bagus meant Rick Nielsen was now the sole guitar player in the group.

JIM ZUBIENA *In between songs I would reach forward with my drumstick and turn off Kenny Bagus's amplifier, and we'd do two or three songs before he would know it and it would really piss him off.*

Keyboardist Grant Johnson had been replaced by another Guilford student named Ross Anderson.

ROSS ANDERSON *I was in a little band called The Newcastles—a little garage band with some guys I knew as a sophomore in high school—and I started taking lessons from an organist that Rick knew. He worked at Rick's Dad's music store, so he recommended me to Rick. I played organ and saxophone. I had an alto sax and a tenor sax and my organs went from, I had a Farfisa mini-compact—that's what I could afford when I was in the Newcastles—and then when I was in The Grim Reapers I got a Hammond M3, and after that a hammond C3. A C3 is* *like the Hammond B3 that jazz organists use but the B3 had spindles, you know, legs, as opposed to the Hammond C3, which was like your continental looking church organ, but once we got done adapting it with Leslie speakers and mic'd through the PA, you know, we went on decibels in the early days.*

On Friday, September 8, 1967, the Sherwood Lodge in Rockford hosted the much anticipated rematch: The Grim Reapers vs. The Paegans in a Battle of the Bands, 7:00 to 11:30, admission $1.75. That same month, The Grim Reapers won a student vote to serve as entertainment for the homecoming dance at Freeport High School, home of The Pretzels. The school's slogan: 'You can eat us, but you can't beat us.'

The Grim Reapers had become the biggest band around, and their stage production approximated that of a national act.

RUSS FREIMAN *Because [Rick] had his dad's music store, they had equipment onstage that would just make your mouth drop at the time if you were in a band. I remember seeing Willie Walsh one night at the Sherwood Lodge, and he had two bass amplifier cabinets together, with a top, and to be a bass player at that time and to have the affordability to even purchase a bass—let alone having a bass and then a bass amplifier, which were kind of expensive at that time—bass players were in high demand at that time, and here's a guy who has not only a bass and a bass amp, and a good one, he has two amp cabinets, which at the time was unheard of. And it was just that little seed, the beginning of things to come where amps would grow and volume would start growing.*

ROSS ANDERSON *Our decibels buried the competition.*

All things considered, The Grim Reapers never cultivated much of an image. Even so, Rick Nielsen always stood out in pictures, with the most expressive face, unruliest hair, and loudest outfits.

JIM ZUBIENA *He was always weird. Rick always dressed weird.*

RUSS FREIMAN *He definitely had his style. The persona being kind of comical, cracking jokes, making his hair look a little bit different than the next guy. I seem to remember Rick being one of the very first musicians who ever parted his* *hair down the middle. Because back in the day you're patterning things off of the Beatles who had these long bangs, combing the sides and Nielsen, he'd part his hair down the middle, he'd wear his guitars lower than most guys. He had just that little bit of difference to him, which truly made him stand out, and whenever you watched the band your eyes were more focused on what he was doing. I think he had a knack for that, and through the years he had the ability to craft that on a stronger level. I think he was into music that was a little bit in front of a lot of kids our age—he was into those bands like The Yardbirds, The Who, those kind of experimental, fuzztone, a little bit louder, cartwheel your arm, kind of 'visual effect' bands that were just kind of starting to come over. You know, he for some reason had tapped into that a little bit earlier than most people, and I think he had that advantage of getting that in front of people before they really realized where it was coming from.*

A couple of students from Harlem High School in nearby Loves Park, Brian Beebe and Robin Zander, never forgot the cold December night they caught The Grim Reapers at Sherwood Lodge, which was located just northeast of Rockford, adjacent to Loves Park. 'Rick had a strobe light flashing on him and it was his birthday,' Robin remembered. 'He was playing a keyboard with one hand and throwing a birthday cake in the air with the other, catching bits as it fell down and eating them. It was pretty far-out.'

BRIAN BEEBE *They were doing 'My Generation' by The Who. He put his guitar up on top of his amp and just let it feed back, and he started eating birthday cake on the stage and throwing it around ... we were fifty feet away at least, and we could feel pieces of cake and crumbs landing on us, and every once in a while the drummer would reach over and bang on Rick's strings, so it kept on feeding back all the way through. Grim Reapers were a great, great band.*

As Nielsen once explained, 'I didn't want to be one of The Beach Boys.'

3

So the story goes...

The Twin Beech aircraft was just five years old when Otis Redding purchased it from James Brown in 1967. Otis happened to be learning to fly himself, and he liked to sit in the cockpit with pilot Dick Fraser. It was there that he situated himself on the morning of December 10, 1967, when he and most of his band, The Bar-Kays, boarded the plane for a flight from Cleveland to Madison, where they were scheduled to perform that evening. The weather report out of Wisconsin was less than ideal—rain and fog—but Otis prided himself on never canceling a show. The four-hundred-mile trip should take about two hours. They were airborne by one o'clock.

At 3:25pm, Fraser radioed the flight tower in Madison and was given clearance to land. Soon after, a cataclysm occurred. It has been postulated that a thick crust of ice that accumulated on the airframe caused the autopilot to disengage when the landing gear was deployed, after which the confused pilot lost control. A witness on the ground saw the plane's left wing dip as the engine sputtered. Bar-Kays member Ben Cauley, the only passenger to survive, awoke to a desperate situation. He lurched from his seat, an ill-advised move that probably saved his life. He later described a 'funny spinning sensation of falling through space.' The plane hit the water with a loud boom, half a mile from shore, and remained mostly intact, floating for a moment before it sank.

Bob Mehr, who wrote an article about Cauley for the *Memphis Commercial Appeal* in 2017, described what happened next:

> Surviving the impact of the crash was only the first hurdle. Cauley, who'd never learned to swim, was now struggling in the waters of the frigid lake.

Somehow, in between blacking out and rising to the surface of the water, he'd gotten hold of a seat cushion, which was keeping him afloat. Amid the waves, he lost hold of the cushion, but then another cushion floated by and he grabbed onto it. In the chaos, confusion and cold, he glimpsed some of his fellow passengers: Carl Cunningham surfaced for a moment without speaking; Ronnie Caldwell cried out for help. Cauley urged him to hold on, but his attempts to get to his bandmates were defeated by the hard, lapping waters.

A rescue team arrived within twenty minutes, and the bodies of pilot Dick Fraser and eighteen-year-old Bar-Kays guitarist Jimmy Lee King were found floating in the ice-cold water. When the fuselage was brought to the surface the next day, poor Otis was still strapped to his seat.

At the time of his death, Redding was booked to appear on *The Ed Sullivan Show*, *American Bandstand*, and *The Tonight Show*. There was a new single in the can, '(Sittin' On) The Dock Of The Bay,' for which Otis had high hopes. An extremely distraught Steve Cropper mixed the song that night, and Volt Records (a subsidiary of Stax) released it two weeks later. The single sold a million copies in a month and became the very first posthumous no.1 single, according to *Billboard*.

Had the Twin Beech landed safely, Otis and his band were expected to arrive any minute at the Factory on Gorham Street in Madison, a club owned and operated by area promoter and booking agent Ken Adamany.

KEN ADAMANY *The band had not yet appeared, but we had been told they were coming on a bus. I got a phone call and the detective asked if I had been expecting an orchestra on a plane. I said no, of course. I wouldn't have thought of them as an orchestra, and we were expecting a bus.*

As cold as it was, fans had lined up on the sidewalk outside. One was Jeff Grob, future drummer for seventies rock groups Looking Glass and Starz (as Joe X. Dube), accompanied by additional members from his band The Denims, one of the many groups represented under the umbrella of Ken Adamany's agency. Meanwhile, within the walls of the Factory, there rose a mounting dread. Half an hour before showtime, confirmation came that Redding and most of his band were either missing or deceased.

KEN ADAMANY *They called back and asked if I would come in and identify the bodies.*

Adamany delegated the unenviable task.

KEN ADAMANY *I sent a guy from Buddy Miles's band, Bobby Jones.*

The dire news had to be communicated to the increasingly impatient fans who were huddled shivering outside. The Factory staff put their heads together and composed a statement. The *Wisconsin State Journal* described what happened next:

> Gary Karp, a UW student and member of Madison's White Trash Blues Band, took his friend's scrawl up to the second floor. He spoke through a microphone [actually a police sergeant's megaphone]. The obituary was eight terse sentences. 'May I have your attention. May I have your attention.' Below, the crowd hushed, looking up expectantly. 'There was a plane crash in Lake Monona today. Otis Redding was on the plane. So were the Bar-Kays. Eight were on the plane altogether. They've only found one alive so far. Two are definitely dead. The rest are missing.'

KEN ADAMANY *The Madison Police Department asked that we stay open that night, fearing the worst. We started refunding tickets immediately, and opened the doors for a free show.*

The city had been on edge since October, when the Dow Chemical Company, which produced napalm, sent a recruitment team to the university and sparked a student protest that turned violent. Adamany scrambled to secure a last-minute replacement, and a band called Lee Brown & The Cheaters agreed to drive in from Milwaukee. The Grim Reapers, suddenly saddled with a tragically appropriate moniker, went on first, as planned. 'People were walking around in a daze,' Rick Nielsen told the *Wisconsin State Journal*. 'Instead of locked doors, we played.'

JIM ZUBIENA *I still get sad thinking about it because at that moment we were looking forward to listening to and opening for, at that point in time, the most powerful, emotional singer in the world.*

Forty years later, Madison weekly the *Isthmus* published a short article about the now iconic poster Adamany commissioned for the show from college student William Barr. Barr was one of those waiting in line outside the Factory on what he called a 'dark and foggy night.' 'We got on with our lives,' he told Kristian Knutsen, 'and the tragedy is they didn't get a chance to grow old with the rest of us.' Otis Redding's funeral, held a week later in Macon, Georgia, attracted 4,500 mourners.

The Jimi Hendrix Experience performed at the Factory two months later, and Rick Nielsen was present, eager to learn. 'When I was growing up, in high school, my Mother would go to Europe and I would tell her what records to get—stuff you couldn't get here,' Rick Nielsen remembered. 'My mother happened to be going to Germany. I said to her, Get me any copies you can of Jimi Hendrix. Because I loved the shiny covers.'

An eerie feeling must have permeated the venue when Hendrix and company, like Redding and the Bar-Kays, were late. Running behind and lost, a truck loaded with Hendrix's gear ended up double parked in front of Adamany's apartment building on Gilman Street, and one of Ken's neighbors hustled over to the Factory to advise him that some pissed-off English roadies were about to kick his door down. It was eventually all worked out, and Hendrix blew minds at the Factory with his wall of ten SUNN amps and newly acquired King Vox-Wah pedal.

'Hendrix had it all: the voice, the songwriting, the guitar playing, and the weirdness. He was from outer space,' Rick Nielsen told the *Quietus*. 'Jimi Hendrix really drove me crazy,' Tom Petersson agreed. 'I must have five copies of his first record. Every time I'd go into the store I'd get so excited I had to buy it again.'

Two weeks later, The Grim Reapers opened for soul belter Wilson Pickett on the same stage. Adding Joe Sundberg to the mix had enabled the group to expand their set list beyond the scope of Gary Schuder's limitations, meaning they could satisfactorily entertain a crowd like Pickett's. Joe Sundberg became available after The Bol Weevils hit a rough patch.

DENNY ORSINGER *There was some interest—major interest to take us on the road with Paul Revere & The Raiders at the time and do some stuff with Dick Clark Productions—and the Myers' parents, you know, they thought it was a nice hobby, the music, but they didn't think it was something that the boys should do,* *so that kind of fell apart. My girlfriend moved to Connecticut, and I couldn't go anywhere in music and I got bummed out, because I really liked the music and promotion business, so I went to Florida, to college.*

Denny's departure meant The Bol Weevils needed not only a new singer but a whole new rhythm section, since drummer Mike Myers, about to be drafted, had enlisted instead. In January 1968, the Viet Minh and North Vietnamese carried out a series of coordinated attacks on more than a hundred cities and outposts (including the American embassy in Saigon) throughout South Vietnam, known as the Tet Offensive.

Craig Myers and Tom Petersson already knew who they wanted to replace Mike on drums: Chester 'Chip' Greenman, from another local band called The Society.

CRAIG MYERS *Chip was Buddy Rich–inspired, so he had all this technique, and we hadn't seen technique at all.*

Greenman accepted the offer, much to the chagrin of the rest of The Society. A threat was made to break Craig's very important fingers, but cooler heads prevailed. The band was still short a bass player.

CRAIG MYERS *The music we were attempting, like the Yardbirds stuff, had really good bass playing, so we needed a good bass player.*

And so, Tom Petersson made the fateful switch from guitar to bass.

CRAIG MYERS *He was willing to do it, out of necessity but also very willing. He just got very good at it very fast.*

'I was a rhythm guitarist when I started out,' Tom Petersson told *Bass Player*. 'I was never great at playing fast stuff.' He explained, 'When I started, I played bass like a rhythm guitar. It wasn't the way a bass teacher would teach you to play, but it gave me my own style and sound.' The first electric bass Tom owned was a Jazz, Fender's follow up to the very first electric bass, the Precision. 'I never liked it,' Tom told *Vintage Guitar*. 'In 1969, I bought a blue Rickenbacker 4001 to replace the Jazz.'

CRAIG MYERS *Chip, Tom, and I rehearsed often in Tom's parents' basement. It was at this time that we went from getting better to just exploding ... we could predict what each other was gonna do, and it became sort of like a natural chemistry that people just don't get very often—it was special.*

As for a singer, they found one in a local folkie named Ron Holm, fresh from a stint with an ensemble called The Liberty Numeral Music Company. He soon realized that this band was operating at another level.

RON HOLM *Tom was so innovative. I kind of felt like I fell into a group of these super-talented people, all with their own style, their own sensibility—Chip with his double bass drums and Craig had great stage presence, he'd sling his guitar low, and he had a really great feel for those blues licks.*

Like most other musicians in and around Rockford, Holm was a regular at the Ralph Nielsen Music House (later called Ralph Nielsen's Music), where Craig's brother Mike had once been employed alongside Ralph's son Rick.

MIKE MYERS *Rick and I would do all the piano deliveries and organ deliveries. We'd go off to Indiana to pick up trumpets at the factory.*
The first time I ever took acid was with Rick Nielsen. We took it together: I think we were on the way back from picking up trumpets, we stopped in Chicago at the Kinetic Playground, saw The Finchley Boys. That was a crazy band.

To flesh out the entirely revamped Bol Weevils, they enlisted another Music House regular, Curtis Wright, on keyboards. An African American from Beloit, Wright was older than the rest, in his mid-twenties, and a navy veteran. An energetic performer, he infused the group with personality.

This would be a very different band from The Bol Weevils. Craig Myers, like many of his contemporaries, had recently experienced a paradigm shift after hearing Eric Clapton play a Gibson Les Paul through a Marshall stack on the *John Mayall's Bluesbreakers With Eric Clapton* album, colloquially called 'The Beano Album.'

CRAIG MYERS *I learned how to play along with Clapton, note for note, on that album. Nobody was playing fluid leads like that. None of the kids in my school,*

in my pocket, knew anything about blues or anything, but I got a copy of
that record. That's how I got the jump on everybody, playing what became the
standard rock'n'roll style of playing, which was all blues stolen. I was able to do
that in '67—the vibrato on the strings and stuff like that. There were people that
were starting to pay attention to the way I played guitar, which helped me a lot,
spurred me on.

As for the set list, the new band decided to shake things up, incorporating a lot
of R&B and traditional blues. In that spirit, they playfully dubbed themselves
Toastin Jam (possibly Toast & Jam, then altered).

RON HOLM *A lot of what we did we were hearing through contemporary records. I*
really liked James Cotton, and we would play tunes by him, so that would be like
a second generation, but some of the songs we did were third generation, learning
from Spencer Davis and Stevie Winwood and the Stones.

Toastin Jam developed a few originals but performed mostly covers, the
intended style being 'shuffle blues' (as Ron described it) with a Hendrix song
or two thrown in for good measure, performed as a three-piece with Tom
Petersson on vocals.

RON HOLM *Kind of our signature piece was our arrangement of 'Back Door Man.'*
Among other people, The Doors recorded that song, but we had a totally different
take on it, more up-tempo, and Curtis Wright, he was large, he was a big guy,
but he was a very adroit dancer, and in the middle of 'Back Door Man' Chip
would play a drum solo and Curtis would not just jump off the stage—he would
do a complete 360-degree somersault off the stage, and then go into a St. Vitus
Dance. It was a hoot.

That spring, Martin Luther King Jr. and Robert F. Kennedy were both
gunned down. Things looked bleak, yet the rock snowball kept rolling. In
July, a nineteen-year-old Rick Nielsen flew to Cleveland to catch a weekend
engagement by the Jeff Beck Group (rounded out by Rod Stewart, Ronnie
Wood, Mick Waller, and Nicky Hopkins) at La Cave, a small basement club
on Euclid Avenue. 'There were eight people there to see 'em, and I sat there
spellbound,' Rick told Nick Perri.

The July 9–11 dates were booked by Ken Adamany for a total fee of $1,250. At the end of July, The Grim Reapers traveled to Estes Park, Colorado for a week-long residency at a place called Jax Snax. A letter to the *Coloradan Alumni Magazine* described Jax Snax as 'the place to go for 18–21-year-olds spending the summer working or visiting in the tourist town. It was a rowdy place, constantly in trouble for noise violations, and it was eventually closed down.'

On August 28, 1968, the *Rockford Register Republic* reported that a group called 'Toast And Jam' would be competing in a battle of the bands against The Esquires, The Brotherhood, The Seeds Of Doubt, and The Grim Reapers in the Rockford College Gymnasium. This meant Joe Sundberg, now with The Grim Reapers, found himself battling against his former bandmates from The Bol Weevils.

Those stakes might have seemed high, but elsewhere nearby they were much higher. That same night, fifteen thousand hippies and yippies who had gathered in Chicago to make their voices heard during the Democratic National Convention unwittingly marched into a melee with Chicago police. At issue, of course, was the war in Vietnam. Former Grim Reapers frontman Gary Schuder was about to be sent there.

The assault that the police launched against the demonstrators came to be called 'The Battle Of Michigan Avenue,' and the entire bloody mess culminated in the controversial 'Chicago Seven' trial the next year. Just eighty miles to the north, a different kind of skirmish ensued in the Rockford College Gymnasium. It is unclear as to which band was crowned victorious, but it is clear that members from two of the competing bands, Toastin Jam and The Grim Reapers, would soon join forces—but not just yet, because on October 12, 1968, Toastin Jam signed a management contract with Ken Adamany's RAM Productions.

RON HOLM *I recall the day we signed it. It was a beautiful, cool, crisp fall day.*

Ken Adamany grew up in Janesville, Wisconsin, and gained his earliest management experience while securing dates for his own combo, The KnightTranes, made up of guitarists Frank Ellefson and Steve Sperry, saxophonist Robert Shebesta, and drummer Bill Fullmer, with Adamany on keyboards. The KnightTranes performed throughout Wisconsin and northern

Illinois during the late fifties and early sixties. 'Ken had been booking bands around that area for a while and he'd built up The KnighTranes into his top-of-the-line act, the one he could charge the most money for,' Adamany's future bandmate Boz Scaggs remembered. 'They'd been a real band at one time, everyone wore gold lame vests and black pants. A little corny, but it worked.'

In 1960, Adamany moved to Madison to attend the University Of Wisconsin, and there he met fellow musicians Scaggs and Steve Miller, out-of-staters who had cut their teeth with a blues band called The Marksmen back in Texas. Adamany recruited the pair for a revamped version of The KnighTranes.

KEN ADAMANY *The KnighTranes played all the summer dates and a few school time dates with Boz, Steve, Denny Berg, and Ron Boyer. When school resumed in the fall, they became The Ardells, without me.*

'We got $80 to $100 a night to perform, which was a lot in those days,' Ron Boyer remembered. 'We were one of the top bands in the market. Others only got $25 a night. It was really a good time.' Future filmmaker Michael Mann, in Madison studying literature at the time, was a part of the friend group.

The next summer, Ken called on the boys again.

KEN ADAMANY *I converted The Ardells to The KnighTranes to play summer resorts in Lake Geneva, Twin Lakes, Fox Lake, Illinois, and other towns around Illinois and Wisconsin.*

According to Scaggs, 'Ken could still get bookings for the band. Whenever he did, he'd call me and Steve and another guitar player and say, Look, we've got to be The KnighTranes. And we'd all show up wearing black pants and gold lamé vests and do jivey Louis Prima lounge stuff and Top 40 songs and our versions of R&B songs. It was a great learning experience, because you were constantly learning new material and having to work four or five sets a night.'

Adamany eventually retired The KnighTranes name, after which The Ardells made another haphazard go of it. Natasha Kassulke described how that turned out in a 1999 article for the *Wisconsin State Journal*:

Boyer recalls that Miller dropped out of college and started living out of his van, surviving on peanut butter and crackers. 'Those guys had almost no money,' Boyer says. 'I had a job, so I was the only one with a steady income.' Boyer says the focus turned to women and partying, two things that he, as a married man with a family and a business, shied from. 'We were playing a lot of shows but we didn't make a record,' Boyer says.

Adamany's focus became his booking agency, which he came to call Ken Adamany Music Enterprises. As of March 1964, he represented more than fifty acts, groups with names like The Disciples, Vantells, Driftwoods, Knightbeats, Crossfires, Chordairs, Seven Sounds and Bel Airs. The list grew ever longer—within two years, Ken Adamany Music Enterprises represented more than one hundred artists, including The Grim Reapers, Bol Weevils, and Paegans.

At the beginning of 1968, Adamany sold his booking department to a company out of Neenah, Wisconsin, called Bacchus Productions, as detailed in an article published by the *Post Crescent*, which noted that Adamany had made the sale 'in order to devote more time to management and promotion of the top rock bands currently in his agency.'

* * *

On October 11, 1968, the night before Toastin Jam signed that management contract with Ken Adamany, Rick Nielsen watched from the grimy floor at Kinetic Playground as Jeff Beck's roadie dropped Beck's guitar and snapped the neck. 'He sat his guitar on the top of his amp and the roadie picked it up by the body, accidentally knocking it down,' Nielsen recalled. 'I don't think anybody else in the place noticed except for me as I was totally glued looking at all of his gear.' Nielsen passed the roadie a note offering to sell Beck a replacement. 'I said, You don't know me, but Jeff Beck is my favorite guitar player and I collect guitars.'

A couple of weeks later, Rick's phone rang. It was Jeff Beck calling. He was in Philadelphia for a two-night stand at Electric Factory (October 25 and 26) and had decided to take Rick up on his offer. Mike Myers accompanied Nielsen on the flight to Philadelphia, the round-trip tickets costing just $21. They brought along five guitars for Beck to choose from. 'Some Juniors and some Standards,' Nielsen recalled. 'When I got to the club, Ronnie Wood was sharing out tea from an antique set he got from a store.' Nielsen sold Beck a '59 Les Paul Sunburst with a Bigsby vibrato, serial number 91864, for $350 ($2,600 when adjusted for inflation). Today, that guitar would be worth at least half a million dollars. Nielsen had originally traded a Gibson SG and $25 for it.

* * *

Facing a significant backlash over the war in Vietnam, President Lyndon Johnson decided not to run for re-election. His Republican counterpart, Richard Nixon, who had lost to John F. Kennedy eight years earlier, was finally victorious that November, in part thanks to his promise to end the draft.

The Nixon administration might have scaled things back, but the war raged on for years.

* * *

There were plenty of paying gigs to be had in the Midwest for groups like The Grim Reapers and Toastin Jam, and they were making money and entertaining people, but if the boys aspired to build an actual career in the music industry, the cover-band circuit was a dead end. They had invested a massive amount of time and energy and become proficient musicians and seasoned performers. It was time to take the next step.

JOE SUNDBERG *Rick and I wanted to start a band that played original music.*

CRAIG MYERS *Rick Nielsen and my brother Mike came to the Dalton Youth Center, it was either in Rockton or Beloit. Toastin Jam was playing there, and they came up and heard the band and Rick was kind of floored, and he talked to me after that about forming a new band with him and Joe and Tom and myself and Chip Greenman. We got together with the purpose of writing songs. We were gonna write our own music and try to record.*

There was only one problem: that other band. If Rick Nielsen wished to join forces with Toastin Jam, he would have to dissolve The Grim Reapers.

JIM ZUBIENA *There was no tumultuous event that caused the breakup. I just walked into rehearsal, unbeknown to me what was going on, so it had to have been something that was planned that was kept from me personally. I never looked at what we were doing like Rick did. Rick Nielsen looked at it like it was going to be his profession. He had every intention of making this what he was going to do for the rest of his life.*

ROSS ANDERSON *Rick was the driving force in all of our work and practice, leading by example. Rick was constantly playing his guitars, new riffs. Even if he wasn't plugged in, he couldn't put the guitar down.*

And yet 'put the guitar down' is precisely what Rick Nielsen did, as by all accounts Craig Myers was a virtuoso on the instrument and would undoubtedly be the lead guitarist in whatever band he was in. Nielsen's predominant role in the new band would be as keyboardist.

It went like this:

1. The Grim Reapers broke up.
2. Rick Nielsen and Joe Sundberg joined Toastin Jam.
3. Toastin Jam changed their name to The Grim Reapers.

Consider this exchange between Rick, Tom, and Ira Robbins:

RICK: Grim Reapers was my band.
TOM: Right. You used the name just because it was popular.
RICK: Because we were more popular.
IRA: So, Tom, you joined The Grim Reapers?
TOM: He kind of got rid of everybody.
RICK: I got rid of everybody and then we started over with ...
TOM: And used the name because it made sense for getting bookings.

They seem to have briefly considered making a fresh start with a new name, sharing with a newspaper at the time that two contenders were The Yankee Dogs and Mello Carmello Palumbo, which was the title of the B-side to a 1968 single called 'Love-itis' by the Canadian group Mandala. 'Love-itis,' which later turned up in the early Cheap Trick live set, was written and originally performed by Harvey Scales, another client of Ken Adamany.

Curtis Wright was the only member of Toastin Jam to be excluded. As David Brent might say, he had been made redundant.

RON HOLM *It was an awful call. I felt really bad.*

Rick Nielsen, supplanted by Craig Myers, in turn supplanted Curtis Wright.

Meanwhile, the first rehearsal for the new band was attended by both singers, Joe Sundberg and Ron Holm, conforming to a precedent set when Sundberg joined The Grim Reapers alongside Gary Schuder (who by this point was busy being sent to Vietnam).

RON HOLM *I don't know what they talked about with the Reapers, but the notion we talked about with Toastin Jam was that we would do something kind of unusual—we had two singers, and Joe and I would try to work out duets and harmonies. I was also a harmonica player, so we could have me play the harp and do that grungy blues stuff. So, the first rehearsal happened, and I sensed this was gonna be a lot of work.*

Holm was keenly aware of the harsh reality that someone like Gary Schuder faced and knew he had to keep his college career on track if he wanted to avoid a similar fate.

RON HOLM *I just didn't go to the next rehearsal. I think that was probably fine with them. I had a draft deferment, and if I tried to do music full time I entered into a whole different world of draft letters, draft physicals. It was so looming.*

Thankfully, Rick Nielsen faced no similar dilemma. 'My dad had asthma his whole life, and I've had asthma my whole life, but not so bad where I worry about it,' he told *Illinois Entertainer*. 'It helped me get out of the draft. There were three busloads of volunteers in 1968 or '69, and we went from Rockford to Chicago for selective service. And out of the three busloads, a midget, a huge fat guy, and myself, were the only ones that were rejected.'

He immediately stopped attending classes at Rock Valley Community College. 'I wouldn't go one more minute because I knew what I wanted to do,' Rick admitted. His former bandmate had no choice: Gary Schuder enlisted in the Army on November 24, 1968. Mike Myers was about to do the same, but not before one last fling with Rick and Tom.

MIKE MYERS *Rick was going to England, so I went with him and Tom Petersson, we all three went to England in 1968, right before Christmas, and we went to London for two weeks. It was great—the flight and the hotel, I think it was a couple hundred bucks. I sold my car. On January 1st I was to report to the Army.*

Rick Nielsen sold a couple of guitars to help fund the trip. 'We got off the plane and went to stay in the Bayswater area, at the Inverness Court Hotel, where you had to put shillings into the meter,' he remembered. 'Later that week I went to the Marquee and saw Love Sculpture with Dave Edmunds, then I bought four Sound City stacks, because that's what he used. It was all so exciting.' Love Sculpture's 'Sabre Dance' was in the Top 10 at the time. Rick, Tom, and Mike hung out at the Roundhouse and the Marquee, where they saw bands like Jethro Tull (whose first album had only been out for two months), Barclay James Harvest, and Bakerloo Blues Line. They also saw Gun, whose 'Race With The Devil' was a recent Top 10 hit, in the Chalk Farm district of north London; and Skid Row, featuring a young guitarist named Gary Moore. Nielsen remembered, 'Halfway through their set everybody left the stage except Gary. He got on the drums, played the guitar and sang all at the same time. Wise guy. It was unbelievable.'

It is interesting to note that on December 7, a Scottish band called Dream Police played the Marquee (just three days before a band called Led Zeppelin— billed, in parentheses, as 'New THE YARDBIRDS'). Perhaps Rick spied the phrase on a lingering poster and filed it away for future use?

'At that time, The Beatles' *White Album* had just come out,' Petersson recalled. 'And then the Stones' *Beggars Banquet* came out when we were over there ... so we bought them there and we had to buy a turntable to listen to it in our crummy little room. But it was the greatest thing I had ever heard. It was just fantastic. It was just really a dream come true.' *The White Album* came out at the end of November and *Beggars Banquet* the first week in December. According to Nielsen, 'We walked about a block away to a used electronics store and bought a little, not even a hi-fi, it was just a little record player, and we sat in the room, freezing cold, and listened ...'

MIKE MYERS *He was buying all these records, all the latest English records and playing those.*

'Listened to them on acid. American acid,' Nielsen recalled. 'Then we went to the Roundhouse and took the guy we bought the turntable from, and we never saw him again ... our acid was LSD from Owsley, the real stuff, and we brought it over. We were eating it like candy. And that's what we gave to the guy who sold us the turntable.' (Owsley Stanley was the soundman for the

Grateful Dead and one of the first people to mass produce LSD.)

Cliff Cooper had recently opened his Orange Music shop in London's West End, primarily to help defray the costs of running a recording studio in the basement, and it was there that Rick purchased his famous Mellotron. According to Rick, 'It was the dual keyboard Mellotron, the kind that Mike Pinder of The Moody Blues had. It weighed a ton. I got a used one and it was a mechanical behemoth. And I had it shipped back from England.' Cooper was not yet selling his now famous amps. 'He was telling us all about his plans of putting out a line of amps which he was building in the back of the shop,' Petersson recalled. According to Tom, the first band he saw with Orange amps was Fleetwood Mac. 'They came to the US in '69, and it was so great. At that time they had those really big ones, you know, giants. The cabinet was like ten feet tall, it was a joke. After that, we all just absolutely loved Orange Amps, and I've loved them ever since.'

Nielsen dropped Adamany a line from London, scribbled on stationary from the Mandeville Hotel and dated December 25. It read, 'Hi Ken. Beck and the owner of the Marquee to hear the tape Monday. Should get jobs at Marquee. Groups so far are terrible.' It is unclear as to what tape Rick was referencing or who might have actually heard it, but as soon as the boys returned from London, the newly formed Grim Reapers dove headfirst into songwriting. 'Rick was leading the band and he had a vision of what he wanted as far as our musical style,' Chip Greenman remembered. 'He was really into the British scene like King Crimson, The Move, Jeff Beck, The Yardbirds, and Yes.'

CRAIG MYERS *All of our biggest influences were British. We were after that heavy rock Brit sound. Not to be confused with metal, that came later. Rick was the catalyst…*

Rick had just turned twenty, Tom was eighteen, Craig was seventeen, and Joe and Chip were sixteen. The band rehearsed in a tiny room at Chip's parents' house, crammed with Rick's new double stacks of Sound City amps (which cost half as much as Marshalls), two Ampeg bass amps, a Hammond B3 organ, a Mellotron, Chip's large custom drum set, and a Sunn Studio PA. Neighbors reportedly complained that the equipment somehow interfered with their television sets.

The new lineup was something to behold, and Adamany signed on to manage them. Winter and much of the spring were spent writing songs and rehearsing them, with the odd gig at the Quarry in Appleton or the Cellar in Arlington Heights. By summer, the band seemed ready for whatever opportunity might present itself.

On June 7, 1969, Adamany landed them a supporting slot with The Who at Majestic Hills in Lake Geneva, Wisconsin, a venue first opened as a ski resort in 1957 on land once occupied by owner Bill Grunow's family's chicken farm. Grunow eventually constructed a bandstand on the property, which, as he described it, became the highlight of the business. Quite a few legends performed on that stage, and The Grim Reapers played with a few of them, including, previously to The Who, The Yardbirds.

ROSS ANDERSON *A lot of our fans followed us there for that and we had pyrotechnics. Rick had constructed a huge looking amp that we called 'The Taint' because it 'tain't an amp' and it was just full of pyrotechnics and so forth. He could smash in the speaker and projectiles would come out and explosions in the back, and I would hold the Farfisa mini-compact over my head. I think Jim had a replaceable front head to one of his bass drums, and Rick or somebody would kick that in or hit it with their guitar. Rick had guitars that were cheap guitars that he could switch out and he would break that guitar.*

JIM ZUBIENA *I remember our final song was 'My Generation.' That was Rick's signature song every night and, of course, since his dad owned a music store and could repair the guitars, he proceeded to smash it into small pieces and use it to trash one of his amplifiers. I remember one of the Yardbirds coming up onstage and, in a rather complementary way, saying on mic, 'We have to follow that?'*

Of course, it was an almost entirely different band called The Grim Reapers that opened for The Who. Still, the Brits had no trouble following them. Rick Nielsen once ranked The Who's performance that night as the best live show he ever witnessed. 'They were pure excitement. Pure wild,' he told Richard Bienstock for *Billboard*.

The stage at Majestic Hills was wide enough for more than one band to be set up, minimizing the wait time between sets. After their performance, The Grim Reapers and friends sat huddled together on the side of the stage to watch The Who. *Tommy* had just been released, and songs from the rock opera made up two thirds of the set. It all ended, of course, with the destruction of the band's equipment. Roger Daltrey swung his microphone around and around, sturdily taped as it was to the end of its cord, while Keith Moon dangled from the limb of the tree growing through the stage, scratching at his armpit. The Who were a month away from performing at Woodstock.

Also that summer, Adamany launched a new label called Smack (as in 'hit') in order to release a single he produced for The Grim Reapers, with a version of Leiber and Stoller's 'Hound Dog'—popularized, of course, by Elvis Presley—on the A-side. 'We did a version that we sort of stole from a band called Plastic Penny,' Nielsen admitted. Plastic Penny were an obscure UK band active from 1967 to 1969. Their sludgy arrangement of 'Hound Dog' was a precursor to early Black Sabbath. The Grim Reapers' version kicks in differently, upbeat and frenetic, but soon segues into the Plastic Penny rip-off. For the B-side, they recorded a generic blues number credited to Sundberg and Myers called 'Cruisin' For Burgers.' Adamany sent the single to most major record labels at the time and managed to conjure up some interest, including from Epic.

KEN ADAMANY *They liked the single I produced and asked for more songs. I sent additional songs and they agreed to come to see the band, if I could get them a date in a major city.*

4

I wonder what life will be...

FUSE. GARY SCHUDER. VIETNAM.

The brick building on North Clark Street in Chicago has at various points housed a casino, restaurant, jazz club, bowling alley, and skating rink. In 1968, a twentysomething transplant from Brooklyn named Aaron Russo turned the ballroom into a venue and nightclub he called the Kinetic Playground. A post to Answers.com describes the club as having 'a huge balcony, eight sound towers, a kaleidoscope of full-length mirrors, an amoeba-shaped stage, and meditation booths,' while a regular attendee described the typical vibe:

> Movies and various light show magic projected on large screens arranged in a circle around the staging area, which also had the house sound behind them. That place was absolutely insane, the party atmosphere was irresistible. Entering the front door after giving up your ticket or cash, you entered a curved wall maze of mirrors. Into the showroom, large carpeted geometric shapes rise from the floor around the perimeter of the varnished wood-planked main floor, always crowded but the rarely unfriendly audience awaiting the start of the show. Once the show had begun it could be extremely difficult to safely navigate through the people seated on the floor, because of the light show and nearly impossible if you were up and walking when they turned on the brightest strobe lights known to man, running around the bottom of the circular control/projection booth suspended from the center of the showroom's ceiling. A trip to the washroom could be a long and interesting journey.

For a few years, the Kinetic Playground was a regular stop for touring acts like The Byrds, The Who, The Animals, Steppenwolf, Blue Cheer, Iron Butterfly,

The Grateful Dead, Deep Purple, The Velvet Underground, Led Zeppelin, King Crimson, and many others.

JOE SUNDBERG *It was a dream that we'd eventually play there.*

Ken Adamany secured a booking for The Grim Reapers at the Kinetic Playground for Thursday, July 24, 1969—Led Zeppelin performed on the same stage less than a week earlier—and convinced three representatives from Epic Records—Mort Hoffman, Larry Cohn, and Rick Blackburn—to fly in from New York. 'Epic were going to be there sometime during our performance, but we didn't know when and we didn't know who to look for,' Rick Nielsen recalled. 'We were pretty nervous.' The pressure was on, but the performance went well. *Chicago Tribune* correspondent Sally Simpson was struck by The Grim Reapers' 'rock version of Borodin's Polovtsian Dances,' a piece from the second act of Alexander Borodin's opera *Prince Igor* made popular by the fifties musical *Kismet*.

According to Nielsen, 'Epic liked us and signed us on the spot.'

KEN ADAMANY *Not exactly. The band was fantastic that night, but negotiations started a few days later.*

CRAIG MYERS *It was in Aaron Russo's office where they decided to sign us.*

KEN ADAMANY *... discussed signing. But they were completely knocked out by the band.*

CRAIG MYERS *[Larry Cohn] said we were the most British-sounding American band he had heard, and that I was America's answer to Jeff Beck.*

Conversely, that same month, former Grim Reaper Gary Schuder was given his very grim assignment, as a rifleman with the 101st Airborne. Having survived basic training, where he was made proficient with hand grenades and an M-14 battle rifle with fixed bayonet, Gary was shuffled through the 'Repot Depot' in Oakland, where he was handed a stack of jungle fatigues designed to be lightweight and fast-drying, and flown to the Tan Son Nhut air base near Saigon. From there, he was ferried to the nearby Bein Hoa base for additional training at SERTS (Screaming Eagle Replacement Training School), at which point his M-14 was probably upgraded to an M-16, which Gary was trained to take apart and clean, all the while thinking, Why me?

Gary's next stop was Camp Evans, just north of the Vietnamese city of Hue, where he was issued a rucksack with aluminum frame, padded shoulder straps and waist belt. Soon enough, a helicopter dropped him 'in the field' with Alpha company. Gary surely understood why he was there: to replace a recent casualty. More than four hundred members of the 101st airborne had been killed or wounded at Hamburger Hill in May. Gary spent most of the next year or more 'in the field'; while his former bandmates were living the dream, he was experiencing the ultimate nightmare: ground combat in Vietnam.

Bill Higgins, a member of Charlie company, 1/506th, at the same time Gary was a member of Alpha company, 1/506th, described the daily burden for soldiers like them in an article for 506infantry.org:

> We carried load bearing equipment (LBE) that was essentially a belt and harness to hang items such as grenades, canteens, canteen covers (filled with grenades), etc. We also had bandoleers of M-16 ammunition strung on top of the LBE … this was the fighting gear if you made enemy contact. On top of this, we carried rucksacks with food, water, ammunition, IV bottles, claymores, gas masks, etc. The rucksacks could be in the range of 50–80 pounds.

The 101st Airborne Division suffered the second highest casualty rate of the war, and Gary was in the thick of it. Almost fifty members of his company lost their lives during his tour of duty, casualties to operations with names like Montgomery Rendezvous, Louisiana Lee, Republic Square, Randolph Glen, and a fierce, months-long battle at Firebase Ripcord. At one point, a bullet reportedly grazed Gary's ear—much too close for comfort. There in the jungle it was all so terribly real, but back home the war was, for many, just an abstract concern. Luck of the draw.

On the last weekend of July, Rick Nielsen attended the Midwest Rock Fest in Milwaukee. Every former Yardbirds guitarist performed at the event: Jimmy Page with Led Zeppelin on Friday, Eric Clapton with Blind Faith on Saturday, and Jeff Beck with his group on Sunday. Rick claimed on the *In The Trenches* podcast that he attended the Midwest Rock Fest instead of Woodstock, but Woodstock happened two weeks later.

The Grim Reapers returned to the Kinetic Playground in early August, but now they were called Fuse (introduced from the stage as 'formerly the Grim Reapers'). The record deal had come with a caveat: change the name, which was 'too dark.' After the band said no to Thunderclap, Epic convinced them to go with Fuse. According to Joe Sundberg, 'Their creative department came up with it.'

The name change occurred just as the Zodiac was sending his first letters to the San Francisco newspapers and Manson's savage flunkies committed the Tate/Labianca murders. In that context, ditching the morbid moniker made a certain amount of sense. At the Kinetic Playground, Fuse performed on the same bill as Terry Reid (now a labelmate at Epic) and Blues Image. Jeff Beck had been scheduled to headline but canceled.

On August 9, Fuse opened for Frank Zappa & The Mothers Of Invention at Majestic Hills. 'Those guys pulled up in two Rambler station wagons,' Rick Nielsen told Ira Robbins. 'I don't know where you can rent two Rambler station wagons.' The show was bookended by Manson murders: Sharon Tate, Jay Sebring, Abigail Folger, Wojciech Frykowski, and Steven Parent were murdered in the early morning hours of August 9 and Leno and Rosemary LaBianca in the early morning hours of August 10. Oblivious to the carnage back home, Zappa watched Fuse from the side of the stage and thoroughly enjoyed himself.

KEN ADAMANY *He came up to me after the set and expressed great interest. Then he went on to complain that the place was oversold and proceeded to get onstage and kick out the stage lights after blasting Bill Grunow, the owner of Majestic Hills. I kept in touch with him and sent tapes to him and his manager.*

Rick Nielsen remembered Zappa saying, 'I really liked your band. I wanted to know if you want to be signed to Bizarre.' Bizarre was Zappa's eccentric complement to his primary label at the time, Straight Records, which had just released the first Alice Cooper album, *Pretties For You*, in June. Fuse had no choice but to regretfully decline Zappa's untimely offer, having just signed a contract with Epic. The boys were bummed. If nothing else, Zappa would have let them remain The Grim Reapers.

* * *

Epic promptly reissued the 'Hound Dog' single as a Fuse release, a development Nielsen expressed mixed feelings about when speaking to the *Rockford Register Republic* in September. 'It was something we did in one cutting,' he said, 'and we don't think it represents what we can do. We've asked Epic not to push it. We'd rather wait and stand on the album.'

KEN ADAMANY *Rick just does not remember. We were there a very long time and there are quite a few takes for each song, and we even put the background vocals through a Leslie 122 cabinet. I certainly did not ask Epic to bury the single.*

At that point the band were in the midst of recording their debut album at CBS Studios on McClurg Court in Chicago with producer Jackie Mills—a pairing the Fuse members came to regret. According to Rick Nielsen, 'The guys that were working at the company, except for maybe the top people, they were hired because they had long hair.'

JOE SUNDBERG *The guys at Epic turned out to be idiots. They gave us a producer who was horrible, he had never produced any kind of heavy rock band like we were so the sound came out really tinny and hollow, he didn't know what he was doing.*

To be fair, Mills had previously produced quality psychedelic rock records for Kaleidoscope and The Floating Bridge. Fuse, on the other hand, had been a band for less than a year, and all but Rick were still teenagers. Their inexperience showed when Mills was able to convince them that having a manager was a superfluous expense. The boys fired Adamany (though he was eventually re-hired), and Epic was none too happy about it.

KEN ADAMANY *Craig's parents and Rick's parents, they decided that they were going to manage the band.*

* * *

On November 15, Gary Schuder's name appeared in the *Rockford Morning Star* beneath the headline, 'Rockford Man Set To Pass Second Yule In Warzone.' (Gary was not the 'Rockford Man' specifically referenced.) Less than two weeks later, the same newspaper published an article about Fuse: 'January Release Set For Album By Rockford Band.'

Fuse complements the usual supply of drums, guitar, organ, bass and voice with the unusual quality of a Mellotron. The Mellotron, according to Nielsen, first plays and records the order and length of a succession of musical notes and then replays the same succession using only one or two keys during an actual performance.

Rick Nielsen did not play a lick of guitar on the *Fuse* album, just keyboards. His eventual notoriety as a guitar player has led to some confusion about this, to the endless chagrin of Craig Myers.

CRAIG MYERS *He didn't touch a guitar on that album—that's me. I'm doing the rhythm parts, I'm doing the acoustic parts on a few songs, all the leads. That's my guitar playing.*

The *Morning Star* framed its article with individual pictures of each band member, and ironically, considering the passage above, Myers was identified as 'big on bass' while Tom Petersson was labeled 'guitarist.' Later that day, the same article (minus the pictures) appeared in the *Rockford Register-Republic* with a different headline: 'Rock Band Fuses Into Record Group.' In it, Nielsen described the band's sound as 'hard and loud like that of a lot of other groups, but the music is original. It's all ours.'

On November 19, Jan Bergstrom penned an article about Fuse for the *Valley Forge*, Rock Valley College's student newspaper. The headline: 'Two Players From ROCK Valley: FUSE Blows Out On POP Record.' The 'two players' referenced were Rick Nielsen and Tom Petersson.

According to Peterson, 'The hardest part about recording the album was that we all had to record on different tracks which means by ourselves. It's hard to hear what you really sound like without the rest of the group behind you.' The producer of the album, Jackie Mills, is a free-lance producer from Los Angeles and was hired by Epic to do the album. He was quite impressed with the group. 'They were a very easy group to work with,' Mills confided. 'They cut the album quite fast. It was really surprising.' According to FUSE's manager Ken Adomany (sic) there is a possibility that the group may tour England over the Easter holidays. While working on the album CBS filmed a five minute news short on how a rock'n'roll group records their first album.

'They filmed for about three hours altogether,' Nielsen explained. The short has been shown on Chicago television and should be shown soon in Rockford, the fast-rising musician added.

In the end, the boys were bitterly disappointed with how the *Fuse* record turned out, but it has its moments. 'Across The Skies,' by Sundberg and Nielsen, is an atmospheric epic, if poorly mixed. The influences are readily apparent: Led Zeppelin, The Zombies, Deep Purple. 'Permanent Resident,' by Myers and Sundberg, is heavy on bass and keyboards, as is most of the album. The drums are buried in the mix, and Myers's guitar work fades in and out. The Easybeats sound like an influence, perhaps Vanilla Fudge. 'Show Me,' by Nielsen, is a generic groover. 'To Your Health,' also by Nielsen, is a six-minute instrumental strewn with riff after riff, accompanied by screaming guitar breaks. 'In A Window,' by Sundberg and Nielsen, is also six minutes but, even with lyrics, far less interesting than the instrumental; '4/4 3/4' by Myers and Sundberg is a galloping rocker that never arrives at a catchy melody. 'Mystery Ship,' by Myers and Sundberg, features nice lead fills from Myers but drags to a slog. 'Sad Day' by Nielsen closes the album. A heavy approximation of a ballad, it was pretty late in the game to finally treat the listener to the album's prettiest moments and strongest melodies.

The *Fuse* album in no way foreshadowed what was to come with Cheap Trick. According to Tom Petersson, 'The band was much better than the album indicates. When it came out we were disgusted.'

KEN ADAMANY *The album they recorded was not well received because they brought in Jackie Mills to produce. About two thirds of the way through the recording, Rick called to say it would not be necessary for me to come back down to the sessions in Chicago. Recording at CBS was a weird setup. That was a union studio, and you could only record for three or four hours and then you had to take a break. You can't do that because you're starting to put stuff down on tape, and a guy comes in and says, 'Union break, everybody out of the studio.' It was very strange.*

'The whole thing turned out to be a joke,' Rick Nielsen lamented. 'We had no say in the record's production, distribution or promotion.'

KEN ADAMANY *When their parents started managing them, I was still in touch with Epic because the record company didn't know what to do, or how to work the release of the single and the album nationally. Apparently they were finding it difficult coordinating with the parents. That was probably a big reason why the band's option was not picked up. Basically, they didn't have a manager.*

JOE SUNDBERG *It stopped the momentum because the record label found out about us warring with the manager, and they didn't like that, so it just really screwed things up.*

CRAIG MYERS *The record was fine, but live the band was kickass. Live, the band could really put it out there.*

KEN ADAMANY *They were an excellent band.*

Future entrepreneur Paul Hamer saw Fuse during this period and agreed.

PAUL HAMER *I had a friend named Gary Gand who had a light show, he called it 'The Incredible Light Show.' I started working for Gary, and he used to do a light show on the weekends, out of a place called Heads Up in Round Lake Beach. Lo and behold, this band shows up, they're called Fuse, they have a record, and I'll never forget the way they walked into the show that night because we had to get there early to set up all of our stuff, and when they walked in, they looked like they were from England, they looked like The Beatles.*

'They were fearless,' Hamer told Steve Matthes. 'Each set was played perfectly.'

* * *

On December 1, 1969, CBS News aired a special report from correspondent Roger Mudd, live from Selective Service headquarters in Washington, DC. 'Good evening,' said Mudd. 'Tonight, for the first time in twenty-seven years, the United States has again started a draft lottery.' So much for Nixon ending the draft.

Twenty-seven million young American males became eligible to be drafted during the Vietnam era. Only a quarter of them were conscripted or enlisted, and less than two million of those actually saw combat, but the prospect of an untimely death in a far-off jungle hung like a dark cloud over every young man at the time. My own father was drafted, and, though he did not see combat, he relinquished his freedom for almost four years of the prime of his life. Former Grim Reapers frontman Gary Schuder was forced to endure a torment that left him scarred, in more ways than one, for the rest of his abbreviated existence.

On December 6, The Rolling Stones staged a free, daylong concert at the Altamont Speedway in California. The event ended in disaster when an audience member brandished a pistol and was stabbed to death by a member of the Hells Angels. Two weeks later, on the eve of his twenty-first birthday, Rick Nielsen married Karen Lindstrand. A month later, on January 26, 1970, Epic released the *Fuse* album, dead on arrival. Perhaps 'The Grim Reapers' was more appropriate after all.

5

Be around for the ball...

On April 10, 1970, Paul McCartney all but admitted in a press release that he saw no future for The Beatles. Paul's candor caused a firestorm in the media, like this *Daily Mirror* headline: 'Paul Quits The Beatles.' We know now that John Lennon had beaten Paul to the punch months earlier.

The tale of the band that started it all was ending, but for many others it was just beginning; there was no quelling the rock'n'roll tsunami that The Beatles had quaked into existence.

Consider this: even after the disastrous climax at Altamont, numerous aspiring promoters forged ahead with schemes to replicate the success of Woodstock, dreaming that the summer of 1970 might be the Summer Of The Rock Festival.

They faced a great deal of resistance. As the summer unfolded, newspapers across the country published articles with headlines like 'A Law To Control Rock Festivals,' 'Rules Needed For Rock Festivals,' 'Adopt County Regulations To Thwart Rock Festivals,' 'Ask Injunction To Prevent Rock Festival Advertising,' 'Rockfests Held Despite Court Bans,' 'Fears Of Rock Festival Invade Jefferson County,' 'Giant Rock Festivals Growing Out Of Tune,' 'Officials To Discuss Growing Controversy Over Rock Festival,' and 'Senate And House Committees Hear Reports On The Rock Festival.'

Fuse were booked to perform at their first of these festivals at the end of April. Called Sound Storm, it was held on an eight-hundred-acre farm in Mt. York, Wisconsin, near the village of Poynette, the land owned by a seventy-nine-year-old grandmother named Irene York, who the local newspaper quoted as saying, 'I like this style of music. It has a good beat.' The Grateful Dead headlined the festival, which was organized by 'Golden Freek Enterprises,' aka ex-cons Pete 'Bobo' O'Branovich and Sandy Nelson. From the book *RADS* by Tom Bates, about Bobo:

> His police record was like a seismic printout of his movements across the country: larceny in Erie, Pennsylvania; grand larceny in Los Angeles; car theft in Wheeling, West Virginia, and in Cleveland; disorderly conduct in San Antonio; and morals, marijuana, and firearms violations in his hometown of Buffalo. In a tavern brawl two years earlier, he had cut up a man's face with broken glass. One of his business associates considered him psychotic, and yet he had a very convincing way about him. 'He is the only person I ever encountered who could sell you suicide and you would feel you got a good deal,' said an associate.

Tattooed on Bobo's arm was a blue flower with the deranged motto *I have loved, I have suffered, now I hate.* Bobo and Nelson, according to Bates, 'raised the $60,000 they needed to launch the Poynette festival by selling hot-dog rights and other concessions. Local authorities were none too happy about two such characters putting on a rock festival in God's Own Country.' They booked more than thirty bands, hired crews for stage and sound, and enlisted a team of lawyers to fend off the aforementioned authorities.

In the end, about thirty thousand bohemians made the trek to Poynette, but, to the organizers' dismay, a huge number of them bypassed the entry fee by hiking to the site through the surrounding woodlands. It was a free-for-all. Vastly outnumbered, local law enforcement ignored rampant public nudity and drug use, as reported in the *Chippewa Herald Telegram* the next day:

> Many persons in it were in states of delirium from the caterwauling guitars and the drugs and marijuana. One naked young man danced atop a U-Haul van beside the four tier stage. An 'Earth People Beach' was established beside a creek that meanders through the 660 acre wooded farmland two miles west of Poynette. Dozens of young men and women peeled off their clothes and frolicked in the water. One young woman in the teeming crowd, unabashed by the photographers who approached her, sun bathed nude save for her rose colored glasses.

Fuse never made it to the stage at Sound Storm because 'the schedule was running so far behind,' according to an article published in the *Rockford Register-Republic* in July 1970 with the headline 'Drummer Knocks Rock Festivals.'

The life of a rock festival musician is not an easy one. You're plagued with long waits, hot sun and dirty conditions, according to a young Rockford drummer. 'Playing at a rock festival is very uncomfortable for the musician,' Chip Greenman, 17, 2128 Spring Brook Ave., said. Chip is the drummer for the rock group 'Fuse,' which recently released an album. 'Musicians don't really get good accommodations at the festivals,' he said. 'You can't clean up because there isn't much water close by and the johns are dirty. You just get a real dirty feeling.'

A week later, some trigger-happy National Guardsmen opened fire on a crowd at Kent State University, cutting down four students. Just three days after that, Fuse performed inside the Exhibition Hall at the Pecatonica Fairgrounds as part of a 'Giant Dance And Concert' presented by local radio stations WRRR and WYFE, an event headlined by The Jaggerz, fronted by Donnie Iris, who had recently scored a Top 10 hit with 'The Rapper.'

At the end of May, Fuse took part in the Kickapoo Creek Rock Festival, held on a farm in Heyworth, Illinois, and organized by a bail bondsman named David Lewis (his family owned the land). A promotional handout read:

RESERVE YOUR PLACE WITH THE SUN NOW. There's a limit even to the best things. Even to the three hundred acres of wood and meadowland along the Kickapoo, where all blithe spirits will gather in the green glow of spring's full bloom. Things will run smooth if we both know ... you, no way to miss this heady scene; us, with proper viands for body and soul. The electronic miracles and the human sounds of the soul meet to get acquainted Friday 29. Their love affair begins full song on Memorial Day. The road leads to Kickapoo Creek. See you there.

Lewis hired future bigwig Irving Azoff, then a booking agent and promoter out of Champaign, Illinois, to manage the festival. Azoff requested Ken Adamany's help booking Jimi Hendrix, who they offered $20,000 to headline. Unfortunately, Hendrix was already committed to play the Berkeley Community Theatre that weekend with Tower Of Power. Hendrix or no, a reported sixty thousand miscreants descended upon rural Illinois for the bacchanal—a nightmare for the neighbors. For security, Lewis enlisted a biker gang called, funnily enough, The Grim Reapers.

The day before the festival was set to kick off, the local state's attorney attained a court injunction blocking it, but the injunction was ignored. The *Freeport Journal Standard* reported that 'six undercover policemen were at the Kickapoo Creek Rock Festival over the weekend gathering information on illegal activities, but the McLean County state's attorney has not yet decided what action will be taken on specific offenses.' Fuse performed at noon on Saturday, May 30. Ted Nugent & The Amboy Dukes went on later that same day.

Additional acts on the three-day bill included Canned Heat, Delaney & Bonnie, The Paul Butterfield Blues Band, and B.B. King. Local favorites like The One Eyed Jacks, REO Speedwagon, The Finchley Boys, OZ, and The Litter also performed, surrounded by the requisite nudity and drug use.

A local reverend named Eddy Cunningham described what he supposedly witnessed: 'I saw a naked lady wearing a raincoat who wanted to trade her baby for a tank of gas. People were sliding down the Kickapoo with no clothes on, nude, like animals. I saw sex orgies which I could not photograph. These were young college students. They were somebody's baby. It was an absolute net of evil and wickedness.'

That quote came from a blog called *djtees*, as did this entertaining blurb:

Residents of Heyworth (whose idea of hippies was the Charles Manson family) awoke finding people, some naked, asleep on their front lawns, on their porches, in their cars and tool sheds ... when it was all over, there was a warrant for the promoter's arrest. The courts ordered Lewis to turn over the profits from the illegal event and seized his bank accounts. By then, the farmer had disappeared with his teenage secretary and two sleeping bags stuffed with cash ... he was never heard from again. Leaving his hometown, his wife and child, the family farm and a one year jail sentence behind him.

Lewis reportedly skipped town with $250,000—almost $1,700,000 in today's dollars. Ken Adamany, who was there representing a band called OZ, bore witness to the spoils.

KEN ADAMANY *I went in to get paid for them and it was in a pumphouse with a* *windmill next to it. Three farmers in bib overalls with shotguns and Irving Azoff standing there. Piles of cash stacked up all over the place.*

Fuse were also booked to perform at the People's Fair in Iola, Wisconsin, near Stevens Point, at the end of June. A headline in the *Post-Crescent* warned those who lived in the area to 'Gird For "Hippie" Invasion.' The article described how 'the site of the People's Fair is 200 acres of rolling country, located one-fourth in Portage County and the remainder in Waupaca County. It is secluded. Only a narrow lane leads to the property. A crumbling barn, filled with bales of molding hay, is the only structure.'

The festival got off to a rocky start when, on Friday, June 25, the only road in was backed up for ten miles, the sound system failed, and the drinking water ran dry. Not to mention the fact that the mosquitos vastly outnumbered the toilets. Some of the issues were fixed by Saturday, and about forty-five thousand dropouts tuned in over the course of the weekend to the sounds of Chuck Berry, The Stooges (an unbilled surprise), Brownsville Station, Terry Reid, and others. Mike Hughes described the goings on for the *Fon Du Lac Commonwealth Reporter*, calling the festival 'a blend of bikinis and bubble blowers, beauties and blanket salesman, and camper trucks and long-haired capitalism.'

It all went to shit on Sunday, not long after Fuse took the stage. Once again, festival organizers made the ill-advised decision to hire bikers for 'security.' The People's Fair aspired to be the next Woodstock but came closer to being the next Altamont, as described in a 2010 article on the website The Hits Just Keep Comin':

> The bikers did anything they wanted and took anything they wanted. Saturday night, a group of them got onstage while the Amboy Dukes were playing and scuffled with a security guard. The bikers tossed the guard off the stage, and he broke his collarbone. Even law-abiding bikers were intimidating, with knives and firearms openly displayed. Promoters eventually asked some of the bikers to leave. But with police involved mostly in controlling access to the area and no uniformed force on the grounds, there was no way to make the bikers go. … Just before 7:00 Sunday morning, people up the hill began throwing bottles at the bikers below. Amid the barrage, a few bikers mounted up and charged.

'We waited all night to get onstage … we were just into our second number when it seemed like a wall of people moved from the center of the crowd and then we heard gunshots,' Chip Greenman remembered. 'Some guy ran on to the stage and grabbed Joe's microphone and screamed, The revolution has begun! State Police quickly escorted us off the stage.' Three people were wounded when the armed bikers opened fire. The crowd revolted, pelting them with rocks and bottles and setting fire to the motorcycles they abandoned.

The *Wausau Daily Record* quoted Marathon County Sheriff Louis Gianoli as stating, 'These gatherings must be stopped before they get a start. Once 50,000 people gather it is impossible to maintain control.' And yet, by the end of July, Fuse found themselves booked at another of these festivals, this time in Wadena, Minnesota, on the banks of the Galena River. Some of the other acts on the bill: Johnny Winter, Little Richard, Hot Tuna, The Guess Who, Albert King, Poco, Terry Reid, The Flying Burrito Brothers, and Buffy Sainte-Marie. Once again the locals tried (but failed) to put the kibosh on the revelry, as evidenced by the headline 'Despite Court Injunction … Wadena Rock Festival Gathering' in *Estherville Daily News* on July 31, 1970.

Flashlights flickered in the dark like fireflies early Friday as a crew of about two hundred rock music fans worked through the night to finish preparations for their controversial festival. There was much to be done and a court injunction banning the event didn't seem to hinder anyone's efforts. The Iowa Highway Patrol continued late Thursday night to block entrances to the site of the festival. A 250-acre farm overlooking the Volga River two miles south of here. However, rock fans from throughout the Midwest streamed in on foot, knapsacks on their backs … Iowa Supreme Court Justice C. Edwin Moore issued an injunction banning the festival Tuesday. Clayton County Dist. Judge T.H. Nelson Thursday modified the injunction to allow the event provided health and safety regulations—which include having a toilet for every 25 persons—were met.

'We were to be the first band to play,' Chip Greenman remembered. 'The stage was not covered, it was over 95 degrees in the beating sun, and I was wearing black leather pants and a dark shirt. … About halfway through our first number I started to get sick, stopped playing, got up and staggered to the back of the stage and hurled major chunks!'

Iowa Lieutenant Governor Roger Jepson shared his thoughts on the festival with the *Sioux County Index* a few weeks later: 'The Wadena incident was a drug festival and calling it by any other name is not accurate.' He described the event as a 'sick money-grabbing island of lawlessness' and contended that it only served to make 'a few shady characters rich.' As much as $450,000 in ticket sales (three million dollars today) was reportedly collected.

Wadena was the last rock festival Fuse would play. They were booked for another at the end of August, the Spoon River Rock Festival in Washington County, Pennsylvania, set to feature a who's who of Detroit rock (MC5, The Stooges, Bob Seger, Alice Cooper, Brownsville Station), but a three-judge panel issued an injunction preventing the event from being held at the Big Country Ranch Resort in West Finley Township. Representatives from the community successfully argued that the festival would create 'a hazard of pollution and disease.'

Histrionics like this prevailed all over the country, including in the Town of Dunn in Wisconsin, where Ken Adamany tried to mount a festival of his own, in partnership with a character from New York named Charles Gottlieb, as described in an article with the cleverly alliterative headline 'Adamany Adamant On Festival,' published by the *Janesville Daily Gazette* on March 12, 1970:

> Kenneth Adamany of Ken Adamany Enterprises, Janesville, said this morning that plans for a Music and Art Fair this summer, tentatively planned for a 600-acre tract in Dunn Township, Dane County, will go ahead whether the fair is held at the proposed location or in some other area. 'We have received offers from other areas,' he said, 'if we find that we cannot legally conduct the event in Dunn Township.'

The locals fought back, irritating Jack MacManus, whose land Adamany contracted to rent, as detailed in the *Wisconsin State Journal* on April 6, 1970:

> 'There is a lot of hate towards me,' [McManus] stated, in the form of anonymous threats like, 'We'll see you get it!' and phone calls informing him he is 'a partner of the devil' and that 'God will punish you!' ... 'To me, the festival is kind of exciting,' he said. 'I thought it would be a helluva lot of fun if it's run right, and I don't believe there will be a bunch of rapists and people

on hard stuff [heroin] out here.' ... He said he 'can't quite understand all this moralistic concern suddenly,' given the adult forms of entertainment in the area. 'They have go-go joints in the Town of Dunn and a race track four miles away. If adults can go down and swill their booze and watch girls take off their clothes, young people can have their art festival,' he said, adding that he was not against 'adult' forms of entertainment, either.

Less than two weeks later, the deal fell through.

KEN ADAMANY *Charles and I then set our sights on fifteen-hundred-plus acres in Black River Falls, Wisconsin.*

Yet Ken and Charles proved unable to make their 'Art & Music Fair' a reality.

KEN ADAMANY *... a very long story that should be made into a movie someday.*

In the end, at least thirty additional rock festivals planned for the summer of 1970 never took place; only eighteen actually happened. A few of those were quite successful, but most operated at some level of dysfunction. Two festivals planned for early August offer examples of the opposite extremes. In Middlefield, Connecticut, residents successfully convinced a state judge to issue an injunction blocking a festival called Powder Ridge from taking place at a local ski resort. According to the poster, 'This Festival will take place within the natural amphitheatre of the slopes of the mountain. At the base of the mountain is a ski lodge whose roof will serve as a stage.' Sounds cool, but it was canceled. But, to the dismay of the residents of the wealthy mountain town, thirty thousand of the bedraggled ticket holders still showed up.

From a 2020 *Connecticut* magazine article by Mike Wollschlager:

On what would have been the first day of the festival, NBC's Huntley-Brinkley Report informed the nation what was happening in Middlefield. Standing in front of a crude map of Connecticut, David Brinkley delivered the following: 'Even though there is no music, and won't be, Powder Ridge seems to have become a kind of outdoor folk ritual, or puberty rite, and a social scene offering a variety of fun and games.' On-site reporter Liz Trotta called it more of an 'overcrowded country picnic' than a rock festival.

Consider the headline for a 2017 article at Timeline.com: 'Rich neighbors tried to cancel Powder Ridge, but the hippies came anyway.' The article goes on to describe them 'descending like a swarm of tie-dyed, hallucinating locusts. That's when everything went wrong. "A few rich people have said that we cannot have our festival," one circulating leaflet read. "Are we going to accept this and leave?" One young man told reporters, "I've got to get my twenty dollars' worth somehow."'

The non-festival turned into a 'three-day drug fueled extravaganza' with 'few bathrooms or other facilities, little food—but plenty of drugs. … When a baby was born on the premises, it was declared that all the festival goers were godparents. There had been impromptu drum circles and plenty of singing, even if most of it was not done by professionals. One man summed it up, "It all goes to show that you can have a rock music festival without rock music."'

Conversely, the Goose Lake International Music Festival in Leoni Township, just outside of Jackson, Michigan, was a roaring success. From a 2020 article by George Bulanda for *Hour Detroit*:

> The idea for the outdoor festival was hatched by three metro Detroiters: Richard Songer, who made a mint in construction; Russ Gibb, WKNR disc jockey and owner of the Grande Ballroom on Grand River; and Tom Wright, Gibbs' manager at the Grande. Held a year after 1969's Woodstock, Goose Lake was much more organized than that free-spirited gathering. An ingenious touch was a revolving stage so that there wouldn't be a lull between acts. The promoters initially hoped the crowd would reach around sixty thousand, but Goose Lake ballooned to more than two hundred thousand music lovers.

From a 2017 article by Todd McGovern for Pleasekillme.com:

> Billed as a better-equipped version of Woodstock (which was held exactly one year earlier), the Goose Lake Festival included showers, restrooms, kitchens and strong fences to keep out those who might bum rush the show. Tickets for the three-day event were $15, and if you didn't have the bread, you could work in the park for admittance.

Security for the event was handled by the White Panthers, along with some bikers (of course) from Detroit and a 'Youth Patrol' made up of 'local hippie peacekeepers.' Acts on the bill: The Faces, Jethro Tull, Chicago, Ten Years After, The Flying Burrito Brothers, Mountain, James Gang, Bob Seeger, MC5, The Stooges. Michigan's governor publicly denounced the event, and Songer was indicted for 'promoting the sale of drugs' (he was acquitted), but Goose Lake went off without a hitch.

In September, the *Los Angeles Times* published an article about that summer's craziness with the headline 'Giant Rock Festivals Growing Out Of Tune.' Author David Swaney asked, 'This was supposed to have been the Summer of Rock Festivals. What happened?' He went on to explain:

> Across the nation law-making machinery reacted by grinding out ordinances, mandates, rulings and injunctions. … Basically, 'straight' people are uptight about festivals because: (1) kids run around nude at them; (2) kids use dope at them; (3) traffic gets tied up around them; (4) land in the surrounding area gets damaged during them; (5) the Mafia might be involved in them, and (6) heaven knows what they'll do next at them.

* * *

The Paegans, despite their success, split up in May of 1968, while they were still attending high school. Half the band wanted to stick with the pop music that made them money on weekends while the other half wanted to explore the more abrasive and inventive side of rock'n'roll, inspired by the likes of Cream and Jimi Hendrix.

Drummer Bun E. Carlos's brother Mark, also a drummer, was in a band called Crystal with Russ Freiman, Rick Pemberton, Mark Swanberg, Bob Lamb, and Steve Summers—that is, until Mark decided to join the Guilford High School football team, after which Carlos began filling in for Mark on Friday nights. He also subbed for Chip Greenman once, during a Fuse gig at a church festival.

BUN E. CARLOS *His sister was in the hospital, and he got in the car and left.*

After high school, Carlos enrolled at Rock Valley College. 'People used to go to college to stay out of the army,' he later told the *Wisconsin State Journal*. 'I studied business administration for lack of anything better to do.' It was there that Carlos met fellow musician Brian Beebe, who was on the lookout for musicians in need of some extra cash.

BUN E. CARLOS *Brian told me, 'Yeah, me and this guy have a duo. We're looking for a band to back us so we can play these rec nights in Rockford. The park district wants to hire us.'*

BRIAN BEEBE *I said, 'Well, I got a singer.' He says, 'I can get a couple guys.' And we formed this band just to play these jobs.*

Carlos drafted Russ Freiman and Rick Pemberton from Crystal to play guitar and bass; Beebe brought along a high-school friend named Robin Zander.

RUSS FREIMAN *Robin and Brian were a duo, they were both singers, they were doing Beatles songs at Ground Rounds.*

At the time, Zander and Beebe were billing themselves as Two Of Us.

BRIAN BEEBE *We played a lot of colleges around Wisconsin and Minnesota and Illinois.*

RUSS FREIMAN *There were a lot of guitar players, there were some bass players, some drummers, but singers were kind of hard to come by.*

Now they had two. The quintet dubbed themselves Phrenz.

RUSS FREIMAN *The name of the band was simply contrived from the fact that that's what we were: we were just people that knew each other, cross-pollination, we knew songs that were quick to throw together and we did and we made a few bucks.*

Remember that concept: cross-pollination.

BRIAN BEEBE *I played a little keyboard and sang, and Robin was the lead singer. We made $19 a man. There were five of us, so I think it was $95 for the band to play three hours and haul our equipment around in the snow.*

RICK PEMBERTON *We played for four or five months. We played every Friday night at different high schools and junior high schools.*

Pemberton recalls them tackling 'Down By The River' and 'Cinnamon Girl' from Neil Young's recent *Everybody Knows This Is Nowhere*. Freiman remembers Phrenz playing several Kinks songs, and Beebe remembers 'stuff off of Rod Stewart's *Gasoline Alley*.'

RICK PEMBERTON *We did a bunch of Who stuff, 'Summertime Blues' and 'See Me Feel Me,' and Cream, we did a number of Cream songs. Bun E. and I liked to play The Who and the Cream stuff, and those guys knew The Beatles stuff a little more, so it was kind of a blending of maybe the heavier stuff maybe meets The Beatles stuff.*

Pemberton and Carlos had another project going at the same time, the byproduct of various late-night jam sessions that they called Buns Carlton's Air Farce, a reference to Ginger Baker's Air Force (launched by Baker and Steve Winwood after Blind Faith).

BUN E. CARLOS *Me and Rick were messing around making tapes and we thought, let's make a tape like Beach Boys Party! where they all sit around and play songs and different guys sing.*

RICK PEMBERTON *Bun E. would sit with a tape recorder, he'd play guitar and then I'd try to play some lead guitar on top of it and we'd play some blues stuff, Robert Johnson or the Rolling Stones, and from there that evolved to, 'Okay, let's get maybe a couple other people, let's get someone who's maybe a good singer.'*

BUN E. CARLOS *First I had a little two-track open reel, where you could record on one track and overdub on the next one, and then I got a TEAC 33/40, a four-track, so we could do it a little better. I played rhythm guitar on most of it, on the basics, and then if there were drums I'd overdub the drums later at my parents' house, in the basement.*

Robin Zander became a regular at these sessions. His vocals are present on recordings of 'Two Of Us' and 'Here Comes The Sun' by The Beatles; the

Patsy Cline classic 'I Fall To Pieces'; 'Peaceful Easy Feeling' by the Eagles; 'Don't You Lie To Me' by blues legend Tampa Red; Neil Young's 'Down By The River,' sung by Robin and Steve Summers from Crystal; and a version of Eric Clapton's 'Let It Rain,' which Robin sang together with a friend from Loves Park named Randy Hogan—another repeat offender.

RANDY 'XENO' HOGAN *One New Year's Eve we got together early and recorded 'Eve Of Destruction' with an oratory that was hilarious.*

That 'oratory' was a chaotic run through of 'Hot Tamales & They're Red Hot' by Robert Johnson, which segued into the Barry McGuire hit. Fuse frontman Joe Sundberg can also be heard on the tapes, along with Pezband leader Cliff Johnson, who sang Leslie Gore's 'You Don't Own Me.' Other songs recorded include: Chuck Berry's 'Let It Rock'; Smokey Robinson's 'You Really Got A Hold On Me'; The Beatles' 'You've Got To Hide Your Love Away'; Cream's 'Badge'; Chuck Willis's 'I Feel So Bad,' made popular by Elvis Presley and hard rockers Cactus; Patto's 'I Got Rhythm'; Badfinger's 'We're For The Dark'; Canned Heat's 'On The Road Again'; the blues standard 'Key To The Highway,' as interpreted by Derek & The Dominos; an approximation of the jazz fusion instrumental 'Uranus' by German group Passport; and, last but not least, a Craig Myers original, sung by Craig, which featured the chorus 'You were gonna be a free girl and I was gonna see the land / But you became my carpenter and made my banana stand.'

BUN E. CARLOS *Sitting around smoking shitty weed and coming up with a shitty song.*

There was at least one more original tune to be found on those tapes, written and performed by Robin Zander and called 'Every Friday Night.'

BUN E. CARLOS *I had a tape of Robin and Brian. When I first met 'em, they came over and played some tunes for me on acoustic, when we were talking about getting a band together.*

* * *

Fuse opened for Rod Stewart and the Faces at the Scene in Milwaukee on October 18, and at Dewey's in Madison on November 3. A nice bit of exposure, but after being dropped by Epic, the band was splintering. 'So there we were: no manager, no record company, no booking agent, just attorney bills rolling in on a regular basis,' Chip Greenman recalled. They rehired Adamany, who placed them on the Rod Stewart dates, but it was too late.

CRAIG MYERS *Some heads started to swell. Everybody in the band was underestimating everybody else in the band.*

JOE SUNDBERG *We had five egos and ideas to please. So, while I would have loved to try different things, we had to be a unit.*

They had enough material for a second album, but no label to release it.

JOE SUNDBERG *I think we were evolving as songwriters. We just didn't have enough time as Fuse to grow.*

Greenman announced his departure from the band, and a farewell show was booked at Sherwood Lodge for the day after Christmas (four days after Rick turned twenty-two, five days after his first wedding anniversary). They broke the attendance record for the venue.

CRAIG MYERS *We put seventeen hundred into a building that holds about eight hundred. If that band had stayed together and gotten over all the stupid, petty differences, and just played the kind of music we were capable of, we would have been huge.*

On the very last day of 1970, Paul McCartney filed papers at London's High Court, seeking the immediate dissolution of The Beatles' business partnership.

6

Been wrong maybe once or twice...

Nazz formed in Philadelphia in 1967, after guitarist Todd Rundgren and bassist Carson Van Osten split from a group called Woody's Truck Stop. They snagged singer Robert 'Stewkey' Antoni from a band called Elizabeth and found drummer Thom Mooney pretending to go to college. Within a year, Nazz had a record out. It flirted with the charts but never took off. A second album was recorded, but Rundgren jumped ship before it could be released. Not long after, Rick Nielsen encountered him at the Marquee in London.

'He was there with Miss Christine from the GTO's,' Nielsen told *Guitar Heroes*, 'and we saw Yes. I think it was a Christmas party or something.'

Yes performed at that venue on the day after Christmas 1969, just five days after Rick and Karen were married, and Rick has linked the memory to his honeymoon. 'I talked to him then, and a few years later I ran into him again and he gave me his phone number because I was trying to get a hold of the other guys who were in The Nazz,' Nielsen remembered. All Rundgren could tell him was that Thom Mooney was in Los Angeles.

THOM MOONEY *I was staying with Nazz's first manager, who had moved out there and was running a chain of record stores, and at one point he asked me, he said, 'One of my record store managers is cheating me so I fired him, so can you go sit there for a couple of days while I find somebody?' So I went to this record store and one day I got a phone call and it was Rick—he had somehow tracked me down through somebody and found out that I was staying with Jack Warfield in Los Angeles and called Jack. Jack gave him the phone number of the store, and he called me and he wanted me to come to Rockford and check out his band. I didn't want to do it, so we spent the next couple of months, I guess, exchanging letters.*

Nielsen wore him down. What did he have to lose?

THOM MOONEY *I went to Rockford, and it was Rick and Tom and a guitar player named Craig Myers and a singer named Joe Sundberg.*

In other words: Fuse. After jamming with the guys, Mooney asked a friend to ship his drums out from Los Angeles, and for a short time the dynamic seems to have been that Thom Mooney replaced Chip Greenman in Fuse, although Mooney surmised that Nielsen had ulterior motives.

THOM MOONEY *Rick wanted two things then: he wanted to get rid of his Rockford guys, except for Tom, and Tom wanted the same thing; and he wanted to be the guitar player. At first I thought they just wanted to replace their drummer, and then, when I got there, slowly I began to realize he wanted to get Stewkey up there too.*

Stewkey and Mooney had kept the Nazz train rolling for a while after Rundgren left, but the band fell apart after they moved the operation to Texas.

THOM MOONEY *We were living in Dallas at the time. Our last show was November 1 or 2, 1969, in El Paso, Texas. A bunch of things had recently happened in the band that just burned me out. So, back in Dallas a few days later, I called a meeting and quit, effectively ending the band. Stewkey liked it there [in Texas] and stayed.*

STEWKEY *I was poor, I had no money. I was working for my dinner, actually, but I was having a great time, it didn't matter. I enjoyed myself in Texas. I have a lot of good friends down there and I did a lot of growing up down there.*

After some prodding from Nielsen, Mooney reconnected with Stewkey (whose stage name came from a bastardization of Ringo Starr's unabbreviated surname).

THOM MOONEY *I knew where Stewkey was in Texas, and I called him.*

STEWKEY *I'm always waiting for the next phone call, it seems like.*

Mooney filled Stewkey in on this new opportunity in Rockford, and it was compelling enough that he headed north and moved in with Mooney at a house owned by Rick Nielsen, into a downstairs apartment that was previously occupied by Tom Petersson's grandparents. Nielsen happened to be renting out the upstairs as well, which meant he was unable to live in his own house, which he purchased in 1970 for $18,000. 'I really couldn't afford it, because obviously I never got any money from them,' he later told *Noisey.*

On March 3, 1971, a photo of a four-piece band consisting of Rick, Stewkey, Mooney, and Tom Petersson appeared in the *Rockford Register-Republic* with the following caption:

Appearing at Dennis School as part of the music-in-the-schools program was the Rick Nielsen Rock Band, above. The project is sponsored by the Rockford Cultural Council and is being tested this semester at Dennis and Whitehead Schools. Sharon Davenport, left, likes the dance step, and Carolyn Stanley digs the music during the visit to Dennis School by Rick Nielsen's rock group.

They had performed as Fuse in February, so it is unclear as to why the newspaper referred to them as 'The Rick Nielsen Rock Band' in March. Perhaps because Craig Myers quit after Stewkey replaced Sundberg, and they tried to leave the Fuse name behind for a brief moment. Then Myers rejoined, even though he told me that he felt the band had 'lost that spontaneous edge.' On May 4, they opened for legendary blues musician Taj Mahal at Dewey's.

On June 4, an interesting article appeared in the *Rockford Register-Republic*, beneath the headline 'Police Team To Confront Hippies Here.'

A major confrontation is expected Sunday between Rockford police and a group of self-proclaimed hippies. They'll play slow pitch softball in Black Hawk Park. The hippies, who bill themselves as The Shaw Street Smackers, are band members of FUSE, a local rock music group, and their equipment men. Magistrate Judge Richard DeGunther will be the umpire, according to Steve Schuder, 26, one of the game's organizers.

Steve was Gary's brother. The next day, an article appeared in the *Rockford Morning-Star* with the headline 'Hippies Fall To Cops 13–2.' There was an immediate rematch, as reported by the *Rockford Register Republic* on June 7, beneath the headline 'Hippies Finally Win Battle With Police—8–7.'

It was a gas, said the victors. Bright sunshine. A perfect day for a game. And the combatants were the same as usual. Hippies and the police. This time the hippies won, but the cops want a rematch. 'I think we'll give them another shot in two weeks,' said Stukey [sic], hippie team spokesman. His red bandana drenched with sweat, his face flushed with the joy of winning. Stukey has traveled a lot, goes under the single name and belts the lead vocal line with the FUSE, a local rock band. 'I'm from the East,' he says, all the explanation there is. … During the game, one of the hippie players joked, 'If we win, they'll probably search us after the game.' Up in the hippies section of the stands, a blond long-hair suggested, 'Stash it now, man, before the search starts.' … The hippies, mostly members and equipment men of the rock band FUSE, needed extra innings to whip the cops. It could have flip-flopped the other way. When it was over, not all the police went over to shake hands with the hippies. That's life.

A week later, Fuse broke up again. On June 11, 1971, the *Rockford Morning Star* published a photo of the band along with the caption, 'Fuse, a local rock combo, will play its final engagement as a unit tonight at Sherwood Lodge. The group that specializes in "Tomorrow's Music" will disband after the concert-dance that begins at 8 and runs to midnight. Among members of Fuse are, from left, Rick Nielsen, Stewkey (the vocalist), Tom Peterson and Thom Mooney. Another member, Craig Myers, is not shown in the photo.'

If Friday, June 11, indeed marked the end of Fuse—this version of Fuse, at least—then a booking for the following Monday and Tuesday at Flo's Inn must have been canceled, which seems to indicate that the dissolution of the band was sudden or unexpected. 'We were never too serious about it. We never rehearsed and we weren't all that good,' Nielsen told *Trouser Press* in 1978. 'It could have been real good, but we were very into alcohol and other things. We never could get it together.' The members planned to scatter, as reported by the *Rockford Morning Star* on June 13, which stated, 'Nielsen will be leaving for Australia, Stewkey for Texas, Peterson for Germany, and Mooney for Los Angeles.'

Coincidentally, June of 1971 was the same month that a pair of singers you might remember from the Buns Carlton's Air Farce sessions, Robin Zander and Randy Hogan, graduated from Harlem High School, five miles north of downtown Rockford, having previously appeared together in Harlem's production of *Annie Get Your Gun*.

RANDY 'XENO' HOGAN *We sang in choir, folk groups, bands, high school musicals, whatever. I remember the days of putting Robin on the handlebars of my bicycle with a guitar and riding over to band practice.*

Zander told Dan Rather that he was in a band with Randy and Randy's sister.

RANDY 'XENO' HOGAN *I guess you could call it a band. We were kids. I think my sister played bass for maybe a year. We had to be twelve, thirteen years old. I'm sure we played a few shows together. He and I and our friend Liz Hughes sang at weddings.*

Brian Beebe had graduated from Harlem High School a year ahead of Randy and Robin.

BRIAN BEEBE *My mother was the secretary at Robin's grade school and he actually would sing over the PA after the announcements sometimes. He had a beautiful soprano voice. The first time I ever laid eyes on him was at a spelling bee, a fifth grade spelling bee, and the way I remember it is he had a white shirt with a black bolo tie and a red sport coat and his arms around two different girls at the same time. As soon as Robin graduated, we went up to Wisconsin Dells and played as a duo.*

They dubbed the act Zander & Kent (Brian's middle name).

* * *

As reported by the *Rockford Morning Star*, Rick Nielsen had decided that his post-Fuse future looked brighter Down Under. 'I tried to emigrate to Australia in 1971,' he told the *Sydney Morning Herald* in 2018. 'I'd never been, but I was an adventurous, young, crazy-stupid guy, and the music scene was awful in the United States. And they said if you moved there they would grant you ten acres of land or something. I was declined.'

The main impediment seems to have been his dog, an epileptic Borzoi named China. 'I couldn't go there because at the time, before I had any kids, I had a dog, and dogs were not allowed because of quarantine,' Rick told *AV Club*. 'You couldn't bring animals into the country. So that's why I didn't move there. I actually did my research and tried to get kind of like a working visa for

Australia. It always seemed like it was the land of opportunities. The same size as the United States with one tenth of the population.'

China found her fifteen minutes of fame a few years later, when she was mentioned in the *Rockford Register Republic*:

> Lost dog stories are common, but Rick Nielsen has one that's a little out of the ordinary. Nielsen's two dogs, China, a Russian wolfhound, and Bela, a poodle, either strayed or were stolen from his garage at 122 Shaw St Wednesday. The unusual part is that one of the dogs, China, is epileptic and Nielsen was concerned that without her daily pills she would have a seizure and be thought rabid. The story has half a happy ending. China was found wandering around East High School Thursday afternoon and is now home, none the worse for the experience. Bela is still missing, however. He's one of the small white varieties of poodle. Nielsen would appreciate the call if anyone sees the dog.

Rick's walkabout wouldn't happen, but Tom and Thom made good on the paper's predictions: Petersson jetted to Germany straightaway, and Mooney hit the highway soon after, headed back to California.

THOM MOONEY *I got into a Volkswagen Bug with the former lead singer of Fuse, Joe Sundberg, and my girlfriend and my dog, and we drove to LA.*

Sundberg needed a change of scenery and bummed a ride out west (he returned to Rockford soon enough). Petersson made his way to the city of Worms on the Rhine River, where his friend and former bandmate Mike Myers (Craig's brother) was stationed.

MIKE MYERS *I went to Vietnam, I came back, they sent me to Germany, and Tom Petersson showed up at my apartment out of the blue. I used to write to Rick and Tom, keep in touch kind of, but Tom showed up one day and stayed there for about six months or so.*

At that point I had kinda gotten run out of my apartment by the German police, so I was living with a friend in the army and his wife, and then Tom showed up and they liked Tom, so Tom and I had the one bedroom and we made a bunk bed—we took a door and put it on legs and had a bunk bed.

Mike was riding out the final year of his enlistment. He and Tom landed jobs at a frozen food warehouse, where they worked alongside German prisoners. On some weekends they took the train three hundred miles north to Amsterdam to unwind. They caught a Velvet Underground show there on November 19, 1971 (minus Lou Reed, the lineup was Doug Yule, Mo Tucker, Walter Powers, and Willie 'Loco' Alexander).

* * *

On July 10, 1971, a recent hole-in-one was announced in the *Rockford Morning Star*'s 'Tee Kettle' column: 'Bob Reitemeier, 714 N. Highland, Rockford on par three, 41 yd. no. five at Iron Oaks with a nine iron. Witnessed by Rick Nielsen, Stewkey and Willy Walsh.'

There they were, Rick and Stewkey, still stuck in Rockford. In order to get something going, they linked back up with Craig Myers and enlisted the services of former Paegans drummer Bun E. Carlos. This lineup gigged for the summer under various names, like The Bunbirds or Ozzie & Harriet, with Rick Nielsen (not Nelson!) on bass.

BUN E. CARLOS *Rick called me up and said, 'Yeah, I'm gonna switch over to bass, Craig'll play guitar, Stewkey will sing, and you can drum. We'll have a band.' So we did that for a few months.*

CRAIG MYERS *We would just play under a different name each time we played. We were getting silly. Manchurian Blues Band, all sorts of stupid stuff.*

BUN E. CARLOS *We just changed our name for each gig because nobody really cared. Everybody was like, Oh, it's just the guys from Fuse.*

A poster for an Ozzie & Harriet appearance at the Sherwood Lodge attempted to list every band the various members had ever been associated with:

FORMERLY: FUSE, NAZZ, PHAETONS, GRIM REAPERS, TOAST & JAM, PAGENS [sic], BOLWEEVILS, MANCHURIAN BLUES BAND, NOMADS, RICK NIELSEN'S 20/20 ROCK BAND, CRAIG MYERS EXPERIENCE, BUNS CARLTONS AIR FARCE, STEWKEY'S UNDERGROUND.

At some point, Rick and Stewkey grew restless and decided to chase after Tom Petersson.

BUN E. CARLOS *[They] went over to Europe with their spouses. I went to work at the roofing company my dad had.*

The dog might have kept Rick out of Australia, but Germany let him bring it.

MIKE MYERS *Eventually, Rick and his wife and his dog and Stewkey, a bunch of 'em showed up at my place, presumably to start a band, but I'm in the army, just trying to finish my time, so they got kinda bored with that.*

Rick Nielsen's mother-in-law had grown up in Germany, and her mother, Karen's grandmother, still lived there. 'I actually lived with her in Nuremberg,' he told the *Illinois Entertainer* in 2021. 'I went there with the idea of finding seclusion, but that turned out to be impossible.' Rick saw Rory Gallagher— 'one of the best guitar players I ever saw'—at the Messehalle in Nuremberg on December 16, 1971. He also recalled running into Mike Harrison, the singer from Spooky Tooth, in a German club. 'I saw him at a club and asked him if he wanted to join our band,' he recounted for Ira Robbins. 'He didn't know who the heck I was, and I was bold enough and nuts enough to ask him. And he just laughed it off, Thanks for the offer.' Nielsen's attempt at recruiting Harrison was a bad omen for Stewkey.

These excursions to Europe were later spun into an elaborate mythology, for example this excerpt from the Rockford weekly *Lively Times*:

> In 1971, Rick and Tom moved to Munich, Germany. Very impressed by the German breweries, 'we'd play in the cities with the best beer, not the best clubs.' They found the Germans did not appreciate their 'off' sense of humor and were thrown out of Berlin for gross performances. 'We'd tell you what we did, but our manager would kill us! Literally kill us!'

* * *

Back in Rockford, Craig Myers formed a new band called Toons with Chip Greenman, Rick Pemberton, Robin Zander, and Mark Dahlgren, a cousin to Bun E. Carlos. The cousins had previously played together in a band called

Ego, formerly Lost Souls. Dahlgren, along with Mike Novak and Joe Guarino, had carried over from Lost Souls to Ego, with Carlos and guitar player Bob Creagan as the new guys.

BOB CREAGAN *I believe Bun E. joined at the same time, and the decision was made to ditch the Lost Souls name in favor of Ego. I replaced Tim Porter.*

Carlos played with Ego from 1969 into 1971. They played mostly covers of songs from the likes of Steppenwolf, Iron Butterfly, Led Zeppelin, and a killer Swiss band called Toad, i.e. the heavy stuff that broke up The Paegans.

BOB CREAGAN *Bun E. was always a pro, as well as a great drummer, and had his sights set on something big. Bun E. would change up his drum kit often, it seemed like every gig he'd have a different set-up.*

JOE GUARINO *We were somewhat active on a local level, but it wasn't anything that we could make a career out of at that time. It was more of a hobby band, something like that.*

BOB CREAGAN *At some point, Bun E. decided to leave for good, and Pat O'Brien became his permanent replacement. I believe this is when the band name evolved to Albatross.*

JOE GUARINO *Ego, I would say, was just a pop/rock band. Mostly what we did was after-game high-school things, general events, parties. That sort of thing. No big concerts or anything. Just a Top 40 pop band. Didn't do many originals or anything. It was when we went into Albatross that we started doing the prog-rock stuff and doing a lot of our own material.*

Albatross went on to release a highly collectible progressive-rock album in 1976. But I digress. Let's return our attention to Toons, the band made up of Craig Myers, Chip Greenman, Rick Pemberton, Robin Zander, and Mark Dahlgren.

CRAIG MYERS *That was before they called cartoons 'toons.' It was basically teens. We wanted to come up with some name that was like 'for teens.' Toons was just a band that practiced in an old building my Dad had downtown, it was an* *apartment building, it was a fourplex, he had an office in one of them and we had a room we could practice in upstairs in the other and it was just a band that was practicing, trying to be good, we only played one or two gigs, I think.*

BUN E. CARLOS *They learned about eight songs in about ten practices. They did one gig at the Lyran Hall, and they did one set and there were about twenty people there.*

Brian Beebe was one of those twenty people. He remembered Toons playing a 'rock'n'roll version' of Tony Bennet's 'If I Ruled The World.'

Bands like Phrenz and Toons are perfect examples of the cross-pollination that Russ Freiman previously referenced: here we have Robin Zander, several years prior to joining Cheap Trick, collaborating with Rick and Tom's former bandmates from Fuse in one band (Toons), after playing with future Cheap Trick drummer Bun E. Carlos in another (Phrenz). After Toons folded, Robin linked back up with Brian Beebe, and the duo accepted an offer to perform as Zander & Kent for the entire summer at the Lookout Lounge in Wisconsin Dells, a resort town 120 miles north of Rockford.

BRIAN BEEBE *We met a friend of a friend, basically, who was working in the Dells, and he thought we would go over good up there because it's a very entertainment oriented area. A vacation destination. So we went up there and banged around and auditioned at a few places, and we got hired in a downtown bar there and started working six nights a week, six hours a night.*

Also booked in The Dells that summer was a group called FAWN, named for an acronym derived from the surnames of its members: singer and guitarist Mic Fabus, guitarist Gordon Anderson, bassist Jim Williams, and drummer Bill Natale. Originally formed by Mic, Gordon, and Jim as Deep Fork in 1969, they became Fawn once Natale joined, but by 1971 he had been replaced by drummer Rich Hazdra. FAWH did not have the same ring to it. Fawn performed nightly for the summer at a club called the Where House.

MIC FABUS *The place was literally sinking in the mud. Sparks flying off the microphones.*

Brian and Robin lived out of a van but spent most of their waking hours at the Lookout Lounge. Zander was a skilled mimic, able to sing just like John Lennon, Neil Young, Robin Gibb, or David Bowie. Together, he and Brian nailed the harmonies for songs by Crosby, Stills & Nash. After a six hour stint at the Lookout Lounge, Zander could often be found propped up outside the Where House, listening to Fawn.

MIC FABUS *We'd heard about Robin and his partner Brian, but we never got over there because we were always working, and they were working while we were working. I think they had an earlier gig, so Robin used to come and sit outside the club—he was underage, so he couldn't get in, but he'd sit out in the little beer garden they had there, and he'd listen to us.*

RICH HAZDRA *When we were through we would go back to their trailer, and we would sit all night and smoke weed and acoustic guitars would always come out, and we'd always be singing harmony.*

MIC FABUS *It was just astounding. We were playing these impromptu campfire gigs or on the pier gigs that weren't really gigs, they were just get-togethers, you're talking four and five part harmony and I looked at Rich and the rest of the guys in the band like, Woah, this is really something.*

It was a summer to remember, but the resort town basically shut down after Labor Day. 'Our first summer of playing music professionally comes to an end, and we've had a ton of fun,' Brian Beebe remembered. 'Suddenly, we sober up and Robin and I are looking at each other like, What do we do now?'

Then they remembered an invitation from earlier in the summer: some army reservists stationed at nearby Camp McCoy had said, 'Come on out to Denver. We'll get you a job. We'll even put you up for free.' Impulsively, Brian and Robin drove through the night, found a phone booth in the morning, and called the number one of them had scribbled down. Luckily, one of the reservists answered, remembered them, and was actually happy they came. He put them up in a condo in Aspen and finagled them a week-long residency at the Aspen Inn, but it was a rough gig.

'It was a big place, and our job was to play three times a night for thirty minutes or so, in between sets by a big ten-piece band called Stoneground,' Brian remembered. Stoneground featured Sal Valentino, former singer for The

Beau Brummels. 'They had a huge sound and got people all fired up,' Brian continued. 'Then they left the stage and two guys with acoustic guitars came out and sang Neil Young songs trying to be cool. Most people ignored us.'

* * *

It was December of 1971, and Fuse was on ice. Chip Greenman was about to enlist in the Army. Rick Nielsen had followed Tom Petersson to Germany. Remaining members Joe Sundberg and Craig Myers attempted to relaunch the band with Rick Pemberton on bass and a drummer named Dave Kenney, another Guilford alum who was a big fan of Fuse. Kenney (who now goes by Ted) decided to be proactive and booked some gigs, including one at Madison East High School.

TED KENNEY *From bands I had been in previous to that, I got contacted about playing some gigs … so I went ahead and booked the gigs, figuring, 'Yeah, this is gonna happen.'*

Then Sundberg dropped out, and with him went Myers. But commitments had been made, and Kenney recruited some friends to make good on them.

TED KENNEY *They got played with a substitute band, and that's kind of embarrassing to me, but that's the story of what happened. They were played with Russ Freiman on bass, Pemberton on guitar, me drumming, and I think we had Robin and Brian Beebe.*

Bun E. Carlos attended the show at Madison East and, in addition to Zander and Beebe, also remembers Randy Hogan singing. Carlos himself was invited to play drums for a few songs, including on Neil Young's 'Down By The River.'

TED KENNEY *The Johnny Cash TV show—he'd start, turn around and say, 'Hello, I'm Johnny Cash'—Robin walked out and said, 'Hello, I wish I was Johnny Cash.' We all thought that was funny.*

So here we have Robin Zander and Bun E. Carlos performing together in some version of a band called Fuse, which was Rick and Tom's band. If this show counts (and that's a big if), then all four members of Cheap Trick performed in Fuse. Russ Freiman has a photo of himself from that night with a Sun City stack behind him, 'FUSE' stenciled on the side in white paint. It looks fresh. What a racket.

* * *

Gary Schuder somehow survived Vietnam and returned to Rockford with a pair of Purple Hearts. No medals were issued for the psychological scars, which were often far worse.

MIKE MYERS *He was pretty screwed up.*

CRAIG MYERS *He came back pretty well toasted from Vietnam. It was a shame.*

Even so, Gary wanted to get back in the game, and he soon linked up with a band called Tugboat Annie, captained by a guitarist named Clark Colborn.

CLARK COLBORN *We had the typical 'basement band' problems with members coming and going, and at one point we found ourselves looking for a singer. I posted ads all around town and put the word out to every musician I knew that we were looking for a singer. I cannot remember if someone gave me Gary's number or if he responded to one of the ads, but we connected initially by telephone. I remember that Gary sounded very confident on the phone, and I think in one of our very first calls he even sang a few lines of one of the songs I had mentioned we were covering, and I thought he sounded amazing. At first, he did not name-drop any of the bands he had been in before, nor mention 'Nam; he just said he had a fair amount of experience. I gave him a list of some tunes we were playing, and we agreed to get together in my parents basement for an audition. When he showed up, we were all surprised that he was quite a bit older than the rest of us, but we didn't care as long as he could sing and didn't mind hanging with younger guys.*

He was great—he simply floored us. We thought he was way out of our league, but he really liked what we were doing and was extremely interested in working with us on originals. The only thing he asked was that we learn and perform 'Sympathy For The Devil' by The Rolling Stones. So he became our singer, and we started rehearsing several times a week and working on writing songs and getting bookings. It took a few months to get ready for gigs, but we got there, and the whole band thought we sounded pretty damned good.

As the weeks went by, Gary began to talk about his time in The Grim Reapers, and some other bands, and a little bit about his time in Vietnam. The rumors we heard over the years indicated that he did have substance abuse issues, but if he was doing anything while in the band he hid it well. I would agree that he had PTSD, looking back on it. Of course, back then, that was a relatively new concept, and we were not familiar with the term until many years later. I know Gary told me he lost many friends during the war, one killed by a sniper as Gary was handing him a cigarette.

At some point, after Gary Schuder went into Downey, I returned his conga and other percussion stuff to his parents' house. All they said was that Gary had suffered a nervous breakdown of sorts, related to the war. Gary may have told me that when he called to say he was in the hospital, but I'm not certain. I know he was in and out of Downey for years.

Downey was a neuropsychiatric facility run by the Veterans Administration, thirty-five miles north of Chicago. It was the largest facility of its kind—so large, in fact, that the compound had been assigned its own zip code. A troubled veteran might be housed there indefinitely—institutionalized, in other words.

Downey was self-contained, with its own movie theater, bowling alley, golf course, and swimming pool. The patients were housed in brick two-story buildings with iron bars on the windows and put to work bagging spoons in the spoon factory or digging compost in the greenhouse. Downey's above-ground structures were connected via a series of shadowy underground tunnels, an area the staff tended to avoid. The facility had no elevators, and the stairwells were lined with cyclone fencing to limit the likelihood of an incident. Radiators supplied heat in winter, but the buildings lacked air-conditioning and became like brick ovens in the summer.

A former orderly wrote about the place on his blog, Oldfoolrn:

> There was definitely a Halloween atmosphere with bizarre shadows and spookiness throughout. The souls of over one hundred schizophrenics all in one poorly lit area … almost every patient had the same diagnosis (SCU) or schizophrenia, chronic undifferentiated. About two percent of the population was bipolar and added some spice to the mix. All patients smoked constantly while in the dayroom producing a dense ever present haze. Smoke Eater machines mounted on the ceiling did little to clear the air. A typical ward

included the day room with connecting hallway to the dorm which was just a huge open room with beds. Just off the hallway was a restraint room with four heavy beds bolted to the floor. The beds were usually all occupied. My claim to fame at Downey was teaching a couple of very violent patients a self-restraint technique. I got them to the point when they felt like slugging someone to come to me and ask to be put in restraints. I readily complied with their request and let them decide when they should be released.

The degree to which a soldier of misfortune like Gary Schuder 'survived' combat is debatable.

TED KENNEY *He was constantly in a crazed state. You'd see him walking up and down the street in the bad part of town, with that 'lost in la-la land' look. I don't know if it was because of drugs to keep him going, or drugs that he was on to get high. He was on some kind of medication from doctors, but I think he used any other money he had to supplement that. There's a guy who could have gone far.*

Gary died in 1992, at the age of forty-four. Tom Petersson reflected on the era that wrecked Gary for *The Pop Culture Show* in 2021: 'Everything seems crazy now but when we were growing up, it was crazy too. Vietnam. Nixon. Kent State. Somebody said to me, Was it much better then? It was bad then. Was it polarized? Yes. Was it frightening? Yes.'

* * *

By January of 1972, Rick Nielsen was back in Rockford and again being written up by a local newspaper, this time the *Rockford Morning Star*, in an article by Dave Zimmerman with the headline 'Success? Stay Footloose And Musically Free.'

He's written about 100 songs and has 'bits of another hundred in my head.' 'I'll probably never sell a million (records) because I've never written a love song,' he said. Most of his material is personal and involves a sort of cynical humor. 'I've tried those 'love question' songs but they sounded phony,' he explained.

A picture published alongside the article revealed Rick to have shoulder-length hair and a scruffy beard. ('I look bad with a beard. I look bad with no beard.'—Rick Nielsen.) The article covered the fizzling of Fuse and Rick's overall disappointment with the major label experience, but also his plans for the future. 'Among Nielsen's goals are more writing, forming a new group and buying a four track studio which would enable him to record his own work with complete orchestration. He has one person in mind for that group, former Fuse bass player Tom Peterson, whom Nielsen had recently visited in Austria.'

On Saturday, January 29, 'The Original Fuse' (Craig, Joe, Rick, and Chip) played a one-off reunion show at the Barr on Highway 41 in Oshkosh. Tom was still in Germany, so Rick Pemberton filled in. The poster listed Ken Adamany on bass, but it was a joke.

That spring, Rick Nielsen occupied himself with writing songs and woodshedding them with a band called Mannequin, which had spun off from another Rockford band called Scag (featuring Stew Erickson, Mark Swanberg, Dudley Goetschel and Rick Michaelson) that opened for The Grim Reapers/ Fuse multiple times. Stew was a friend of Rick's whose parents also owned a business downtown (selling office furniture).

BUN E. CARLOS *Rick did a couple of gigs with [Mannequin] where they did some of Rick's tunes that he'd written since Fuse. Nothing was happening with that, so Rick and I put a band together.*

Me and Rick and Rick Pemberton would rehearse down at Nielsen's Music Store. Joe [Sundberg] came down to sing one week. Lee Kelso, this guy from Belvidere, he sang for a week. We would work on stuff Rick was working on.

Lee Kelso went on to form a band called Cotton Mather (later Zap) with Dave Kigar, Philip MacNames, Tom Leary, and drummer Pat O'Brien, the guy who replaced Bun E. Carlos in Ego/Albatross.

RICK PEMBERTON *Rick said, 'Hey I'm trying to work on some arrangements, do you guys wanna come and jam?' I had nothing better to do. So it was Bun E. drumming, I'm playing bass, Rick's playing guitar, and we're going through original stuff and we would try an arrangement, then a couple days later we'd get together, 'Okay, I changed the arrangement, it's gonna go like this now.'*

BUN E. CARLOS *In May of 1972, me and Rick and Rick Pemberton played a wedding reception.*

RICK PEMBERTON *I think that was Rick's way of getting us fifty dollars each to help defray our time. I believe it was at Rockford College.*

BUN E. CARLOS *Me and Rick and Craig went down to Macomb in Western Illinois and did the Hay Days Of May as a trio. So we were doing gigs, gigs, side projects, rehearsals, gigs, all through 1972.*

Also in May, The Move scored a Top 10 hit in the UK with a song called 'California Man.'

BUN E. CARLOS *We played once at Sinnissippi; we played a couple bar dates; we played a couple parties; we played at a high school in Janesville, Wisconsin, for an after-game dance one night. That was our last gig.*

* * *

Meanwhile, Robin Zander and Brian Beebe performed nightly as Zander & Kent for a second summer at the Lookout Lounge in Wisconsin Dells.

BRIAN BEEBE *We both wrote songs and we played them. People were receptive to things like that—it didn't matter if they didn't know the song. Sometimes we'd even tell them it was an original song. The regular fans took to it really well.*

Fawn had also returned for the summer. As the season came to an end, Robin asked drummer Rich Hazdra if he could crash with him temporarily, at his mom's place on Union Avenue in Chicago.

RICH HAZDRA *He wanted to be in Fawn.*

Fawn gigged regularly around Chicago, and they let Robin roadie for them once or twice. Then a gig had to be canceled when Robin's friend's pickup broke down with all of the band's gear in the back. They started thinking they might be better off just letting him join.

While Robin was living with Rich, Fawn was in turmoil. A falling-out between founding members Jim Williams and Mic Fabus resulted in Jim quitting and Mic taking a hiatus, leaving guitarist Gordon Anderson as the only original member. Rick Young, younger brother to J.Y. from Styx, replaced Williams and the band added a keyboard player named Tom Busch. They also gave Robin Zander a shot on vocals, even though Mic Fabus returned shortly thereafter.

RICH HAZDRA *We did some great stuff with Robin—that's when we started doing different stuff. We did 'Roundabout' by Yes, and that's when Robin moved into my brother's room right across the hall. I could hear him all night practicing that intro, over and over, because he wanted to know it perfectly. Robin would go back to visit his mom and sister on and off, so I would drop him off at the Greyhound station—he would take the greyhound back, visit with his mom and sister for a couple days.*

Robin didn't have a car, nor even a license. Punctuality was an issue.

MIC FABUS *We had some pretty amazing rehearsals, it was really stunning how good it all sounded, and I honestly, truly do believe that Cheap Trick was the beneficiary of our youthful impatience because, to make a long story short, Robin had a hard time getting to rehearsals on the south side of Chicago in a timely fashion, so we foolishly let him go.*

As the *Chicago Reader* put it, Robin 'joined the group for a minute—though he got booted for habitually arriving late from Rockford.'

* * *

For Nielsen and Stewkey, Rockford had become a kind of purgatory. They intended to leave, then stayed (except for that trip to Germany), but a proper band failed to coalesce. At the end of his rope, Stewkey hatched a plan to return to Philadelphia. He invited Rick to tag along.

BUN E. CARLOS *Stewkey had a manager [Steve Bruno] who thought they could get a record deal with Columbia.*

STEWKEY *Having a reputation in Philadelphia, I thought we had a chance of landing something.*

BUN E. CARLOS *So Rick went out to Philadelphia. I carried on working at the roofing company.*

THE GRIM REAPERS   EXCLUSIVE REPRESENTATION **KEN ADAMANY, LTD.** · A. C. 608 868-7673 · JANESVILLE, WISCONSIN

Get all the latest music supplies from RALPH NIELSEN MUSIC HOUSE, 404 7th St., 963-7693.

TOP Grim Reapers promotional 8x10, 1967. L–R: Rick Nielsen, Willie Walsh, Gary Schuder, Jim Zubiena, Joe Sundberg, Ross Anderson. *Courtesy of Ken Adamany.*

ABOVE A newspaper ad for Ralph Nielsen Music House (featuring Rick Nielsen, middle).

RIGHT The Paegans at the Meadow in Janesville, 1967. Back row: Jerry Parlapiano, Rick Schneider, Bill Nicholson, Steve Carlson. Front row: John Furland, Bun E. Carlos. *Courtesy of Bun E. Carlos, all rights reserved © 2022.*

ABOVE The Grim Reapers at the Kinetic Playground, July 24, 1969: Rick Nielsen, Tom Petersson, Craig Myers, Joe Sundberg.

OPPOSITE TOP Fuse at Memorial Union Terrace, Madison, 1970: Rick Nielsen, Craig Myers, Joe Sundberg, Chip Greenman, Tom Petersson.

OPPOSITE BOTTOM The Grim Reapers at the Kinetic Playground, July 24, 1969. *All photos by Bob Koonz, courtesy of Ken Adamany.*

ABOVE Sick Man Of Europe outside (Stewkey, Bun E. Carlos, Tom Petersson, Rick Nielsen) and inside (Stewkey and Rick) their rehearsal space at 3rd & Race in Philadelphia, 1973. *Both photos courtesy of Bun E. Carlos, all rights reserved © 2022.*

RIGHT Poster for Fuse mk II (Craig Myers, Rick Nielsen, Stewkey, Tom Petersson, Thom Mooney) at Flo's Inn, 1971. *Courtesy of John Calacci.* Below that, newspaper ads for Sick Man Of Europe opening for the Raspberries, and the very first booking for the original Cheap Trick lineup (with Xeno and Rick Szeluga), for which they were billed as 'Reapers.'

SICK MAN OF EUROPE

Ken Adamany
Hilaria Music, Inc.
P.O. Box #4263
Madison, Wis.
608 257-1026 255-7875

TOP Sick Man Of Europe promotional 8x10; photo taken upstairs at Artemis, Philadelphia, early 1973. *Courtesy of Ken Adamany.*

BOTTOM The original Cheap Trick lineup at the childhood home of Bun E. Carlos, summer 1973: Bun E. Carlos, Rick Szeluga, Xeno, Rick Nielsen. *Courtesy of Bun E. Carlos, all rights reserved © 2022.*

RIGHT AND BELOW The original lineup rehearsing in Rick's parents' garage at 4101 Spring Creek Road, Rockford, summer 1973.

OPPOSITE The original lineup at Bun E. Carlos's childhood home, 1973. *All photos courtesy of Bun E. Carlos, all rights reserved © 2022.*

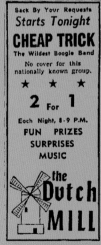

ABOVE Cheap Trick (Rick Nielsen, Bun E. Carlos, Xeno, Tom Petersson) performing at the Sterling High School post-prom, Sterling, Illinois, May 18, 1974. *Courtesy of the Sterling High School yearbook.*

FAR LEFT An advertisement for Cheap Trick's second residency at the Dutch Mill in Minot, North Dakota, October 15–20, 1973. *Courtesy of Ken Adamany.*

LEFT At the Rock & Roll Revival in Minneapolis, November 25, 1973, Cheap Trick performed as The Rock & Roll Revival Band.

BELOW The band's first two logos, created by Dave Muldowney.

7

A lifetime away from your home...

Philadelphia was one of those early hotspots for rock'n'roll. Bill Haley started out as musical director for a radio station in Chester, less than twenty miles outside the city, and his earliest live performances happened in Philly. *American Bandstand* started as a local Philly show called *Bandstand*, hosted by disc jockey Bob Horn on the local affiliate WFIL Channel 6. Another local, Dick Clark, filled in for Horn from time to time and took over when Horn was fired in 1956. *American Bandstand* was produced out of Philly until 1963, when the operation moved to Los Angeles. Philly natives Bobby Rydell, Frankie Avalon, and Chubby Checker racked up a combined seventeen Top 10 hit singles in the rock heydays of the sixties.

At the dawn of the seventies, Philadelphia still ranked as one of the nation's five largest cities, but the exodus to the suburbs was underway. White flight carried prosperity with it, and upkeep became a struggle. In Philadelphia, abandoned buildings beckoned as canvases for graffiti artists, while street gangs waged turf wars with literal packs of wild dogs. All of the unrest culminated in the election of a gruff high-school dropout named Frank Rizzo to the office of mayor in 1971. People were hungry for a scapegoat, and Rizzo, who was more than willing to court controversy during his volatile three years as police commissioner, was practiced in racial antagonism. His reign as mayor was no less volatile; as civil rights attorney Larry Krasner put it, 'Rizzo kidnapped the fucking city, that's what he really did.'

And yet, amid the turmoil, at the heart of downtown was Center City, and at the heart of Center City was Sansom Street: 'The city's original bohemian enclave,' as author Stephen Fried describes it in his book *Thing Of Beauty*:

The street's rebirth had begun in the mid-sixties, supposedly as a Philadelphia version of London's Carnaby Street, and it maintained a foppish air even after some of the mod, fashiony shops were replaced with hippie and glitter-rock stores. But Sansom Street was more than just stores. It was a scene, the site of the city's first stationary freak show of painted hippies, outlaw bikers and drag queens. Those extremes made the street a place where Philadelphia's traditionally less powerful—the young, the black, the female, the homosexual—could feel powerful, or at least relatively safe in numbers.

In early 1971, an entrepreneur named David Carroll cut the ribbon on his renovation of a former fire station and plumbing warehouse at 2015 Sansom Street and unveiled a restaurant and nightclub he called Artemis (named for the Greek goddess of the hunt). It was a narrow structure with a deep interior (built to house a fire engine) and stood three stories tall. Jonathan Tarkiff described the interior in an article for the *Philadelphia Daily News* dated April 16, 1971:

The natty front room is dominated by a long, antique bar, brick floor and several large booths upholstered in brown and lime, steel-studded canvas (custom built, natch). A massive (and eye-popping) stained glass window keeps it all kosher. Dark and cool, the low-ceiling middle room offers casual (romantic?) seating at little box tables and a bird's-eye view into the small, stainless steel kitchen. In the airy, white-bricked back room is where it all happens on Friday and Saturday nights, when the eclectic gang of center city sophis, pretenders and gays gather to dance on the saw dust to Otis and Led Zep. The multi-speaker installation by Natural Sound is first-rate. For those who prefer to gawk, padded benches and butcher block tables circle the perimeter, zapped-out paintings by local artists (like Tom Palemore's Giant Red Gorilla) are a visual gas and stereo headphones at each table offer further sonic sensations. Plenty of hanging greenery, theatrical lighting and pastel-hued trim keeps the glow warm, but soft.

Another article celebrating the opening of Artemis by Elaine Tait appeared in the *Philadelphia Inquirer* the same day:

The long, narrow interior is divided first into a bar space, with a few booths and a stained glass window. Next comes a long, narrow, cocktail loungish room with continuous bench along the wall and small, painted cube tables every few feet. A big dining area is in the rear, a light, attractive room with big window, hanging greenery, sawdust-sprinkled floors and butcher block-effect tables. Two huge paintings dominate the decor and if your taste in art is conservative, you might think twice before sitting across from the one depicting a King Kong-sized ape reclining on a fuchsia sofa.

Joe Sharkey profiled Artemis for his 'On The Go' column in the *Inquirer* in late January:

It's packed every night, not just weekends and Wednesdays. 'It's like a party every night,' said David Carroll, who runs Artemis. The back room was pulsing with dancing, jammed elbow-to-elbow with people who all seemed to know each other. 'It doesn't look like it, but we have eighteen staff people in here working to make this thing click,' he said.

Those eighteen staff members included local musos Timi Tanzania and Bobby Startup.

TIMI TANZANIA *When I first went to the Artemis, I lived in North Philadelphia, which was a really rough part of the city. I got tired of the gang war and all that, so I came downtown to Center City, where most of the night scene was—and your clothiers, haberdasheries, things of that nature—and at night I would stop into the discotheques in the early seventies and check out the music. And at that time it really was unique to hear a lot of the sounds that Bobby Startup was playing in the discotheque—he was playing a lot of sounds from England, so that attracted my ear—and shortly after I stopped in the club I wound up working there during the daytime, because it was a French restaurant during the day that served French cuisine, and at night it was a discotheque. So, the Artemis had a dual history, an eatery in the daytime and a party club at night. The personnel was mostly young people who were either artists or musicians or artists and musicians.*

Bobby Startup was one of the major draws in the club because everybody came to hear the music—the music that wasn't ordinary neither in Philadelphia nor the United States. A lot of the songs that Bobby Startup played, he searched out, and he was playing the big hits from England and the underground scene from England.

BOBBY STARTUP *It was a very popular club—all of the high-end nightlife people would hang out there. You had a real mixture of people, and that was one of David's great talents: getting together people from all parts of society into one place. You had musicians, you had drug dealers … Rohrer was the company that made quaaludes, and that was right outside Philadelphia, so I remember there was an influx of them because it turned out that one of the security guys would sell barrels—industrial-size barrels of the ones that were supposed to be destroyed because there was an imperfection for some reason, if they were slightly irregular they would throw them away, so he would sell barrels of those to the local drug dealers. They were like fifteen cents apiece in the beginning, I remember. So, everybody would come to the club with pockets full of them. It was pretty wild back in those days.*

Philadelphia Magazine published a nostalgic article about Artemis in May of 2016, when the old building went up for sale.

Spencer Zahn described it as the place where everybody went. 'It was Studio 54 before there was a Studio 54,' he said. 'Teddy Pendergrass, Daryl Hall, John Oates, they all came here,' along with other notable musicians; Zahn wouldn't swear to this, but he thinks he may have bought a young Bruce Springsteen his first legal drink at the club.

Springsteen turned twenty-one in 1970, so probably not.

* * *

Not long after arriving in Philadelphia, Stewkey and Nielsen landed jobs at Artemis.

STEWKEY *It was the only place, basically, in Philly. Everybody went there. It was located right near Rittenhouse Square, which was the big hang out for all the hippies back in those days, it just was happening.*

Stewkey first came to Philadelphia from Rhode Island with friend Steve Bruno in the mid-sixties, when they formed a band called Elizabeth with drummer Hank Ransome, who also worked at Artemis.

STEWKEY *I'm sure that Hank had something to do with probably introducing me to people I needed to talk to to get the job.*

Stewkey was also familiar to David Carroll, the owner of Artemis, having previously worked at a bar Carroll owned called Peanuts. Artemis hired Stewkey as kitchen staff and Rick Nielsen as busboy and bartender.

HANK RANSOME *Just picture him behind a bar. Rick's got that personality, man. That's all you gotta say. He was as animated as a bartender.*

Hank had a band called Good God who were signed to Atlantic Records, and Stewkey and Nielsen recruited three of its members (Hank on drums, Hank's twin brother John on bass and Cotton Kent on piano) to help record some demos at the small recording studio Steve Bruno ran down on Brown Street. (Nielsen has also claimed they did some work at the legendary Sigma Sound.)

HANK RANSOME *Then we went to New York, and we went into Columbia Studios. I'm under contract with Atlantic Records and this stuff was all being done at Columbia, so when we went in to do the demos I had to use a different name.*

They recorded an audition tape, and Columbia passed. 'They turned us down,' Nielsen told the *Milwaukee Sentinel* in 1978. 'I guess they wanted more groups like Iron Butterfly.' Technically, the act under consideration at Columbia was Stewkey, the singer from Nazz, as a solo act (Steve Bruno's idea)—not a band, per se, even though Nielsen wrote the songs. As Nielsen told Ira Robbins, 'We did the audition for Stewkey.'

Three of the Columbia demos later surfaced on a Nazz bootleg called *Retrospective Foresight*, mislabeled as 'He Was,' 'Ready I Am,' and 'But I Ain't Got You.' They were actually called 'Bean,' after Thom Mooney's dog; 'I'm A Surprise,' which later became a Cheap Trick song called 'So Good To See You'; and 'Ain't Got You,' also performed later with Cheap Trick.

After the 'Stewkey solo' pitch failed, it was decided that they would make a go of it as a band. But they would have to do so without the gents from Good God.

HANK RANSOME *John moved to Florida so we didn't have a bass player so I said to Rick, 'Do you know any bass players?' He says, 'Yeah, Tom ...' He was living in Germany. I said, 'Well, get his ass over here.' So then Tom flew back from Germany to Philly.*

According to Tom Petersson, 'Rick said he got this thing with Stewkey. He said, Do you want to come back and go to Philadelphia? So I came from Germany right to Philadelphia.' They had a job waiting for him at Artemis, as a waiter. Tom brought a band name with him: Sick Man Of Europe, a designation the European press thrust upon whatever country was experiencing the most economic difficulty or impoverishment at the time. When Rick and Tom were in Germany they saw a headline that labeled Italy as such. In 1996, Petersson told Ira Robbins that he still had the article. So, even though Rick Nielsen would eventually call it 'the world's worst band name,' they used it.

HANK RANSOME *And then myself—under contract with Atlantic, playing with Good God—I had to go on the road. Four-month tour. So I said, 'Rick, I'm gone for four months, you gotta find somebody else, do you know any drummers?'*

BUN E. CARLOS *I went out to visit in September, took a vacation from my job. Dad, I'm tired of roofing. I'm taking a vacation! I'd been roofing for about a year, and I went out there. They told me, 'We need a drummer!'*

HANK RANSOME *So Bradford Carlson came from Rockford to Philly.*

BUN E. CARLOS *... with Rick's brother-in-law. That's when I joined Sick Man Of Europe. It was either be a drummer or be a roofer and work for Dad. I said, 'Give me a couple of years, Dad.'*

Now they had a band. There was no steady gig at Artemis for Bun E., but he worked there periodically as a DJ.

BUN E. CARLOS *Billy Mousseau was the regular DJ, and I'd sub once or twice a week. In those days, before disco and shit, it was basically 'Brown Sugar' and rock tunes that you could dance to. Stuff like 'Do It Again' by Steely Dan got a lot of airplay because it had a basic straightforward beat, and 'Superstition' by Stevie Wonder.*

Gary Glitter's 'Rock And Roll Part 2' was another favorite spin. Carlos was also tasked with mixing sound sometimes, if Artemis booked a live act.

BUN E. CARLOS *I mixed for Robbie Basho one day, and Carolyn Hester—folkies, mostly, so it'd be, mix a guitar mic and a vocal mic on their tiny little PA they had.*

Sick Man Of Europe performed at Artemis once, in the fall of 1972.

BUN E. CARLOS *I went down to 8th Street Music and bought a conga drum. We did our hour's worth of tunes, and it wasn't very exciting. A prog-rock band playing acoustic.*

Carlos recorded the show. The performance of a Nielsen original called 'Mandocello' can be found on Youtube.

BUN E. CARLOS *That was a tape I made at the Artemis, and only the piano and Rick's mandocello and Stewkey's vocal mic were on the tape, so a week later, at Tom's apartment, I had a stereo tape recorder, and me and Tom overdubbed the bass guitar and conga on the other track.*

At the end of 1972, David Bowie rented out the upstairs at Artemis and threw a private party to mark the end of that leg of the Ziggy Stardust tour—this after a three-night stand at the Tower Theater.

BUN E. CARLOS *The next day, I asked Rick at practice, 'What kind of beer was he drinking?' 'He was ordering Budweiser.' And we were all kinda like, 'Ewww, he drinks Budweiser?' We were kinda disappointed to hear that.*

It was during this period that Tom Petersson started calling him 'Bunny,' and it stuck.

BUN E. CARLOS *My nickname was from Paul Bunyan, I got it when I was a kid—like, four or five—because I liked this Paul Bunyan book or something, and everyone called me Bunyan or Bun or Bunnifer, stuff like that, different variations on Bun. And then Tom started calling me Bunny out in Philadelphia in 1972, when Sick Man was getting together.*

KEN ADAMANY *When they were in Philly as Sick Man they asked me to fly out to see them, which I did for two days. I saw some rehearsals when I got in and was introduced to Hank's group, Good God, at the time. They gave me photos and literature. Met their manager, Bill Eib.*

BILL EIB *I booked them a couple of shows as Sick Men. Rick had a suit made of the Sunday comics cloth. He started early on with the goofy costumes.*

KEN ADAMANY *Tom drove me to the airport for my return. I was seated next to Jim Belushi on the return flight to Chicago, as I recall.*

Jim Belushi was nineteen at the time. His older brother, John, had just relocated to New York to join the Off Broadway cast of *National Lampoon's Lemmings* alongside Chevy Chase and Christopher Guest, among others.

On January 27, 1973, the Selective Service finally announced an end to the draft (Nixon waited until after he had signed the Paris Peace Accords to make good on his campaign promise). Back in Rockford, Craig Myers and Joe Sundberg made another attempt to resurrect Fuse with Rick Pemberton on rhythm guitar, Mike Myers on bass, and Roger Wiley (from a band called Wheezer Lockinger) on drums. Chip Greenman was stationed in Germany at the time, where he joined a band called Frantic Dwarf.

CRAIG MYERS *We played a few gigs as Fuse. Not many, maybe ten. All covers.*

At the same time in Philly, Sick Man Of Europe were gearing up to start playing the clubs. They signed on with a local guy named Tony Messina.

BUN E. CARLOS *He knew all the Italian club owners in Jersey. He was a manager straight out of central casting.*

Messina booked them for the first weekend in February at a club called T's Zodiac in Gloucester Heights. An advertisement in the *Philadelphia Daily News* billed the band as: 'Formerly the NAZ [sic], star of HELLO, it's ME.'

'Hello It's Me' was only a minor hit for Nazz, but by year's end Todd Rundgren would crack the Top 10 with his solo version. Coincidentally, the very first live performances by KISS (sans makeup, or at least that makeup) took place that very same weekend, less than a hundred miles away at the Popcorn Club (soon renamed Coventry) in Sunnyside, Queens.

On February 8, Sick Man performed at 'some high school in Philly' for $400, according to Rick Nielsen's notes. Also in February, they landed a pair of choice supporting slots at the Satellite Lounge in Cookstown, New Jersey, opening for The Raspberries and then Foghat. The former bill was advertised in the February 7 edition of the *Philadelphia News* as 'Rasp Berrie & Nazz.'

ERIC CARMEN *There were a lot of errors when it came to our name. Among my favorites were 'Nazzbennies' and 'Le Fromage' in France. I guess it sounded a little bit like 'Framboise.' Raspberries, cheese, whatever!*

By February 9, the ad was corrected—not 'Rasp Berrie' to Raspberries but Nazz to Sick Man Of Europe, with, in smaller print, 'Formerly Nazz.' The Raspberries' second album had been out since November, and the first single had cracked the Top 20. They had just returned from a short tour of Europe.

BUN E. CARLOS *They were loud and in your face—two guitars, bass, and drums. The different thing about the Raspberries that we thought didn't do them any favors was they'd do the concert and they'd play three original tunes, then they'd play 'Honky Tonk Women' and 'All Right Now.' They did a buncha cover tunes.*

Two weeks later, Sick Man opened for Foghat at the same venue, a seedy haunt owned and operated by a colorful character named Carlo Rossi. Once promoted as the largest club in New Jersey, with a capacity of two thousand, the Satellite Lounge, housed in a converted bowling alley, was a regular stop for regional and national acts, despite Rossi's volatile reputation. His temper flared during Foghat's set, according to a *Weird N.J.* article:

Stories abound about Mr. Rossi's various interactions with the bands that played in his club over the years, one of the most famous in local lore being the time that he shot out the sound system during a performance by the band Foghat. As the story goes, he had repeatedly told the band to turn down their volume, then finally emerged from his office enraged and brandishing a handgun. He then proceeded to shoot out the band's amplifiers.

Lucky for the Sick Men, none of them had stuck around to catch the headliner. A few days later, a magnitude 3.8 earthquake shook the region, its epicenter near the Delaware and Pennsylvania border.

HANK RANSOME *I was at 21st & Walnut and Rick and his wife were across the street, and I felt the ground shake and I get a phone call from Rick across the street. 'You feel that?' I said, 'Was it just an eighteen-wheeler?' Then I get a call from Tom Petersson, who's way down on 12th street. 'You feel that?'*

A report from the Delaware Geological Society detailed the rattling of windows and doors, overturned or falling objects, and rare instances of cracked plaster or glass, with the consensus being that the most frightening aspect of the event was the intense noise, which witnesses described as 'explosive' or 'booming.'

Tony Messina next informed the band that he had booked New York mainstays Blue Öyster Cult to perform at Great Valley High School in Malvern, Pennsylvania on March 4, and Sick Man would be opening. BOC had one record out at the time, but the follow-up, *Tyranny & Mutation*, was about to be released. Sick Man played (in the gym with no stage) but as soon as the headliner started, they sensed there was a problem.

BUN E. CARLOS *When they went on we noticed they were just jamming, and didn't look like a headline rock act. BOC were just getting a name and we didn't know what they looked like, but after a few minutes it was apparent to us, and a few audience members, that the band was a fake. We got out of there, fast.*

When confronted the next day, Messina 'made some excuse about not being able to finalize getting BOC,' according to Carlos. Apparently, rather than cancel the show, he had gone with an unannounced replacement, assuming the audience would be none the wiser.

They immediately severed ties with Messina. Plans had already been made to return to the Midwest for a 'small tour' booked by Ken Adamany, with shows at the Joint in Fon du Lac on March 9, the Shorecrest in Jefferson on March 11 and 14, two consecutive nights opening for John McLaughlin and The Mahavishnu Orchestra: first at Beloit College Fieldhouse on Wednesday, March 21 (a poster for the gig declared, 'Former members of Fuse Rick Niebon

[sic], Tom Peterson, also former singer from Nazz, Now from Phil. P.A.'); then at Albee Hall at UW-Oshkosh on Thursday, March 22, where a newspaper ad referred to Sick Man Of Europe as 'Columbia Recording Artists.' Sick Man recorded an audition tape for Columbia, so technically …

Speaking of recording, several trips were made to Sauk City (on March 12, 13, and 21) to lay down some tracks at Cuca, a sixteen-track studio just a half hour drive from Madison. Demoed were 'Bean,' 'Maid Out Of Wood,' an instrumental called 'Ultramental' ('basically taken from *The Inner Mounting Flame* by Mahavishnu Orchestra,' according to Nielsen—check out 'The Dance Of Maya'), and a fresh take on the Screamin' Jay Hawkins tune 'Bite It,' wholesomely reimagined as 'Suck It.' As for the Oshkosh show with Mahavishnu, some dweeb named Keith LaGraves unleashed a scathing review of Sick Man in the *Advance Titan*:

> The backup band, Sick Man Of Europe, was just that—sick. Featuring the former bass player from 'Fuse' and the lead singer from 'Nazz,' this group was so bad they would have trouble making music in any country. They were offensive from the moment they stepped onstage. It was great to see them leave after a half set of unadulterated garbage.

BUN E. CARLOS *It was a nice way for Ken to see how we would do in front of a big audience … and it didn't do very well.*

Regardless, they thoroughly enjoyed watching the headliner. 'They blew my mind all over the place,' Rick Nielsen recalled. 'It wasn't music that I could play or would play. It was so innovative that all you could do was be stunned.' Bun E. Carlos also paid close attention, learning a few tricks from Mahavishnu's ambidextrous drummer Billy Cobham.

Sick Man Of Europe next brought their unadulterated act to the 'Hall Of The Mountain King' at Norse Chalet, an 'Authentic Scandinavian Smorgasbord' in Stoughton, Wisconsin on March 23 and 24, where they played their hearts out to the accompaniment of the clatter of knives and forks.

BUN E. CARLOS *We died the death at pretty much every gig. It wasn't really dance music for bars. No one knew who the band was, so there would hardly be anybody there.*

They made a return trip to the Joint in Fon du Lac on March 25, then performed at a familiar haunt, the Stardust Lounge in Rockford, on March 26, after which they trekked to Milwaukee, booked to perform at what would soon become another familiar haunt, Humpin' Hanna's on Locust Street. Advertisements for the club always called it simply Hanna's, presumably because newspapers in the seventies refused to print the entire name. On March 29, they entertained the students at Parker High School in Janesville, for which they were paid $150. It was a fruitful trip home, but they headed right back east, booked to open for Quicksilver at Neshaminy High School, half an hour outside Philadelphia, on March 30.

* * *

At the end of April, the boys attended a performance by Stewkey's former bandmate Todd Rundgren at the University of Pennsylvania.

BUN E. CARLOS *King Crimson opened for him, and they blew him off stage. Todd did his first song, and at the end of the song they had this long fade out, it was real quiet, and Tom Petersson stood up, we were in about the tenth row, and he goes, 'Boo! You stink!'*

STEWKEY *Todd and I didn't get along back then.*

Rundgren's eclectic *A Wizard, A True Star*, padded with tunes like 'Rock'n'roll Pussy' and 'Dogfight Giggle,' had just come out. Writer Peter Key referenced the show in a *Philadelphia Business Journal* article in 2013, asserting that Rundgren was 'more weird than good.' Still, his star was on the rise, while Stewkey and his bandmates could barely get a toe in the door. Witnessing the scope of Rundgren's success, despite his eccentricities, must have been frustrating.

STEWKEY *I don't know why [Sick Man Of Europe] didn't take off.*

Then reality came crashing down. As Nielsen would tell Chris Jericho, 'I was living in Philly, no money, no insurance, and I don't know what, but my wife got pregnant.'

HANK RANSOME *When Karen got pregnant, that's when everything fell apart. She* *didn't wanna have her first baby without her mother, so she said, 'I'm going back to Rockford. I need my mom.'*

One problem: the move back required funds that the Nielsens did not have. Then fate intervened. 'I got a call from Paul Hamer, who knew of me as a guitar collector,' Rick told *Premier Guitar*. 'He wanted a Sunburst Les Paul Standard, and I had one to sell. It was pretty faded out, as I recall. He gave me $2,500 for it … that money allowed us to return to Illinois. Paul sold that guitar, and that became the working capital that helped start Hamer.'

PAUL HAMER *[Fuse's] guitar player [Craig Myers] had a guitar that was really valuable—as a kid I didn't know it was a valuable guitar, I just knew it was the guitar I wanted. When you were a musician in the sixties if you wanted to play anyplace you had to belong to a union, so Gary [Gand] and I joined the Waukegan Musician's Union because it was cheaper than the Chicago Musician's Union for dues, and the union put out a book that they sent out with news in it, once a quarter or something, and I had heard that Fuse had broken up and I started thinking about this guitar that the guitar player was playing, which was a Sunburst Les Paul, and then one day I see in the musician's union book that Rick Nielsen is selling Mellotrons in Rockford and has a listing with a phone number, and I thought, I wonder if that guitar player wants to sell that guitar. And I called the phone number and it turned out it was Rick's Dad's house—Rick had moved to Philadelphia, I by that time was a mailman, and I had been buying guitars and reselling them, primarily to British rock bands, so I remembered the Sunburst Les Paul, I called the dad, the dad gave me the number in Philadelphia, I called Rick up to see if the guitar player wanted to sell that guitar, and Rick said, 'I lent him that guitar, that's mine.' And I said, 'You want to sell it?' And he said, 'Sure.'*

RUSS FREIMAN *That guitar, from what I can remember, came in the music store one day, I think it was Rick's father who talked to the gentleman. The gentleman had this guitar and he wanted a Gretsch Country Gentleman, and it could have been because of The Beatles. He had this older guitar and he wanted a Gretsch Country Gentleman, and there was a guitar teacher at Kay Coster's guitar store—she was on 7th street as well, about three blocks down—and one of her music teachers had a Gretsch Country Gentleman and Nielsen ended up trading* *him a guitar that went through our hands, back and forth, for that Gretsch Country Gentleman, because he knew he could then call that guy up and trade him the Gretsch Country Gentleman to get that Sunburst Les Paul.*

'I always bought used guitars. Any place I could find these six-string orphans. And I found them all over,' Nielsen told *Vice*. 'You had to travel around. I'd get newspapers and be looking at the want ads: I'm a farmer living out in the sticks. I'd go out to see him and get a guitar he bought in '63 or '59. Back in the day, people would come into my dad's music store and trade their guitars. They didn't buy a new one. Even car dealerships would take guitars on trade for a Ford. So I'd get guitars from car dealerships, appliance stores, you name it.'

PAUL HAMER *So I flew to Philadelphia, I spent a weekend with them and they were so nice, they were so much fun, they were also incredibly funny all the time, it was just a joy to be with them—you had to be the brunt of jokes, but if you gave back and let another band member be the brunt, they accepted you.*

Money in hand, the band followed Rick and his pregnant wife back to Rockford.

STEWKEY *Everybody was getting a little frustrated. I guess it was costing too much to live in Philly, so they went back—I guess we all went back.*

'Ken Adamany, who'd been my agent off and on since 1965, suggested we come back to the Midwest and he'd guarantee us work,' Nielsen told the *Lexington Leader*.

BUN E. CARLOS *So we decided, yeah, we'll all move back to Rockford and carry on. We moved back in May. Stewkey got rid of his real nice apartment. Stewkey and Lisa sold all their furniture. We had a truck, and me and Stewkey threw all our crap in a truck, and the three of us drove back to Rockford. Tom and Rick drove back to Rockford with their stuff, and after about a week of practicing, Rick and Tom and Ken got together one night and decided to fire Stewkey and told me the next day and I was like,* Oh, good, thanks for letting me know, you know we got gigs booked in three weeks. *Because Ken booked a bunch of dates for June, to start playing in the Midwest.*

STEWKEY *We moved back to Rockford and I got fired. But that's all right. Shit happens, you know?*

BUN E. CARLOS *He was steamed. They got rid of all their furniture and stuff, and a week after moving to Rockford: 'You're fired!' So he packed up and moved back.*

Why did they fire Stewkey? For starters, Adamany cites the scathing review from the Mahavishnu Orchestra show in Oshkosh.

STEWKEY *You don't really ask why, you just kind of say, 'Okay.' I had a great time. I had a fun time in that band.*

A cross-country move, followed by the almost immediate dismissal of the singer, left the band in complete disarray. Exasperated, Tom Petersson made a hasty exit of his own.

BUN E. CARLOS *'I can't stand Rockford! I'm going back to Philly!' He had a chick out there or something. It's always a girl.*

Stewkey did not return to Philly, at least not right away. In a further twist, Rick and Karen were not the only couple who were expecting.

STEWKEY *I actually went home to Rhode Island for a while. My wife was pregnant at the time. I had to work. I had a kid right after that, so my life changed a whole lot, and I didn't do anything musically for a long time after that.*

Stewkey's daughter was born in February of 1974. So was I.

8

I hope everyone missed you...

CHEAP TRICK MK I. ADAMANY AND TOLER. CHEAP TRICK MK II.

The departures of Stewkey (involuntarily) and Tom Petersson (voluntarily) sounded the death knell for Sick Man Of Europe. The sickness had proved fatal. The homecoming was off to a rocky start.

BUN E. CARLOS *Me and Rick got together the day they drove off. We called Ken, and he said, 'You got dates here in two and a half weeks.'*

Dates Ken had booked for Sick Man Of Europe. When asked about Sick Man by *Circus* in 1978, Nielsen dismissed the group as 'second-generation garbage.' His plan was to build the new band from the ground up. As he explained it to Chris DeMakes, 'I'd already had a taste of failure, so I wanted some more failure.'

KEN ADAMANY *Next day, he wants me to locate the singer of The Lemon Pipers and also the singer from One-Eyed Jacks.*

The Lemon Pipers from Ohio had a no.1 hit, 'Green Tambourine,' in the late sixties, but frontman Ivan Browne had since relocated to San Francisco. Mike Murphy from The One Eyed Jacks had joined REO Speedwagon. Nielsen realized he would have to settle for an unknown, at which point Bun E. Carlos reached out to Robin Zander, his former bandmate from Phrenz, only to learn that Zander was under contract for another summer at the Lookout Lounge in Wisconsin Dells. Robin suggested that Carlos contact his friend Randy Hogan.

RANDY 'XENO' HOGAN *I got a call from Bun E. Carlos, who said, 'Do you want to come over and sing with me and Rick Nielsen?' Well, of course, they were the older guys and I had seen The Grim Reapers, so I jumped at the chance. This was the summer of '73. So we started rehearsing in Rick's parents' garage, and they brought out all these records—it was a lot of English stuff that I didn't know. And the next thing I knew I was singing all these songs and I was playing the Mellotron.*

BUN E. CARLOS *[Randy] was going to Rock Valley and taking classical guitar and he says, 'Yeah, I'll join you guys for three months and then I'm going back to college,' and we were like, 'Yeah, sure, get in the band.' And he got in the band.*

Hogan was far from a novice, having joined his first band, The Noblemen, when he was still a pre-teen.

RANDY 'XENO' HOGAN *That's when I decided I was gonna be a musician. When I was in seventh grade I was playing with the ninth graders. Big difference, you know, at that age. Some of these guys could actually drive. I'm in seventh grade, all gangly and geeky, walking down the halls with my geeky friends and the varsity cheerleaders stop and say hello to me. Right away I went, Hmm, I think I might want to be a musician.*

My parents were not musicians, but my grandmother played organ in the church for sixty years, and I had an uncle who was a part-time musician, and my parents were always big music fans. They could both sing, but they didn't even know they could sing. My parents were from the South and they'd have these parties—you know, real casual, play cards, what have you—and they'd have their friends come over and at one point somebody would pick up a guitar, somebody that they knew, and they'd start all singing these old country songs, and my mom and dad would blow my mind. I'm six, seven years old, and they'd get up and sing three-part harmony.

After high school, Randy joined a band called Probe alongside John Furland from The Paegans, and after that he was in a band called SFZ with Jerry Parlapiano from The Paegans; more of that cross-pollination. Furland told the *Rock River Times* that Robin Zander was also briefly involved with Probe: 'When [guitarist Mike Olson] left the band in fall of '71, we played as a trio until bringing Hogan and Zander into the group. After a few practices we decided to keep it a four-piece and kept Hogan till disbanding.'

It was essentially an audition process, and Hogan, who was the superior double threat at the time, guitar and vocals, beat out Zander. Rick Nielsen was also impressed with Hogan, and invited him to join the new band—then promptly rechristened him Xeno. Back in Philly, the guitarist from Good God went by Zeno Sparkles, which sounded more rock'n'roll than his real name, Larry Cardarelli. Bun E. told *Legendary Rock Interviews* in 2012 that Rick 'stole that name and made it Xeno.'

HANK RANSOME *I never even thought about that. That's hysterical.*

For Hogan, the unwieldy moniker became a blessing in disguise.

RANDY 'XENO' HOGAN *I'd had the name for a while, and upon talking to a friend of mine who was teaching English at a local community college, he said, 'You know, that's a Greek name, Xeno from Xenos, meaning stranger or alien,' I went, 'Oh, I think I'll keep it.'*

With Tom Petersson AWOL, they still needed a bass player, so Nielsen rang up his pal Stew Erickson from the bands Scag and Mannequin.

STEW ERICKSON *We got together in Rick's father's garage and started hammering out songs. Rick gave me a list of things to learn and we practiced the next few weeks, with me on bass. I can remember doing Badfinger and Patto.*

BUN E. CARLOS *We had about ten days before our first gigs were starting, so we started practicing in Rick's garage, and after three or four days Stew Erickson's wife told him he couldn't be in the band.*

According to Dave Hopkins, a friend of Stew's on Facebook, 'Stew's wife made him quit because making it in music was just a childish pipedream. The divorce happened a couple years later. Stew never enjoyed talking about those days much, other than to say, It was just a few minutes of life and I can't spend the rest of my life dwelling on those few minutes.' Stew was barely (if even) in the band, yet he was technically the first person to play bass in the new, post–Sick Man Of Europe project.

STEW ERICKSON *My wife at the time asked me if I wanted to raise our son and be a father or be a rock star, much to my dismay. I had always known the boys would be famous, honestly. I had to let Rick know that, given that choice, I had no choice, so I suggested they give a friend of mine Rick Szeluga the position.*

BUN E. CARLOS *So he quit, and we called up Szeluga. He joined with about three days to go. So we practiced for three days and we went and started playing.*

RICK SZELUGA *I got a call from Nielsen, asking me if I wanted to come over and play bass, and I said yes, and I think he had probably been misinformed and told that I was this hotshot bass player because I was real energetic.*

Back in High school, Szeluga was in a band with Tom Petersson's older brother Jim on vocals and another Jim, Jim Girling, on guitar, along with drummer Dave (now Ted) Kenney, called Steeled Blues. Young Tom used to watch them practice in his parents' basement.

TED KENNEY *We were actually quite ahead of our time. I was in tenth grade, those guys were in ninth grade, '67, '68, we're doing Cream, Hendrix, Yardbirds, Traffic. Nobody'd heard of that stuff.*

Jim Peterson went on to become Cheap Trick's first sound guy, and Jim Girling replaced him.

KEN ADAMANY *I remember Rick called and said, 'We've finally got the band together, come down to a rehearsal.' It was at Spring Creek Road [Rick's parents' house], and it was Bun, Szeluga, Xeno—who I had never heard sing before—and Rick. They played a bunch of songs and I really liked it a lot, I was impressed. So we started booking them, but they were so different. Very difficult to get them in places. Fortunately, I had an agency with some bands that were really popular, like Dr. Bop & The Headliners—fifties band, popular all over the country.*

Dr. Bop & The Headliners were drummer Mike Riegel, the band's namesake; bassist Ned Engelhart, who went by Ferret de Monte Christo; and guitarists Ken Champion and Bob Kenison, or Speedo and Troy Charmell, respectively.

Kenison also played keyboards. Dr. Bop's frontman, Al Craven, called himself The White Raven.

AL CRAVEN *Dr. Bop was the hammer of the agency.*

BUN E. CARLOS *They opened more than a few doors for us.*

KEN ADAMANY *They did help Cheap Trick a lot. Never objected, even though the band was really different, just starting out. The Dr. Bop guys were always there for Cheap Trick.* Sure, put 'em on. We like those guys. They're fun.

Dr. Bop & The Headliners essentially resurrected Adamany's management career. He had pondered leaving the business entirely in the early seventies.

KEN ADAMANY *I had just gone through a divorce and had two little girls, ages two and three, and was playing two nights a week with The Tim Davis Band, but knew that I had to do something else. Bill Sherrick said, 'Hey, why don't you come and work with me for a while, until you decide what you're going to do.' And that's where I met Chuck, and Chuck was so optimistic. Because I had connections with all the big agencies, I was promoting bands from way back, popular bands.*

Ken accepted the position with Sherrick's company, Midcoast Management, while he considered his options. Also working for Midcoast at the time was an obsessed rock fan from Beloit named Chuck Toler, who had long been a fixture on the local scene. Toler first introduced himself to Adamany at a Cream concert that Ken booked at Beloit College for March 21, 1968, on Cream's farewell tour.

CHUCK TOLER *Of course I was there, backstage, and Ken later in life said to me, 'You know, you were always that pesky kid, hanging around.'*

When Led Zeppelin performed at the Kinetic Playground in 1969, Toler staked his claim right in front of the stage. When Jimmy Page sauntered out to check on his gear he noticed him there, nodded, and said, 'Hey, Chuck.' Everyone was mightily impressed, including the guys from The Grim Reapers, who were standing nearby. (A week later, they performed for the Epic reps at the same venue.) Page recognized Toler as the Ledhead who had been following the band on tour.

Chuck flirted with booking concerts out of his parents basement in Beloit, which is where Adamany tracked him down one day to ask for his help booking an REO Speedwagon show. It would be their first collaboration. Then came Midcoast Management, where they were colleagues. Then came a partnership (for a few years).

CHUCK TOLER *Ken said, 'Well, you know, I might start my own thing.' Which I thought was a bluff. And I told him, 'Well, if you're interested, I'd partner with you.' And he goes, 'Oh, no way, you're a kid. I'm not gonna partner with you.' And then he decided to partner with me, and we went on from there. And that's how we kind of built the alliance of the agency, management company, the whole nine yards.*

Adamany points to Dr. Bop & The Headliners as the inspiration.

KEN ADAMANY *Mike Riegel kept calling me to come see them at The Nitty Gritty. They talked me into being their manager, and it turned out to be one of the best things I've ever done.*

Ken and Chuck's first step was to purchase the Midcoast Management name from the Sherrick brothers, but they eventually went with 'Adamany & Toler.' Which brings us to June of 1973, when Adamany piggybacked Rick Nielsen's new band onto a Dr. Bop & The Headliners booking at the Riviera in Lake Geneva, Wisconsin—a lakefront facility with a marina, beach, and large Italian Renaissance–style building. The ballroom on the top floor had served as a concert venue since the thirties, hosting acts as prestigious as Benny Goodman, Louis Armstrong, Frank Sinatra, Billie Holiday, and Stevie Wonder. In the seventies, former state senator George Borg sublet the space and repurposed it as a discotheque called the Top Deck, as described by Anne Morrissy in a 2019 article for *At The Lake: Geneva Lakes Area Magazine*:

Borg invested a significant sum of money to reconfigure the interior and convert it from a ballroom to a slick bar and nightclub called the Top Deck. When Borg died in a motorcycle accident the following year, Buzz Braden bought the Top Deck Corporation, just as Wisconsin changed state law and lowered the drinking age from twenty-one to eighteen. Thomas 'Murph' Morrissy worked as a bartender at the Top Deck from 1972 to 1974. 'When that change went into effect, the place was packed, especially on the weekends,' he remembers. 'Some weekends we had 1,000 people in there. On weekend nights in the summer, we had seven bartenders on shift at once, seven different bar stations, each with our own register. On good nights, I would take in $1,000 in a single night at my register alone.'

Rick Pemberton and Pat O'Brien served as temporary roadies, helping the new band lug all their gear, including a Diapason upright piano and Mellotron, up the many stairs to the venue. The band hauled those keyboards around with them for a couple of years before realizing they were dead weight. Nielsen might have used them a couple times per set—for example, playing piano on Free's 'Heavy Load' or Mellotron on Manfred Mann's 'Meat.'

Advertisements placed with the *Lake Geneva Regional News* for the Top Deck engagement billed the new band simply as 'REAPERS.'

BUN E. CARLOS *We called ourselves The Reapers for about three weeks because we didn't have a name.*

The new band rolled into town two nights before Dr. Bop & The Headliners, as they were booked for six nights and Dr. Bop for just four. The very first public performance by the new band took place at the Top Deck on Tuesday, June 6.

BUN E. CARLOS *I'd be yelling chords to Rick Szeluga because he didn't know half the stuff.*

Unfortunately, the new band's act was not tame enough for the Top Deck's sophisticated clientele, and they were asked not to return—i.e., they were fired. A 1972 article from the *Lake Geneva Regional News* might shed some light on why the booking, the new band's very first, was cut short:

Manager Scott Braden explains, 'People come here to have a good time. The entertainers we feature provide danceable, fun music, and the atmosphere is informal.' Hard rock music is seldom found at the Top Deck. 'We want our customers to have a good time dancing and talking. So we offer more of a sock hop, early 1950s-type music that is easy to dance to and not quite so loud,' Braden added.

KEN ADAMANY *Simply stated: they were just too strange for the Top Deck. Rick was wearing a top hat, he was playing Mellotron and guitar. They were too loud.*

RANDY 'XENO' HOGAN *We had a screaming rock'n'roll band. Rick with his flying V, playing The Who, and I'm pretty sure that's not what they had in mind.*

RICK PEMBERTON *Some people thought maybe they were a little weird. It was maybe a little glam looking, not that there's anything wrong with it but maybe for Lake Geneva, Wisconsin it was a little different.*

Nielsen donned a top hat for part of the show, years before Slash. Owner Buzz Braden told Adamany, 'That's not gonna work.' Adamany was not discouraged.

KEN ADAMANY *I knew they were going to be really good. Really good!*

He had something for Saturday: a date he'd booked for Sick Man of Europe back in May, at Memorial Union Terrace in Madison, an outdoor venue right on the lake. The contract called for three forty-five-minute sets for a fee of $150. It was an inauspicious launch for the new band: rejected by the Top Deck and right back to being called Sick Man Of Europe.

The following Wednesday, they drove an hour and a half northwest of Rockford to the small town of Benton, Wisconsin, where they were booked as entertainment for a Fourth of July celebration in a small park adjacent to a cornfield.

KEN ADAMANY *As I recall, it was a makeshift stage set up between Benton and New Diggings.*

BUN E. CARLOS *Rick gets up there and goes, 'Is everybody here bent?'*

In other words: 'Is everyone in this rural enclave of less than a thousand people, once called Swindler's Ridge, a homosexual?'

BUN E. CARLOS *We're laughing it up in the band and everybody's just kind of staring at us. They just wanted to kill us. I was thinking to myself that it just couldn't get any worse.*

The band persevered, at some point deciding to call themselves Cheap Trick. Xeno remains adamant in his recollection that the name was born out of a moment when he caught Rick copping a Grand Funk riff during a rehearsal in Rick's parents' garage—a cramped space clogged with gear, drums, and clutter, wires and cords crisscrossing the cement floor, a record player on a short table next to them (for learning songs), doors left open to mitigate the summer heat (neighbors be damned). The phrase 'cheap trick' was uttered, and it stuck.

RANDY 'XENO' HOGAN *I can tell you exactly how it happened. We're at rehearsal one day, and Rick is playing this Mark Farner lick, to which I said, 'Hey, that's a cheap trick,' to which Rick replied, 'That's a great name for a band.'*

BUN E. CARLOS *I remember just bandying names about at practice. We were talking about different variations. What about cheap? Because we didn't have a show, we didn't have a big stage act, we didn't have a gimmick. It was like, 'Well, we could call ourselves, you know … cheap something.' And I remember Rick goes, 'How about Cheap Trick or Cheap Tricks?' And we were all kind of like, 'Yeah, that's not bad.' And it was like, 'Okay, it'll be Cheap Trick.' It wasn't like we had forty names listed and we cut it down to twenty and we cut it down to ten. There's no great story like that.*

The phrase, be it churlish or snide, aligned with the simpler, dirtier sound the new band was going for, away from the proggy elements that held Sick Man Of Europe back.

BUN E. CARLOS *We were clearing dance floors. When Cheap Trick started, that was one of the only rules we kind of formally made: let's do songs people can dance to, so we won't get fired from any more gigs. The prog end of it kind of went out the window.*

When asked to reflect upon the nuance behind the name by the *Wisconsin State Journal* in 1997, Carlos deemed it a 'reaction to art-rock goofballs.' This was to be a new kind of band. New look. New sound. The name needed to embody that.

RANDY 'XENO' HOGAN *I was like a glam guy and that's basically what the band was in the beginning, that's why it was a cheap trick, because it was a glam band.*

Tom Petersson has been wont to spin a different yarn, linking the name's inception to a moment of inspiration at a Slade concert, when he turned to Rick and said, 'These guys are doing every cheap trick in the book.'

BUN E. CARLOS *They would stop every song. 'Come on, everybody! Put your hands together.' The songs would just stop and start all fuckin' night long—it was kind of a headache to watch. That was their schtick.*

One problem: Petersson wasn't even in the band at the time the name was conceived, a fact he openly acknowledged when speaking with a magazine called *Super Rock* in 1978:

SUPER ROCK: Where did you get your name?
BUN E: Cheap Trick?
SUPER ROCK: Yeah.
BUN E: We just kind of …
TOM: I don't know, because I left …

Exactly: he didn't know, because he left. He was back in Philadelphia when it all came together.

Nielsen has been guilty of spinning even more outlandish yarns about the name, at different points attributing its origins to an encounter with extraterrestrials, a session with a ouija board, or a tribute to Linda Lovelace, she of the deep throat. Xeno's recollection, clear and concise, rings true: he said, 'Hey that's a cheap trick,' and Rick said, 'Hey that's a band name.'

RANDY 'XENO' HOGAN *If Robin had been the original lead singer, they would never have been called Cheap Trick.*

The name made it feel all the more real—time to take it to the next level.

BUN E. CARLOS *Ken was just booking us any place that would hire us for one hundred bucks or whatever, and then he says, 'You guys should go to North Dakota and break the band in. You do five sets a night for a week or two, and you'll come out of there knowing how to play.'*

It was half a day's drive to Minot, North Dakota, for an extended residency at a roadside diner called the Dutch Mill, beginning Monday, July 23. They arrived in town on Sunday, just in time to attend the final day of the North Dakota State Fair.

RANDY 'XENO' HOGAN *We were in Minot for two weeks, just to tighten the thing up.*

BUN E. CARLOS *Get the cobwebs out, get the act together.*

Five sets a night (a twenty-minute intro followed by four forty-minute sets) for six nights, one day off, then six more: $750 per week, plus accommodations:

BUN E. CARLOS *One motel room with four beds and a cot. It was the four of us with Ron Short, our roadie—a guy we went to high school with that roadied for Fuse. He roadied for us the rest of that summer, and then he quit to be a cable guy.*

It was bar-band boot-camp, yet they still managed to assert themselves, as Rick recollected for *Chris DeMakes A Podcast*: 'They were telling us to turn it down all the time, after every set, Would you turn it down? Yeah, okay, we will. We never did.' Pyle!

RANDY 'XENO' HOGAN *There was a windmill, and I sat in that windmill and wrote letters to home.*

RICK PEMBERTON *Early Cheap Trick was a mish mash of this and that, but they figured it out pretty quickly.*

* * *

After a visit to the Dynamite Lounge in August, the band crashed at the Traveler Motel in Bettendorf. Two rooms. In the memo line on the first invoice, Rick Nielsen wrote 'Sick Man Of Europe,' and in the memo line on the second, he wrote 'Cheap Trick.' The 'world's worst band name' still lingered, having also turned up on an Adamany & Toler roster printed in July.

KEN ADAMANY *There was a transition period where we were booking both names.*

On Sunday, August 26, 1973, Cheap Trick performed in the parking lot of an apartment complex called Ridgewood Trace in Madison, opening for Looking Glass (featuring Jeff Grob, who we met earlier, outside the Factory, on drums) and Dr. Bop & The Headliners. The set was all covers:

```
'Dealer Dealer' (Manfred Mann)
'Rock And Roll Queen' (Mott The Hoople)
'Down On The Bay' (The Move)
'Rich Kid Blues' (Terry Reid)
'Cold Turkey' (John Lennon)
'It's All Over Now' (The Rolling Stones)
'Wam Bam Thank You Ma'am' (The Small Faces)
'Second Generation Woman' (Family)
'Let It Rock' (Chuck Berry)
'My Wife' (The Who)
'Vacation / Walkin' On Sunset' (John Mayall)
'Love Me Do' (Badfinger)
'Waiting For The Man' (The Velvet Underground)
'Suffragette City' (David Bowie)
```

The opening song, 'Dealer Dealer,' was in fact a very cool mash-up of two different Manfred Mann tunes, 'Dealer Dealer' from 1967's *Manfred the Musicmann* and 'Prayer' from the 1972's *Manfred Mann's Earth Band*. All four Sick Men Of Europe attended a Manfred Mann's Earth Band show at the Bijou Cafe in Philadelphia on December 18, 1972, and witnessed a performance of the unreleased arrangement. In fact, Bun E. recorded it.

BUN E. CARLOS *Manfred Mann was doing the announcements and he goes, 'This song was on our last record, it's called Prayer, but we had these other lyrics we like a lot better, from the song called Dealer, but we didn't put 'em on the record because we would have had to pay the guy royalties.' So they were doing the* *song live, but they never actually had this version on a record. And it was called 'Dealer Dealer.'*

They were endorsing Hiwatt amplifiers, and I had an instamatic with me and I took a roll of film, shots from this little balcony in this tiny little club, and after the gig the Hiwatt guy came up and goes, 'Can we borrow your film and we'll get it developed? We wanna use a couple of pictures for these endorsement ads, because this is the last gig of the tour and we didn't get any pictures.' So we got to go in the dressing room and meet the band. That was kinda neat. Of course, I never saw my pictures.

Cheap Trick were the odd band out at the Fabulous Fall 50s Rock'n'Roll Revival on September 15. Dr. Bop & The Headliners, well, headlined, along with three additional throwback acts from the Adamany & Toler roster: Ziggy & The Zeu, The Shakers, and The Illusive Sounds. On September 20, Cheap Trick (possibly—there was a ticket at Rick's Picks) opened for The Ides Of March at Armstrong High School in southern Illinois. The Ides had almost topped the charts with 'Vehicle' a few years earlier, but they were now two months from splitting up. (Leader Jim Peterik would remain a fixture on the Chicago rock scene, eventually launching Survivor.)

The next night, Cheap Trick played the Red Lion Inn in Bloomington, Illinois, for a well-lubricated audience, thanks to 'Super Happy Hour'—15¢ beers from 4:00 to 6:30. On September 28, they played Ted's Warehouse in Charleston, Illinois. A newspaper ad declared them 'A Dynamite Group' called 'CHEAP TRICKS.' Also on the bill was a southern (Illinois) rock band called T.S. Truck. Printed at the bottom of the ad: 'WELCOME PARENTS.' It must have been orientation week at EIU.

On September 30, Cheap Trick performed at the other Red Lion Inn in Champaign, where they stayed overnight. It was in the car the next day, as they headed back north, that tensions flared, specifically between guitarist and bassist.

BUN E. CARLOS *Szeluga was getting loonier and goofier as the summer went into the fall.*

Rick and Xeno were up front, with Bun E. and Szeluga in the rear, and Szeluga was talking a blue streak.

BUN E. CARLOS *Nielsen was like, 'Shut up, I'm driving.'*

Szeluga did the opposite, while waving around a Bible he'd purloined from the previous night's motel.

BUN E. CARLOS *He gently tapped Rick in the head with the Bible, like to get his attention and Rick made a fist and turned around and popped him one, he got pissed at him. 'Knock it off, Sluggo!' We called him Sluggo because you couldn't have two Ricks in the band—you'd never know who you were talking to.*

Sluggo got slugged.

BUN E. CARLOS *It was just like, 'Well, we're getting a new bass player.'*

RICK SZELUGA *I knew I was done, but I knew I was done before that. You know, I just wasn't cutting it. So I drank more and had a good time in my own way and kind of just separated myself and helped facilitate the move to a new bass player.*

BUN E. CARLOS *So we called Tom. He'd been back in Philly for four or five months, and he was ready to get out of Philly.*

Tom Petersson described his thought process when the call came: 'Oh, you're actually working? Well okay, then I'll do it. What the hell, I'm not doing anything, either.' He returned to Rockford the first week in October and attended one of Szeluga's final performances, at Someplace Else on Water Street in downtown Milwaukee. Tom took a seat at a table with Ken Adamany, close to the stage, not far from where the guy that he was replacing was performing, crossed his arms, and stared. Szeluga—aka Kid Korvette, aka Sluggo—bowed out gracefully, seeming to have always understood that the position belonged to Petersson, if and when he wanted it.

RICK SZELUGA *I was good enough at least to get the band going, but I wasn't good enough to stick around long because I hadn't been playing, and we're talking about guys who played all the time. So it was four months of Cheap Trick, and then I was out.*

Tom Petersson made his debut with Cheap Trick on Thursday and Friday, October 10 and 11, at Humpin' Hanna's in Milwaukee. Next came back-to-back nights at the Red Lions, Champaign on the 12th and Bloomington on the 13th. Immediately following the Sunday night show, they hit the road, headed back to Minot, North Dakota, for a second crash course at the Dutch Mill. They barely made it out of Bloomington before the car conked out—luckily, next to an operating farm.

BUN E. CARLOS *While the rest of us waited at a grain silo, Rick got a ride to Rockford, one-hundred-plus miles north, and drove another car back to Bloomington, where we unhitch the trailer from the broken-down car and hitched the trailer up to the replacement car and left at around 6am and drove to North Dakota.*

A newspaper ad for the band's encore engagement at the Dutch Mill declared, 'Back By Your Requests. The Wildest Boogie Band. No cover for this nationally known group.' Nationally known? If you say so. They did get a raise, from $750 per week to $1,000, plus those luxurious accommodations. This time they were only in Minot for a week, performing nightly from October 15 to 20. They then drove three or four hours to the east—which was at least in the direction of home—for a weeklong engagement at McGuire's Bar ('Where a drink is a drink') in downtown Grand Forks, October 22 to 27.

A set list from Grand Forks:

```
'Wam Bam Thank You Ma'am' (The Small Faces)
'Ain't Got You'
'Ultramental'
'Slow Down' (The Beatles via Larry Wilson)
'Shake' (Sam Cooke)
'You Can't Judge A Book By Its Cover' (Bo Diddley)
'My Generation' (The Who)
'Route 66' (Chuck Berry, Rolling Stones)
'Burlesque' (Family)
'Move Over' (Janis Joplin)
'Waiting For The Man' (The Velvet Underground)
'Rock And Roll Queen' (Mott The Hoople)
'Speak To Me' (Jackie Lomax)
```

```
'Tom's Blues'
'I Got Rhythm' (Patto)
'Rock And Roll Part 2' (Gary Glitter)
'Dealer Dealer' (Manfred Mann)
'Wipeout' (The Surfaris)
```

A few tunes from the Sick Man Of Europe days had re-entered the set. Sick Man played mostly originals (like 'Ain't Got You,' 'Ultramental,' and 'Tom's Blues'), but the bulk of the material performed by Cheap Trick over the course of the first couple of years would be covers. In addition to the songs that have been previously listed, other tunes they tackled during this period included 'Revolution' and 'Get Back' (The Beatles), 'Stupid Girl,' 'Let It Bleed,' and 'Honky Tonk Women' (The Rolling Stones), 'You're Lookin' Fine' (The Kinks), 'Boris The Spider' and 'Shakin' All Over' (The Who), 'The Stealer' and 'All Right Now' (Free), 'Jeepster' (T. Rex), 'I Hear You Knockin'' (via Dave Edmunds), 'Tin Soldier' (Small Faces), 'Love-itis' (Mandala), 'Midnight Rider' (The Allman Brothers),' 'Rock And Roll' (Led Zeppelin), 'Lookin' Back' (Bob Seger), 'River' (Terry Reid), 'Will It Go Round In Circles' (Billy Preston), 'Messin' With The Kid' (via Rory Gallagher), 'I Know' (Gary Wright & Wonderwheel), 'Coz I Luv You' and 'Mama Weer All Crazee Now' (Slade), and 'Hang On To Yourself' (David Bowie). The award for Most Covered Band goes to Badfinger: 'No Matter What,' 'Love Me Do,' 'Suitcase,' 'Rock Of All Ages,' 'I Can't Take It,' and they at least rehearsed 'Without You.'

It did not make for your average Top 40 bar band set, and things were about to get weirder, as Rick Nielsen arrived at rehearsal one day with the first two original songs he wrote specifically for Cheap Trick: 'Daddy Should Have Stayed In High School' and 'Hot Tomato.'

BUN E. CARLOS *Rick wrote those two and presented them to us when we had Xeno in the band. 'Daddy' was first, or right around the same time, because I remember we started practicing them with Rick Szeluga. We also had learned 'Mandocello' and 'Ain't Got You' and a couple other Sick Man tunes—there was one called 'My, My, My.'*

Returning from North Dakota, the band found themselves right back at both Red Lions, Bloomington on November 2 and Champaign on November 4.

On November 9, they opened for Climax Blues Band in Oshkosh. Posters for the event billed them as 'Formerly Known as Nazz,' with a newspaper ad boasting 'formerly of FUSE.' Soon there would be no need to harken back to such … past glories?

Next up, a three-night engagement at the Stone Toad in Milwaukee, followed by a Thursday night show at the Barn, a longstanding nightclub attached to a literal barn on the Mary-Le-Lakes estate in Sterling, Illinois, and then Friday and Saturday night performances at Bachelors III on Main Street in Madison, named in tribute to owner Pierce Nolan's three sons.

Bun E.'s former bandmate from Phrenz, Robin Zander, came out to Bachelors III on Saturday, and they hung out afterward. Meanwhile, Tom Petersson, thrown to the wolves, had to get his groove back post haste.

BUN E. CARLOS *We gave Tom this big list of tunes, and I remember one of the first gigs he got to, Tom says 'Living In The USA' is the toughest song in the world to learn, 'You know that Steve Miller thing goes on for eight minutes!' And we're like, 'No, the Chuck Berry song. Three chords.' Tom was like, 'Jesus, that took me forever to fuckin' learn, and you guys don't even do it!'*

Speaking of Chuck Berry, Dr. Bop & The Headliners were booked to open a big show at the Minneapolis Auditorium, The Rock & Roll Revival featuring Del Shannon, Freddy Cannon, and Bo Diddley, with Mr. Berry closing. The promoter was looking for a ready-to-go ensemble capable of backing up all four legendary rockers, and Adamany volunteered the services of Cheap Trick. The show was originally set for November 10 but rescheduled (thanks to Berry) for November 25. Cheap Trick caravanned to Minneapolis and performed for the duration as 'The Rock & Roll Revival Band,' with Adamany on Hammond B3 organ.

Dr. Bop & The Headliners went on first, after which Cheap Trick performed a song or two before Xeno took a seat in the audience for the rest of the show. The band squeezed in a bit of rehearsal time with Shannon and Cannon, but it would be a trial by fire once the big names hit the stage. Del was a nice guy, and the short set went well. Freddie, on the other hand, was a firecracker.

KEN ADAMANY *Freddie thought Tom was dicking everything up. He was not fond of me playing B3 either.*

They stumbled through Cannon's hits: 'Tallahassee Lassie,' recently covered by The Flamin' Groovies; 'Palisades Park,' written by game-show host Chuck Barris.

BUN E. CARLOS *Freddie would be, 'Thank you very much!' He'd turn around, 'You motherfuckers are killing me!'*

There was no time to recuperate. Up next was Bo Diddley.

RANDY 'XENO' HOGAN *Bo Diddley was hysterical, he was really funny. I remember he came into the dressing room and he had that old guitar, and Rick Nielsen asked him what kind of strings he had on there, and he said, 'I don't know, they've been on there for twenty years.'*

When Bun E. approached Diddley to ask for some guidance, all Bo had to offer was, 'Don't play none of that tom-tom shit.' Come showtime, Diddley ambled out onstage in a tailored lime green suit, savoring the spotlight.

KEN ADAMANY *Every time Rick would take a solo, Bo would stand right in front of him.*

'After Bo Diddley drank root beer and ate beans, I played guitar while he farted,' Nielsen quipped to *Rolling Stone* in 1979. In a *Cheap Licks* bonus video, he added, 'It was just a lot of rhythm, making a lot of noise with the guitar. Pretty cool.'

Chuck Berry was late, of course. And difficult.

RANDY 'XENO' HOGAN *Berry lived up to his reputation. He pulled that whole thing that he used to pull: 'You don't have my amplifier, you owe me the other thousand dollars.'*

BUN E. CARLOS *The rider says, 'Two Dual Showmans—unaltered.' So he goes over to his amps and there's been a repair made on one, so he unplugs his guitar and walks off.*

KEN ADAMANY *One thousand dollars later, he's back. Cash.*

Cheap Trick's take for the entire event was five hundred bucks. Berry doled out terse instructions: keep it simple, follow his lead. Nielsen described the pre-show huddle for John Rzeznik on *Chorus & Verse*: 'He said, *I don't need your band. I can play without you.* You know, giving you confidence right before you go play with him.'

KEN ADAMANY *He wanted to tune his guitar to a mid-octave B-flat on the organ, and insisted I have the Leslie cabinet on high speed.*

Berry took no prisoners, machine-gunning the crowd with a barrage of hits, including his most recent one, 'My Ding-A-Ling.' 'He would start the song,' Nielsen recalled during a *Cheap Licks* bonus video, 'never tell you what key it's in, never tell you what song he was gonna do, so I'd have to look over and see what he was playing and yell at everybody else.'

Not very deep into the breakneck two-hour set, Carlos had the gall to cap a song with a Charlie Watts–style power fill.

KEN ADAMANY *Berry went up to him and said, 'They [the audience] don't know what I'm telling you, so just smile!' And he read him the riot act.*

BUN E. CARLOS *His head swivels around and he jumps up on the riser and gets in my face and goes, 'I told you when my leg goes up in the air you stop. When my leg goes down, the song's over, don't play that shit no more or I'll throw your ass out of here. I don't need you up here, I'll kill you!' And then he goes, 'There's twelve thousand people out there. Smile!' And I go, 'Yes, sir, Mr. Berry!' And he goes, 'Now laugh!' And I go, 'Yes, sir!'*

Berry lightened up once they found their groove. As Tom Petersson told the *Austin Daily Texan* in 1977, 'Chuck Berry let Rick do more solos than he did. He gave Rick the spotlight, and Chuck Berry was all smiles.'

BUN E. CARLOS *I got Chuck's autograph that night. Rick had him autograph the back of his flying V.*

Pulling off an impromptu set as Chuck Berry's backing band was tantamount to earning a degree from Rock'n'roll University. Berry commandeered the stage with a heedless confidence, hammering out his concise songs, bracingly to the point—just a short burst of magic and on to the next. He spurned the superfluous. The flash was in the deftness and clarity.

BUN E. CARLOS *We learned not to do a bunch of shit that we were probably doing in Sick Man Of Europe. When we got done with Chuck, two hours onstage with that guy just kind of drilled it in.*

Put simply: Simplify. Trim the fat. Tom Petersson echoed this sentiment when interviewed by Salley Rayl in 1977: 'I learned more about the feel of rock'n'roll from Chuck Berry than from almost all the years I've played the instrument—guitar, bass, anything. You can't really explain it, but the man—he's got a feel for it.'

As the night unfolded, a rumor made its way through the venue: John Lennon was in town and might make a surprise appearance. He did not.

BUN E. CARLOS *We went over to the Holiday Inn afterward to see if he was there.*

He was not.

9

You're not
the last one...

The war in Vietnam did not end well, exacerbating American doldrums as the economy floundered. A years-long recession followed, and then came Watergate. Meanwhile, for Cheap Trick at least, things were looking up. November 30 marked a return to the Top Deck, where this time they were allowed to complete the engagement. Next on the itinerary: weekend bookings at Someplace Else in Milwaukee and the Pack & Hounds in Green Bay, with a gig at Joker's Wild in Madison in between. Christmas meant a day off, but the next night—the same night *The Exorcist* opened to much controversy in theaters—Cheap Trick opened for Dr. Bop & The Headliners at the National Guard Armory in Prairie du Chien, Wisconsin.

The band's first engagement of 1974 was a long weekend at Humpin' Hanna's in Milwaukee, as recalled by Steve Grimm from the bands Crossfire and Bad Boy:

STEVE GRIMM *[Hanna's] was almost destructive in that they would have Monday penny-beer nights and they would have a band, so every drunk and the dregs of the city would come there and get totally annihilated. It was I guess more European than anything else because the place smelled of urine. Looking back at it, it was adventuresome but not very healthy for anybody.*

Tom Petersson settled in and was soon antagonizing rural Midwesterners with his idiosyncratic approach to androgyny.

BUN E. CARLOS *Tom brought an element of trouble, things we didn't have with Szeluga. He was wearing whiteface makeup and curling his hair and looking real* *weird. The first couple months he was with us, we'd go into these bars and people would want to kill us. They thought Tom was some sort of weirdo. They used to look at Xeno and call him names, but we could deal with that. Tom just put these people over the edge.*

Tom's new look, with his powdered face, eye makeup, nail polish, and lipstick, resembled (but predated) Frank-N-Furter from *The Rocky Horror Picture Show.* 'We would almost never stop between songs,' he once noted. 'There was never a lull where people could hurl insults at us.'

BUN E. CARLOS *I remember we played Macomb one night, and a bunch of frat guys wanted to beat us up. Tom was in whiteface and had his hair all frizzed out, and we were doing some song and I jumped off the drums in the middle of the song and grabbed a mic stand and stood at the top of the stairs onstage left and was like, 'Come on! Come on!'*

Tom was trying, but it took years for Cheap Trick to settle on a 'look' or 'image.' In the early days it was a free-for-all. Xeno approximated the lanky charisma of Mick Jagger, but with a cheaper (yet somehow more extravagant) wardrobe. His sister's mother-in-law, an 'old Italian lady' who 'spoke hardly any English,' was a seamstress, and Randy enlisted her services to accentuate his stage garb.

RANDY 'XENO' HOGAN *I used to go fabric shopping with Rick Nielsen, we'd go into these fabric stores and look for the weirdest shit we could find and bring it to her, and she'd make suit coats and pants and things for us. She would fit me two, three, four times until what I had fit like a glove—tailormade, and she would charge us, like, twenty dollars. I had quite a wardrobe at one point.*

For example: a glossy purple jacket decorated with half-peeled bananas.

KEN ADAMANY *This was a different-looking band back then. We had to wedge our way into places.*

Rick Nielsen found ways to stand out with The Grim Reapers and Fuse, but he'd struggled to find his niche in the seventies. As Tom Petersson would tell *Vintage Guitar,* 'Back then, people used to tell us, Wow, we like your band, but when are your drummer and guitarist going to get with it?'

Seventies rock evolved into a different kind of animal, and while Nielsen may have exuded his own brand of charisma, funny and weird, his thinning hair was not going to cut it (pun intended). Bun E. shared a similar fate, but soon sorted it out.

BUN E. CARLOS *Me and Xeno went to Milwaukee in the fall of '74. This hairdresser wanted to dye Xeno's hair blonde, so we went out there and she dyed his hair blonde and I had shaved my beard off a week earlier, and she goes, 'Let me give you a haircut, it'll look a lot better.' My hairline was just starting to move back a little, and I was like, 'Yeah,' because I wasn't looking too good in the long hair. So she cut my hair real short.*

Inspired by this drastic change to develop an entirely new look, Carlos eventually scavenged some dress clothes (collared shirts, slacks, and ties) from thrift stores and added an additional accoutrement, the ever-present cigarette, inspired by a Rockford band called The Daiquiris, whose members puffed while they played.

* * *

Cheap Trick had New Year's Eve 1973 into 1974 off, leaving Tom Petersson free to tag along with Ken Adamany on a drive up to Detroit to see Dr. Bop & The Headliners open for the New York Dolls at The Michigan Palace. Dr. Bop had performed at the Whisky A Go-Go during the same week as the Dolls a couple of months earlier, and singer Al Craven was in for a shock when the Dolls hit the stage in Detroit.

AL CRAVEN *They did a song that they had seen us do at the Whisky, which was called 'Stranded In The Jungle.' When I was writing out my set before the show, I said, 'I don't know about "Stranded In The Jungle," this crowd is definitely not gonna like that song.' So I X'd it out. So I was standing with Ken and Tom and they started doing 'Stranded In The Jungle,' and I just remember saying, 'They do this song!?' And I was so happy that I didn't put it in my set. I would have really looked like an asshole, you know?*

Attendee Michele Saint Thomas shared her recollections of the show with the *Detroit Metro Times* in 2011:

'Detroit! Are you ready to ring in the New Year with the New York Dolls?' Everyone in attendance stood, cigarettes on lips, hands clapping; a joyous roar filled the air. The Dolls crashed out their first song, the Motor-City hit 'Personality Crisis,' and it was here that my eyes and ears first zapped into the sight and sound of guitarist Johnny Thunders. Amid a kaleidoscope of colorful outfits, fishnets, and platforms stood Thunders, provocative in leather pants and swastika armband, slamming feverishly on the strings of his guitar. Notes crashed, ocean waves on rocks. His smirk taunting the crowd, he rode a watershed of sound that bounced off the theater walls and ricocheted back to him before evaporating mid-air.

The show ended in a melee.

KEN ADAMANY *The stupid band invited everyone onstage, and the crowd just started climbing up on the stage. Tom was one of the first ones, and he went up there and started kicking out the lights, the floor lights.*

Tom was forcibly removed from the venue.

* * *

After a third consecutive summer performing six nights per week at the Lookout Lounge, Zander and Beebe floundered. They'd weathered the autumn with the odd gig at a bar or college party, but with another long, cold winter approaching, the pair decided they might as well take their chances in the UK. Brian's future father-in-law owned a flat in a converted mansion just a few blocks from Princes Street in Edinburgh, Scotland, in a neighborhood called Leith Walk. They flew over and crashed with him. The first week there, Robin was mugged.

Times were rough in Edinburgh. Violent gangs prowled the streets, inspired in part by the 1971 film *A Clockwork Orange*. Some even adopted the look. Robin and Brian ventured outside Scotland as well, performing in Wall's End and Newcastle, which is also where Robin caught a Neil Young concert in November. Opening was a new band from California called The Eagles. Young performed his forthcoming album *Tonight's The Night* in its entirety and closed the show with an extended version of 'Cinnamon Girl,' which 'got a great reception from the crowd, who were pleased to hear something familiar,' according to an attendee who blogged about the show.

Edinburgh was four hundred miles from London, where the wide-eyed duo tried to make some contacts. After an audition at Pye, they were advised to 'go back home and practice.' At some point they caught the attention of a huckster who bankrolled some studio time and signed them to some sort of publishing deal, but nothing came of it. Zander remembered attending 'Alex Harvey's Birthday Party,' 'which turned into a drunk fest.'

The Sensational Alex Harvey Band performed at the Empire Ballroom in Leicester Square on February 11—six days after Harvey's thirty-ninth birthday—but the show was advertised as a 'Valentine's Rock Ball.' The poster promoted a '£50 PRIZE FOR THE MOST ORIGINAL COSTUME.' The event was reviewed by *Sounds*, which concluded, 'Alex will try anything—anything—to get the audience off. He's so anarchic, so reckless, that you wonder sometimes whether he's not a little deranged. The crowd were like a football crowd: the atmosphere was raucous, talkative and sceptical even of their hero.'

The excursion was an adventure, but the boys found no break to catch. They had little choice but to retreat back home for a fourth summer as a featured act in Wisconsin Dells.

* * *

The first weekend in February, Cheap Trick returned to Milwaukee for an engagement at the Stone Toad. A newspaper ad declared, 'TONITE! And Every Thursday it's SINK or SWIM! 5¢ BEERS—25¢ DRINKS.' The second weekend of February saw them at Sammy G's Circus in Kenosha. Toward the end of the month, Rick Nielsen received a check in the mail from Green Apple Music in Hollywood, for Fuse-related royalties, totaling 66 cents. He framed it.

February was an interesting month: Peter Benchley's novel *Jaws* arrived in bookstores, heiress Patty Hearst was kidnapped, Iggy & The Stooges broke up, Mel Brooks' *Blazing Saddles* opened in theaters, and the first KISS album was released.

Rush's debut album came out on the first day of March. Cheap Trick performed at Someplace Else in Milwaukee. Queen's second album came out on March 8. Cheap Trick returned to Humpin' Hanna's the next night. A week later, they were back at Someplace Else. The last day of March witnessed the very first public performance by a new band called the Ramones. That spring, Van Halen graduated to the Sunset Strip, Led Zeppelin launched Swan

Song, Sparks released the revelatory *Kimono My House*, the New York Dolls' second album *Too Much Too Soon* ('Stranded In The Jungle' included) came out, and David Bowie made his final foray into glam rock with *Diamond Dogs*.

Cheap Trick found time to record some demos at Cuca Studios in Sauk City, including versions of 'Hot Tomato,' 'Daddy Should Have Stayed In High School,' and a song from the Sick Man Of Europe set called 'Maid Out Of Wood,' which included the lyric, 'You look like a woman but act like a man ...'

On May 18, they provided entertainment for the Sterling High School post-prom in Sterling, Illinois. A photo of the band even made it into the school's yearbook, Bun E. with his trademark cigarette and Tom the embodiment of a grinning vampire, giving a spooky thumbs up.

* * *

In early June, an interesting article appeared in the *Rockford Morning Star* beneath the headline 'Duo Stays Busy, Hopes For Break.'

Popular music is a grueling, fiercely competitive profession, and Brian Beebe and Robin Zander are grateful for having achieved a measure of success in it that most self-taught musicians from North Park, Ill. [actually Loves Park] never achieve. But there's always the chance of 'making it,' and they keep pushing for it, performing, writing, traveling, meeting influential people and hoping. It's the life of a pop musician. Brian, 22, and Robin, 21, are Zander & Kent, a vocal-instrumental duo that has been making the rounds of college towns and cocktail lounges in Illinois and Wisconsin since the summer of 1971. They mix popular standards with their own compositions.

The article in no way foreshadowed that the partnership was on its last legs.

A couple of breaks might be breaking for them. One is the likelihood that one of Brian's songs, 'Wait For Me,' will be recorded in England. The two recorded it in a London recording studio during a European visit last winter, and it attracted the attention of John Schroeder, owner and producer of Alaska Records. 'He said the song will be released sometime in the near future, sung by an English singer,' Brian said. 'We don't know her name, but she's not too well known yet.' But the duo have signed royalty agreements with Schroeder, and the royalties will be coming in as soon as the record is released. Alaska would release it worldwide. The other possibility for records are some tapes of other songs the duo recorded at a studio in Lake Geneva, Wis. These are being reviewed by record producers …

That article was published on June 9. The very next night, Cheap Trick performed at Uncle Sam's (formerly the Depot and later First Avenue) in Minneapolis. Tom Murray, drummer for the much-respected Midwest psychedelic-rock group The Litter, happened to be there. Murray had a new band called Straight Up and was on a quest to find the perfect frontman— someone with both a big voice and a knack for the theatrical.

TOM MURRAY *I was going through singers. Mark Gallagher for a little while, who was in The Litter, he was in it before, and I had a couple of other singers, and I just couldn't find the right singer. That's when I saw Xeno, and I said, 'That's the guy I want.' His voice matched the music we were writing. He had a signature voice for the band. And his performance, as I was watching it, he had a theatrical side to him when he was performing, so when I did talk to him and told him what the band was all about and would he enjoy doing this, playing a character in a song, he went, 'Yeah.' You know when you see someone and you just know they're perfect for what you want to do with them? If that makes sense. It was like magic. That's why I asked Rick: I said, 'I want and I need your singer, man.' And he said, 'Okay.'*

One might have reasonably assumed that Rick Nielsen's response to 'I want your singer' would have been, 'Well, you can't have him!' Murray was confused, if not pleasantly surprised, when Nielsen just shrugged.

TOM MURRAY *So I went up to Xeno and I said, 'If you ever leave this group, give me a call. I'd like to put you in my band.'*

The seed was planted, but took time to germinate.

BUN E. CARLOS *After the gig we went to some party in St. Paul. We didn't get out of there until about two in the morning, so we didn't get back home until eight in the morning the next day, probably. It was a long-ass night, I remember.*

Cheap Trick closed out June with a weekend engagement at a club in Madison called DJ's. On July 8, they played the Stardust Lounge in Rockford. A handmade poster for the event promised a 'Hollywood Party' featuring a 'Gay Paree Floor Show' and 'GIRLS GIRLS GIRLS.'

On July 13, Cheap Trick performed in the daylight on an outdoor stage at Summerfest in Milwaukee, behind them an amateurish backdrop of green, yellow, and orange (matching the band's Orange amps). Overhead loomed the skeletal frame of an unfinished roof.

RANDY 'XENO' HOGAN *There was no covering on the stage. It was 107 degrees that day and we did a ninety-minute set. Well, somebody, some crew member there, decided they were gonna help us out by putting a covering over the stage of clear plastic. So we went on and did the show—it had to be 127 degrees on that stage—banged it out. That night we played the Black Knight in Lake Geneva, went down there, and I ended up passing out from heat exhaustion. I was so wasted I caught the measles and was out for two weeks.*

The Black Knight was one of their regular haunts. Every time the barkeep rang up a sale on the cash register it buzzed through the PA.

STEVE GRIMM *The stage was right on top of the bar so the guy was always bitching that he couldn't get drink orders because the band was too loud.*

That same month, Ken Adamany sent a tape of the Sauk City demos to a friend named Jim Charne, who was by then gainfully employed with Epic Records in New York.

JIM CHARNE *I've known Ken forever, since I got to Madison in 1968 or probably early '69. I was working as a Columbia college rep in Madison from September 1969 on, and I knew Fuse when they came through Madison. When I graduated from the University of Wisconsin, CBS Records offered me a job in Minneapolis as a local promotion manager for the Epic Records line. I was in Minneapolis for a year when I applied for a job in New York as Epic Records product manager. Epic and CBS were affiliated labels. I got the job and moved to New York.*

Ken's package for Jim included a note that read, 'We recorded in Sauk City on antiquated equipment and, as a result, have had trouble with the vocal mix, but I think the music speaks for itself.' Ken shared the same tape with Robin McBride, employed by Mercury Records out of Chicago. But neither Charne nor McBride was able to foster any interest in the band from his superiors.

At the beginning of August, Rick Nielsen and Craig Myers flew to Los Angeles at the request of Jackie Mills, who produced the *Fuse* album, to perform on sessions for an ultimately unreleased project with Rod Richards (ex-Rare Earth). Leland Sklar played bass on the sessions.

While they were in LA, Rick and Craig, along with Ken and bodyguard Vic Buff—a perfectly monikered biker from Milwaukee—stayed at the infamous Riot House on the Sunset Strip. Also in residence at the time was another Rod, Rod Stewart, along with his former producer, Lou Reizner.

KEN ADAMANY *They were going over songs and were staying just down the hall from us. Lou produced the Dick Campbell album for Steve Sperry and me on Mercury Records back in 1965.*

At some point, someone caught a glimpse of Led Zeppelin by the pool.

KEN ADAMANY *From memory, it may have been just two of them, but lots of girls.*

They also hung out at Rodney Bingenheimer's English Disco, a glam-rock dance club opened by Rodney on the Sunset Strip in 1972. In January of 1974, *Newsweek* described the venue's dance floor as 'a dizzy kaleidoscope of lamé hot pants, sequined halters, rhinestone-studded cheeks, thrift-store any things and see-through every things.'

LA Weekly published a look back at the legendary establishment in 1998:

Alice Cooper lost his snake there. Sean Cassidy played his first show there, opening up for Iggy Pop (who proceeded to slash himself to bloody ribbons onstage). David Bowie pranced and posed on an empty dance floor to the sounds of Elvis Presley there. (The King himself came to check out the hotspot a couple of times, too.) Chuckie Starr had his picture taken there, wearing the world's tallest platforms (14 inches), thereby launching the '70s big-shoe craze. When Led Zeppelin came to LA, they'd drive there straight from the airport. It was the Sunset Strip's palace of wanton escapism, glittery facades, and never-before-heard glam sounds.

They also visited the Whisky A Go-Go, catching performances by The Bar-Kays on August 4 (Ben Cauley, the lone survivor of Otis Redding's plane crash, had relaunched the group in 1971) and Rory Gallagher on August 5.

The sessions for Rod Richards never amounted to anything. The boys were lucky to even get paid, as the first check Jackie sent bounced.

KEN ADAMANY *I eventually collected.*

* * *

On August 9, Richard Nixon became the first President of the United States to resign from the office. Cheap Trick were busy at the Black Knight. An ad for an August 16 appearance at Sammy G's redundantly proclaimed, 'Cheap Trick's Music Is Even Better Than Their Music.' They returned to Sammy G's a month later for 'Sammy's Birthday Party And Corn Roast.' No cover.

On August 27, Cheap Trick opened for Fanny at Snoopy's (later Stone Hearth) in Madison. Fanny had appeared with Todd Rundgren at Rockford Armory two nights earlier, with Dr. Bop & The Headliners opening. Meanwhile …

BUN E. CARLOS *In August 1974, we decided Xeno wasn't working out. I again suggested Robin Zander, just like I did in May 1973.*

Carlos possessed numerous examples of Zander's vocal prowess in his tape collection: Phrenz shows, Robin and Brian demos, the Air Farce tapes, even a Toons rehearsal.

BUN E. CARLOS *So I made a little thirty-minute tape of the stuff Robin just sounded killer on, played it for Rick and Tom, and said this is the guy we need. He's got a great voice. He can learn shit in five seconds. He looks good.*

Intrigued, Rick, Tom, and Ken met up in Wisconsin Dells to check out Zander & Kent.

BUN E. CARLOS *The next day, Rick and Tom said Robin wasn't too good a singer and the long-haired kid had a better voice. I laughed and explained they had Brian and Robin mixed up. They said, 'We don't know if he's frontman material.'*

Zander & Kent's fourth consecutive summer residency was about to come to an inauspicious end. Concurrently, Tom Murray had continued to court Xeno for Straight Up. Murray's overtures culminated in a telephone conversation between Adamany and Straight Up manager David Vieths on October 7. Ken, acting as Xeno's representative, negotiated the singer's exit from Cheap Trick and new partnership with Straight Up.

RANDY 'XENO' HOGAN *I was in a place in my life where I wanted to get away from the people I was working with, I wanted to get the hell out of the town I was in. I'd never been anywhere. I'd never done anything. I loved the Twin Cities and they called me and they bugged me about it, and eventually I just made the decision.*

Straight Up offered Xeno a salary of $250 a week—more than he was making with Cheap Trick—and he would be the star of the show, not just singing but performing, with props and effects.

TOM MURRAY *I saw the actor in him, and the voice matched. He was kind of like David Bowie, to me, when I first saw him. I didn't think I would be able to get him, but it was the right moment. I really do believe that Rick was going to replace him anyway. It was perfect timing.*

Xeno had grown ever more disillusioned with his circumstances in Cheap Trick.

RANDY 'XENO' HOGAN *I don't think they were happy with me, and I wasn't happy with them. And you have to realize, at the time, there was a discrepancy between people who lived in one part of town and people who lived in the other part of town. They were from Rockford and I was from Loves Park, which was considered low-class.*

Brian Beebe backs up Xeno's assertion that people from Loves Park were sometimes treated like hicks by the city people from Rockford, but, in all fairness, Robin Zander was also from Loves Park.

Xeno's last show with Cheap Trick happened at Madison East High School on a Saturday night, October 12. Exactly one week earlier, Bon Scott performed for the first time with AC/DC at a Masonic Lodge in a suburb of Sydney.

RANDY 'XENO' HOGAN *I stayed in Madison that night, hopped on a plane—it was like a prop plane—flew me to Iowa, from there I made a stopover and flew right to Minneapolis. To me, it was the Emerald City. Big, beautiful shining city with all of these lakes. I loved it. I fell in love with it immediately. So that played a big factor in it too.*

The guys from Straight Up picked me up and took me off to Minnetonka, where I stayed, right away. I was still wearing my stage clothes.

Xeno fronted Cheap Trick for more than a year—hundreds of shows—but they were mostly a cover band. Realistically, Straight Up presented a better opportunity (at the time), and he was ready to move on.

RANDY 'XENO' HOGAN *I really wanted to get out of Rockford and I had the opportunity to do that when I joined the Straight Up band and they did this big theatrical thing, which I was very into. I ran away and joined the circus. Literally. Circus boy, that's me.*

I helped [Cheap Trick] become popular. We were very, very popular. We'd just pack the places. I think I made a contribution ... I was the guy who helped start the thing. I was very young, very inexperienced. I go back and listen to that stuff now and I cringe a little bit because I'm over-singing, not paying attention to tonality.

Nielsen later called Xeno's departure 'kinda mutual.' Their paths diverged. Xeno performed with Straight Up for more than three years—twice as long as he was with Cheap Trick.

RANDY 'XENO' HOGAN *I was Alice Bowie. Costume changes, little skits ... it was pretty outrageous for its time.*

TOM MURRAY *I really do believe that Xeno really dug being in Straight Up.*

RANDY 'XENO' HOGAN *That was a huge, huge thing in my life, to just pick up and leave and start over. The amount of emotional growth, maturity and growth, the things I learned along the way, I made lifelong friends, it was quite an experience. I wouldn't trade that for anything—it was awesome. Still my favorite band that I ever played in.*

After Straight Up, Xeno enjoyed brief stints with some other Minneapolis bands, like Dare Force and Harlot, before moving to Milwaukee to join local legends Bad Boy, formerly Crossfire, with whom he still performs to this day. He never experienced the same level of success as Cheap Trick, but it's all relative. Xeno has maintained a lifelong career as a professional musician.

RANDY 'XENO' HOGAN *Somehow I've managed to do that by just staying fluid and diversifying and working very hard. When I started doing this, I thought I was gonna rock'n'roll all night and party every day. Little did I know I was gonna work my ass off.*

Xeno has no regrets. He made the sensible choice at the time, financially and otherwise. Chances were exceedingly slim, even then, for a band like Cheap Trick to transcend the local circuit and 'make it.'

RANDY 'XENO' HOGAN *That's a one-in-a-million shot, and they were really lucky. Of course, they were talented and really good, but, hey, I've managed to make a living making music my whole life, which was the point when I started. How many people get to do what they love for their whole life?*

TOM MURRAY *I respect Xeno so much. He's so talented.*

KEN ADAMANY *Even with the configuration with Sluggo, the band was really good, and Xeno was on top of his game.*

* * *

Finally, the pivotal circumstances were concurrent:

1. Cheap Trick needed a singer.
2. Robin Zander was available.

'I remember going to a battle of the bands at this place called Sherwood Lodge, where kids would go and vote on their favorite band,' Zander once reminisced, 'and I would see Rick's band at the time, The Grim Reapers, and Tom's band, The Bol Weevils; I'd see Bun E. Carlos's band, The Paegans. I didn't think we'd ever get together as a band, but it happened. It was a dream come true, in a way, to see the best guys in each band suddenly in a band that wanted me as their singer. I was like, Wow! This is pretty cool!'

And what about Zander's longtime partner, Brian Beebe?

BRIAN BEEBE *We'd done everything. We'd been to Europe a few times, just banging around, trying to make contacts. I said, 'I'm gonna do something else if we're not famous by the end of '74.' Come November, I opened up a bar, and he joined Cheap Trick. It was kind of foretold. I remember the feeling of going— this is just a few months after Robin and I had played for four years together, we're like brothers, and all of a sudden I go to hear them in Madison and the spotlight's on him, and nobody even knows who I am because it's all Cheap Trick, and Robin's now part of that. It wasn't his intent to shut me out or anything. It just happened.*

10

One boy in a thousand...

HELLO ROBIN. CHEAP TRICK MK III.

In 1974, the city of Pewaukee, twenty miles west of Milwaukee, was still just a town, population four thousand. On October 19, a mild Saturday afternoon, the Pewaukee High School football team, the Pirates, 0–4, faced off against the Kettle Moraine Lasers, also 0–4. Little was at stake, or so it seemed. Pewaukee happened to be celebrating its homecoming that weekend. Unfortunately, the Pirates failed to capitalize on multiple scoring opportunities and fell to the Lasers 12–0. Pewaukee coach Jim Morrison (not the Lizard King) came away convinced that his players had been treated unfairly by the refs, airing his grievances the following Monday in the *Waukesha Freeman*. The article was given a very matter-of-fact headline: 'Kettle Moraine Ruins Pewaukee Homecoming.'

Late in the first half Pewaukee had a second down at Kettle Moraine's fifteen-yard line, quarterback Gary Baumann passed to Rick Murphy in the end zone for an apparent touchdown but officials ruled Murphy did not have full possession of the ball before going out of bounds. Morrison was incensed and later sputtered, 'You can't win when they steal touchdowns on you. You might expect to see it somewhere else but not at home especially. Both his feet were in bounds but those leakers took all our momentum away with that call saying he didn't have possession.'

Regardless, the homecoming dance commenced that evening at Pewaukee High School, with entertainment provided by a musical group out of Illinois called Cheap Trick. The band's fee: $300.

BUN E. CARLOS *We did three or four sets that night.*

None of those in attendance could have understood the significance of the occasion: Cheap Trick's first public performance with their new singer, twenty-one-year-old Robin Zander—this after just three rehearsals in Rick's parents' garage.

BUN E. CARLOS *There was a bunch of stuff Xeno sang that Robin wasn't really good at, at that point. He didn't quite have the high scream that Xeno had. Rick sang 'Daddy' and a couple other originals because Robin didn't know them, and Tom sang 'Tom's Blues.' On the break we went and smoked a joint with a couple teachers.*

A student dance was a covert way to initiate a new singer, hidden as it was from cynical rock connoisseurs and rowdy bar patrons. The true test would come when the prying eyes watched and booze flowed freely.

* * *

Autumn in Madison can be wonderfully serene, a slight chill in the air as a gray sky hovers over the modest city surrounded by lakes. It was on just such an evening that a pair of roving musicians named Richie Ranno and Jon Parrot ducked into a club called the Boardwalk on West Gorham Street in the middle of the University of Wisconsin campus. Black plastic letters on the marquee out front spelled 'CHEAP TRICK.' Both had seen the band with Xeno but remembered Tom Petersson telling them this was Cheap Trick's first gig with a new singer. (It was one of the first, but technically the fourth.)

After the homecoming dance, the band invested in another week of rehearsals before tackling a weekend engagement at the Black Knight, Friday and Saturday, October 25 and 26. A Sunday night at the Boardwalk was a low-key way to introduce Zander to Cheap Trick's home away from home in Madison, but he definitely made an impression, as Ranno and Parrott each still vividly recall that night four decades later. Just a few years earlier, together in a band called Bungi, they had made a run at the same Midwest club circuit that Cheap Trick were about to conquer. Bungi even played with Fuse, at a free show sponsored by the UW Oshkosh student government. It was just two days after Jimi Hendrix was found dead in London, and Richie performed the 'Star Spangled Banner' in his honor. Ken Adamany, who was there representing Fuse and two other groups (OZ and Crowfoot), was impressed and offered his agencies' services to Bungi. He even bought them a van.

JON PARROT *That's right—he gave us the red van! That's where that came from! I eventually drove that red van down to Florida [where he still resides].*

Bungi eventually employed a pair of roadies: Jolly (like the Green Giant) Shaw (a Vietnam vet Ranno met at an anti-war protest in Oshkosh) and the perfectly named Patrick Ampe, both of whom would end up working for Cheap Trick. Bungi's only single, 'Six Days On The Road,' foreshadowed what was to come when the band imploded after a disastrous attempt at an East Coast tour in the summer of '73.

RICHIE RANNO *We booked the gigs and we'd get to the place and they wouldn't pay us. We were eating out of people's gardens.*

Ranno opted to stay behind rather than return to Wisconsin with Jon and Steve, crashing with his parents in New Jersey until signing on with Ian Lloyd and Stories, who were riding high on the chart success of 'Brother Louie.' The gig was short-lived, and Ranno soon found himself back in the Midwest, cajoled by Parrot into returning to join a new band called Eden Stone.

RICHIE RANNO *I believe they actually asked the guitar player to leave to make room for me. I played with them for six or seven weeks and then realized it really wasn't going to go anywhere.*

Ranno ditched Eden Stone and headed back east, where he eventually joined a band called The Fallen Angels, formerly Looking Glass, who scored a big hit with 'Brandy (You're A Fine Girl)' in 1972. The Fallen Angels became Starz.

But back to the fall of 1974, when Richie Ranno and Jon Parrott bore witness to Robin Zander's Madison debut. John Masino, another fixture on the Midwest rock scene, was also present that night. A couple of years earlier, when Masino's band Chunky Pie was in need of a frontman, following the departure of namesake Michael 'Chunky' Allen, Masino accompanied Chuck Toler to Wisconsin Dells to scope out Zander & Kent.

JOHN MASINO *My impression was that they were two hippies. Robin had an army coat on and real long, kind of scraggly hair, and they were playing Elton John and Bee Gees and stuff. I don't know if we caught them on an off night or* *something, but the impression that we got, that night when we saw them, we didn't think a lot of it. We passed on them, which was probably the stupidest thing we ever did. We ended up hiring some guy named Charlie from South Beloit instead of asking Robin, and then Charlie was short-lived in the band, and we didn't end up with a singer at all, in the end.*

Masino took over those vocal duties himself, and was now shocked to discover that the hippie from the Dells had joined Cheap Trick.

JOHN MASINO *They were up above the bar on the second level, and it looked really cool because you could watch them from a balcony, and I know that Robin was brand new because he had a music stand. He brought his acoustic guitar and he played some acoustic songs alone by himself, but what struck us was that here was this guy that we saw in the Dells with the army coat and scraggly hair, and all of a sudden he had this green suit on and a shag haircut, and we were like, Is that the same guy!? And then of course as soon as his mouth opened and we heard him sing, we were like, We didn't hire HIM!?*

It had been decided that a proper way to introduce Robin Zander to Cheap Trick's fans would be to nudge him out from behind the curtain to start the show, just him and an acoustic guitar.

BUN E. CARLOS *For the first week or two he would come out and do two songs, acoustic, by himself. Just for the three or four bars where we had a following.*

JON PARROT *He had the balls to get up in a rock club and play an acoustic set.*

Of course, Zander had amassed a great deal of experience as a lounge act, six nights a week for several summers in Wisconsin Dells. What required balls for Robin in 1974 was fronting a loud, abrasive rock band. He had the look and the voice but not the disposition of rock'n'roll ringleader.

Rick Nielsen was ready, willing, and able to fill any void that resulted from Zander's reservedness, but did he prefer it that way? Michael Seymour from *Illinois Entertainer* seemed to think so: 'Trick needed a singer that had no stage presence. Nielsen insists on being the focal point.' And yet, even after Zander joined, Nielsen still tried to recruit someone else.

George Faber was a regional star, the frontman for a wild, crusty blues band out of Champaign called The Finchley Boys (you may recall that Nielsen saw them at the Kinetic Playground with Mike Myers … on acid). Faber wore a boa constrictor around his neck years before Alice Cooper did. When The Finchley Boys broke up, Nielsen invited Faber to join Cheap Trick.

GEORGE FABER *I turned him down …*

That was the first time, after Xeno left, and Bun E. lobbied for Zander. Faber declined, and Rick went with Robin, whose transition from lounge act to rock star was gradual at best. For Nielsen, an only child, patience was rarely a virtue, so he asked Faber again.

GEORGE FABER *They got Robin in the band and they still asked me to join the band, and I had heard Robin by this point and I thought he was a perfect fit for them, and he said, 'No, Robin's too conservative. We're gonna keep him in the band, but we'd have him play acoustic guitar and sing backgrounds, and we want you up front.'*

BUN E. CARLOS *Rick and Tom said Robin could 'wear a tux and play acoustic and sing the high parts,' standing back by the drums.*

A Nielsen-led combo with not one singer but two was not without precedent. When Joe Sundberg joined The Grim Reapers, he'd joined alongside Gary Schuder; and when The Grim Reapers merged with Toastin Jam, Ron Holm attended the first rehearsal alongside Joe Sundberg.

George Faber performed with Cheap Trick at least once, as reported by Doug Peterson on the Illinois Alumni website:

Chances R was packed, with smoke hanging low over the raucous crowd, as the band Cheap Trick prepared to begin its set. It was the early 1970s, and looking down on the stage from one of the club's multilevel balconies were Geoff Poor from the group Feather Train and George Faber, the shaggy-haired lead singer of The Finchley Boys. Faber was also one of the most electrifying showmen in the area, so he didn't walk down—he leaped from the balcony, harmonica in hand, just as Cheap Trick launched into 'Train

Kept A-Rollin'.' He landed on the stage like a bolt from the blue and hurled himself into the music as the crowd erupted.

Paul Wood reported on the same incident for the *Champaign News-Gazette*, and quoted Poor as saying:

They called out to George and he went right over the railing and dropped down to the stage. They went right into 'Train Kept A-Rollin'.' They kept asking him to join the band but I talked him out of it. I told George for their kind of music, Robin was the best singer. Rick kept pestering him, saying, 'We'll have Robin sing background.'

But Faber had been there and done that.

GEORGE FABER *I had just broken away from The Finchley Boys, which was a very guitar-dominant band, and wanted to do something a little bit more rhythm & blues-style and be the leader of a band. I thought that my style and Rick's were a little bit at odds as far as what I wanted to do and where I knew Cheap Trick was going.*

Faber's focus was on his own aspirations and, it seemed, opportunities: he thought he was going to get signed himself. After a Faber demo tape made it into the hands of Lowell George from Little Feat, Lowell gave Faber a call in the middle of the night and sang one of his songs to him over the phone, after which Faber flew out to California to crash at Lowell's place in Laurel Canyon. Lowell held some sway with Warner Bros and hoped to produce an album for Faber, with Little Feat as his backing band. Tragedy intervened, but Faber does not regret rebuffing Nielsen's advances.

GEORGE FABER *I cannot visualize Cheap Trick without Robin, so it's hard to look back on it and think, What if? Well, what if maybe we wouldn't have made it, you know?*

Robin Zander's Rockford debut took place at a popular restaurant and bar called Charlotte's Web (formerly a Swedish church). Also on the bill was a recently formed band called Silver Fox, featuring Joe Sundberg, Craig Myers and Chip

Greenman from Fuse, along with Rick Pemberton on bass. It was a Halloween show, so Nielsen dressed as Woody Allen, Petersson as Eddie Munster, Zander as—who else—the boy wonder, and Carlos as … Buns Carlton.

BUN E. CARLOS *I just wore a Buns Carlton shirt and said I was Buns Carlton of Buns Carlton's Air Farce. It was for charity. We took requests that night for songs, and I remember some guy gave us twenty bucks to play 'Louie Louie.'*

Raucous gigs like a November weekend at Ted's Warehouse in Charleston really put Zander to the test, as did a week-long engagement at the Brewery in East Lansing that December. The Brewery was an infamous club on the Michigan State University campus. A great article entitled 'Beers, Bands & Brawls: The Story Of The Brewery' by Rich Tupica, published by the *Lansing City Pulse* in June of 2015, included recollections from journalist Jack Bodnar, who remembered the Brewery smelling 'like stale, spilled beer no matter how much they cleaned up.'

'It had a definite look,' Bodnar said. 'With the crazy brick as you walked in, the barn wood on the walls, the cavernousness of it, the darkness of it. Above the bar was this narrow walkway where the VIPs, record execs, press and girlfriends of the bands would sit. That little row only fit ten or twelve, and it's also where the soundboard and some of the lights were. It was the best vantage point.' As for the capacity, it was technically seven hundred— though Bodnar said some nights would break a thousand. But, he said, it never felt uncomfortably crowded. 'It was a huge place, hell, it had been an indoor golf range,' he said.

Sometimes the mess would spill outdoors, leading to malicious-destruction and assault-and-battery cases. 'There were some really bad fights out in the parking lot, cars were getting smashed,' Bodnar said. 'It was a roughneck place. But, really, it was also a great time. It was like the Wild West. Anything could happen. You could steal somebody's girl, maybe there would be some fists exchanged and drinks thrown. Whenever you have that much passion and energy, where people are just totally wired and want to have a good time, things can go awry.' Awry as in: someone rolling a live grenade out onto the dance floor. One of the club's three owners, Rick Becker, described the

Brewery as 'very poorly lit' and 'dangerous,' 'a haven for the stoners, rebels, misfits, thrill seekers and music lovers.'

A week later, Cheap Trick performed at a recently opened club called Space Shanty, described in newspaper ads as an 'Annex to Parmer Horseshoe Bar,' eight miles west of Monroe, Wisconsin in a hovel called Browntown, population less than three hundred. They celebrated Christmas Eve at Sammy G's Circus in Kenosha. A festive newspaper ad listed the band members at the bottom: RICK—ROBIN—TOM—BUNNY.

Sammy G's was a diamond in the rough on Sheridan Road in Kenosha, just a couple of blocks from Lake Michigan, owned and operated by its namesake, a colorful character named Sammy Gerolmo.

SAMMY GEROLMO *'Hi Pie.' That was my slogan. It was for the girls. We called the young girls Pie. We weren't politically correct back then. I had a big sign out back welcoming the Pies, lit up, it was a beer sign saying, 'Hi Pie.' I had the world's only hand-painted dance floor. It was a lit Plexiglas dance floor with a big tiger in the center.*

Cheap Trick performed there regularly for the two and a half years that Sammy G's was open.

SAMMY GEROLMO *Somebody saw them, it was my door man's brother, and I think it was in Milwaukee. He told me about them and I booked them immediately afterward.*

BUN E. CARLOS *This guy that worked for Sammy G, he'd come up to us and he'd go, 'I love that song you do, Talkin' 'bout a place called Moo Moo.'*

Someone figured out that the confused fellow had misheard 'Second Generation Woman.'

KEN ADAMANY *Xeno belted it out on that one with the band roaring behind him. It always raised the roof.*

SAMMY GEROLMO *Cheap Trick had a classy crowd. It was more intimate. It wasn't like where you couldn't get in. There was plenty of room in there when Cheap*

Trick played. You could dance. It wasn't an overflow crowd, but it was always a good crowd. It wasn't the biggest moneymaker, but the clientele was nice and they were a great band.

Writing for Prosoundweb.com, Greg DeTogne begged to differ: not about the band but about the vibe. He described Cheap Trick at Sammy G's as 'cutting through the bad vapors and smoky miasma that poisoned the place with potent original material as well as hardcore covers they made their own.'

SAMMY GEROLMO *They always stayed overnight. I had rooms up above the Circus, and Cheap Trick stayed there every time they played. They'd come in on Friday and leave on Sunday. Bun E. had room number one—he always stayed in room number one, a little room there, give him his comic books and there he'd be. Throw him his hamburgers and comic books. He was a great guy, Bun E. What a drummer.*

BUN E. CARLOS *It was an old road house because there were bedrooms upstairs and we used to stay over so we didn't have to drive back. One night we were getting feisty, we threw a guy out, a guy bit him or someone on the ear or he bit someone in the ear, someone whipped a gun out and shot the tree outside the entry and we were upstairs, it was right after the show ended and we hit the floor. It got a little wild up there.*

CHRIS CROWE *That was an interesting place. You know, these were tough places, some of them. Sammy G had his ear bitten off one night and went out the door firing a .45 at the perpetrator, which is loud. Didn't hit him, thank god.*

SAMMY GEROLMO *Oh yeah, I bit somebody's ear off. I did the biting. They charged the place, a bunch of guys, so I picked the biggest guy and I cornered him—there was a little corner, to come into the bar there was one door that swung out, and you couldn't get out once you got him into this little corner. So I got him down there, the biggest guy, I got him on the ground and I bit his ear off and in front of all his buddies. I drug him out and I spit his ear in front of them and I said, 'Does anybody else want any action?' So they all went running, then I ran up and got my gun and I started firing it up in the air. They were definitely after me because there was a jealousy issue in town, with all the girls coming in there. It was over the Pies.*

It was an incredible time in my life. Loved every second of it. All the action. I was twenty-seven when I opened it up.

STEVE GRIMM *He was an interesting guy. He made himself very visible while the band was playing.*

It was by way of repeat appearances at haunts like Sammy G's Circus and Humpin' Hanna's that Cheap Trick steadily built a following, doggedly winning over fans like Chris Crowe, a twenty-six-year-old aspiring writer from Racine.

CHRIS CROWE *They were vastly different, I thought, than what one was used to seeing in the provinces in terms of the creativity and the quality of the thing. Really a very impressive deal.*

11

Put on a brand new shirt...

LOGO. MARSHALL MINTZ. MOTHER'S DAY. LOU REED.

After graduating from Milwaukee's Layton School of Art in 1972, Chris Crowe ventured east for a year or two before returning to his hometown of Racine, an unfinished novel in his suitcase, citing 'New York neurosis' as the reason for his retreat. He turned the novel into a screenplay and promptly sold it to a Hollywood production company for $50,000, as reported by the *Racine Journal Times* in October of 1974:

'It was probably one of the quickest sales of a script ever made,' said Jim Gibson of J. Carter Gibson in Los Angeles. 'That's almost unheard of in a beginning writer.' J. Carter Gibson will act as Crowe's agent from now on, Gibson said. 'Christopher is a very, very talented young man.'

Crowe dismissed the notion of taking his chances in Hollywood:

'I'd never want to live out there,' he said. 'It's too bizarre.' He currently is working for his father's advertising agency the Jack Crowe Studio, and also his own agency, Agency 90. Both are in Racine. 'I love Racine,' Crowe said. 'This is where I was born and raised. Hopefully, I'll be able to write here, and just go to California when I sell a screenplay and work on rewrites during production.'

Crowe's reticence was short-lived, as by the end of 1975 he had moved to Los Angeles, where he built a successful career writing for film and television, but before he left, Crowe bid adieu to the Midwest in a most ingenious way. A recent convert to the cult of Cheap Trick, he longed to manifest the creative kinship he felt.

CHRIS CROWE *They were out there alone, doing this thing, creating it on their own without a guide, without a natural slipstream to slide into. This was self-designed and self-wrought, and that's what was so impressive about them.*

It was young artists in hell. We were in these grim, industrial towns going into their rust-belt phase, and it was all pretty depressing. It was really challenging to find kindred spirits and people who weren't beaten down by the whole thing.

Adamany had at some point commissioned two different logos for the band, both designed by Madison-based artist Dave Muldowney. The first was 'CHEAP TRICK' written in a bulbous, oblong font called Orbit Solid. It was unoriginal but exuded a very seventies vibe. The second was 'Cheap Trick' scrawled in cursive, suggestive of a neon sign or, as Tom Petersson pointed out, toothpaste. Also unoriginal, as it resembled, perhaps too closely, the logo for the New York Dolls (lipstick rather than toothpaste).

Muldowney was talented—he also designed the original mascot for Rocky Rococo and logos and artwork for Dr. Bop & The Headliners (Adamany used him a lot)—but the members of Cheap Trick were less than enthusiastic about the toothpaste design. Crowe caught wind of their dissatisfaction and secretly nominated himself to rectify the situation, certain he could conjure up a more appropriate emblem to represent the band. And so, one Saturday afternoon in late 1974, he locked himself away in his father's graphic-design studio and went to work. What Crowe conjured up that day, completely unbeknown to the band, was brash and obnoxious, intriguing and memorable, and undeniably enhanced Cheap Trick's vibe and mystique moving forward.

CHRIS CROWE *That was my graphic response to what I saw. It was not studied. I just thought, on a gut level, This is great. These guys are like I am or wanna be, you know. We're all striving at the time, I'd like to help them in some way, which is to come up with this graphic, so I did it.*

The iconic Cheap Trick logo essentially birthed itself, the spirited creation of an enthusiastic fan as a token of his admiration. Does it get any better than that? The letters in the logo were not produced with a typewriter but rather a Letraset-brand dry-transfer sheet.

CHRIS CROWE *It was a typewriter font from them, but then massively fucked with.*

The Letraset decals were administered by placing the transfer sheet, transparent except for the decals, face down on the target surface—in this case, a piece of paper or poster board—and rubbing over the decals with a stylus or ballpoint pen. The transfer sheet could then be carefully peeled away, leaving the decals affixed to the surface (thereby transferred).

CHRIS CROWE *It was first rendered, just once, in Letraset, then run many times through an overheated Thermo-Fax duplicating machine, until the bleeding and degradation looked just right.*

The Thermo-Fax used radiant heat to reproduce an image. A thin sheet of heat-sensitive paper was placed over the document to be copied and exposed to infrared energy. The image absorbed the energy and thereby transferred itself to the heat sensitive paper.

CHRIS CROWE *Talk about non-digital—this was all fucking bleeding heat and very organic relative to today, and that's why it has some kind of feel, I suppose. It's overheating the machine and making it do what it did, and then cleaning it up and Photostating that and finally getting the original.*

The Photostat predated the Photocopier. The document to be copied was placed, face up, beneath a camera, the image then projected onto a roll of sensitized paper, generating a copy. There was a method to this madness. The overkill was quite intentional. Crowe purposefully employed various redundant processes in order to layer, degrade, saturate, distort. The end product insinuated that the phrase 'Cheap Trick' had been typed obsessively, over and over, one on top of the other, 'like a Brooklyn secretary's final typing assignment before a brutal suicide,' as Cary Baker described it for *Lively Times*.

CHRIS CROWE *Any creative or artistic endeavor, you play with it until you either abort and go, 'This is bullshit,' or you get to that wonderful moment where you say, 'This is fucking good, leave it alone, it's done.'*

A year and a half later, Paula Scher, a veteran graphic designer at Epic Records, recognized and appreciated Crowe's intent when she was tasked with designing the cover for the first Cheap Trick album.

PAULA SCHER *When I saw that logo I thought, This is a black-and-white cover. It was a little bit high contrasty black-and-white, so it was a little bit nasty, and that was all deliberate.*

CHRIS CROWE *That album cover reflected the logo so completely. That stark black-and-white imagery and high contrast.*

PAULA SCHER *We had this aggressive, misrepresented, dripping kind of logo. It was a graphic-design joke. It was making a joke about reproduction, and I thought that was smart.*

CHRIS CROWE *That sounds right, but it was not studied. I didn't think of it that way. I didn't do it intellectually. The way I did it, I mean the physical, you know, stupid process was I set the type, hand set, then ran it through an ancient Thermofax machine, which was a heat process that grabbed an image and regurgitated it by heating some fucked-up film that they used in these machines, and if you overheated it, it would bleed, and so that's the way it was done—that is, it is all about massively stupid reproduction. Warhol used to fuck around with this stuff.*

Crowe's efforts yielded a stunning result. Even so, it took some nerve for him to bring it along to a Cheap Trick show at, he thinks, Humpin' Hanna's.

CHRIS CROWE *It was on a piece of illustration board less than a foot big. Maybe it was eight inches by eight inches or something. By now it's probably peeling and brown, but that's how it was delivered. Camera ready. It was done. God knows where that is, the original graphic.*

BUN E. CARLOS *It was handmade when given to us. He wrote, 'Use any line you like or use them all.'*

Crowe approached Rick and Tom between sets and unceremoniously presented them with their new logo. It was one of those historically significant moments that can only be adequately appreciated in retrospect.

CHRIS CROWE *Rick was ambivalent but kindly. Tom was effusive, enthused.*

'Tom immediately thought it was terrific, and the rest of us were like, Well, it's different,' Nielsen remembered. Petersson intuited that the graphic was something special, later proclaiming it 'a stroke of luck.' In 1979, *Rolling Stone* erroneously credited Petersson with designing the logo himself, but as Tom told Scott Starr, 'I wish I could take some credit for it, but I can't. It was all his thing.'

CHRIS CROWE *I had no idea if I'd ever see the logo again when I left.*

Crowe need not have doubted the merits of his creation. It was a priceless gift. That original design is now recognizable worldwide, having been stamped onto millions of surfaces by this point.

CHRIS CROWE *I've thought to myself, If I had a nickel for every one of those things, it'd pay for my dotage now. That would have been an actual sin against nature, though, because this was us against the world. It was not done for money.*

* * *

On New Year's Eve, Cheap Trick returned to Rockford and the Stardust Lounge, the cover: $2.00. An advertisement in the *Rockford Morning Star* promised 'beautiful go-go-girls' with 'parking in rear.' Parking for cars, of course. The first weekend of 1975 meant a return trip to Milwaukee to entertain the scallywags at Humpin' Hanna's, Thursday through Monday. Opening all six nights was a local band called In A Hot Coma, its members being Jerome Brish (stage name Alex Deluxe) and Martin Krohne on guitar, Jim Keller on drums, Caleb Alexander on sax, and Scott Krueger on bass.

SCOTT KRUEGER *They let us open for them because Jerry was a big fan of theirs, so we used to go see them all the time. He struck up a friendship with Rick, and they were nice enough to let us play with them, which was a lot of fun.*

In A Hot Coma drummer Jim Keller shared a humorous memory from that weekend with the blog *Cheap Rewards: Punk & Power Pop Records*:

It was a jam-packed performance and Jerome was wearing a pair of custom made, skintight leopard pants with nothing underneath. Unbeknownst to him, the entire front seam of his pants had split during one of their final songs. The audience was pointing fingers and the band tried to gesture to him that he had 'fallen out,' but he didn't notice until after they'd completed their set! Thinking he'd be the laughing stock of the city, Cheap Trick guitarist Rick Nielson (sic) assured him after the show that the incident would be talked about for years to come, and that's a good thing!

Scott Krueger recalls a very specific moment he witnessed one afternoon at Dirty Frank's Record Rack in Milwaukee:

SCOTT KRUEGER *I remember Rick Nielsen, in the cut-out bin, picking up that first Big Star album and then asking us, 'Is this any good?' And us saying, 'Yeah, yeah, you gotta buy it, it's fantastic.'*

* * *

At some point, Nielsen must have realized how lucky he was that George Faber turned him down. Zander was a quick study. From Beloit to Manitowoc to the Quad Cities, night spots with names like Red Bird, Jack's Beer Garden, and COD Steam Laundry, weekends at joints like the Uprising in Dekalb or JD's White Elephant in Monroe, from one rickety stage to another, night after night, week after week, Zander discovered more and more about himself and his voice, testing the limits of his range, only to find … no limits.

BUN E. CARLOS *It took three or four months of doing stuff like 'Cold Turkey' and Robin got some sandpaper and grit, and then there was no stopping him.*

PAUL HAMER *I think when Robin joined the band Rick knew he had something great …*

KEN ADAMANY *We all did!*

PAUL HAMER *He always* wanted *to do something great, but he had all of the ingredients at that time to be* able *to do something great.*

'It was like, *Ahh, there's the voice that can sing what I can write,*' Nielsen told the *Savannah Morning News* in 2019. To Redbeard on *In The Studio*, he said,

'When we got Robin, the picture was a whole picture, it was the band.'

Zander became his muse, and the songs poured out of him. With a killer lineup in place and a rapidly expanding catalogue of original material, there was only one thing for Cheap Trick to do: perform constantly.

* * *

At the end of January, Cheap Trick headed back to East Lansing and the Brewery, where they got to hang with former Turtles and Mothers Of Invention members Flo & Eddie, who were in town to spin records at the club. According to Bun E., they all watched *Match Game* at the hotel and played along, wagering quarters.

February saw return trips to Sammy G's and the Stone Toad and a weekend engagement at COD Steam Laundry in Iowa City. A crudely drawn poster for the event declared Cheap Trick to be 'The Best Rock'n'roll Band Iowa City Has Ever Seen.' Maybe so. The last weekend of February was spent at the Uprising in Dekalb, a sketchy bar that had recently reopened after being ordered closed by the mayor, but not permanently. At least not yet.

The first week of March saw Cheap Trick back at Humpin Hanna's. An ad in the college newspaper promised 'Dynamite Rock And Boogie.' The Sunday show was billed as a 'Bugle Benefit,' with the proceeds earmarked to help Milwaukee's independent newspaper the *Bugle American*, whose offices had been firebombed and destroyed that February—a crime that remains unsolved, perhaps because the police themselves might have done it (according to some). Cheap Trick were quite popular with the underground crowd in Milwaukee, including a loyal contingent from the gay community. Also on the bill for the Sunday show was a band called Hurry, featuring old friends Rick Szeluga and Russ Freiman.

On March 13, Cheap Trick landed at the Airway Bar in Marshfield, home to a sunken dance floor called the 'Bull Ring,' then rendezvoused at the Rendezvous Room in Sheboygan. They celebrated April Fool's Day at the Elbow Room in Waukesha. My late uncle Bill might have been there—he was definitely present one of the three times they rocked that particular venue. Bill told a story about ordering a drink at the bar, then, as he turned to leave, colliding with the guy behind him and spilling the drink all over him. Luckily, the drink only cost 25¢. Unluckily, the guy Uncle Bill doused was Robin Zander, and he was pissed.

April saw repeat engagements at Humpin' Hanna's, JD's White Elephant, and Sammy G's Circus—lots of apostrophes. It was about this time that Cheap Trick took part in their first ever professional (or at least semi-professional) photo shoot, the photographer being an acquaintance of Petersson's father named Marshall Mintz. (Both men worked in the iron industry, Mintz for Liebovich Steel and the elder Peterson for Behr Iron & Metal.)

BUN E. CARLOS *We tried to get people to take pictures of us. A girl named Tricia took some pictures of us in my folks' backyard. We didn't like the pictures.*

Marshall Mintz invited the band to his house on Indian Terrace in Rockford, a trendy neighborhood at the time. The shoot lasted a couple of hours. Mintz shot the band in black-and-white against two different backdrops, one black and one white.

BUN E. CARLOS *He didn't take a lot of pictures. He wasn't one of these guys who would take forty pictures of one pose and pick one. He would line us all up and place us and take two shots and then move us.*

At the time, Rick, Robin and Tom's personas were still in flux, but Bun E. had his act together, right down to the cigarette dangling from between his lips in one shot, jutting from between his fingers in another. Rick donned a dark sweater emblazoned with a row of soda (or beer) bottles for one backdrop, a button-down shirt depicting the various phases of the moon for the other. Robin's black long-sleeve shirt blended right into the black backdrop, his hair pulled back. For the white backdrop he let his hair drape past his shoulders. For both backdrops Petersson wore a kerchief or scarf wrapped tightly around his head, for that feminine vibe.

Mintz pursued his photography on the side but was recognized several times for his work, for example this 1971 blurb from the *Wisconsin Jewish Chronicle*:

Marshall Mintz, Rockford, Il., received honorable mention in the B'nai B'rith Israel Photo Contest. His entry, 'Soldier And Boy At The Wall,' was chosen to be the cover photograph of the June 1971 issue of the *National Jewish Monthly*.

The following year, some of Marshall's photographs were exhibited at the local library, as reported in the *Rockford Morning Star*:

Marshall Mintz, sales manager of Liebovich Brothers Inc., visited Israel last year and brought back his memories in the form of color photographs. These are now on view in Gallery 3 of Rockford Main Public Library, 210 N. Wyman St. Character studies of Jewish people, both young and old, are included, as are pictures of the landscape.

Mintz's shots of Cheap Trick were decent, and a couple were used for promotional purposes, but they became obsolete as the band's image developed. As Zander told *Rolling Stone*, 'Early on, I was into David Bowie. Then someone suggested I try a Bryan Ferry type of thing. That's when I started wearing three-piece suits.'

BUN E. CARLOS *Robin got a white suit made and he started wearing that out and he started wearing some nice clothes and suddenly there were a lot of women standing in front of him, not dancing. We used to love watching the dancers, that was entertainment for the band, and once Robin started dressing up and word got out, there would be a crowd standing in front of Robin every night and people stopped dancing.*

Petersson soon followed suit (pun intended), replacing his glam façade with button-down shirts and slacks. Nielsen would be the last member to figure himself out, it took him a while to arrive at the cardigan/bowtie guise.

But they just kept at it, night in and night out, one town to the next. The first bucket of bolts they bounced around the Midwest in was a Pontiac Bonneville that Ralph Nielsen purchased at a government auction, with what looked like bullet holes in the dashboard. They replaced the Pontiac with a relatively new Lincoln Continental acquired on the cheap, thanks to the gas crisis. After another upgrade, to a Cadillac Fleetwood Brougham with a patinated leather interior, they finally graduated to the relative comforts of a van. Rick did most of the driving because, according to him, he was the 'best driver' and 'too antsy to sit in the backseat.'

KEN ADAMANY *Rick Nielsen would often work on writing songs when driving back to*

Rockford after faraway dates, and call the next day with possible lyrics and titles.
At times he would call the office to ask someone to type up his new lyric ideas.

Adamany still has some of these pages, torn from a yellow legal pad, rows of shorthand symbols jotted down with a ballpoint pen. Scribbled at the top of one: 'He's A Whore.'

For a bar band like Cheap Trick, the slow build was a daily grind. Petersson remembered 'little podunk towns with eight people in the audience.' Rick shared a similar recollection with the *LA Times*: 'There'd be seven people in the bar and four of them would be us, and the other three would be fighting on the pool table.' Bun E. concurred: 'You can play for a week and then on Saturday afternoon they can have a polka band in that would draw more people in one afternoon than we did for six nights.' But they stuck to their guns.

'We weren't like anything else,' Petersson told *Bass Player* in 1997. 'People said, These guys suck. They're not disco, they're not punk, and they look too goofy. So at the time we didn't do too well. It's only looking back that we say, *God, we were brilliant!*'

Nielsen described his process as 'setting progressively higher goals for myself and my music, and then making my best efforts to achieve the goals.' Fair enough, but it was a stubborn mission, to build a local following while playing the obscure music they liked, spurning disco and Top 40 and cultivating an outlandish oeuvre of original material. As it turned out, a lot of the barhoppers, *they liked different, liked weird, liked good.* And it didn't hurt that Cheap Trick put on a great show.

PAUL HAMER *In the early days, a lot of the Cheap Trick show was comedy. Rick is such a funny guy—he'd start talking onstage, and ten minutes would go by and then they'd play a song. He'd keep everybody laughing and everybody entertained.*

One example of a joke Rick told from the stage (courtesy of fan John Nelson-Horn):

Q: What's the difference between parsley and pussy?
A: You can't eat parsley.

Speaking of eating parsley, there was also the 'carnival game.' Nielsen commandeered the microphone and declared that he could accurately guess the weight of any female present. The method of discernment was less than scientific: the scale was Rick's face, where a volunteer would be asked to sit. Bun E. Carlos described the festivities for *Rolling Stone* in 1979:

> I'd start up a little shuffle, and Rick would take the mike: 'Ladies and gentlemen, welcome to the Cheap Trick carnival. Tonight, we're asking for volunteers. Do I have a young lady in the audience? Well step right up, and you'll win a prize if I fail to guess your weight within five pounds. Just step right up.'

The stunt backfired (pun intended—you'll see) when a certain member of the audience, as Zander put it, 'must have not bathed too well.' Nielsen detailed the incident for former Sex Pistol Steve Jones on his radio show, *Jonesy's Jukebox*, in 2018:

> RICK: The last one that mounted me, uh …
> STEVE: She broke your nose?
> RICK: Broke, uh …
> STEVE: Broke your face?
> RICK: Broke everything.
> STEVE: She farted?
> RICK: I think so.
> STEVE: That's why it stopped.
> RICK: Ended right there.

Nielsen's stage antics went well beyond the carnival game. John Masino remembers Rick hanging his Strat from the rafters at one club, then kicking it while it swung back and forth. Fan Bill Jordan recalls: 'Rick had those shredded Sound City bottoms, he called them *Sound Shitty*, that he would abuse on a nightly basis. One night he was in the middle of a solo and he stuck his head into one of the cabinets. He was in there for quite a while, with his posterior under the follow spot facing the audience. When he finally emerged he had a large chunk of speaker cone in his mouth.'

Another early fan, Brad Elvis, describes watching Rick find a weak spot in an old wood stage and 'jumping on it throughout the set,' until he finally broke through. He then thrust his guitar into the ragged hole, until just the cord could be seen snaking out, and left it to buzz and feed back.

Rick was infamous for leaving his mark, especially on clubs with low ceilings, like the Pack & Hounds in Green Bay or Night Gallery in Waukegan. Steve Salzman, who worked for Night Gallery, recalls that owner Tom Olsen cut a deal with Nielsen: he could wreck ten tiles per gig. Rick's excuse: the ceiling got in his way. Nielsen explained to the *Milwaukee Sentinel* in 1978 that the destruction resulted from a feeling of confinement. 'We usually played on these really small stages and I like to run around when I'm performing,' he said. 'I used to jam my guitar through the ceiling at a lot of places. I was like a wild animal in a cage.'

Jol Dantzig, who had a band called Heartbreaker, bore witness to said shenanigans.

JOL DANTZIG *I think the amount of people that they would draw into the club outweighed the ceiling tiles. Pretty inexpensive prop.*

Adamany still has the bill that one club sent him for replacement tiles: $15.

JOHN MASINO *Rick was just out of his mind, like he had forty cups of coffee or something.*

Coffee maybe, but there was a hard and fast rule about consuming alcohol. As Bun E. told Robin Tolleson, 'All four of us in the band go onstage dead straight from the moment we get up till the moment we're done playing.' Petersson told *Vintage Guitar* that they 'always waited until the end of the night and then we could drink a few beers. Or several hundred.' Nielsen agreed, telling *Chicago Reader*, 'I drank more beer than anybody I've ever met, but I never drank when I played.' This did not prevent revelrous fans from buying them a round and delivering the drinks to the stage. Rick just dumped them over his head; problem solved.

The band's ingenuity and tenacity paid dividends as audiences expanded. Word of mouth was key.

JOL DANTZIG *Back then, people either liked this kind of music or liked that kind of music, but it didn't matter what kind of music you liked, I could take anyone to see Cheap Trick, and the next time I'd go to see them that person would be there with his friends. They were just so spectacular and different.*

PAUL HAMER *Every time I went out and saw them there'd be more people there and more people there.*

JOL DANTZIG *It almost seemed like they could come into a club and there would be a decent turnout, but by the next time they played that club it would be standing room only—people would just be packed in there because the buzz would be so big.*

They had special cards printed up, to be made available at shows. Once filled out, that person would be added to a mailing list, which enabled Adamany to distribute detailed itineraries straight to the fans. As Nielsen told Temple Ray, 'Before you knew it, we did have a big following and we were doing real well.'

AL CRAVEN *The one thing that I really remember about them is how focused they always were and I always respected that about them, and no matter what the situation was, if they were in a situation where it wasn't necessarily the most receptive audience, they always just stayed focused, they did their show—they were like a ball peen, just really intent upon fulfilling the mission that they believed in, and it wasn't always a smooth road. I could feel the direction that they wanted to go in … they were very true to it.*

STEVE GRIMM *They were unique. There was something enduring, and you wanted to be a part of it.*

JOL DANTZIG *At the time, there was just nothing like it. The stage show was spectacular, the songs were different and sounded great, they sounded different, it was just the kind of thing that people were wowed.*

MIC FABUS *They were really smart about their entertainment value, and they had the musicality to back it up.*

CHRIS CROWE *It was a homogenized genre of their own creation—you really couldn't put them in a box.*

JOL DANTZIG *They were in a whole different league than everybody else.*

MATTHEW PERRIN *People took notice because, when you saw* Cheap Trick *in the clubs, it was intense.*

Perrin worked for another of Adamany's bands, Ziggy & The Zeu, but eventually came on board with Cheap Trick.

BRAD ELVIS *It would go into this white noise, just turn into this fucking roar, then they'd get really quiet. They were really good at dynamics.*

Brad Elvis played in the bands Jet, Star, Screams, and eventually The Elvis Brothers, another band managed by Ken Adamany.

DEONE JAHNKE *They had exuberance and finesse in perfect balance.*

Jahnke was an early and avid fan and photographer.

PETE COMITA *I loved them. They were my favorite band ever. I mean, when they played I was there, right in front, every time I could be. I'd stand there with my mouth open, freaked out about their songs and Robin's singing and everything about them.*

Comita played with Cliff Johnson in D'Thumbs, post-Pezband, and eventually joined Cheap Trick.

Claudia Becker summed it up for the *Madcity Music Sheet*: 'This band was so good, not to mention so much fun, that people viewed them as faith healers.'

BUN E. CARLOS *By the spring of 1975, it sort of all came together.*

* * *

It was Gary Schuder's brother Steve who booked Cheap Trick for the annual Mother's Day concert at Sinnissippi Park in Rockford. They took the middle slot, between The Boyzz and Zap (formerly Cotton Mather). Zap frontman Lee Kelso had jammed with Rick in the basement at Ralph Nielsen's Music when Rick was trying to put a band together after Fuse.

It was reported by the newspaper the next day that five thousand people descended upon the park for the free concert, but the bandstand area could contain only a fraction of that. Before Cheap Trick took the stage—a concrete slab beneath a weathered brown bandshell—a local disk jockey named Mark Larson addressed the onlookers.

'Beer is a no-no. That's what they say. No beer in the park folks,' he began. 'People around the neighborhood may be thinking, *Boy there are a bunch of freaky people just destroying the park*, and you're just conducting yourselves perfectly as far as I can tell.'

Larson plugged the band's upcoming appearance opening for Lou Reed at the Capitol City Theatre in Madison, then introduced them: 'Formerly, a long time ago, the Grim Reapers, then Fuse, and now better than ever ...'

Rick sported the white, Townshend-esque jumpsuit, but the other three had their personas pretty well put together by this point: Bun E. the frumpy accountant; Robin magnetically dapper in dark pink dress pants and white button-down, tucked in; and Tom the sex bomb with excessively flared blue bellbottoms and half-buttoned shirt. They looked great.

Rick bashed out some chords lifted from 'Do Ya' by The Move, an intro they'd developed that segued into an original called 'Down Down Down,' later 'Downed.' As it was originally arranged, the soaring chorus did not arrive until the very end of the song, like a coda. The contemplative lyrics explored the disillusionment Nielsen felt after his hopes of moving to Australia were dashed. Rick claimed to have written the song at a low point in his career, when he had 'no money, no group,' referencing the fallow period between Fuse and Sick Man Of Europe, but the song was never performed with either Stewkey or Xeno. Next came a cover of 'We're Gonna Rock 'N' Roll Tonight' by Roy Wood's Wizzard—another song they'd revisit later, tacked onto the end of *Busted* in 1990.

Before they careened into the third song, Nielsen took a moment to address the crowd. 'We still have a few cards left for our mailing list,' he said. 'Let's see, we have about ten thousand left.' After a chaotic run through 'Daddy Should Have Stayed In High School,' he again approached the mic, this time to offer an apology—not for the schizophrenic song just performed, about a predatory pervert lurking outside of a school, but a preemptive apology for the song coming up next.

'This whole set is fairly related. It's about people that ... what?' Rick paused, distracted, gaze lingering on the many parents present, small children in tow. A nice family outing. After all, it was a free concert in the park. On Mother's Day. Rick finally spat it out: 'It's sex.'

'Yes, yes, yes,' he continued. 'A terrible subject to talk about here in the park.' With all of this buildup, what song could it be?

'We have four demented minds up here, and when you have that you usually run into trouble, so this next one is about a guy that's trying to make out with this beautiful girl even though he's a real dope, and at the end you'll see what happens.'

Bun E. tapped out a steady beat on a cymbal, and then Rick's guitar came crashing in, chug-chugging some chords. It was 'I Want You To Want Me,' clumsily performed and barely exceeding two minutes.

BUN E. CARLOS *It must have been pretty new, we demoed it at the store [Ralph Nielsen Music House] on my four-track that spring.*

No one present in the park that day could have possibly imagined they were hearing a future Top 10 hit and enduring classic.

After that, 'Ain't Got You' from the Sick Man Of Europe days made an appearance as well as 'Hot Tomato' from the Xeno era. Just before the band blasted into a frenzied version of 'The Ballad Of Richard Speck,' a contemplative Nielsen once again addressed the crowd, this time to acknowledge the approaching ten-year anniversary of the infamous murder spree whose perpetrator the song's title referenced. 'We don't condone or condemn the poor man,' he concluded. The sentiment was disturbing, considering the fact that Speck slaughtered eight young women over the course of a few brutal hours.

Nielsen's reluctance to 'condemn the poor man' must be explained thusly: the dominant source of information about the case at the time was a 1967 book called *Born To Raise Hell* (a title Nielsen later lifted for a different song), written by Speck's prison psychiatrist Marvin Ziporyn. Ziporyn crafted a series of excuses for Speck's monstrous behavior, concluding:

The essential elements are: a brain-damaged human being—impulsive, childish, emotionally labile, racked by headaches; drugs, alcohol and barbiturates which excite him—methedrine to make his judgement poor, catalyze latent hostility and enable him to work with great efficiency; a basic obsessive-compulsive personality, rigid, punitive, puritanical, sadomasochistic, containing unconscious hostility to females because of a Madonna-Prostitute complex; hatred of his wife for suspected infidelity and for divorcing him. These elements are all present at the scene of the murders. A hopped-up, brain-damaged drunk, looking for anything and nothing, with a gun and a knife, stumbles into a girls' dormitory near his union hiring hall. The girls are bound and helpless. One of them resembles his hated wife.

Some derided Ziporyn as an opportunist mining Speck's story for fame and a book deal, but regardless of his motives, the depiction of Speck as a victim of circumstance who randomly stumbled upon his victims was ridiculous and disgusting. Speck's unimaginable crimes were clearly premeditated. He knew where he was going and what he was going to do when he walked more than a mile to that townhouse with a gun, a knife, and two extra T-shirts. Still, in 1975, Ziporyn's apologist screed framed the narrative and presumably provoked the guitarist's misplaced sympathies.

Cheap Trick also performed 'Ain't That A Shame' for the crowd of however many at the Mother's Day show, so here we have both hit singles from the band's breakout, triple-platinum live album, performed three years earlier at a free concert in the park. Next up was a song introduced by Rick as 'Baby I'm Yours,' released several years later as 'Take Me I'm Yours.' Rick told the crowd that the song was 'written by that guy with the million-dollar smile right over here to my left, your straight ahead, this guy Robin—he's very good, isn't he? Very good, very good. He's damn good. He's been all around the world, and that's how come his lyrics are very hard to understand, because he's learned all these different languages and he's trying to put it into one, and Robin, we're in America today, so sing in English.' (Zander does have a co-writing credit on the song, along with Rick.)

The Mother's Day set closed with a song called 'Number One,' a frenetic precursor to punk, reasonably similar in style to 'I Want You To Want Me' (at the time) but better (in my opinion). Probably one of the first five or so songs that Nielsen wrote for Cheap Trick, it was resurrected seven years later as 'Love's Got A Hold On Me' for the *One On One* album (the band's first without Tom Petersson).

Less than two weeks later, Cheap Trick opened for Lou Reed and his band (Doug Yule, Bruce Yaw, Marty Fogel, and Michael Suchorsky) at the Capitol City Theatre in Madison, a concert booked and promoted by Ken Adamany's

Last Coast Productions. Also on the bill were Scottish folk rockers String Driven Thing, who broke up soon after. Posters for the event challenged attendees to 'pervert your sense of decorum.'

Reed's career was at a low point: he was nearly broke, and the record label had rejected his most recent batch of songs. The purpose of the tour was to replenish the coffers, but shortly after the month-long string of dates, the self-destructive Reed recorded the infamous *Metal Machine Music*.

Lou might have been a mess behind the scenes (Lester Bangs, once a big fan, had recently described him as a 'completely depraved pervert and pathetic death dwarf'), but the opportunity to open for a founding member of The Velvet Underground was a milestone for Cheap Trick, so they ordered their first ever batch of Cheap Trick T-shirts for the occasion, proudly emblazoned with the amazing new logo. As originally designed by Chris Crowe, the logo used standard black letters against a white background. But Adamany had heard from tour merchandisers and promoter Randy McElrath that black T-shirts sold better than any other color. The decision was made to have the shirts printed with white letters on black.

BUN E. CARLOS *We couldn't find black T-shirts. I remember we found one supplier …*

KEN ADAMANY *The T-Shirtery in Atlanta.*

It was not planned, but the reversal of the color scheme boldly enhanced the impact of Crowe's harsh design. It was incredibly effective.

BUN E. CARLOS *We gave 'em to Lou Reed's crew—that was the first night they were ready. We gave 'em to all of Lou Reed's roadies. One showed up in* Melody Maker *with Mick Ralphs wearing it that year, in the fall of '75. That got the name out before the music got out.*

An invigorated Cheap Trick did their best to upstage the headliner (a less than Herculean task as, according to Adamany, Reed 'was in poor shape and had to be pushed on stage to start his performance').

KEN ADAMANY *Cheap Trick did a very long set, much to the dismay of Lou Reed's band and road manager.*

Partial set list:

```
'Down Down Down'
'Daddy Should Have Stayed In High School'
'Hot Tomato'
'Son Of A Gun'
'Take Me I'm Yours'
'The Ballad Of Richard Speck'
'Tonight'
'Number One'
'Go Go Girls'
```

The performance garnered a positive (if hesitantly so) review from Jay Lengnick for *Bugle American*.

> Trick is an excellent rock band sporting flash galore and a guitarist who resembles John McLaughlin gone bad (in appearance, not style). Their weakness, at this point, lies in the writing which comes up with every cliche in the book. That, in itself is a very minor criticism as most 'great' r&r contains the same elements.

The *Wisconsin State Journal* reported that there were '1,700 sweating fans' in attendance. Reed opened with 'Sweet Jane' and closed with 'Rock 'n' Roll,' when, according to Lengnick's review, 'Lou demonstrated a major disappointment of the evening by holding one chord through three quarters of the song & keeping his back to the audience. Afterwards, Doug Yule said he was tired.'

On May 21, 1975, the *Decatur Herald* mentioned a decidedly less glamorous upcoming appearance for Cheap Trick:

> The Peoples State Bank of Newton will celebrate its 100th anniversary Thursday through Saturday with musical entertainment ranging from rock music to fiddling ... a concert by rock group 'Cheap Trick' from Madison, Wis., will play from 8:30pm to midnight, ending the bank's celebration.

Adding insult to injury, a coupon for a dollar off admission to a performance at Waverly Beach the next month billed the band as 'CHEAP TRUNK.'

12

The weekend is the only world...

SUMMER '75. 'CANDY, WHY DID YOU DO IT?' HAMER. CHECKERBOARD.

The band recorded the Lou Reed set, which Adamany started sending to record labels. The tape elicited 'thanks but no thanks' responses from Tony King at the Rocket Record Company (founded by Elton John and Bernie Taupin in 1973) and Bob Feiden at Arista. Ken's June 18 letter to Kip Cohen at A&M Records bragged about the band's 'wide following' in the Midwest, including the 'Iowa area.' Cohen responded a week later, but no dice.

Ken also sent a copy of the tape to his friend Jim Charne at Epic in New York. Charne had previously heard the Sauk City demos (featuring Xeno) but much had changed since then, and he appreciated the strides Cheap Trick had taken.

JIM CHARNE *I heard it and I felt,* This is fantastic. *I might have been the head of marketing at that point. I went to talk to Steve Popovich, who was our head of A&R, and Tom Werman, who was staff producer, and I gave it to them.*

Werman gave the tape a listen and passed along a note to Jim, who passed it along to Ken. It read, 'Some good stuff, but not really strong tunes after all is played and sung.'

Another executive at Epic, Lennie Petze, gave the tape a listen and passed along a note that read, 'It's good but not great. Material doesn't excite me.'

Disappointed, Adamany stamped the notes as 'Received June 20, 1975' and filed them away. That same night, Steven Spielberg's *Jaws* opened in theaters and promptly ushered in the era of the blockbuster.

In his own letter to Ken, Charne complimented Rick's lyrics and 'interesting concepts.'

On Sunday, June 22, Cheap Trick took part in the '75 Summer Day Session at Kessler's Silver Dome Ballroom in Neillsville, Wisconsin, fifty miles east of Eau Claire. The venue resembled a landed spaceship and housed a one-hundred-foot circular bar. Five additional acts performed that day: The Heartstrings Melody Band, Snoblind, Yancy Derringer, Punch (featuring John Masino, ex of Chunky Pie), and Circus.

Cheap Trick spent the fourth of July weekend at Humpin' Hanna's in Milwaukee, then, on Tuesday the 8th, they introduced Robin Zander to Summerfest. The next day they caravanned an hour south to open for Chicago blues legend Freddie King at the Twin Lakes Ballroom. The weekend saw a return trip to Sammy G's Circus in Kenosha. In mid-July, Cheap Trick traveled north to Lake Delton to perform at the Ace of Clubs, a bar recently opened by Zander's former partner, Brian Beebe.

BUN E. CARLOS *We rarely had played the Dells, so it was kind of an important gig.*

Cheap Trick performed as planned on Friday the 17th and Saturday the 18th, but the performance for Sunday the 19th had to be canceled due to a development that might have been anticipated: Nielsen's very pregnant wife had gone into labor.

BUN E. CARLOS *We were in Rockford and Rick's like, 'Karen's in labor, she's going to the hospital.' And we were like, 'Well, let's just cancel the gig.' Robin was staying up in the Dells, because we were up there the night before, and me and Rick and Tom had driven back. So we were gonna drive up that night, play, and then Robin would ride back with us.*

Rather than immediately cancel, they decided to set out for the Dells and stop along the way so Rick could call home from Adamany's office in Madison.

BUN E. CARLOS *The word was, 'Yeah, get back home. She's having the baby.'*

They called Robin and Brian to let them know, then drove back to Rockford so Rick could witness the birth of his second son, Miles. (A few years later, he would miss the birth of his third son, Daxx, in order to record with John Lennon.)

BUN E. CARLOS *Me and Tom went out when we got back, went downtown to one of the bars and had a couple beers.*

After all, it was a rare night off. Meanwhile, Ace Of Clubs owner Brian Beebe scrambled to secure a last-minute replacement for Cheap Trick, until he suddenly realized that he had a very experienced and professional act right there, ready to go: Zander & Kent. Brian and Robin had spent four years as partners, chasing a dream. Now Robin was making headway while Brian was left to pursue plan B. It was a bittersweet reunion.

BRIAN BEEBE *Robin and I did some of our old songs that night and covered for the band. I didn't feel like he was comfortable with it. Maybe it was me thinking he was different now. He was in this hot rising band and he had learned a lot of new songs. And these new songs were the music of his life now. He was being groomed by people I didn't know to be a different kind of entertainer.*

Just one year earlier, Zander & Kent had been profiled by the *Rockford Morning Star*, described as 'pushing for it' and 'hoping.'

BRIAN BEEBE *We had tried all we knew at that time to get to the top and nothing had happened. I felt that we both just assumed that if one of us made it somehow, the other would make it, too. So I was very happy to see him get an opportunity, and there were several attempts by Robin to get something done to help lift me up to where he was somehow. We discussed doing a solo album for me. We talked about Cheap Trick using one or two of my original songs. The truth of the matter is, I wasn't ready for success. Emotionally or personally.*

So much had changed in so little time, and the out-of-necessity reunion at Ace Of Clubs was anticlimactic for Brian. He would have to wait four decades for the next one.

BRIAN BEEBE *I never talked to Robin about it, but I don't think he felt like he was abandoning me and vice versa. We were both heading into very new things that we didn't know much about.*

Robin and Brian would finally perform together again in January of 2016 at

Monk's Bar & Grill in, of course, Wisconsin Dells, a mere six miles from the former site of Ace Of Clubs. When *Wisconsin Dells Events* reported on the occasion, they caught Robin waxing nostalgic:

'It was the best part of my life because I learned how to live, and how to appreciate things, and, more than anything it was my sort of stomping ground to learn how to be a professional musician,' Zander said between songs during the second half of the second night's show. 'It started with me, pretty much right there. I knew what I wanted to do all my life, as a kid, but it really honed me in the right direction doing this with Brian, and I just appreciate him so much.'

* * *

On July 17, Ken Adamany's office manager, Jeff Messenger, took a message from Jolly, Bungi's former roadie, now employed by Cheap Trick:

Jolly asked that the following information be passed along to you:
1. The owner of the Phoenix told them that he wants them to play ONLY at his place when they're in Rockford and if he can't have them exclusively then he doesn't want them at all
2. Straight Johnson's really wants to sell Cheap Trick T-shirts and wants to know when such an arrangement can be made
3. There's a place in Janesville which also wants to sell Cheap Trick T-shirts

Straight Johnson's was a head shop that sold waterbeds. 'The Phoenix' was Flight Of The Phoenix, formerly the Stardust Lounge.

KEN ADAMANY *We agreed to terms in a signed contract protecting the band's interests.*

Adamany's collection of rejection letters continued to grow. Ariola and Capricorn declined in June. On the 24th, a letter arrived from Bill Traut, co-founder of the Dunwich and Wooden Nickel labels. Traut had previously responded enthusiastically to the Sauk City tape, writing to Ken that Cheap Trick were 'a real good group, best I've heard in the last couple of months,' but the Lou Reed tape elicited a tepid response: 'Sorry Ken, I pass. I know Punk-Rock is supposed to be my field, but it's beginning to bore me.'

On the last weekend in July, the band took a trip down to Oklahoma City to play at a place called Ruby Tuesdays, then back north for a July 30 show at the Likely Story in Aurora, Illinois—a bar whose newspaper ad proclaimed 'Happiness is rock, boogie, or blues.'

August began with a two-night stand at Night Gallery, followed by a Sunday night performance at Turner Hall in Quincy. 'I remember that I could still see Fuse stenciled on some of their gear,' Brad Elvis, who was there, remembered. On Tuesday, they returned to the Boardwalk in Madison, and on Wednesday the Big Horn in Mundelein. The following weekend was spent at a place called Middle Earth in Rockford.

Some context for that summer: on July 30, Jimmy Hoffa disappeared from a parking lot outside of Detroit; on August 14, the *Rocky Horror Picture Show* debuted in theaters; and on August 16, Ted Bundy was arrested in Salt Lake City after being pulled over by police while prowling a neighborhood in the middle of the night with a mask, rope, and knife in his car. Bruce Springsteen's magnum opus *Born To Run* came out on August 25. That same day, Ken Adamany placed an order for one thousand Cheap Trick stickers from Advertising Creations in Madison, but whoever scribbled out the invoice spelled it 'Cheap Tricks.'

KEN ADAMANY *We had these stickers made up that we put up all over the Midwest, all the toll booths. You couldn't get 'em off. We got calls from the state patrol.*

Tom Lounges referenced the rampant vandalism in an article for the *Northwest Indiana Times* in 1998, noting, 'By the end of 1975, nearly every toll booth in Chicagoland was emblazoned with Cheap Trick stickers, as their buzz-saw bubble gum anthems turned them from garage gonzos to kings of the bar scene.'

CHRIS CROWE *They were pasted everywhere.*

* * *

On the final night of a weekend engagement at Humpin' Hanna's in mid-August, Cheap Trick punished the carousers with a meandering, five-minute-long inside joke of a song called 'Disco Paradise,' after which Rick Nielsen addressed the room.

RICK: Tomorrow we're playing in Fairmont, Minnesot-oh. At a rock festival. And I'm sure to see a lot of you there because …

TOM: Minnesot-oh? (laughs)

RICK: … your favorite group besides Cheap Trick is there … Styx.

A number of those present—the still-lucid ones—groaned and booed at the mere mention of the Chicago progsters, prompting Rick to launch into a brief, off-key dismantling of 'Lady,' a Top 10 hit for Styx just a few months earlier. The moment of mockery segued into a searing Cheap Trick original called 'Blow Me Away.'

BUN E. CARLOS *Tom and Robin were dating Playboy bunnies from up in Lake Geneva, and they always used to think that song was the best.*

When it opened in 1968, the Playboy Club in Lake Geneva was the first of its kind in the United States, according to *Lake Geneva Regional News*: 'an urban, pleasure-filled paradise plopped down in the middle of conservative, church-going America.' Back to Humpin' Hanna's, where Cheap Trick followed 'Blow Me Away' with another fierce original, now lost to history, called 'Son Of A Gun.' The song featured a riffy breakdown section over which Robin crooned phrases like 'I'm a mover,' 'I'm a loverboy,' 'I'm a dancer,' and 'I'm a prancer.' Tom seized the opportunity to bust Robin's balls right there onstage, singing 'I'm a [substitute joke here]' up close, so only Robin could hear. Neither 'Blow Me Away' nor 'Son Of A Gun' hung around in the set very long, but the songs were heavy and cool and ahead of their time. If only Bill Traut and Wooden Nickel had devoted some of that Styx money to signing Cheap Trick and releasing an album filled with punchy tunes like these, pre-Ramones.

As promised, Cheap Trick opened for Styx the next day, at an event clumsily dubbed the Southern Minnesota Outdoor Rock Spectacular, mounted at the Fairmont Speedway. The stage was a flatbed truck parked on the racetrack. The Rockford upstarts made an impression on Dennis DeYoung, who remembered Rick Nielsen 'jumping around' and 'thought the band was interesting.' Cheap Trick bailed before Styx went on.

Less than a week later, a brief letter arrived at Adamany's office, postmarked Omaha, Nebraska, and typed on official stationery from *Morris Drea & Associates*.

Dear Sirs:

Please add my name to your mailing list for CHEAP TRICK. I saw the band last Sunday in Fairmont, minn. and I am still perplexed.

Sincerely,

Maurey

KEN ADAMANY *He joined the fan club.*

On August 25, Cheap Trick were hired to perform at a private party in Lake Geneva, hosted by a shady character named Dale (who they met via the Playboy Bunnies). Three sets. No cover. At least, there wasn't supposed to be.

BUN E. CARLOS *There was a long driveway down to the yard and this little house. Some guy stood up there and charged admission and made a few hundred bucks and then just took off with the money.*

Jolly's show report noted that the dressing room was 'Dale's House,' which also supplied the power. Jolly approximated the attendance at two hundred.

Cheap Trick returned to Someplace Else in Milwaukee for shows on Friday and Saturday, August 29 and 30, three sets per night. According to Jolly's show report, the set times were Friday 9:40–10:25, 11:00–11:58, 12:40–1:30; Saturday 10:00–10:55, 11:40–12:33, 1:10–2:00. Approximate attendance: 350 on Friday, 400 on Saturday (Jolly also noted that the club's capacity was 300). *Stage size: None. Dressing room: None. Promoter's attitude: Good.* Jolly's summation: 'I was told that the club had 3x normal business.'

Next up, another outdoor festival on the last day of August (technically, Cheap Trick did not take the stage until the first day of September). They headlined the affair, which was held in Moon Valley, Wisconsin, an unincorporated community in Sauk County, and organized in part by Michael Oosten, who also performed with his band Vajra (along with Chris Utley and Terry Arbegust).

MICHAEL OOSTEN *Even though I was living in very rural Wisconsin, my band attracted a crowd of fans from Rockford, Illinois. Every weekend we played a local club, the Jungle Bar, at the end of a dead-end road. The Rockford crew would show up and party the weekend through. This was early spring of 1975. Jack Anderson, who became Jack Pine once he started to work his carpentry magic at*

Charlotte's Web music club in Rockford, became a regular at my remodeled barn. Jack and I came up with the idea of an outdoor rock concert at the Jungle Bar. He went back to Rockford to float the idea and came back with a plan. A few bands from Rockford agreed to do the gig and Jack also got a backer with some cash. I wanted my friends and brothers in Piper Road Spring Band, a bluegrass outfit, to be on the bill, and as the headliner we decided on Cheap Trick.

Posters for the event promised 'a full 14 hours of music in the outdoors' with 'camping available.' Six bands were booked: Mad Dancers, Illinois Road Band, Faith, the aforementioned Vajra, Piper Road Spring Band, and Cheap Trick.

MICHAEL OOSTEN *We set to work securing scaffolding for the stage and rain canopy, along with volunteers to build the seventy-foot stage. Our band, Vajra, had an all-original set planned, and we were to be third, then Piper Road, then Cheap Trick. The tickets got printed with the wrong band order as the money man wanted his band [Faith] in the number three slot, but we ended up where we had wanted to be.*

The 'money man' was a 'nefarious character' who had his hooks in Jack Anderson. Oosten remembers Cheap Trick 'arriving in their white Caddie' and still marvels at 'how professional they were, out of the box.' Issues with the PA caused multiple delays, a complication exacerbated when Faith (represented by the money man) hijacked the stage for an extended set.

BUN E. CARLOS *They went on and did about three hours and finally I got Jolly or somebody to go up to the edge of the stage and tell 'em, three more songs or we're pulling the plug. And they get on the mic and they go, 'Cheap Trick says we got time for only three more songs! They're trying to get us off stage.' And I said to Jolly, 'I'm going out there and kick that guy's ass,' and started to walk out onstage. Jolly grabbed me and pulled me off stage.*

Jolly's show report confirms this: 'Another band Faith tried to start a fight with us and made bad remarks about us over the PA.'

Given the unreliable nature of said PA, Cheap Trick opted to use their own, over the objections of the money man's stage manager, a 'big Indian.' He might have been big, but Jolly and road manager Sid Wingfield were bigger.

KEN ADAMANY *Sid was in a band called Kinetic Energy that we booked, as a keyboard player, and I thought he'd be perfect as a road manager. We needed a big guy and a smart guy. He was soft spoken, but we got things done.*

As the story goes, Jolly lifted the 'big Indian' off the ground and held him in mid-air until he agreed to a compromise. Meaning: Cheap Trick used their own PA. Still, technical difficulties persisted.

CHRIS UTLEY *They did use my Sunn bass bins to beef up the sound system at Moon Valley, and just as [Cheap Trick] started to play, one cabinet started to smoke, then burst into flames. I've never seen that before. I ran up and pulled the cable on my cabs and the stage manager or guitar tech chased me across the grounds.*

The remainder of Cheap Trick's set went off without a hitch. Oosten remembers Jolly running a followspot, i.e. a very bright, manually operated, targeted spotlight—'nobody was doing that!'

MICHAEL OOSTEN *They did a great job playing to a valley full of campfires and a star filled sky.*

BUN E. CARLOS *It was kind of smoky and moody.*

By the time the reverberating echo of Cheap Trick's chaotic encore faded, sunrise was imminent. Why bother going to sleep?

TERRY ARBEGUST *Me and Chris Utley went in their band van and partied. I remember going but nothing about what happened inside, or coming out.*

CHRIS UTLEY *There were some activities in their Winnebago that are probably best left unsaid.*

The whole shebang culminated in an armed robbery.

MICHAEL OOSTEN *I was back at the barn, a 1913 dairy barn I lived in, when Jack came rushing in with the news that they had just finished counting the gate when a couple of the motorcycle security guys hired by the money dude walked in the* *trailer with a gun and grabbed the take. Nothing ever happened about it. Jack did not want to bring in the police.*

On September 6, Cheap Trick performed three sets at Waverly Beach in Beloit, which lasted, according to Jolly's show report, 10:00–10:58, 11:35–12:25, and 12:45–1:40. *Attendance: 700–800. Admission: $2. Dressing room: Dirty.*

Cheap Trick headlined yet another outdoor concert on September 7, on a farm between Rockford and Belvidere, called the Summer Party '75. That same day a brief article appeared tucked away on page twenty of the *Rockford Morning Star*, beneath the blunt headline 'Rockford Man Found Hanged In Apartment.'

Marshall Mintz, 38, was found dead Saturday afternoon in his second floor apartment at 515 Indian Ter. Police said his body was found suspended in the kitchen of the apartment. It was discovered by Mintz' cousin, Sheldon Liebovich, and the cousin's father, Joe Liebovich, who notified police. Officers said they found the kitchen door secured from the inside with a night lock and chain. They had to kick the door in to gain entry. Mintz had placed a short length of lumber across the top of the open kitchen cabinet doors. He secured one end of a rope to the piece of wood and stepped off a kitchen chair. His ex-wife told police she last heard from her former husband about 1am Saturday when he telephoned her to complain he couldn't sleep. She said Mintz had been depressed for the past ten days and had talked of taking his life.

The couple divorced in 1969, with two young children. Mintz was an army veteran and devout Jew, an artist with a dayjob. His daughter Helene remembers him as 'very quiet, very humble, and very intelligent.'

'My dad did have some bouts of depression,' Helene recalls. 'Mostly related to the merry go round that my mother had him on.' The couple had 'a very toxic marriage, and an even more toxic divorce. Through those years, he struggled with anxiety and depression.' As the summer of 1975 wound down, things took a turn for the worse.

HELENE MINTZ *It's like, something clicked, and for nearly two weeks, he was miserable. He called [that night] because he wanted to see his kids. He called to say that he would kill himself if he couldn't see us.*

Even so: 'People were in disbelief,' Helene insists. 'Shocked that he had killed himself.' For the most part: 'My dad went about his life with a good mindset. A solid frame of mind.'

HELENE MINTZ *He had some really solid friendships, many photography friends. He was really a terrific father. Very hands on. As his daughter, I could do no wrong. His princess. He actively stayed in touch with family. His cousin and uncle in Rockford, who found him dead, were very close to him.*

Not long before Marshall's untimely death, he conducted a second photo shoot with Cheap Trick. It didn't go well. The band posed with a semi-nude model, creating an awkward, uncomfortable vibe. None of the photos were ever used. Marshall never even finished developing them.

A year prior, Marshall had fired off a letter to the editor at the *Rockford Morning Star*, responding to a previously published letter whose author denigrated Rockford's Burpee Art Museum. Marshall begged to differ:

To the editor:
In a recent letter to the newspaper, Dr. Donald Hajek diagnosed the ills of Burpee Art Museum from what appeared to be secondhand information. As far as I know, the museum is not funded by public monies, but rather by a private trust. Therefore, his recommendation that an inquiry be made to see if the public is getting its money's worth certainly seems pointless. He also points an accusing finger at just about everyone, if at no one in particular, for the apparent lack of maintenance. However, firsthand experience on his part, especially during the time he is going to donate to the museum, should reveal to him what are the unique and somewhat hairy maintenance problems facing the museum. Hajek also cites a lack of space in the museum, and no one can disagree with him about that. The time has come, it seems, for a larger museum. And his letter suggests—if, perhaps, for the wrong reasons—the need for that. The many people who have enjoyed the museum and its wealth of activities have been bothered less by dust and more by the lack of adequate space for those activities. If the museum is to be a source of civic pride, as Dr. Hajek suggests, then it needs to be so not only for its attractiveness, but for what it can offer the public. The museum is not a disgrace. For the past few years it has been a great and exciting people place.

It exists for the people. It needs, as Dr. Hajek infers, to be supported by them. But the museum cannot stand still. It becomes a testimonial to none of us if it cannot grow.
– Marshall H. Mintz, Rockford

Forty years later, Marshall would have some of his work displayed at that very same museum, as a part of the Rick's Picks exhibit.

* * *

On September 18, an image of Rick Nielsen, still clad in the Townshend-esque white jumpsuit, appeared in the *Oshkosh Advance Titan*, taken when Cheap Trick opened for blues guitarist Luther Allison (another of Adamany's clients) on the 14th at Shapiro Park, an event billed as 'Another Sunday Afternoon On The Fox,' meaning the Fox River. Ruskin Spear penned a review for the paper:

The second group to play was Cheap Trick. I didn't know much about them, but I had heard they were from Rockford, Ill., played heavy original music, were very talented, musically tight and had a lead guitarist who came on like an outpatient from a mental institution. It was all true, particularly the part about the lead guitarist, Rick Nielsen. Dressed in a white janitor's uniform and playing the most far out shaped guitar I've ever seen, he was constantly in the air, leaping from amp tops, making incredible faces, and playing some very good guitar besides. The lead vocals were done by Robin Zander whose voice was powerful enough to get and hold attention regardless of what insanity was taking place onstage.

In the spring of 1975, Fleetwood Mac embarked on their first tour since uniting with a duo called Buckingham Nicks. The self-titled *Fleetwood Mac* album came out in July and was climbing the charts when the tour arrived in La Crosse on September 23 for a performance at the Mary E. Sawyer Auditorium on Vine Street. Advertisements for the concert promised 'A VERY SPECIAL GUEST, To Be Announced.' The very special guest was Cheap Trick.

The *La Crosse Tribune* reported that there were more than 2,200 fans in attendance—perhaps the largest audience Cheap Trick had performed in front of to that point.

BUN E. CARLOS *'Over My Head' had gotten airplay, their first single. The place was about two thirds full. One thing we did notice of interest was they were all walking around before the show and they all had Heinekens and we were like, Where'd they get Heineken? All we ever get is fuckin' Pabst.*

KEN ADAMANY *Cheap Trick liked Point Beer. We tried to get it for shows whenever possible. The band and I met with the company in Stevens Point to discuss a possible commercial tie-in.*

After the show, Nielsen ventured into the headliner's dressing room, hoping to thank them for the opportunity and to present them all with their very own Cheap Trick T-shirts (guerilla marketing).

BUN E. CARLOS *Christine was sitting there, and he gave her a shirt. 'Here's one of our band shirts. You can wear it at your next gig, or it makes a great tablecloth.'*

John McVie, Christine's husband, who had apparently downed one too many of those Heinekens, angrily confronted Nielsen, who described the altercation to the *Quietus* in 2017: 'We said, Thanks for letting us play. Here are some shirts for you guys, and John McVie threw us out of the dressing room. "Are you calling my wife a cheap trick!?"'

Nielsen told the story as they were leaving and Adamany walked him right back inside and demanded that McVie apologize, then and there. 'It had nothing to do with calling his wife a cheap trick. Give me a break,' Nielsen affirmed. 'How drunk was he?' *Fleetwood Mac* entered *Billboard*'s Top 10 the next week, on its way to no.1.

On the day after the Fleetwood Mac show, at 3:35pm, an ambulance was summoned to a rowhouse at 304 W. Jefferson Street in Rockford. The patient in need was Gary Schuder, 27. The report in the *Register-Republic* did not elaborate; the call was simply one of sixteen requests for an ambulance to be logged for that day.

* * *

On October 10, Cheap Trick performed at a bowling alley called Les & Jim's (a father and son team) in Merrill, Wisconsin. An ad for the show maligned the band as a 'Great Top 40 Show Group.' *Saturday Night Live* made its historic premiere on NBC the next night, hosted by George Carlin. Cheap Trick missed it—they were at the London Inn in Eau Claire. An ad for that show declared the band to be 'A GREAT GROUP … LOTS OF FUN.' A second ad promised they would 'rock & roll you all night long!' The cover: $1.25.

On October 21, a Tuesday, Cheap Trick performed at the Thirsty Whale in River Grove, a suburb of Chicago. A newspaper blurb predicted the band would 'thrill the crowd.' On Halloween, Cheap Trick performed at Bradley University in Peoria, Illinois, a fittingly spooky venue for such an occasion as, according to Wikipedia, 'The Bradley Polytechnic Institute was founded by philanthropist Lydia Moss Bradley in 1897 in memory of her husband Tobias and their six children, all of whom died early and suddenly, leaving Bradley a childless widow.'

That same month, in a public relations coup, an image of a then unknown Rick Nielsen, sporting the T-shirt of his then unknown band, appeared in the very popular *Guitar Player* magazine, as the focal point of an advertisement for Hamer Guitars. The histories of Hamer and Cheap Trick are indelibly linked, all the way back to when Paul Hamer, then a long-haired mailman, flew to Philadelphia to buy Rick's Sunburst Les Paul for $2,500. That windfall became the seed money for Cheap Trick.

PAUL HAMER *Turns out Rick moves back to the Chicago area and he and I, we're the only ones buying and selling old guitars—there's no one else into it at that point, that we knew of anyway. Then, when I opened up my store, I started finding people all over the country who were interested in it, and so later George Gruen opened GTR in Nashville; the Friedmans started buying and selling vintage guitars on 48th Street in New York City; there was a guy in St. Louis; there was a guy up in Minneapolis; and so we kind of all started buying and selling and trading stuff together, and Rick was involved in that.*

Hamer met fellow guitar nut Jol Dantzig via a mutual friend, Gary Gand. For a brief time, all three played together in a band called Bunion Stew. Dantzig eventually formed a band of his own called Heartbreaker (whose singer, Steve Summers, sang with Bun E. Carlos in Crystal) and turned heads with his one-of-a-kind Flying V bass (which he built himself). Paul Hamer opened one of the first vintage guitar shops in the country, Northern Prairie Music, in a suburb northwest of Chicago called Wilmette. A significant chunk of

Northern Prairie's business became repairing or refurbishing old instruments, and Paul hired Jol, who was skilled in such work.

Paul and Jol soon realized they could take their collaboration a step further. It was not a huge leap from repairing guitars to building guitars. Fully aware of how disenchanted players had become with the quality of contemporary instruments, Paul and Jol were willing to bet that they could build a better guitar and sell it at a higher price than the competition, because it would still be much cheaper, and more readily available, than sought-after vintage guitars—or 'used guitars,' as Dantzig notes they were called back then.

Used guitars were in high demand because, as Rick Nielsen would tell John Rzeznik on *Chorus & Verse*, 'Who wanted new? You wanted the mojo in it.' Paul and Jol hoped to imbue the guitars they planned to build with that same mojo. But they had to start somewhere, with help from another shop owner named Jim Beach, who ran Wooden Music on Lincoln Avenue in Chicago.

JOL DANTZIG *He was making all kinds of guitars in the shop. He actually knew how to make guitars—we didn't know anything about how to make guitars, we were just repairing them and selling them. And we bought one that wasn't completely finished.*

They built their prototype guitar using the components they had acquired from Beach. At least, it was supposed to be a prototype.

PAUL HAMER *I told [Rick Nielsen] that I was gonna build a guitar for myself after a fashion, and he said, 'When you get it done let me take a look at it.' And so, after I finished the first guitar, I showed it to him, and he ordered one right away. And then I couldn't build them fast enough, so he decided he'd keep the first one, and he bought it from me …*

JOL DANTZIG *We took so long to make his guitar that we just gave him Paul's to satisfy him.*

'I wouldn't give it back to 'em,' Nielsen told Mark Agnesi on YouTube. 'I said, *This is what I've been looking for.*' When the guitar was put on display at the Rick's Picks exhibit it was posted in the description that: 'Paul Hamer lent it to the firm's first endorser, Rick Nielsen—but never got it back. Admitting that he had fallen in love with the Standard, Nielsen insisted on purchasing it.'

The original Hamer, which Nielsen dubbed 'the ultimate' but the design of which came to be called 'The Standard,' took its 'futuristic' shape from the Gibson Explorer, of which fewer than a hundred were ever produced, but added the flame maple top and bound sunburst body of a Les Paul Standard. It was pointed out at Rick's Picks that the 'plastic and electrical components came from Rick's vintage parts collection.' Once Hamer started taking orders and producing additional guitars, Rick's ultimate was assigned the serial number 0000. Hamer's second and third customers were Ted Turner of Wishbone Ash, who ordered an Explorer shaped bass; and Martin Barre of Jethro Tull.

The company announced itself to the public in October 1975 with the previously referenced advertisement in *Guitar Player* magazine, starring Rick Nielsen. The photo was taken in the showroom of Northern Prairie Music by a Chicago freelancer named Rich Kwasniewski.

RICH KWASNIEWSKI *I was doing a lot of work with magazines and record companies and managers and agencies. I was one of the Midwest guys doing that kind of stuff—there weren't many of us, but I was one of those. I wouldn't say professionally—there wasn't a whole lot of money even back then, but it was fun, and I got published.*

Hamer met Rich at a Jethro Tull concert in Chicago and tapped him to decorate the walls at Northern Prairie Music with a series of enlarged prints of the guitar players he photographed.

RICH KWASNIEWSKI *They noticed that I was the guy who was shooting concerts all over Chicago, so they got a hold of me and they asked me to come over and show them all the cool guitar photos I may have of performances. They were looking for guitar shots where the grain looked good—you know, typical guitar head kind of stuff (laughs)—and they picked out a whole bunch of things, and they were telling me that they were creating Hamer guitars, they were going to make custom guitars.*

The shoot at Northern Prairie was the first time Rich and Rick met. Cheap Trick would enlist Kwasniewski's services soon enough. On that day, Nielsen turned up wearing white pants and a white jacket over a black-and-white Cheap Trick T-shirt. Jol Dantzig took one look at him and a light bulb went off.

JOL DANTZIG *I had a checkerboard strap on my personal 1959 Flying V, and I liked the way it looked, so we used it in the photo.*

Dantzig, cognizant of the fact that the ad would be printed in black-and-white, foresaw that his checkerboard-patterned guitar strap would complement Nielsen's outfit nicely. The strap was a last-minute inclusion, inspired by the immediate aesthetics, but when Nielsen attached Dantzig's strap to Hamer 0000 and slung it over his shoulder, the checkerboard pattern said hello to the Rick Nielsen/Cheap Trick aesthetic.

JOL DANTZIG *Rick liked it so much he asked if he could have it, and I gave it to him thinking I could get another.*

The synchronicity between the Cheap Trick logo and the checkerboard motif must have been immediately apparent. Rick has linked his appreciation of the pattern to watching 'white noise' as a child after the television networks signed off for the night. The flickering black-and-white dots, often called 'snow' but which Nielsen referred to as 'bug races,' was a manifestation of the electronic and electromagnetic 'noise' being picked up by the antenna.

JOL DANTZIG *Rick asked me if I could get more straps. He wanted as many as I could find. Turns out that the company, Bobby Lee Straps, had used some remnant material that Kodak had used for camera straps for the Indy 500, and I had to beg to get them to find some more for me.*

Hamer eventually sold its own branded version of the checkerboard strap. The burgeoning company built a dozen custom instruments in 1975 and twice that many in 1976. By the end of the decade, Hamer's list of customers included Keith Richards, Ron Wood, Pete Townshend, John Entwhistle, Brad Whitford, Mick Ralphs, Mark Knopfler, Joe Walsh, Daryl Hall, Paul Stanley, Nick Lowe, Andy Summers, Johnny Ramone, Dave Edmunds, Lita Ford, Steve Jones, and John Belushi, just to name a few.

* * *

Cheap Trick devoted most of 1975 to building a set list and a following, performing at least twenty nights per month, mostly in Illinois and Wisconsin but also regularly in Iowa and Michigan, amassing an impressive repertoire of original songs: 'Ain't Got You,' 'Hot Tomato,' 'Daddy Should Have Stayed In High School,' 'Lovin' Money,' 'Number One,' 'Down Down Down,' 'The Ballad Of Richard Speck,' 'I Want You To Want Me,' 'Take Me I'm Yours,' 'He's A Whore,' 'Blow Me Away,' 'Son Of A Gun,' 'Tonight,' 'Need A Little Girl,' 'I Was A Fool,' 'Disco Paradise,' 'Punch Ya,' 'Pain Pain,' 'You Talk Too Much,' 'Good Girl,' 'Auf Wiedersehen,' 'Come On Come On,' 'Southern Girls,' 'Taxman,' and 'Fan Club,' which referenced the evening fans Jim and Nancy Sanborn invited the band over for tacos before a show and Detective Nielsen discovered the 8x10 the band had given them hanging on the wall— but in a closet.

According to Nielsen, the band 'really didn't hone stuff. I'd write a song and we'd just do it.'

'We try to flush the idea out. Or flesh it out, I don't know,' he elaborated for the *Coolest Conversation* podcast. 'We try to flush and flesh.'

As a songwriter, Nielsen built upon a unique foundation of influences, mostly British. From the explosive rock of The Who, a band he appreciated for the 'unpredictability'; to the party stomp of Slade and The Sensational Alex Harvey Band, who Rick described as 'a mash of cool stuff' and 'haunting and heavy and fun, all at the same time'; to the schizo blues of Family and Patto, who Rick praised for their 'irreverence'; to the quirkiness of Sparks (expats) and Roy Wood. Rick loved how Roy 'couldn't be constrained; he had to be different … always take things one step too far.' It was a volatile stew, boiled down and refined, the end result something similar but different.

As writer Andy Mellen later put it, 'Cheap Trick has absorbed and assimilated its innumerable influences into a powerhouse hard rock package.' Or, according to Lawrence Keenan, 'Cheap Trick's British rocker sound receives a shot in the arm from some forthright American craziness.'

Wasn't that the essence of seventies rock in the States? An American take on a British take on an American take. Cheap Trick dug deeper. 'Obviously we're influenced and listened to lots of people, but we never really tried to copy anyone. We took the good elements of what we liked from people we liked,' Rick told *Gig For Working Musicians*. Studied and disciplined in the writing but fearless, even reckless, in the delivery, Nielsen's compositions played hard to get but seduced the right listeners. A Cheap Trick enthusiast might feel as if he or she were 'in on it,' an accomplice or co-conspirator.

LEFT Rick and Bun E. standing, Ken Adamany seated at the piano, Cuca Studios, Sauk City, 1974.

BELOW Tom and Xeno, location unknown. *Both photos courtesy of Bun E. Carlos, all rights reserved © 2022.*

ABOVE Shapiro Park, Oshkosh, Wisconsin, September 14, 1975. *Photo by Jim Nowack.*

RIGHT Mother's Day concert at Sinnissippi Park, Rockford, May 11, 1975. *Photo by John Horowy.*

LEFT Advertisements for Zander & Kent, Straight Up featuring Xeno, Cheap Trick opening for Lou Reed, and 'The best rock'n'roll band Iowa City has ever seen!' Iowa City poster courtesy of Ken Adamany.

BELOW Shapiro Park, Oshkosh, Wisconsin, September 14, 1975. Photo by Jim Nowack.

TOP Onstage at the Starwood, November 1975. *Courtesy of Bun E. Carlos, all rights reserved © 2022.*

ABOVE Greetings from Pacific Discount Records on Hollywood Boulevard. *Courtesy of Ken Adamany.*

RIGHT The original advertisement for the Starwood appearance from November 1975, as printed in the *Los Angeles Times*; and, beneath that, the front and inside (after folded open) of the official invitation for the Starwood appearance, as distributed to industry insiders. *Courtesy of Ken Adamany.*

TOP Paul Hamer, Rick Nielsen, Jol Dantzig. *Photo by Rich Kwasniewski.*

ABOVE The original Hamer ad featured in the October 1975 issue of *Guitar Player* magazine.

LEFT An outtake from the photo session for the *Guitar Player* ad, taken at Paul Hamer's store, Northern Prairie Music, in Wilmette, Illinois, 1975. *Photo by Rich Kwasniewski.*

THIS SPREAD Photo shoot at Ralph Nielsen's Music, early 1976. *All photos by Rich Kwasniewski.*

RIGHT A promotional 8x10 from the band's short-lived relationship with International Creative Management. *Photo by Rich Kwasniewski.*

BELOW LEFT A note from Tom Werman, June 1975.

BELOW RIGHT Shorthand lyrics for 'He's A Whore,' taken down by Ken's secretary (with Rick on the phone) so she could type them up. *All photos courtesy of Ken Adamany.*

Jim Charne —
Some good stuff but
not really strong
tunes after all is
played + sung.

T.

TOM WERMAN

'We experimented, tried all kinds of stuff,' Rick said. 'A lot of it we failed at. We played for years with no success at all, but we thought it was good and we kept at it.'

As the songcraft developed, so did the stage show. They persistently pondered the presentation, band members tossing out ideas while they drove from gig to gig.

BUN E. CARLOS *Everybody had their idea of what a great show is.*

Some (not Carlos) felt one aspect of a great show was the drum solo.

BUN E. CARLOS *When a band played in those days and a drum solo began, the dance floor immediately stopped dancing, and everybody hit the bar or hit the pisser. So, if we're gonna do a drum solo, I gotta have a great drum solo.*

He waited for inspiration to arrive, and then it did, when at some point he came across a pricey pair of giant drumsticks. Eureka!

BUN E. CARLOS *I don't know where I found the sticks, but it was like, I'll use these. No one will forget this drum solo. So it would be the shortest, greatest drum solo in rock'n'roll.*

As for Nielsen's guitar solo …

MICHAEL OOSTEN *Rick traveled with a 'Who's Who' of guitars. At any given gig he would have six, eight, or more guitars onstage with him. Most of them were uber collector's guitars. Late '50s Les Pauls, Explorers, and later his custom Hamers.*

For his big moment, he started wearing three guitars stacked one on top of the other, usually a Fender (a left-handed Strat with a right handed neck), on top of Hamer 0000, on top of a custom-built/modified (by Hamer) Les Paul Jr, with 'Rick Nielsen' painted where 'Les Paul' used to be and the words 'You Know You Like It' inlaid on the fretboard. Nielsen lifted the phrase from a pioneering 1970 porno called *Mona The Virgin Nymph*. I suffered through the first fifteen minutes until I heard the reference. Trust me, you don't wanna know.

Rick also had 'KY Jelly' printed on the truss rod cover. 'I thought it was

Kentucky Jelly,' he told Mark Agnesi. 'I goof up these things. I'm dyslexic in one of my eyes.'

* * *

Back in February, all four members of Cheap Trick sat for an interview with Bob Reder for a weekly rag out of Rockford called *Absolutely Free*. The interview just happened to be printed on the same page as an advertisement for the Ralph Nielsen Music House.

REDER: OK, let's find out who everybody is. The members of the group are Rick Nielsen on Guitar, Tom Peterson on Bass, Bunny on Drums, and Robin Zander on Vocals and Guitar. How long has CHEAP TRICK been together?
NIELSEN: About a year and a half now, and three months with Robin.
REDER: Where mostly do you play?
NIELSEN: We play all over. This month we are going to Detroit, Ann Arbor, and Lansing. We are backing up KISS, AEROSMITH, ROXY MUSIC, a lot of colleges, a lot of concerts. We still like bars though. We played at Cobo Hall with the NEW YORK DOLLS once.

Here we have Rick engaged in some myth-building. Cheap Trick 'backed up' none of those bands. Eventually, years later, they played with KISS and Aerosmith, but never Roxy Music. Tom Petersson *saw* Aerosmith in Philly, just like he *saw* the New York Dolls in Detroit, when Dr. Bop & The Headliners opened.

The interview continued:

REDER: Is there any particular kind of music you all listen to?
PETERSSON: No.
REDER: How much do you play in an average week?
NIELSEN: About five or six days. Sometimes we get two or three days off in a row.
REDER: Have you played in any particular place that is your favorite?
ZANDER: Detroit is a pretty nice place.

Zander had only been in the band for a few months, and they had not yet played Detroit.

NIELSEN: Los Angeles. We played at the Whisky, backing up RORY GALLAGHER one night and the BAR-KAYS the night before that. That was good, it's the place where the most action is. We did session work during the day and we played back up at night. Nobody ever knew who we were. PETERSSON: We did session work for NOEL REDDING on some singles.

Rick and Tom are obviously referencing the trip Nielsen took to Los Angeles with Craig Myers in August 1974: session work for Jackie Mills on an unreleased Rod Richards project. Tom did not accompany them. The Bar-Kays and Rory Gallagher performed on back-to-back nights at the Whisky while Rick and Craig were out there. I'm seeing a pattern here: any band they saw, they 'backed up,' as far as *Absolutely Free* was concerned. As for Noel Redding, Rod Richards had a band with Noel called Road. What a tangled web …

The interview continued:

REDER: Have you ever thought about adding a keyboard or a synthesizer and doing some of the more electronic things that have been happening? PETERSSON: We have keyboards. We have a Mellotron and a piano but not a synthesizer. We have been working on them on the side. It takes time. We aren't going to do it until we get it down. REDER: Every time you turn around, you hear about CHEAP TRICK playing somewhere. PETERSSON: A lot of people don't believe that's what we really do. We don't work in a factory during the day or something. People around here don't realize that the reason they don't see us for three months at a time is that we are thousands of miles away from here.

As of February 1975, Cheap Trick had yet to perform outside the Midwest, let alone be gone for three months.

The interview concluded:

NIELSEN: People don't realize that we are as good as we are. REDER: I hope the album comes through. NIELSEN: I don't know what we are waiting for. I guess we are just waiting for what our manager says. He has the final say on everything.

ZANDER: He knows more when we are ready than we do.

PETERSSON: You can't jump the gun, cause that's the only chance you got.

By November, nine months after this interview (a very appropriate period of gestation), Ken Adamany knew they were ready.

KEN ADAMANY *When a band's music starts to work, it starts to work, and that's it.*

JOL DANTZIG *They were so good that it just made you rethink your career.*

CHRIS CROWE *They were brilliant, and brilliance in those oppressive environments is hard to find. And when you find it, it clobbers you over the head. If it doesn't, you're dead. Long before anyone even thought of them making it, I remember a friend turning to me when we were in a basement saloon in Milwaukee, in the middle of a nowhere neighborhood, and saying, 'If these guys can't make it then none of us can.'*

Cheap Trick were a smoldering pyre, poised for the conflagration. But if a tree falls in a forest fire …

They needed the eyes and ears of the right people. Ten cent beers at seedy dives rarely reeled in the powerbrokers, yet witnessing Cheap Trick shake those seedy walls could not be adequately experienced via a cassette tape. The idea, when it came, was a simple one, but expensive. They would stage their own damn showcase. Right there in Los Angeles.

KEN ADAMANY *We decided we had to get some exposure, and the only way was to spend the money and fly out there.*

13

Got a new approach...

When PJ's opened its doors in the early sixties, the club was hailed as Los Angeles's very first discotheque. In 1971, ownership transferred to a formidable trio of investors: Eddie Nash, Dominic Lucci, and Hal Glickman. Within two years, Nash, a dealer and addict now infamous for his role in the brutal Wonderland slayings, had bought out the other two and renamed it the Starwood.

The Starwood rapidly earned a reputation for loud rock'n'roll and everything that came with it. George Lynch, who performed there often with his pre-Dokken bands The Boyz and Xciter, has described the club as a mini-arena. 'It was intense and the PA was loud and you were surrounded by it, it was all consuming,' he remembered. 'It was really a wonderful experience to watch a band there.'

Adamany booked Cheap Trick for three nights at the beginning of November 1975 and sent out a flurry of invitations.

KEN ADAMANY *The band played Hanna's the night before in Milwaukee, and then we drove to Chicago and we flew out and played that next night.*

The trip was no small investment, with more than $2,200 spent on airfare and almost $1,000 to ship the band's equipment via United Airlines, plus more than $600 on hotels.

Ken Adamany Music Enterprises fronted the cash. 'Lose $10,000 and go home. We did it anyway. What else could we do?' Tom Petersson explained. The band stayed at the Sunset Marquis in West Hollywood, where Carlos and Petersson had a memorable encounter with Steve Marriott, who was upset after being ejected from the offices of his record label, A&M, that morning. It had been a tumultuous year for Steve, who was in the midst of recording his first solo album when the record company took it upon itself to cobble together another Humble Pie collection without his knowledge, released as *Street Rats* in February 1975.

Marriott's response: a Humble Pie farewell tour, after which he found himself bandless and broke, having been victimized by a succession of shady managers, all the way back to The Small Faces and Don Arden. Marriott had an inkling that his current manager, Dee Anthony, was more invested in the budding solo career of his former bandmate Peter Frampton. Later that year, A&M unceremoniously released *Marriott* into the void at the same time *Frampton Comes Alive* was topping the charts. Steve Marriott and Peter Frampton represented two very different possible outcomes, and Cheap Trick were in LA pursuing the latter. Just imagine it, a career-making live album …

KEN ADAMANY *When the Starwood thing was about to happen, our guys on the street had placed posters in every record store and, in addition, had distributed Cheap Trick T-shirts to the store employees.*

BUN E. CARLOS *They had the Marshall Mintz poster in the window of Licorice Pizza across the street from Tower. Ken or someone came and took a picture of it in the window, and we made a postcard out of it.*

Pacific Discount Records posted 'WELCOME TO LA CHEAP TRICK' on the sign above the door, facing Hollywood Boulevard. Tower Records and Licorice Pizza, both on the Sunset Strip, posted the same on the signs in their parking lots.

KEN ADAMANY *We really promoted the hell out of it.*

Cheap Trick opened all three nights for a group called Bandit, not to be confused with the British band of the same name whose bassist, Cliff Williams, soon joined AC/DC. This Bandit was a Los Angeles–based five-piece with a halfway decent album out on ABC/Dunhill. Bandit's members were David Della Rossa and Joey Newman on guitar, Kevin Barnhill on bass, Danny Gorman on drums, and Timothy Eaton on lead vocals.

TIMOTHY EATON *It was manufactured. Nobody knew each other. There was a management firm called Schiffman & Larson—they had managed Iron Butterfly and managed Loggins & Messina. They wanted a rock band and they put it together. I was signed to RCA as a solo artist and was on a rocket sled to nowhere, and they said, 'We'll buy you out of your RCA contract if you want to come over and join Bandit.' They had fired their lead singer, and I met him—they were rehearsing with him—and it was Don Johnson, you know, the actor.*

Bandit were at the 'going through the motions' stage of their brief career. The last thing they needed was to have to follow some raw, hungry band who'd traveled halfway across the country to make them look like chumps.

TIMOTHY EATON *They blew us off the stage in every aspect: looks, style, songs.*

'The first night there was hardly anyone there and the next two nights it was jammed,' Nielsen told *Gig For Working Musicians*. 'There were a lot of LA types that we'd heard of but didn't know.' A photo of Cheap Trick performing on the modest stage reveals a clean-shaven Bun E. behind the kit, Robin in a black shirt and pink slacks and rocking some serious bangs, Tom sporting a red long-sleeved shirt and gray slacks, and Rick in a yellow button-down shirt and white pants (finally some color, but still not a sweater).

Cheap Trick were an unknown entity outside the Midwest, but they made a lasting impression.

TIMOTHY EATON *Everybody shit their pants. They took the night. They really were entertaining and special and fearless. So I remember that. You always remember who kicks your ass. It's not like we stunk or we got booed off the stage or it didn't work—we were fine, but they were definitely ready to go.*

Infamous impresario Kim Fowley showed up and predictably flipped his lid. Chris Crowe, a recent transplant to the City of Angels, witnessed a hyper-animated Fowley accost the band backstage.

CHRIS CROWE *He wants to sign them immediately. Blah blah blah. Complete hustler.*

TIMOTHY EATON *Kim was equal part predator and promoter. He never struck me* *as being the most musical guy but very much a predator, very much a creep. A usurious individual, but really a character.*

BUN E. CARLOS *Kim Fowley saw us, and it was 'let me tell you about myself' for the next three days.*

'Kim Fowley wanted to sign us real bad,' Nielsen remembered. 'He was all over us.' Fowley fancied himself an Ideas Man, as Zander explained on *In the Studio*. 'He goes over to Rick, and I'm standing there, and he goes, Hey Rick, you know, everybody looks great up there but listen, we gotta get Bun E. to change his image a little bit, we should dress him up like David Bowie.'

Petersson described Fowley's blustering for *Tangents* in 2017: 'He came up to us and said, I love your band, but you know what you ought to do to really make yourself stand out? Get dressed up and made up like ninety-year-old men! They'd see you come out there with walkers and canes, and then you'd just get out there and just rock out.'

KEN ADAMANY *Afterward he used to call me almost every night. I'd work late at the office. About ten o'clock his time [midnight for Ken] I'd get a call and he's all over the place. He really wants to produce the band. He says, 'Look, you gotta change the name of the band. I got the perfect name and it's gonna work, and I know I can help you get a record deal right away.'*

The name Fowley pitched was The Quick, a name far inferior to Cheap Trick, but also: there was already a band in LA called The Quick, made up of Billy Bizeau, Danny Benair, Danny Wilde, Ian Ainsworth, and Steve Hufsteter. Fowley would be credited as co-producer on their 1976 album *Mondo Deco*. So why did he try to foist that band's name upon Cheap Trick in 1975? He had no claim to it, yet presented it to Adamany as the antithesis to the Grateful Dead, i.e. 'The Quick And The Dead.' According to drummer Danny Benair, his band had borrowed the name from a band Eric Carmen was in before The Raspberries, and they'd been called The Quick for almost two years before they even met Fowley.

Benair's bandmate Steve Hufsteter was not surprised to hear that Fowley was willing to purloin his band's name.

STEVE HUFSTETER *Kim didn't see The Quick until early 1976. Very possibly somebody told him about the band sometime in 1975. He would have assumed the band was worthless because he hated what he called 'failure rock.' So it sounds just like him to steal a band's name if he thought it was good. Kim offering the name to another band makes perfect sense if you put it in the proper timeline.*

Ironically, Adamany eventually booked dates for The Quick (as well as Fowley's much more successful pet project, The Runaways) in the Midwest.

The trip to California garnered Cheap Trick a positive review from Justin Pierce in *Performance* magazine on November 21, 1975:

Co-billed on the program was Illinois-based Cheap Trick. Even though they're the epitome of a flashy Hollywood unit, Cheap Trick's musical game plan has much more in common with that of hard British rockers. The four man group evidences many traces of influences such as Bad Company, The Move, and The Who. Most of the pieces are extended efforts that emphasize precise instrumental work that is highly danceable. Their polished stage presence suggests that the band has spent much time perfecting a professional appearance. The theatrics are never overblown, although the guitarist does seem a bit self-indulgent at times, but the execution is flawless. One of their biggest attributes is their fine two- or three-part harmonies featured in many of their songs. It's an asset that should prove fruitful in the recording studio. With a little more care in the compositions and some more road experience, Cheap Trick may evolve into a group to be reckoned with.

Butch Stone, who managed Black Oak Arkansas, also came out to the Starwood. Adamany and Butch were already acquainted: Dr. Bop & The Headliners opened for Black Oak Arkansas in 1974, and Ken booked many dates for another of Stone's groups, Ruby Starr & Grey Ghost. (Ruby also toured with Black Oak Arkansas as a backing vocalist.) In fact, Butch had already seen Cheap Trick open for Ruby Starr at the Camel's Hump.

KEN ADAMANY *He flew in for one of the co-billed playdates, of which there were many, and expressed interest in working with me to hookup Cheap Trick with Capitol Records, which was Ruby's label at the time.*

BUTCH STONE *I was always looking for new talent. I saw them live and they absolutely blew me away. One of the best bands I've ever seen. They were way ahead of their time. The songs were good, the melodies were great. It was definitely on the cusp of that punk attitude.*

After laying waste to the Starwood, Rick and Tom flew home while the rest remained in LA for a few days. Adamany had a meeting scheduled with Herb Cohen and Frank Zappa, who had a new label called Discreet Records, for November 7.

KEN ADAMANY *I waited in his office for over an hour before they showed.*

That night, Adamany and Zander went to see The Sensational Alex Harvey Band at the Roxy (after a pre-show dinner at the world famous Rainbow Bar & Grill).

KEN ADAMANY *I could not believe how good they were. Unbelievable.*

The show was reviewed by Richard Cromelin for the *Los Angeles Times*:

Lead man Harvey and his group tap the natural theatrics of rock'n'roll rather than coat the surface with a veneer of devices. The forty-year-old Harvey is his own prop, and a good one at that—a gnarled Wallace Beery with a lecherous smirk and a knowing eye. He projects the zeal of a fundamentalist preacher ('Let me put my hands on you' is the grainy-voiced demand of 'The Faith Healer') and the sinister allure of the 'Cabaret' ringmaster. Themes include freedom, responsibility, salvation and escape, but all concerns are subsumed into an atmosphere redolent of the intensity and passion of rock's early days. The subtlety absent from the band's heavy-handed attack is never missed, and the two mobile players serve as handy foils for Harvey's shenanigans.

The LA trip was an expensive roll of the dice, and some valuable connections were made. Better than nothing, but back to the grindstone: Faces in Madison on the 10th, Beach Roamers in Fontana on the 12th, Pendulum in Appleton on the 13th, a weekend at Night Gallery, then a trip to Waukesha to play the Sunset Bowl on the 16th.

On November 17, Adamany sent another tape to Jim Charne at Epic Records with a letter that read, in part:

> I am enclosing a tape containing new compositions that you have not heard; but I am qualifying it by asking you to understand that it was done live at a club and that the recording is far from acceptable. I hope you will find time to listen soon and call me with your comments.

Cheap Trick were scheduled to open for Rainbow at the Riverside Theatre in Milwaukee on the 19th, but that show was canceled.

KEN ADAMANY *My recollection is that Ritchie simply did not want to play the date. He may have refused to play a few others also in that time period.*

Instead, they road-tripped down to Memphis to link back up with Butch Stone.

BUN E. CARLOS *Rick and Ken and Tom went in Ken's Cadillac, and me and Robin drove whatever the band car was. It was raining and getting cold out.*

Stone had offered (with strings attached) to foot the bill for the band to record some demos at Ardent Studios. The sessions were manned by longtime Stax engineer Ron Capone (he had worked with every big name at the label). Ardent is now famous for its association with Big Star, but at the time it was not. Big Star drummer Jody Stephens, who was always in and out of Ardent, remembered that Butch managed a band out of Memphis called Jaguar who had recorded at the studio.

JODY STEPHENS *So he was pretty well versed. Ardent is a place where great things can happen. We certainly had the tools.*

Cheap Trick chose four songs to put to tape there: 'Come On,' 'Taxman,' 'Southern Girls,' and 'Fan Club,' all relatively recent additions to the set list.

BUN E. CARLOS *We must have thought those were our four best candidates.*

The trip took three days, with just one day spent at Ardent. According to Carlos, they 'did a quick rough [mix] and hopped in the car and headed north again.' Nielsen drove on ahead in Ken's car.

BUN E. CARLOS *They drive so fuckin fast that me and Robin couldn't keep up with 'em, and it was starting to snow. They lost us in about ten minutes. We finally met 'em at some truck stop an hour or two up the road.*

The Ardent sessions went well, and Butch presented the recordings to his contacts at Capitol Records, who were impressed.

BUTCH STONE *I did get them a deal and negotiated the deal for them.*

BUN E. CARLOS *We were offered a multi-album deal with Capitol Records with upfront money. I think he had an 'in' with the label. The business arrangement didn't work out because [Butch] wanted a portion of the front money, and we decided that wasn't the way we wanted to do it.*

BUTCH STONE *I did want a commission for what I delivered.*

KEN ADAMANY *Butch actually wanted 50 percent of the publishing income, 50 percent of the possible record company advance, and 50 percent of the record sales royalties. In addition, he was looking for an administration fee for publishing.*

'He wanted to give us a deal sort of like Elvis Presley had: 50/50,' Rick Nielsen concurred.

KEN ADAMANY *I managed to negotiate some of the terms down, but even the revised arrangement was not one we elected to go with.*

Cheap Trick passed on the crummy deal and reimbursed Stone for the Ardent expenses—no hard feelings.

BUTCH STONE *I think they're one of the best American bands ever.*

* * *

Cheap Trick closed out November with a trip to Haymaker's, a popular club in the Chicago suburbs, advertised as 'A Special Thanksgiving Treat While You're On Vacation.' The band performed on at least twenty nights in December: Madison, Portage, DeKalb, Elmhurst, Hanover Park, Waukesha, Cincinnati, Rockford, Wheeling, Janesville, Appleton, Milwaukee, Beloit, Decatur, and Fontana. Michael Oosten's band Vajra performed at Godfather's in Portage on December 8, the night after Cheap Trick, and Oosten recalls noticing that, above the stage, most of the ceiling tiles 'were either missing or out of their rows.' A writer named George Burazer was present at the Yellow Brick Road in Elmhurst, which called itself 'The Western Suburbs No. 1 Club For Live Entertainment,' on December 11, and managed to misspell three of the four band members' names within his review:

> The band was a bit apprehensive. The night before, they played at the III Kings in DeKalb knowing that lead vocalist Robin Zander was straining under a severe sore throat. The band made it through their first number, but the vocals were failing and to the regrets of all the show folded. 'I still have the sore throat,' said Zander, 'but a lot of our friends are here tonight. We've got to play on.' With such a receptive audience, Cheap Trick saw no turning back. The foursome entered, lights dimmed. Casually poised, Bun Carols began a slow roll on drums. The beat grew louder, faster. Rick Nielson's lead guitar began to simmer as did Tom Petersen's bass and Robin Zander's rhythm. Then, lights engulfed the stage, setting afire a vibrant energy which raged in perfect control for two hours of non-stop rock'n'roll.

Burazer appreciated the band's 'unpredictable style' and the way the songs weren't 'limited to redundant chorus lines.'

> They move in strange ways; skipping, sliding or whatever in rhythms various measures making for effective transitions. Though their specialty is ear-buzzing, instinctive rock, Cheap Trick blends a flavoring of soft ballad and blues into their act. From the sounds of their electric, metal music you'd expect a glitter band.

On December 20, they performed at the YMCA in Janesville, an event described by the local newspaper as a 'jam session.' Jolly's show report: *Stage*

Size: None. Dressing Room: Good. Power: Sufficient. Promoter's attitude: Wants return date. His additional comments: *Too many steps, Teeny boppers loved band, Getting home at nine o'clock in the morning.*

On Monday and Tuesday, the 22nd and 23rd, Cheap Trick found themselves at a place called Pendulum, a one-story brick building on the northeast corner of College and Locust in Appleton, originally some kind of warehouse. Inside was a long, narrow room with the bar against the wall opposite the stage. The regulars simply spun on their stools to watch the band.

Cheap Trick took Christmas off, then headed to Milwaukee for a weekend engagement at a night spot called Sugar Mountain at 13th & Lincoln. Sugar Mountain's newspaper ad touted 'a superb stereo system emanating select progressive music downstairs / appreciable bands offering boogie entertainment and dancing upstairs / ascend the sweet heights of SUGAR MOUNTAIN.' The club's less than subtle logo featured an ass-shaped pile of cocaine (which also represented the *m* in mountain) along with the necessary accouterments: razor blade and straw. One waitress wore a custodian helmet (the traditional headgear of a British constable). Every night at closing time, a bartender named Roscoe spun Neil Young's *Everybody Knows This Is Nowhere.*

Next came engagements at Waverly Beach and Beach Roamers, a pair of venues whose names felt like taunts in Wisconsin in December. Cheap Trick rang in the New Year at an after-hours joint in Cedarburg called H&M Five Acres (of Fun). Nielsen left a message with Adamany's secretary the next day: 'The fights closed us down early, which was the best thing about this venue.' The 'FREE BEER' included with the five-dollar entry fee most definitely contributed to the evening's abrupt conclusion. Police cleared everyone out before the stroke of midnight, leaving them to sing 'Auld Lang Syne' on the walk (hopefully) home.

* * *

On the agenda for 1976: finish what they started in Chicago.

JOL DANTZIG *Rick and the guys knew that they had to break the Chicago market if they were gonna make it.*

PAUL HAMER *There were two great bands in the Chicago area in those days: one was Cheap Trick and the other one was Pezband and had you asked us in those days*

which band was gonna make it we would have said, hands down, Pezband—
they're gonna be big.

Cliff Johnson, the frontman for Pezband, exhibited a zany athleticism onstage. He dressed the part, too: T-shirt, shorts, and tennis shoes with tube socks pulled to his knees. Then, as 1975 came to a close, Cliff quit the band.

BRAD ELVIS *Pezband lost a limb … and Trick were now a full package, revamped and energized. It was a pivotal moment.*

Pezband continued on without Cliff (who soon launched his own band called The Thumbs, later D'Thumbs, which included two future bassists for Cheap Trick, Pete Comita and Jon Brant), but in the immediate aftermath of his departure there was a void left in the Chicago scene, and Cheap Trick were equipped to fill it. 'We just kept going,' Tom Petersson told *Rock Cellar*. 'It was kind of this underground scene that we got on top of in our area of the Midwest, Chicago and Madison, Wisconsin; Champaign, Illinois; Detroit. We started to do really well in those regions, and then eventually what really helped was we got really big in the Chicago area. Chicago is so much bigger than Milwaukee and these other places, so it really meant a lot.'

* * *

Cheap Trick's first engagement of 1976 was at Big Horn in Mundelein, not far from Chicago, on January 2 and 3. The next weekend, they rocked Night Gallery in Waukegan, before finishing off January with bookings at Haymakers, Chances R, and Someplace Else. Brad Elvis traveled to Milwaukee that night with the rest of his band, then called Star (later Screams). 'Rick was doing his usual nasal banter on stage and mentioned us, *The band Star is here tonight. They're trying to find Smokehouse to try and borrow some of their flashpots,*' Brad shared on Facebook. 'Smokehouse were known for having a big light show, using flashpots, wearing heavy glam make-up, etc.'

'They used Rick's Mellotron and played 'Violins,' one of the only two times I saw them do that.' At the end of the night Brad remembered Robin and Tom standing at the door, shaking hands and thanking fans.

'On the way back we had stopped at a 7-11 or Convenient Mart somewhere between Milwaukee and Rockford and Trick just happened to stop at the same time in their old white Cadillac. Rick was wearing an old, long womens' fur coat that I saw him wear several times. A funny visual that I remember: both bands standing in line with snacks for the drive.'

A February booking at the Church Key in Madison was moved to March 1, when the local paper slandered Cheap Trick as a 'Chicago-based disco group.' Disco was the enemy, and as its popularity snowballed, the situation intensified, from annoyance to threat. All of a sudden, bars were booking DJs for 'Disco Nights' instead of booking bands.

JOHN MASINO *It was infringing on our gigs.*

In the war with disco, Cheap Trick's weapon of choice would be ridicule. Consider Lawrence Keenan's illuminating article from the *Illinois Entertainer*, published in January of 1976 with the headline 'Shoot Out In Disco Paradise.'

There was a momentary pause and the lead guitarist laughed, 'You people are not going to like this one.' There followed an immense bass riff and a mumbled imitation of Barry White. The drums shadowed closely in Rhythmic xerox fashion as the rapid dip of the instruments drew several extra couples onto the dance floor. What were they singing? Something about dancing in a 'disco paradise?' Suddenly, the guitarist and singer leapt into the audience to bump with the crowd. Lost from sight for a few moments, the lead guitarist is back onstage, climbs atop his amplifier and talks to people in the balcony behind the stage. The song ends and the crowd applauds. The band is looking at each other and laughing.

Extended, indulgent performances of 'Disco Paradise' functioned as a sort of cautionary tale: was *this* what music fans really wanted? The article continued:

Cheap Trick are perhaps the best rock'n'roll band in Illinois. Certainly there are those other innovators but the spirit isn't the same. In most Midwest rock bands, loudness over subtlety has infiltrated virtually everything the Midwest wanted to call its own. It's here that Cheap Trick are in the process of turning things around. Strangely enough, you couldn't tell by looking at them. Rick Nielsen, their lead guitarist, looks like he just got off work at McDonald's …

Published alongside the article was a photo of Rick wearing the white jumpsuit and wielding Hamer 0000.

> Rick has fun at certain moments by hitting the unanticipated wrong notes or shaking his guitar for an elusive extra one. Whereas some guitarists fill the empty space with a concise, even passage, Rick is always doodling.

Near the end of the article, Keenan remarked on the band's skillful approach to the cover, be it Dylan's 'Please Mrs. Henry,' which zoomed along 'at a rollicking pace,' or Fats Domino's 'Ain't That A Shame,' similar in style to John Lennon's version from *Rock 'N' Roll*. Keenan also highlighted two of the group's original tunes: one he called 'Kamikaze' ('with a lead break so crazed and convoluted that it seems lifted from Frank Zappa's "Can't Afford No Shoes"') and the 'maniacal screams' of 'The Ballad Of Richard Speck' ('whose visions are best left to your imagination').

* * *

On January 26, a letter arrived at Ken Adamany's office from Don Ellis, Vice President of West Coast A&R at Columbia Records.

> Dear Ken,
> Irv Azoff passed me a tape of 'Cheap Trick,' and while they are interesting, they don't seem quite ready to us. If you do further work with them or if you feel their touring situation warrants further involvement on our part, please feel free to contact us again.
> In the interest of geography, it might be better for you to contact Mickey Eichner, my counter-part in New York, who could get the band auditioned more easily than I could out here.

Adamany almost landed Cheap Trick the coveted slot of opening for KISS (about five months into the *KISS Alive! Tour*) at Dane County Coliseum on February 5, but the booking fell through when representatives from KISS's talent agency, ATI, insisted that the plum spot go to one of their clients, Point Blank, instead.

Adamany promptly dispatched postcards to the diehards on the mailing list:

NOTICE. Due to a scheduling problem, CHEAP TRICK will not be able to appear with KISS at the Coliseum in Madison, Wisconsin, on February 5, 1976. We hope this hasn't caused you any inconvenience. If you have already purchased tickets and now do not plan to attend due to CHEAP TRICK's cancellation, you may send your tickets to us with a self-addressed, stamped envelope, and we will reimburse you for the full ticket price. ($5.50)

They narrowly missed out on performing for nine thousand KISS fans. It was disappointing, but they carried on, performing that night (and the next) at Pendulum in Appleton instead. After a February 7 performance in Ashland, a small city in northernmost Wisconsin, a disgruntled attendee named John posted a handwritten note to Adamany's office:

Dear 'Cheap Trick,'
I really wish I could have heard you at Northland College, but being that you were to (sic) fucking loud I could neither listen or (sic) dance. I advised your PA man but he had a stick up his ass. Thanx for a headache.

Meanwhile, the rejection letters kept coming: from Pat Pipolo at Island Records, Al DeMarino at United Artists, and Roberta Petersen at Warner Bros. Undeterred, Adamany developed a new plan of action. The Starwood gambit did not result in a record deal but, as Adamany put it, 'we gained a lot of momentum from those appearances,' not to mention exuberant reactions from industry insiders like Irving Azoff, Frank Zappa and Herb Cohen, Kim Fowley, and Butch Stone, which only served to reaffirm Ken's belief in Cheap Trick. They were ready for the big leagues, it was just a matter of getting themselves called up from the minors. How?

Impress a scout. Not a suit but a fellow artist. Someone like … a record producer. The right person might help open the right door for Cheap Trick to step through.

KEN ADAMANY *I checked around a bit, and I came across the name of Jack Douglas.*

14

Slaved and slaved for years...

JACK DOUGLAS. SUNSET BOWL. ACCORDION.

Jack Douglas grew up in the Bronx in the fifties, a transitional decade for the borough. His father found employment at one of the bustling industrial parks and before long arrived home toting a tape recorder for his son. As Jack put it, 'things would always "fall off" the freight trains.' Douglas told *Tape Op*, 'He knew I liked my grandmother's piano. He thought, We can't afford a piano, so here's a recorder.'

As a result, young Jack developed a keen interest in recorded sound, as described by John Bard Manulis for *Ageist*:

Jack seized the opportunity and started recording things, anything, everything: the musical themes from his favorite TV shows, the sound of the elevated train that went by their apartment, even the sound inside of his mother's vacuum cleaner tube, which he'd record at the fast speed and then play back at the slow speed. He was enraptured by the sounds themselves and the ability to edit them into unusual compositions. It was the birth of a sound engineer.

Eventually, an acoustic guitar 'fell' from a train and Jack taught himself. A quick study, he soon graduated to performing live. He told *Ageist*, 'I was playing anywhere I could. Folk music, hootenanny time. That's what got me into music.'

In 1961, a nondescript young Minnesotan named Robert Zimmerman arrived in New York City, and within a couple of years had rechristened himself Bob Dylan and scored a hit record. In Dylan's wake, a gaggle of socially conscious troubadours fomented a movement in the clubs of Greenwich

Village, which then insinuated itself into the culture at large. Jack joined the fray, and after performing at a Young Democrats meeting, mostly to meet girls, he was offered a job with Robert F. Kennedy's 1964 Senatorial campaign, warming up crowds at rallies.

Then came The Beatles.

Jack's obsession with the Fab Four inspired a fraught trip across the Atlantic on a tramp steamer with his school friend Eddie Leonetti. 'We crossed the North Atlantic in the middle of the winter and it was terrible, just terrible!' Douglas remembered. 'I can't describe how bad it was, but it was bad!' Adding insult to injury, when they arrived at the Liverpool docks, the young Americans were denied entry. They'd brought guitars and amps with them, planning to busk, but customs held them at the port. At some point, Douglas snuck off the ship and found his way to the offices of the local newspaper, the *Liverpool Echo*. When the paper published a story about the American musicians being held hostage in the harbor, Douglas and Leonetti were allowed in. *Rubber Soul* had just come out.

Douglas returned home to New York and soon enough, like Dylan, had gone electric, trading in his Martin acoustic for a black Les Paul Custom. He performed with various bands, including tours with Chuck Berry and New Jersey girl group The Angels. Inspired by the advent of Led Zeppelin, he formed a band with Leonetti called Privilege and landed a deal with T-Neck, a record label launched by The Isley Brothers (who were from Teaneck, New Jersey).

Privilege set to work recording an album but were hampered by interference from the Isleys. According to Douglas, 'They brought in girl background singers and horns and conga players.' Hoping to salvage the project, he campaigned to mix the record himself. The Isleys acquiesced, and, once behind the mixing desk, Douglas was transported back to his early years experimenting with that tape recorder. He had found his calling.

The *Privilege* album stiffed and the band dissolved, but Douglas was fine with that. It was the summer of '69, and he tried to get a job at A&R Recording, Phil Ramone's studio on 48th Street. They regretfully declined and suggested he try his luck at a new place called the Record Plant over on 44th. They hired him, first as a janitor and then, to mollify the union, as a 'general worker.'

The Record Plant, name inspired by Andy Warhol's Factory, was born out of a friendship between recording engineer Gary Kellgren (who worked on early

Velvet Underground and Mothers Of Invention recordings, among others) and his favorite client, Jimi Hendrix. They enjoyed collaborating but longed for a more relaxed environment in which to create. Kellgren floated the idea of building their own studio, the way they wanted it, which as Martin Porter and David Goggin described in a 2018 *Rolling Stone* article was 'a new design that was more like a living room than the lab-like label studios of the era. Hendrix didn't really want a typical recording studio; he wanted a nightclub where he could record.'

Kellgren asked his friend Chris Stone, a Revlon sales executive, to partner with him in the endeavor, and together they turned an abandoned garage near Times Square into the hippest studio of its time. The Record Plant was an immediate success, and they soon opened a sister studio in Los Angeles. Douglas was in the right place at the right time; he hung around and made himself useful and it paid off. Eventually, as he recounted to Eddie Trunk, Douglas graduated 'to the tape library to the dubbing room,' where he 'learned to edit jingles from sixty second spots to thirty second spots and make copies for people.' He was good at it, and soon enough the kid who crossed the Atlantic to buy *Rubber Soul* was suddenly working for a Beatle, tasked with transferring two-track demos John Lennon had recorded in England to multi-track tapes ready for overdubs in New York.

Douglas swiftly ascended to the position of assistant engineer, working with Mountain, James Gang, and Don McLean on *American Pie*. For Douglas, this meant, 'Now I'm taking notes on what works and watching producers.' He benefited greatly from the stewardship of chief engineer Roy Cicala, who mentored Jimmy Iovine during the same period.

'We had sixteen-track machines, but Roy Cicala would not let you move past four tracks until you mastered it,' Douglas told *Milwaukee* magazine. 'That was school for us. You had to learn balances and mix and bussing. You had to get it together, and it was a demo so it wasn't all that dangerous. Roy would listen to what you were doing, and you didn't move, or you were out of there if your shit was terrible. So it was about microphone placement, microphone choice. We were always learning from the staff engineers at Record Plant.'

Douglas later remarked to *Sound On Sound* that he 'was totally obsessed with the whole thing, and I would sleep there at the studio.' His big break came in early 1973, when Mercury Records booked time for a flamboyant group of ne'er-do-wells called the New York Dolls. Todd Rundgren, riding high off the success of *Something/Anything* and Top 10 hit 'Hello It's Me,' signed on to produce. As Douglas put it, 'it was a bit of a mismatch.'

Jack, who was a regular at haunts like the Mercer Arts Center and Max's Kansas City, was a big fan of the Dolls and requested he be made chief engineer on the project, though the significance of his role expanded over time. 'Todd made great records,' Douglas told Ben Yakas, 'but they were productions, and this was not going to be a production. This was going to be raw and nasty, you know, and Todd was sitting next to me the first day or so and was like, *Oh my god, these guys can't play.*' As Rundgren described to *Classic Rock*, 'The sessions involved politics, psychology, and crowd control, and at a certain point I had to surrender to the process and accept that the surrounding insanity was going to be a part of the character of the record.'

'He got in over his head with those guys. They were pretty hardcore,' Douglas remembered. Dolls frontman David Johansen told the *Houston Chronicle*: 'Jack essentially did the grunt work. Rundgren would just throw up his hands and say, Call me, and Jack would take over. He has this natural, psychological knack of bringing things together out of chaos into a cohesive form.' According to Douglas, 'They were totally disorganized. They had the songs when they got to the studio, but recording them was really tough. Don't forget, everything was foreign to them, including working with headphones, trying to keep a tempo without speeding out of control, and not making horrendous mistakes in the middle of a take.'

Douglas felt like the *New York Dolls* album sounded 'like it was made in a wooden box,' but what mattered was that he delivered a finished product with which the label could be satisfied. 'No one thought it could be done.'

He did it, and the right people noticed, like Bob Ezrin, who encouraged Douglas to pursue a production career and helped him land his first job, producing an album for Canadian blues-rockers Crowbar. Satisfied, Ezrin stepped aside and allowed Douglas to helm the sessions for the final album by the original Alice Cooper Group, *Muscle Of Love*. Meanwhile, neither had Leber & Krebs, whose agency represented the New York Dolls, forgotten about Douglas. 'My reward for recording New York Dolls was their baby band, which was Aerosmith.'

This was big, and Douglas needed an ally as an engineer. He had often assisted a great one, Jay Messina. 'When I started producing, I wanted to work with someone whose engineering skills and bedside manner in the control room I admired,' Douglas recalled. 'I wanted to be able to deal with very difficult personalities without having to have arguments in the studio over stupid stuff.' A great partnership was born. 'From Jay, I really learned how to get it done,' Douglas remembered. 'Make a decision and dedicate the sound to tape.'

Get Your Wings, recorded at the Record Plant in December of 1973 and January of 1974, vastly improved upon the sound of the band's debut. 'Doing the record was a bit of a training session for all of us,' Douglas remembered. 'On both sides, we were getting our wings.' It was the next album—*Toys In The Attic*, recorded in early 1975—that really put Aerosmith, and by proxy Jack Douglas, on the map. Little did they know. 'By the time I finished *Toys In The Attic*, I could barely listen to it,' Douglas once said. 'I was like, *Uhhh, this is the worst piece of shit.*' He grew to love it after it spawned a Top 10 hit and sold millions.

Douglas was mired in the muck of producing Aerosmith once again when Ken Adamany tracked him down at the Copley Plaza Hotel in Boston.

KEN ADAMANY *It took a long time, but I did get through.*

Ken dispatched a package to the hotel, along with a note that read, 'I am enclosing two tapes of CHEAP TRICK. The live one was done over a year ago and understandably, the group is much better now. All compositions are original, as are an additional 25 not on good quality tape.' The 'live one' was the opening set from the Lou Reed show in May 1975.

The follow-up to *Toys In The Attic* was being recorded in a cavernous warehouse in Waltham, Massachusetts, but Douglas still found time to give the tapes a listen, and he was impressed enough to agree that, when he had a chance, he would fly to the Midwest to observe the Cheap Trick animal in its natural habitat.

At the suggestion of Kim Fowley, Adamany also sent the same tapes to Betty Edell at Columbia Records, and on March 13 received a rejection letter that read: 'I am sorry to tell you that after careful consideration and evaluation, Columbia would not be interested in releasing this artist.' That night, Cheap Trick performed at the Shindig in Mosinee, Wisconsin, where Xeno and Straight Up had performed just one week earlier. Mosinee was two hours north of Madison, where The Who happened to be performing that same night at the Dane County Coliseum. Mayor Soglin had declared it 'WHO-MANIA DAY.' Band and entourage were driven to and from the venue in limousines rented from Ken Adamany, who by then had a small fleet at his disposal. Ken had one of the drivers distribute Cheap Trick T-shirts to the band.

The very next day, March 14—a Sunday—Jack Douglas landed at the small airport in Waukesha, a suburb of Milwaukee, where his sister happened to live. Waukesha had a population of about 48,000 at the time.

BUN E. CARLOS *We flew him out and rented a limo.*

Douglas was delivered to the Holiday Inn on Moreland Road, where they had booked him a room. That evening, Adamany picked him up and drove him across town to the Sunset Bowl on Sunset Drive, less than two miles from the childhood home of Les Paul. It was Cheap Trick's fifth engagement at the bowling alley since November of 1975. They would return at least five times before the end of 1976. 'There was another room that was a bar with a stage,' Tom Petersson recalled. According to Douglas, 'They had a lounge and the place was packed to the rafters.'

BUN E. CARLOS *He sat down in the club with a pad of paper and a stopwatch.*

Adamany spied Douglas unpacking a metronome. 'You're not going to need that,' he told him.

MATTHEW PERRIN *We put a special show on for Jack. I wasn't officially the lighting guy for Cheap Trick yet—Jolly was the lighting guy at that point. I had built a lighting system for Cheap Trick and Jolly would run it. I was working for another band called Ziggy & The Zeu [also represented by Adamany and Toler] and I had a really big lighting system for them, probably the biggest lighting system that anybody used in the clubs in those days, and Ken hired me to come in and make a spectacle with the two lighting systems at the same time.*

'They had a show that was more like a carny show than it was a rock show,' Jack Douglas remembered. 'They did schtick onstage. They acted out a lot of the music that they did, and there was a lot of falling down and a lot of running into the audience.' He described it as bawdy: 'a combination of a carnival and a cartoon, and it was really wonderful.' He 'couldn't believe how good they were,' and was 'just knocked out by these four characters. They had been playing for a long time before I saw them, so they had it honed in.'

BUN E. CARLOS *He stayed for all three shows, and I gave him the show tapes afterward so he could digest what he heard.*

'It was really loud and all of the songs that I had heard from their demos sounded even better and so I knew that I wanted to do something with the band,' Douglas recalled. A tentative business arrangement was hammered out, right then and there. 'Basic deal points,' according to Adamany.

'Everything about them was tremendous,' Douglas remembered. 'I told them that night, I'm going to get you guys a deal. We're going to do this.' Yet the grind continued, with weekend gigs at the Red Lion in Bloomington and Ted's Warehouse in Charleston. A newspaper ad for Ted's described Cheap Trick as 'extreme high-energy rock' with 'a sound all their own.' Apt descriptions.

On the following Monday, far away in the Tunisian Desert, George Lucas and crew began principal photography on the tentatively titled *The Star Wars*. A March 26 appearance by Cheap Trick at the Northwest Community Center in Rockford resulted in a series of photographs being published by the *Rockford Morning Star* the next day: a bareheaded Rick Nielsen, clad in a cardigan and bowtie (the look!), onstage with his son Erron, a blonde toddler.

There was plenty of music and lots of laughs Friday night for the audience attending a fundraising concert at the Northwest Community Center. Three bands were on hand, Phoenix, Albatross, and Cheap Trick. Rick Nielsen of Cheap Trick seemed electrified, above, at the appearance of son Aaron [sic] … he just took those great big drumsticks and did his own thing, beating out some licks on an instrument case at one side of the stage. The drummer kept a close watch on this budding competition.

The newspaper had it wrong. The third band on the bill was Cold Shot, not Phoenix. Cold Shot featured Marty Ross and Tim Roe, along with two guys named Mike (according to Marty).

MARTY ROSS *That job was offered because Rick came over to Tim's house where we were rehearsing in the basement, and he listened for a while and left. I think he thought we would be a good opener, plus Tim's older brother Paul's band Albatross was on the bill. [Rick] was always kind of pissed at Tim and Paul Roe, who lived down the street from Rick—somehow, both of them on the right day, sometime in around 1965 or '66, came into the Ralph Nielsen music store, and there were two 1959 used Les Pauls and they bought them. Rick was always chasing the Roe brothers' guitars. Those are the ones that got away.*

TED KENNEY *Actually it was earlier than that, it was a '53 or '54, an early one with the stop tailpiece, but not a Tune-o-matic. It could have even been a '52. Regardless, it's a Les Paul and it's one of the first ones. Tim still has that guitar. Rick had routed it and put PAF's in it.*

Rick used to have some of his guitars—not on display—but they were out, in case somebody came along, 'Oh, I'll trade it for this or that.' It was before the vintage guitar thing really hit.

Tim walked in there, Rick wasn't around but Ralph was there and Ralph'd sell anything. Tim said, How much for that used guitar in the window? And Ralph said, 'Oh, is it one of mine or is that one of Rick's?' 'I don't know.' And Ralph sold it to him.

Rick came back and … 'Hey, where's my old Les Paul!?'

* * *

At the end of March, a letter arrived at Ken Adamany's office from Jack Douglas's attorney in New York, Joseph Zynczak.

RE: CHEAP TRICKS
Dear Ken:
I am the attorney for Jack Douglas and his company, Waterfront Productions, Ltd.
Jack has informed me that he is to be engaged by the artist 'CHEAP TRICKS' to produce an album for them this summer …

Also in March, the Rockford weekly *Lively Times* published a brief 'article' about Cheap Trick that read like a fan letter and was purported to have been written by a sprightly young female fan named Heather Ransome.

'Cheap Trick' is the hottest act to emerge in a long time. They're what I've been waiting for! They write 90 percent of their material, and everything about the band clicks. The band looks great; they've got the sound; they play perfectly together; and most important, their material is the best. It's hard to believe, but I like every song they do. They should be seen now, so you can say you saw them when. All the songs have catchy melody lines, and you find yourself humming the songs much later. They go everywhere from pure pop fun, 'Southern Girls,' to the perverse 'Ballad Of Richard Speck' (screams included) to classic rockers like 'Auf Wiedersehn' [sic]. If you're sick of all the trashy rock groups you see, don't be discouraged. 'Cheap Trick' has the magic it takes to give you chills.

Heather just happened to be the name of Hank Ransome's six-year-old daughter, back in Philadelphia. According to Steve Johnson, co-publisher of *Lively Times*, 'Rick wrote it.'

They're what I've been waiting for!
It's hard to believe, but I like every song they do.
'Cheap Trick' has the magic it takes to give you chills.

HANK RANSOME *Rick wrote it and used her name because he couldn't say it was written by himself.*

* * *

In April, a strange photo graced the cover of *Performance* magazine: a black-and-white image of Rick Nielsen, mouth agape, nostrils flared, aggressively (almost suggestively) fingering the keys to an accordion. The image was captured by Rich Kwasniewski at Ralph Nielsen's Music.

RICH KWASNIEWSKI *That's a photograph that never, ever should have happened. The story is that Ken wanted some new band photos. We clear out a huge area of the store so I could shoot, I'm setting up the background paper, I'm starting to set up my lights. Luckily I had a camera on a tripod. I'm still setting up my lights, we're nowhere near ready, and all of a sudden Rick just walks into the background paper set with an accordion and he just starts playing it and singing and I'm like, Holy crap, I hope my exposure is gonna be close to* *something, and I just quickly snap about a dozen photos and he walks away, and that's it.*

At some point, Tom Petersson wandered into the frame as well.

RICH KWASNIEWSKI *Tom had this habit of going through his pockets looking for stuff, which a lot of local bands mimicked. I photographed a lot of local bands at the time too, and they were always doing the kind of stuff Cheap Trick was doing in their photos because they thought it was cool. So yeah, Tom was in the background going through his pockets for like two or three shots, that's it.*

That accordion shot really helped them when it was the cover of Performance *magazine, because people had no idea who Cheap Trick was. And then there's this interesting cover of some guy with an accordion, and they were like, 'Who is this?'*

Nielsen loved the random weirdness of the photo.

RICH KWASNIEWSKI *Probably for a year or so, if not longer, he kept walking around with that photograph in a frame.*

15

There's still a chance for a better life...

RECORD LABELS. BROKEN ARM. HANK RANSOME.

'I called up Tom Werman at Epic and I said that I had something really special,' Jack Douglas recalled. Werman, most notable at the time for his production work with Ted Nugent, worked in the A&R department at Epic Records, a subsidiary of CBS launched in 1953 as an eccentric sister to Columbia. Epic originally focused on jazz and classical, but the label's roster expanded in the sixties. After scoring hits with acts like The Dave Clark Five, Donovan, and The Hollies, Epic was ready to rock come the seventies.

'We were looking for talent as quickly as we could because the record business was exploding,' Werman remembered. 'So Jack called me and he said, I ran across a band from Rockford, Illinois called Cheap Trick and I'd like to make a record with them and I think you should go see them.'

Wheels were in motion, but Cheap Trick must have felt like they were spinning theirs, performing on at least seventeen out of the thirty nights in April at a collection of dives named for anthropomorphic double entendres: Camel's Hump, Thirsty Whale, Big Horn, and Horny Bull. Even with Jack Douglas on board, Adamany continued to pursue other options. At the end of April, onetime Beatles associate Nat Weiss, who co-founded Nemperor Records with the late Brian Epstein, attended a gig at the Sunset Bowl. The interaction did not end well.

KEN ADAMANY *There was an incident, and we'll leave it at that!*

Tom Werman was scheduled to fly to Ann Arbor to see Cheap Trick at Chances R on the first of May, but he had to reschedule. East Lansing was an hour from Ann Arbor, and Cheap Trick swung through for a May 2 gig at the Silver Dollar Saloon (formerly the Brewery). The venue bore witness to a daring afternoon heist. While the crew was setting up, some joker slipped into the bar, grabbed a Gibson Firebird III and a Telecaster, and skedaddled, piling into a getaway car. With an irate roadie in pursuit, the panicked purloiners tossed the Firebird out the window.

'Get this—it didn't break!' Rick Nielsen later laughed. 'We filed a police report, and the next day got a call from a pawnshop where the guy had dumped the Telecaster for $50.'

Tom Werman flew to Illinois a few days later to catch Cheap Trick at a club called Catacombs. Adamany's assistant, Lynee Hovde, a striking Nordic blonde, drove down from Madison to greet him.

TOM WERMAN *I saw them in a club in a strip mall in a town called Quincy, Illinois. Big club, and packed, and they were extraordinarily loud—they were louder than Ted Nugent. It was so loud that I actually spent part of the evening just outside the door because I could hear the music so much more clearly from there.*

They had him at 'Hello There.'

TOM WERMAN *That's still probably my favorite track of all time from Cheap Trick.*

'I've seen bands come out and begin their concerts with these long, slow, boring songs,' Rick Nielsen once observed. 'Are they kidding or what?' The short but sweet tune, with its caterwauling riffs, evolved out of an instrumental bit (later titled 'Oh Claire') that the band had been using as an intro or opener, the idea being to have something there, at the beginning of the set, to give the soundman time to adjust the levels.

As far as Werman was concerned, this was the first time he was hearing Cheap Trick, but he had heard them before. Less than a year earlier, Jim Charne had passed along a cassette, to which Werman had listened and responded, 'Some good stuff, but not really strong tunes.'

So, Adamany's plan worked: Douglas's enthusiasm piqued Werman's interest, and he made the effort to see the band live, which he described as a 'very extreme experience.'

TOM WERMAN *They were so kind of out there, wild, completely different from anything I'd seen. I was really taken with them, and when I went home I told my boss, Steve Popovich, he had to see them.*

That very same week, Aerosmith's fourth album, *Rocks*—the album Jack Douglas was working on when he made the fateful detour to Waukesha and the Sunset Bowl—came out, and within a month was one of the top five best-selling albums in the country.

After wowing Werman in Quincy, Cheap Trick caravanned down to Oklahoma for a week of gigs at the Wharf, 'Tulsa's Rock & Roll Club,' at 21st & Mingo. It was a good market, with a great many college students and popular clubs, and Ken's agency had connections.

BUN E. CARLOS *It was in a shopping center. This big place. They had all these cool exotic fish in this huge tank by the door.*

Adamany's assistant, Lynee, flew down to chaperone another visit from a record label rep, this time Mark Spector from Columbia—the same label that rejected Cheap Trick two months earlier.

KEN ADAMANY *From Jack talking to different labels that had already said, 'I don't think so,' there started to be interest.*

Spector flew to Tulsa on May 12, a week after Werman saw them at Catacombs.

MARK SPECTOR *I knew Tom [Werman] very well even though he worked for Epic and I worked for Columbia, but we worked in the same building and were part of the same sort of extended group of young A&R people. There was a lot of fraternal rivalry between Columbia and Epic, particularly during the seventies. There was a period where Epic had an enormous roll of big hits with all kinds of different artists.*

Spector enjoyed Cheap Trick quite a bit.

MARK SPECTOR *They were certainly one of the most original bands playing on the circuit at that time.*

KEN ADAMANY *He expressed interest in signing the band, but wanted more time to discuss with me and to go see them again.*

The hard work was paying off. There was a definite buzz, and Adamany intended to amplify it. He also sent tapes to A&M's vice president of A&R, Kip Cohen, and the label's West Coast A&R rep, Roger Birnbaum. Cohen shared the tapes with the M in A&M, Jerry Moss, and Jerry, intrigued, sent someone to investigate.

DAVID STEFFEN *I was doing local promotion for A&M, so I called on local radio stations and newspaper reviewers and some record stores who reported to Billboard. I did that for about three years in Chicago, and then I moved into the sales department, and it was in that bridge time that I was moving into sales that, at the time he was president of A&M, Jerry Moss called me. And as you can imagine, when a young twentysomething guy who is almost at the bottom of the totem pole at A&M, gets a call from Jerry Moss, it's like,* Oh shit, what have I done?*

He said, 'There's a band playing in your area. Will you be able to go see the band?' And I said, 'Sure, is it somebody we've signed?' And he said, 'No, no, no. I'm looking at them. I'm talking to their people. We're interested in them.'

Jerry was listening to everything. He was always involved. I think that was part of the charm of A&M, that Jerry and Herb [Alpert] were such people, real genuine people that loved music.

Steffen reached out to Adamany and was invited to see Cheap Trick at Night Gallery in Waukegan, a sizable suburb thirty-five miles north of downtown Chicago. Night Gallery was a strange venue. Acts were contracted to perform a series of sets, all through the night, right up until closing time at 6am. 'It was a long night,' Tom Petersson remembered. 'Get there at 4pm, we'd go on at 10pm, we'd go on at 2am and we'd go on at 4am. Then six in the morning rolls around. I don't have that many fond memories because it was such a drag with the hours.'

As former Pezband and later Off Broadway (also managed by Ken Adamany and produced by Tom Werman) member John Pazdan recalled, 'They had wooden shutters on the windows, and when you opened the shutters you expected half the club to evaporate like vampires. The Great Lakes naval base was nearby, and all of the drunken sailors would come in and try to pick up girls along with the typical rock crowd. It was kind of a dreadful place.'

All the same, the money was good. 'We always had a larger pool to pick from out there in the suburbs,' Rick Nielsen explained. Robin Zander agreed: 'It seemed like the bigger clubs were in the suburbs. You could get a thousand people into a club in the suburbs, and, with a cover charge, you're making some money.'

Mary Stevens described those days for the *Chicago Tribune* ten years later:

In 1976, long before video monitors became as common as Old Style in our local bars, and long before the denizens of Chicago's 'New Nightlife' decided the suburbs were a form of hell on earth, Wheeling and Waukegan were bright satellites in the hip universe of North America's most lucrative live rock club circuit. Then and there, spacious venues such as Haymaker's and the Night Gallery (both now defunct) were among hundreds of successful night spots within a 100-mile radius of the Loop that offered live rock to enthusiastic crowds six or seven nights a week. The drinking age was nineteen, high-quality regional talent was abundant, and anyone with an ounce of worldliness was riding the wave of excitement generated by still-rising stars such as Cheap Trick, Pezband, and The Thumbs. For a brief, bright period, Chicago and its suburbs seemed the ultimate market for young, hopeful rockers. Here was a booming metropolis that offered big-time visibility, as well as steady gigs, while waiting for the 'big break.'

DAVID STEFFEN *So I went there and I didn't know what to expect. It was a much larger venue than I thought—it wasn't just strictly a bar.*

Steffen made the rounds, rubbing shoulders with the sailors and vampires.

DAVID STEFFEN *Any time I went to see a band on business, I always worked my way through every part of the crowd, just to see if everybody likes them or what the deal is. The vibe was very good, the people were very into either the band or the night or some measure in between.*

As soon as Cheap Trick hit the stage, of course, his attention was drawn to Rick Nielsen.

DAVID STEFFEN *I thought he was outstanding as a player, but most importantly as a performer—he just was magnetic on the stage, he seemed goofy and brilliant all at the same time, and the crowd loved it. People were just into his antics onstage.*

I thought the band was very good, they all had a certain personality, I thought Robin was definitely a perfect front vocalist for the group. They had a really good set. I was probably there an hour, hour and a half, and then I left, and the next morning I called Jerry.

I said, 'As a unit they were very good, but I guess what bothered me about the whole evening was, I didn't hear like a string of three or four standout songs that just slayed me.' I said, 'I thought as a performing group, they're terrific, they're dynamic onstage, they could be really good, I just don't hear the music yet.'

There was this pause for, I don't know, fifteen seconds on the phone, and I'm a young guy working for this label and talking to the owner, and I'm thinking I've said something terrible—because he's just been silent, and, as you can imagine, fifteen seconds in that phone call seemed like an hour—and then he said, 'You know, I think you're right.' He said, 'That's what I'm stuck with, I don't hear the songs yet.'

It's one of those classic moments. You either get it or you don't, in that moment, and so much of the industry, particularly in the seventies and eighties, was that kind of a thing to me—you either got it instantly or you were never gonna get it, and I didn't see the larger nature of the band, and Jerry didn't hear it in the music and that was that.

* * *

Adamany had the ear of another Chicago A&R guy, Robin McBride from Mercury Records. McBride heard the band as far back as the Xeno days, when he wrote to Adamany that 'the group displayed a certain degree of competence with respect to material and performance' but he was not 'knocked out.' McBride came around once Zander joined the group.

ROBIN MCBRIDE *In my hanging out with Rod Stewart [who was signed to Mercury] when he was in town, because I was scheduling his sessions, or anything of that sort, I knew a few groupies. Not intimately, but they were around all the time, and they were around the people that I was around, and I forget her name but there was one time we were hanging out and she said, 'You know, Cheap Trick is going to come to a club on the far south side next week,' and I said, 'Oh, I didn't* *know that, I'd love to see them,' and she said, 'Well, would you take me?' And I said, 'Well, yeah, but why do you wanna see Cheap Trick?' And she said, 'I've got to meet Robin Zander.' So I picked her up and we went down there, and that's when I met the band. I loved what they did and the music, and so I got a hold of Ken Adamany and got into seeing them regularly.*

McBride talked the band up to his superiors, but it was not until the other labels started sniffing around that he was finally able to convince the Mercury brass to properly consider signing them.

KEN ADAMANY *Mercury was right there saying 'no, no, no' for two years, and then all of a sudden saying 'yes' and offering us a contract.*

On May 24, 1976, McBride rang Adamany's office to discuss a potential deal with Mercury. Office manager Jeff Messenger took the call, and his notes tellingly referenced Mercury's policy of 'not making huge money advances.' Nevertheless, McBride wanted to 'record the group in a couple of weeks.' One week later, he attended a band rehearsal in the basement of Ralph Nielsen's Music. McBride remembers the date, June 2, because it was also his birthday. Interestingly, the song from the band's arsenal that made the greatest impression on him that day was 'I Want You To Want Me.'

'We sat down at practice and did that song about forty times while Robin [McBride] was there, and he was offering suggestions about the arrangement,' Bun E. Carlos recalled. 'He was like, We've gotta get a better arrangement. He could never quite get it.' The song begged to be tweaked, but McBride heard its potential.

ROBIN MCBRIDE *I arranged for the principal executives at Mercury to go out and see them perform with me, and they were impressed as well. I started talking to Adamany about a contract, and I heard from Adamany that Epic Records was also interested in them. I was talking about how I'd work with them and what I would do with them and so on and so forth, and Ken calls me and says, 'I've got an offer from Epic for the group, they'll give us an advance.' It was either $125,000 or $250,000 as a signing advance.*

KEN ADAMANY *Not quite, but close enough.*

ROBIN MCBRIDE *I think I recall Ken saying, 'If you'll match that, we'll sign with Mercury,' so I had no reason to think that he was leading me on, and so I thought I had a deal.*

KEN ADAMANY *I said, 'If you'll match that, we'll consider signing.'*

ROBIN MCBRIDE *I walked into [Mercury co-founder Irwin] Steinberg's office, brought him up to date on what I knew, and I think I can quote Steinberg's response correctly. He said, 'I will never give that kind of money to an unproven act.' And that was the end of that.*

If they had signed with Mercury, the first album would have turned out quite differently, most likely with 'I Want You To Want Me' prominently featured.

KEN ADAMANY *[McBride] and I discussed having Glyn Johns produce, but later he seemed interested in producing the first record himself.*

Adamany also invited Rupert Perry, vice president of A&R at Capitol Records, to attend a performance at the Sunset Bowl, as per a letter dated May 28:

Dear Rupert
I'm sorry that I missed your return call today. CHEAP TRICK will be rehearsing new compositions next week, but will be performing next Sunday, June 6, in Milwaukee (Waukesha) at the Sunset Bowl (the room in which Jack Douglas saw the group).
We would be most appreciative should you be able to review the group at that time. My assistant, Lynee Hovde, will be happy to make the arrangements from this end, pending your confirmation next week.

Note the reference to 'rehearsing new compositions next week.' It was one of those rehearsals that Robin McBride attended.

Perry responded to Ken's invitation, but too late. Instead, plans were made for Mark Spector and two additional representatives from Columbia, Don Ellis and Mickey Eichner (both of whom had previously rejected Cheap Trick), to attend the June 6 show at the Sunset Bowl.

* * *

That summer, Cheap Trick garnered a mention in a special issue of *Phonograph Record* magazine, wherein local scenes from cities across the country were highlighted. The segment about Chicago, written by Al Rudis from the *Sun-Times*, was titled 'Not Since The "Ides Of March" Has It Been So Intense.' In it, Jim Peterik made an admirable attempt at describing the Chicago rock sound:

> No offense, but it's a lack of soul. The vocals are just laid on there real hard. Chicago has always been in that stage of being neither New York or LA. Therefore we try harder and that comes across on record. We're singing so earnestly into that microphone. Our harmonies are bigger, our echo is echoier. We don't have a sense of cool.

Rudis characterized Chicago rock as 'mostly punk and pushy' and related that the city was in the midst of 'another golden era, the kind of time that isn't really appreciated until it's gone.' He explained that 'the name of the game is clubs, and they come in all shapes, sizes and locations.' Peterik agreed, declaring Chicago to have 'the best club scene in the United States.' According to Rudis, 'Chicago likes heavy-metal rock, boogie rock, basic rock, and theatrical rock best.' Several Chicago-area bands were highlighted, including Cheap Trick.

> Says Peterik, 'They play heavy metal rock'n'roll with a sense of humor. This crazy guy named Rick Nielsen, the lead guitarist, looks like a refugee from a mental institution. You hate to look at him, but you're drawn in anyway.'

Coincidentally, Ed Sciaky's segment about the Philadelphia scene spilled over to the same page and included a reference to a Philly band called Snow ... 'with Hank Ransome of Good God.'

As fate would have it, Hank was about to re-enter our story. On June 5—the night before the three representatives from Columbia were booked to fly to Wisconsin to see Cheap Trick at the Sunset Bowl—Bun E. fell and broke his left arm. The accident happened at the end of a long night at a windowless roadhouse in Jefferson, Wisconsin, called the Char-Bar, named for its original owner, Charlie Hartmann. The bar occupied the east wall of the building, with fifteen or twenty tables between it and the small stage in the northwest corner. Cheap Trick's take for the night was $650.

MATTHEW PERRIN *He actually tripped over the dimmer pack that I made for them.*

As the crew were packing up in the dimly lit club, the small black light box had been placed on the floor near the stage, between two tables.

BUN E. CARLOS *I landed on my knees and my arm. I thought I busted my kneecap. I limped to the car, and we drove back to Rockford.*

They drove for an hour before dropping Bun E. off at his apartment. By then, he knew something was seriously wrong.

BUN E. CARLOS *I drove myself, one-armed, in my Volkswagen, to the hospital.*

The knee was only bruised, but the arm was broken near the joint. Even so, after several hours at the hospital he was sent home with just a sling. His outraged mother called the family doctor, who met him back at the hospital the next morning to apply a temporary cast.

BUN E. CARLOS *I had to get surgery a couple days later ... there were some bone fragments.*

Just in time for his twenty-sixth birthday on June 12.

* * *

The injury to the drummer occurred at a most inopportune moment for the band. Mark Spector and Mickey Eichner were scheduled to fly in from New York, Don Ellis from San Francisco.

KEN ADAMANY *Rick called me at 3:00am, and it took him about fifteen minutes to convince me that he wasn't kidding. The executives were leaving in four hours from New York and the West Coast, and Rick wasn't kidding. I was able to contact the Columbia offices on both coasts in time for the three of them to not leave for their flights. They wanted to reschedule when the band began to perform again.*

But when would that be?

KEN ADAMANY *We were dead in the water and over $100,000 in debt. We sat around for a while.*

They had far too much momentum built up to rest idle for long. A few shows had to be canceled, including weekend stints at Horny Bull and Camel's Hump (cue the *Beavis & Butt-Head* laughter), while the band figured out what to do. The search was on for a temporary replacement.

BUN E. CARLOS *We tried a guy in Rockford, Pat O'Brien.*

O'Brien had already replaced Carlos once, in Ego/Albatross.

BUN E. CARLOS *Pat was a good drummer—he was a natural born drummer, he had tempo, he knew how to play, he didn't overplay, if anything he underplayed a little—and I went to Pat and I said, 'You should audition for the band.' He showed up at Rick's garage and tried drumming and he didn't have the confidence, so that didn't work. I knew one guy that had a beat, but he froze up at practice.*

They kept looking.

BUN E. CARLOS *We called the guy from Wings. He told us to fuck off.*

That would be Denny Seiwell, who was the first drummer with Paul McCartney's post-Beatles band, Wings, but left in 1973.

DENNY SEIWELL *I was in Chicago producing an album for Bill Quateman. Cheap Trick's management contacted Quateman's management, and I politely declined.*

'Fuck off' vs. 'politely declined'—same difference. The situation was becoming desperate.

KEN ADAMANY *After sitting around for a week and a half, everyone was pulling their hair out. We were all going crazy, and they would call sometimes twice a day, asking questions and floating ideas. There was nothing we could do.*

Finally, all of them decided to get a friend of theirs in, so they could at least rehearse. They brought Hammerin' Hank Ransome in from Philadelphia, and started rehearsing.

HANK RANSOME *I get a phone call at 1am on a Friday night and it was Tom Petersson. Tom never called me in his whole life! [Author's note: except for that earthquake.]*

Hank remembers Tom saying, 'Hank, we got a problem. You gotta come out.' Hank jumped on a plane and flew to the band's rescue, then things failed to gel at rehearsal. It was not an easy task, replicating and sustaining Carlos's signature rhythms, be it 'ELO Kiddies' or 'Hot Love' or 'Southern Girls.'

BUN E. CARLOS *Hank was a good drummer, but he hadn't drummed in a couple of years. He was running out of steam or dropping beats.*

Hank played guitar in his current band, Snow. As a drummer, he was out of practice, but there was no time left to waste.

BUN E. CARLOS *I was thinking for the next two, three weeks I get to go to all these Cheap Trick gigs and sit out in the audience, go smoke a joint in the parking lot, sit around and drink beer and watch the band play—this'll be a nice healing holiday for my arm. Day before the first gig, 'Bun E., we'll bring both drum sets, you gotta sit up there with Hank and play along with him ...' So we didn't have to worry about the song falling apart or creaking to a halt.*

HANK RANSOME *I started out playing by myself, and then Bun E., actually with a broken arm, we played together.*

KEN ADAMANY *We had two sets of drums onstage, both had Cheap Trick logos, and we had a drummer and a half.*

BUN E. CARLOS *We had a drummer and a half for a month and a half. All the benefits of double drummers without having two guys do all the rolls, just one guy. It sounded really neat because it was a big beat, but it didn't have the clumsiness of two drummers.*

KEN ADAMANY *Boy, did it work. It was amazing. What an amazing sound.*

BUN E. CARLOS *You didn't have two guys doing the licks, so you didn't get this dancing elephant effect like two drummer bands often have—it just sounds like a tank marching down the road, no swing.*

KEN ADAMANY *It was so good that I immediately called Werman and asked him to come back out. I told him that we had [Columbia] coming out to see us, but Bun E. broke his arm. Werman said, 'Good.' He said, 'I don't mean it that way, but it gives me some extra time to get my people back out, because we want the band.'*

16

Now you can say that you own me...

International Creative Management (ICM) was co-founded in 1975 by two former attorneys, Ralph Mann and Marvin Josephson, both veterans of World War II. Mann worked as a lawyer in Washington DC and, according to his obituary, 'proudly took an active role in the initial efforts to censure Senator Joseph McCarthy' before transitioning to the entertainment industry with jobs at NBC and later MCA. Josephson worked as an attorney for CBS before moving into artist management. Together, they orchestrated the merger of two top agencies (Creative Management Associates and International Famous Agency) and formed a new company, ICM. By 1976, the agency boasted clients as disparate as Henry Kissinger, Steve McQueen, and Lorne Michaels. ICM's music department represented the likes of Aerosmith, Eric Clapton, Linda Ronstadt, James Taylor, and Crosby, Stills & Nash.

Cheap Trick's attorney, Richard Shelton, knew Ralph Mann. From Shelton's obituary, published by the *Chicago Tribune* on June 3, 1985: 'During the 1930s and 1940s, Mr. Shelton was leader of the Dick Shelton band, a popular ballroom dance group. As an attorney, Mr. Shelton represented show business personalities, including Bob Newhart and The Smothers Brothers.' Shelton also represented The Ohio Players, signed to Mercury Records.

Adamany was a known quantity to ICM thanks to his extensive efforts as a regional promoter, and Shelton helped convince the agency that Cheap Trick might be a worthwhile entity to represent.

KEN ADAMANY *The president of ICM and two of his key agents flew into Chicago to see the band at Haymaker's on June 26, 1976.*

Below is an excellent description of Haymaker's from a 1977 *Chicago Tribune* article:

The audience is young—twenty-two is the average age, according to manager George Swanson—and there was a line of even younger people at the door finding out that their fake IDs weren't fooling anyone. (Haymaker's is patrolled by a group of smiling bouncers whose size and muscular development would do credit to the Chicago Bears' front four.) Inside the large room a rock band named Prism was playing at a moderately deafening volume level while some couples danced and stag groups of both sexes congregated around the bar, waiting to make contact. Towards the back, the pinball machines, video games, and Fooz Ball tables were perking. The room seemed active, but Swanson explained that by normal standards this was a slow night, probably because of the rock concert that afternoon at Soldier Field. 'When we have one of our more popular bands—like Cheap Trick, Thumbs, or The Boyzz—it's wall-to-wall people. It can take you five minutes to get from the door to the bar.' For all the beef of the security men, Haymaker's seems like a friendly place—kind of a cross between a singles bar and a sock hop.

Ralph Mann arrived at Haymaker's accompanied by two of his associates from the ICM music department, Shelly Schulz and Chip Rachlin.

CHIP RACHLIN *There was some buzz on the band. Ken was telling us they were selling out big clubs.*

Haymaker's was a familiar stamping ground, and Cheap Trick tore it up.

KEN ADAMANY *Watching Ralph, Chip, and Shelly during the performance gave me the impression we would be working together.*

CHIP RACHLIN *The place was full and they were great. Cheap Trick checked all the boxes for us. It was not an agonizing decision. Let's get this done. We liked 'em. We wanted 'em. You played hunches if you liked what you saw.*

KEN ADAMANY *We signed with a major agency before we even had a record deal.*

Not long before.

* * *

The Haymaker's show was Saturday. Cheap Trick returned to the Sunset Bowl on Sunday, took Monday off, then on Tuesday, June 29, Jim Charne and Tom Werman arrived from New York, along with the head of A&R at Epic, Steve Popovich.

KEN ADAMANY *Werman was trying to get Steve to come in when all of a sudden Columbia got very interested, and they then agreed to all fly out here.*
I have to confess: I spent about a week on State Street giving every good-looking girl, and I mean every one, free tickets.

JACK THIBAULT *Ken wanted the place packed.*

'The place' was the Stone Hearth (formerly Snoopy's, later the R&R Station, then Paramount), Madison's largest nightclub at the time, located next to the viaduct on Park Street. Regulars affectionately referred to the place as the 'Stone Barf.' Patrons' shoes stuck to the floor even though it was carpeted, saturated as it was with cheap beer and Coca-Cola.

Jack Thibault worked for a booking agency out of Minneapolis called Thumbs Up Music and first became aware of Cheap Trick during the Xeno era when Chuck Toler called him regularly looking for gigs. Thibault found himself at the Stone Hearth on June 29 by chance.

JACK THIBAULT *I just happened to be in Madison. The show that night was off the charts. Up to that point, I had never heard them better.*

KEN ADAMANY *Tom Genetti, who was the local CBS Records guy, was there too.*

Genetti was a Madison undergrad who parlayed his fandom into a job working part time for Epic as a marketing rep, targeting college students.

TOM GENETTI *I'm enamored, dumbstruck. I'm with people from Epic Records, seeing my favorite band about to get signed.*

Madison was Cheap Trick's home turf, and dominating the Stone Hearth was second nature.

JIM CHARNE *They were sensational. Sensational visually. Their songs were great. They had a great sound. There were two drummers onstage, you know, Bun E. with his arm in a cast and playing with one arm, and the other guy who was filling in.*

Lighting coordinator Matthew Perrin installed flashing lights in the three steps up to Nielsen's platform for the occasion, by request. The idea for Rick's platform 'came from playing clubs, where I used to stand on monitors and smash them, not intentionally,' Nielsen told the *Boston Globe*. 'So I said, all right, let's design something.'

Steve Popovich echoed the enthusiasm of Charne and Werman. 'When you see Cheap Trick in a club in Madison, Wisconsin, you see what they do to motivate a crowd,' he told *Record World*. 'It was a combination of great songs and they were fun to look at. You left the show with a great feeling. After we saw Cheap Trick we made the decision to sign them on the spot.'

Post-gig, the representatives from Epic, along with band and entourage, invaded Paisan's Italian restaurant around the corner (just off University Avenue) for a celebratory feast. The principals (Adamany, band, execs) then reconvened a mile away at the Edgewater, at 666 Wisconsin Avenue (yes, the number of the beast), a resort hotel overlooking Lake Mendota, within view of the Capitol building.

KEN ADAMANY *... Until well after bar time.*

JIM CHARNE *Steve Popovich talked to Ken and they made a deal and the band was on Epic. It was very fast.*

KEN ADAMANY *He said, 'Let's do it!'*

In the space of just four days, Cheap Trick signed with a major talent agency and record label—all with the drummer on the disabled list. Epic beat Columbia to the punch and Cheap Trick belonged to them indefinitely. As Rick Nielsen put it, 'I've always liked to be exploited in the right way.'

MARK SPECTOR *I always felt like, you know, I should have moved a little faster. I mean, they were great.*

* * *

With the protracted quest to secure the elusive record deal complete, the triumphant group took a couple of days off to celebrate. But, lest Rick Nielsen's head get too big, his mother, Marilyn, was there to keep him grounded with an article she wrote for the *Rockford Morning Star* titled 'Music Reflects US History,' published on July 2, a mere three days after her progeny finally saw his years of hard work validated.

As I listen to the strains of a current 'rock' tune being played by Cheap Trick, our son's rock band (they sometimes use our garage for a rehearsal room), I can't help but wonder about the life span of this particular song. Unless it has the special appeal of The Beatles' best tunes, 'Yesterday,' I would give it a rating of three on a measuring device of one to ten. Some of the new tunes make the grade for a few months or even a few years before they become obsolete. I am sure that none will survive the next hundred years until our great country celebrates the Tricentennial. On the other hand, when I play a patriotic tune on a music box or a recording of 'Yankee Doodle,' our two-and-a-half-year-old grandson recognizes it immediately as a lovely tune to march to.

Three out of ten!? The next night, Cheap Trick were back at Waverly Beach, 'Yankee Doodle' absent from the set list. They celebrated the Bicentennial at a private party in Delavan, Wisconsin—not as guests, but entertainment.

KEN ADAMANY *Our contract called for $425 plus catering, with a $100 advance.*

Rick Nielsen sported an elaborate ensemble for the occasion: a cream corn cardigan over a pink satin bowling shirt monogrammed 'Debbie,' with a light pink collared shirt underneath. He wore a bowtie, but not a black one, and was bare-headed (he would start wearing a ballcap soon enough). The stage was the freshly mowed lawn, Rick, Robin, and Tom out front with the dynamic duo of Bun E. and Hank drumming behind them, a white garage as a backdrop. Legend has it the band could be heard from up to two miles away.

Cheap Trick performed on July 5 at a place called Bear Lake Disco in Braidwood, Illinois, an hour south of Chicago, on July 6 at the Ford County Fair in Springfield, and on July 7 at a place called the 18th Amendment— cheekily named for the document that established Prohibition—in Shorewood, a suburb of Milwaukee, where they spent the weekend at Fantasy's 2nd Avenue at 35th & Burleigh. A former patron described Fantasy's as a 'total fire-trap.' A steep staircase delivered revelers to the underground establishment, which had once been called Beneath the Street.

* * *

Something Hank Ransome remembers fondly from that summer is the development of the song 'Surrender.' The band first performed a version of the tune as early as May, a month before Hank arrived. 'I wrote it at home late one night,' Rick told *Guitar Player*. 'I was playing an unplugged electric guitar, and I had a rhythm thing going on.'

'It just rolled off at one sitting,' Rick remembered. 'Those opening lines— "Mother told me, yes, she told me I'd meet girls like you"—that's like advice to the lovelorn, and obviously inspired by the old Shirelles hit, "My mama said that there'd be days like this." It's a good way to start a song, if you can make it go with a chord progression.' As soon as he heard it, Bun E. Carlos 'thought it was a really interesting lyric.'

Interesting is one word, *risqué* another. Nielsen's early drafts were strewn with vulgarity, which he eventually cleaned up as the words evolved. 'Indonesian shit' became 'Indonesian junk.' 'Dykes, old maids, or whores' became 'old maids for the war.' 'Murderers and queers' became 'losers of the year.'

The second half of the third verse gave him some trouble. Then one day at rehearsal, they started telling stories and something came up—something that happened back in Philadelphia, where they met Hank.

BUN E. CARLOS *Heather walked in on her parents on the couch doing the deed and we had a big laugh about it, and three years later Rick remembered it and put it in the song.*

An early version of those last two lines went like this: 'When I woke up Mommy's nude and laying on the couch / Daddy's barking like a hound dog, I think he's going to pounce.' Less than subtle.

HEATHER RANSOME *I don't recall a particular moment seeing them rolling around on the couch, but I do have a lot of feelings about that song. My parents were one of the only couples that had kids, and I was kind of like the trophy kid for lots of my musician aunts and uncles. Rick and his wife Karen would babysit me, as did Tommy Petersson.*

The eventual lyric—'rolling on the couch, rolling numbers, rock'n'rolling'— conjures up an image of a teenager walking in on frisky parents who have raided more than just his or her stash of records. Whatever that final couplet ended up being about—whether Hank and his wife were the ones rolling on the couch, or the ones that 'just seemed a little weird,' or neither—Hank remains proud of his daughter's perceived connection to the perennial classic. He calls it 'Heather's song.'

HEATHER RANSOME *I remember that we moved from our apartment across the street from Rick and Karen. The new house we were renting was on a street full of kids and they liked to call me and my parents weird, since we were a rock'n'roll family with colorful people coming in and out of the house at all hours of the day and night. It hurt my feelings, and I really tried to be perceived as normal, which was absolutely impossible. Later in life, not until high school, I was told that the song was in part about me. I listened to it a little more carefully and had a little epiphany about what it means to be an outlier. Yes, I was raised oddly—me and my parents were not a traditional bunch—but I needed to embrace it, not be embarrassed by it. My life was unique, and I survived an interesting childhood, and that is something to own. I think the popularity of that song and how people feel about it makes me realize that living a weird, or non-traditional life, means being exceptional, and I would rather be exceptional.*

A sample of Nielsen's handwritten lyrics, seen on display at the Rick's Picks exhibit—red marker on a torn section of manilla envelope—revealed that Rick's original thought was 'GOT MY QUEEN RECORDS OUT' before he crossed out QUEEN to scribble KISS above it.

* * *

The contract with Epic was still just a handshake deal, but Cheap Trick were essentially off the market. Yet the July 10 issue of *Cash Box* contained this confusing blurb: 'Look for a Wisconsin band called 'The Cheap Trick' to be the next Kim Fowley follow-up after his current involvement with the Runaways and The Quick.'

Kim Fowley was famous for self-promotion, infamous in terms of veracity. The Runaways' debut came out June 1. As for The Quick, they released a very Sparksian album with Mercury called *Mondo Deco*, but it sold poorly, and they were dropped. Steve Hufsteter joined The Dickies and Danny Wilde and Ian Ainsworth formed Great Buildings with Phil Solem (their one album, *Apart From The Crowd*, is a power-pop classic). Wilde and Solem went on to form The Rembrandts.

Cheap Trick spent the rest of July gracing stages at places like the Airway Bar in Marshfield, Mr. Lucky's in Stevens Point, the Uprising in Dekalb, and He & She in Milwaukee—a disco club shoehorned into a shopping center.

On July 28, Cheap Trick returned to Rockford for what seems to have been a very significant evening at Flight Of The Phoenix. Significant because, according to longtime fan and peer Brad Elvis, at some point during the show an unknown member of the audience tossed a tan painter's cap onstage and Rick Nielsen bent over, picked it up ... and put it on. As Rick later told *Zig Zag*, 'You can lose a lot of body heat through your head.' Brad Elvis is adamant in his belief that in this moment Rick Nielsen donned a cap such as this, with a brim visor, onstage for the very first time.

BRAD ELVIS *Rick played with it on and off the rest of their set. Probably three sets. I saw them a week or two later and Rick still had that same cap but didn't take it off. The next time I saw them, he wore a black cap with a big 'Point Beer' badge pinned to it.*

Bun E. suspects that Rick might have worn a hat similar to this at some point previous, but I have seen no photographic evidence of Nielsen wearing a ballcap before the end of July 1976. Could the final piece of the 'Rick Nielsen' costume have fallen into place so randomly, flung from the crowd like a fateful frisbee?

By now, Nielsen had developed an elaborate schtick, bouncing and flailing and flaunting the elasticity of his face, strapping on multiple guitars while peppering the audience with pick after pick after pick (one writer called the flurry of picks 'Cheap Trick popcorn'). Patrick Goldstein referenced the raining plectrums for the *Chicago Daily News* in 1977, calling Nielsen 'surely the first guitarist to use his picks as props—they bombard the audience like guided missiles, as Nielsen bounces them off his nose and knees into the crowd.'

'We were kind of the perfect band to have a tchotchke,' Nielsen astutely observed. He told *Vintage Guitar*, 'It's my business card.' Rick would not have picks with his face printed on them until 1978. 'For the first couple of years, everybody thought my name was Fender,' he quipped to *Illinois Entertainer*.

As for his stage garb, Rick seemed drawn to anti-fashion. 'I wasn't a sex-god, lead-guitar kind of guy,' he admitted to the *Quad City Times*. 'I'm half-nerd and half-noodling.' The cardigan/bowtie getup was the ultimate solution, and the cap was the capper. Whether he was unwilling or unable (or some combination of the two) to conform to the seventies rock aesthetic, or aesthetics, what he needed was a niche, and he found it. The physical manifestation of 'Rick Nielsen' came together piece-by-piece over the course of 1976. He finally had a vessel for his every whim and quirk. The only child. The class clown. Hijinks harnessed. Antics amalgamated. A brazen buffoon. A demented raconteur. The hat was the cherry on top of the goofball sundae.

'Do you know what people say behind my back?' Rick asked the audience at NAMM, then supplied the answer: 'What an ass.'

When Jack Douglas saw Cheap Trick at the Sunset Bowl, when Tom Werman saw them at Catacombs, when Ralph Mann saw them at Haymaker's, when Steve Popovich saw them at Stone Hearth … Rick Nielsen was hatless. Then someone tossed a painter's cap onstage at Flight Of The Phoenix.

* * *

It was not long after Rick Nielsen put the hat on that Bun E. Carlos's cast came off.

BUN E. CARLOS *There was a little kerfuffle then.*

Having been the band's drummer since their inception, Bun E. reasonably assumed that as soon as his arm healed, Hank would be heading back to Philadelphia.

HANK RANSOME *I was basically helping out some old buddies. That was the plan.*

All of a sudden: new plan.

BUN E. CARLOS *Rick and Tom wanted to carry on with two drummers, and I said, 'No fucking way.'*

He was shocked at his bandmates' desire to undermine or diminish his role in such a way. Not to mention the inherent clumsiness of a band with four arms drumming, rather than three.

BUN E. CARLOS *Clunky drum rolls, two guys trying to play along with each other, flamming like crazy—when the drums don't quite hit at the same time and it ends up sounding sloppy and crummy.*

But Rick and Tom remained steadfast. Why not? It was such a killer sound! A resentful standoff ensued. And then …

BUN E. CARLOS *They said, 'Okay, we'll try it with one drummer, but without you. Stay home.'*

KEN ADAMANY *They didn't bring me in on that part of it.*

BUN E. CARLOS *'You're fired. Can we borrow your drums?'*

The fracas fractured the lineup just as Cheap Trick were about to cross the finish line.

Cheap Trick rehearsed with Hank Ransome as sole drummer and seem to have even played a gig with just Hank (possibly in Iowa). Then, reminded as to why they had asked a one-armed Carlos to bash it out alongside Hank in the first place, they flew Thom Mooney out from Los Angeles to see if he could make it work. They rehearsed with Mooney at Full Compass in Madison, but encountered the same problem: the songs simply did not feel or sound the same without Carlos behind the kit. Cheap Trick, like most (or all) bands, was the sum of its parts. Oh, and one more thing: very soon, the members of Cheap Trick were scheduled to sign on the dotted line a legally binding recording contract with Epic Records.

BUN E. CARLOS *[Epic] wanted nothing to do with it, with two drummers. They said, 'No, we signed the four man band. Bun E. and Rick and Tom and Robin,* *that's who's making the record. Not four guys plus an extra drummer.' They didn't wanna know about two drummers. Neither did Jack Douglas.*

And so, Rick and Tom capitulated.

BUN E. CARLOS *They called up and said, 'One drummer is fine, and you'll be fine as the one drummer.' And we went back to work.*

On the first day of August, Rick Nielsen, Robin Zander, Tom Petersson, and Bun E. Carlos convened at the offices of attorney Richard Shelton in Chicago and put pen to paper, making things official with Epic Records. It was probably at around this time, as they were about to ascend to the next level, that Tom Petersson added an extra 's' to his surname and Brad 'Bunny' Carlson scrambled the letters in his name to become Bun E. Carlos.

Ron Alexenburg, who was Senior Vice President and General Manager of Epic & Associated Labels at the time Cheap Trick were signed, remembered those days fondly.

RON ALEXENBURG *Epic Records was on fire. In '76 we signed bands that nobody really wanted, like Boston and Meat Loaf and Kansas, and some little kid I signed called Michael Jackson, and Cheap Trick was right in there.*

KEN ADAMANY *We negotiated a very good deal ... both good front money and strong label support guarantees. There had to be a decent amount of front money on signing and also with all of the option pickups, because we were an organization that had poured a lot of performing income back in just to keep things going. We were totally self-contained with trucks, a GMC motorhome, a road crew, and also owned our own equipment. No other band had that at the time around here. We had the whole thing.*

RON ALEXENBURG *We had a young staff, the best staff in the record business, and they wanted Cheap Trick.*

When Cheap Trick finally found a home, it was ironically the same home that Fuse had been evicted from.

KEN ADAMANY *Everything in between was just the band playing incredibly well and playing a bunch of dates all over the place. Touring constantly. Going back to Chances R in Champaign twenty times, Ann Arbor twenty times, Milwaukee, Madison, Chicago, The Fox Valley, The Twin Cities, back and back and back, and all of a sudden the $200 dates were $2,000 dates, before the band was even signed. And getting ICM—a major agency, one of the two largest—to sign this band without a record deal was big, too. This was all before Epic came into the picture.*

The same week that Cheap Trick signed with Epic, Aerosmith's *Rocks* was nestled in the Top 10 on *Billboard*. Interestingly enough, both of Ken Adamany's former bandmates from The KnighTranes, Steve Miller and Boz Scaggs, also had albums in the Top 20: *Fly Like An Eagle* at 11 and *Silk Degrees* at 15.

The day after inking the deal, Cheap Trick hit the road for an abbreviated East Coast tour.

BUN E. CARLOS *My arm was fully healed by then, and it was like, Let's take Bun E. out for a week or two and make sure his arm works. Ken took the band about eight hundred miles away to do these gigs, just in case it didn't sound too good. He didn't wreck the band's reputation in the Midwest.*

The reconstituted Cheap Trick played Chances R in Ann Arbor on August 2, then drove six hours to Henrietta, New York (just south of Rochester) for a booking at Orange Monkey on the 3rd. They played two sets that night.

First set:

```
'Down Down Down'
'Daddy Should Have Stayed In High School'
'Speak Now Or Forever Hold Your Peace'
'ELO Kiddies'
'I Was A Fool'
'Taxman Mr. Thief'
'High Roller'
'Hot Love'
'Please Mrs. Henry'
```

Second set:

```
'Surrender'
'Fan Club'
'Southern Girls'
'Tom's Blues'
'Come On Come On'
'You Talk Too Much'
'Ain't That A Shame'
'Cry Cry'
'Auf Wiedersehen'
```

They next headed to Lockport (thirty miles northeast of Buffalo) for two nights at a club called After Dark—the type of joint that had a mechanical bull and 'pit' where ladies mud wrestled—then twenty miles west to Niagara Falls for a gig at a club/restaurant called the Switchyard on August 5. They cut across Ontario and down through Michigan to make it back in time for an August 9 engagement at the Stone Hearth, then played the Thirsty Whale in Chicago the next night. Cheap Trick performed at least fourteen more nights in August, all at familiar venues: Red Lion, Electric Ballroom, Waverly Beach, Chances R, Big Horn, Sunset Bowl, Haymakers.

On August 21, Cheap Trick performed for their largest audience yet at an outdoor concert on the Summerfest grounds, the Milwaukee skyline for a backdrop. No soundcheck. Nielsen played part of the show hatless, but donned a black Hamer cap for much of it.

BUN E. CARLOS *We did thirty minutes. The audience didn't give a fuck who we were.*

One member of that apathetic bunch was Carol Line, who reviewed the six-hour concert for *Bugle American*. 'I never expected Daydream's advertised special guest to be The Band or Bruce Springsteen,' she wrote, 'but neither did I expect a Cheap Trick ... which is exactly what was delivered.' Carol deemed the band's lyrics 'totally distorted' and music 'redundant.' But she remained optimistic, imagining that one day 'the group's musicians might scrape away the decibels and power chords to unearth what I suspect is some musical talent lying dormant.'

Next on the bill was Gary Wright, whose hard-rocking 1972 single 'I Know' was featured often in Cheap Trick's set in the early days. At this point, Wright was riding the wave of his sappy hit 'Dream Weaver,' and his live band featured three keyboardists (including Wright) and zero guitarists. Carol Line called his music 'comfortable' (and she seemed to have meant it as a compliment). Bachman Turner Overdrive were up next and, irony of ironies, their drummer performed with his arm in a cast. Line dismissed the Manitobans as 'masters of mediocrity.'

In the middle of BTO's set, the crowd suddenly went wild, girls screaming, convinced they'd just caught a glimpse of the heartthrob headliner peeking out from behind the curtain.

KEN ADAMANY *It was Tom Petersson, and this was after he and I were asked to move away from the fence to the right of the stage because the crowd thought he was Peter.*

'We were standing backstage and the fans were about a hundred yards back behind a chain-link fence,' Tom remembered. 'I unwisely jumped up on top of a limo and started waving at the fans, and they thought it was Frampton.'

Frampton Comes Alive was at that very moment perched atop the *Billboard* charts, and a throng of twenty thousand greeted Peter Frampton, the headliner, when he finally took the stage. Carol Line, who described herself as 'an opinionated almost 30-year-old lady,' harkened back to the heaviness of Humble Pie before accusing Frampton of 'pandering to the robot-faction of society.'

* * *

On August 16, 1976, Jim Charne delivered an official-looking 'Memorandum' to Dan Beck, the director of press and public information at Epic.

DAN BECK *Epic's staff at the time was quite small, and the interaction between A&R and marketing was very close.*

Charne's memo read:

Cheap Trick is certainly the most bizarrely commercial new act ever signed to the Epic label. They have developed an extensive following throughout the Midwest (although their music sounds like it comes directly from the European continent) and they are now preparing to record their first album with Jack Douglas.

In mid-August, Jack Douglas met up with Starz, who were on tour, in Chicago. Douglas was in between producing the first and second Starz albums, and he sat in on rehearsals at SIR. Monday, August 23, was a day off, so the Starz tour bus ferried producer and band down to Burbank, twenty miles south of Chicago, to catch a run-of-the-mill Cheap Trick show at a dive called the East India Club.

RICHIE RANNO *Nielsen came up to us and he was wearing that outfit, his Cheap Trick look, which was something I had never seen before.*

Ranno was startled by the strange new persona, having known Rick since the Fuse days.

RICHIE RANNO *I said, 'What's with the get up?' And he said, 'What do you mean, I've always looked like this.' He said it to me and Dube, who knew better. And we just laughed. We knew he was kind of being facetious when he said it.*

Ranno 'got it' once the band hit the stage—as did his bandmates, guitarist Brendan Harkin and drummer Joe X. Dube (Jeff Grob from The Denims).

RICHIE RANNO *They were great that night, as always.*

BRENDAN HARKIN *I was blown away by them. They were so funny. They were like cartoons.*

JOE X. DUBE *I love 'em. I absolutely love 'em to death.*

A few days later, Jack Douglas headed up to Madison to rendezvous with Cheap Trick at Full Compass, a professional sound studio in operation there since 1971.

KEN ADAMANY *The opening of the studio was the best thing that happened for local* *and area bands and individual musicians. They were always busy and had an excellent staff. Cheap Trick, Dr. Bop, Luther Allison, and others we represented, rehearsed and recorded there. A few years later, George Martin and Geoff Emerick came in from London to do pre-production work with Cheap Trick there. The engineering staff at Full Compass seemed very pleased to have both Jack Douglas and then the team of George Martin and Geoff Emerick working with Cheap Trick in their studio.*

Most of August 25, 26, and 27 were spent at Full Compass, a routine exercise called pre-production—an opportunity for them all to get to know each other, personally and professionally while, in between, Douglas observed and advised. In the process, they churned out a slew of two-track recordings, capturing the cream of the crop of Cheap Trick's tried-and-true material.

BUN E. CARLOS *About thirty songs, just demos with him, band up, vocals down in the mix. Just running down songs so Jack could take them back to New York and figure out which ones we should actually track for the record.*

It would be left up to Jack to decide which songs were contenders for inclusion on the first Cheap Trick album, to commence recording in less than two weeks in New York City.

* * *

'One of our last shows before we [recorded the album] was with Tom Petty opening for us at a place called B.Ginnings in Schaumburg,' Rick Nielsen told *Guitar Aficionado*. 'It was kind of a big club, and I think we made $10,000 that night.' Ka-ching!

Tom Petersson, for one, was quite fond of the place. 'B.Ginnings was really good,' he remembered. 'It had a good stage and it sounded good in there. That's when we really started getting success as a local act. We weren't just playing for eight people in some Pizza Hut in Bettendorf, Iowa.' Robin Zander concurred: 'Before we even made our first record we had a following that had grown from three people standing on their heads to 1,500, 2,000 people in a nightclub.'

B.Ginnings was a high-end establishment owned and operated by Danny Seraphine, drummer from the band Chicago. Jane Rozek penned an excellent description of the club for a blog post titled 'Only The B.Ginning Of The Nightlife Scene In Schaumburg.'

> The interior of the club was decorated by set designers to resemble the streets of Chicago Seraphine had grown up on, with building facades, stoplights, 'el' tracks, and real street signs. A replica of the Chicago Theater marquee was backlit on the ceiling above the main bar, another bar was set up to look like an old-fashioned newsstand and one wall was painted with the Chicago skyline. The club featured three bars, a restaurant, a sunken stainless steel dance floor …

Upon learning that a band called The Heartbreakers would be opening, the boys assumed it was the Johnny Thunders band.

BUN E. CARLOS *We were like, Oh, the Heartbreakers are opening for us! This oughta be interesting! Of course, it turned out to be some guy from Florida named Tom Petty and his band.*

The date was August 29, 1976, and Petty remembered it well. As quoted by biographer Warren Haynes, 'I'll tell you another band that really astounded me, and when I first saw them I hadn't even heard their stuff. I didn't know anything about them. We were playing a club outside Chicago, in Schaumburg, Illinois, and we were going down pretty well at this point. But that night we just didn't get much of a response. The place was packed, we were playing good, but we just weren't getting much back.' As Bun E. Carlos told *Ugly Things*: 'They were good, but they weren't really slamming people in the face or really hard-rockin' or anything like that. They weren't beating them to death like the Chicago bands did.'

　'So I'm talking with this guy afterwards, saying how weird this seemed,' Petty recalled. 'And he says, This is Cheap Trick's audience, man. I said, Cheap Trick? Wait until you see this, he tells me.' Roadie Rich Torres commented on Facebook that Heartbreaker Benmont Tench once told him, 'You don't open for U2 in Dublin, Springsteen in New Jersey, or Cheap Trick in Chicago.'

　'They hit the stage and it was fucking mind-bending,' Tom Petty declared. 'Robin Zander was one of the most powerful lead singers I'd seen, sang like one of The Beatles. The sheer energy of the thing on the stage was so great. I thought, *This band is going to be enormous.*'

* * *

Toward the end of September, Richard Cromelin reported in the *Los Angeles Times* (under 'Additional Pop News') that 'Patti Smith has completed her second album, *Radio Ethiopia*. Her producer, Jack Douglas, is also at work on a Chicago group called Trick Baby (sample titles: "The Ballad Of Richard Speck," "I Like Go Go Girls") …'

Lynee from Adamany's office immediately typed up a letter:

Dear Mr. Cromelin:

In the Sunday, September 26th issue of the *LA Times* you made reference to a group Jack Douglas is producing called 'Trick Baby.' We do appreciate the mention, however the name of the band is CHEAP TRICK.

When Patti Smith walked into the Record Plant on 44th Street between 8th and 9th, barely a block from the depravity of Times Square in the seventies, she was pissed and looking for Jack Douglas. The critically acclaimed punk poet had selected Douglas to produce her second release for Arista specifically because she hoped that the resulting album would get her on the radio, thereby moving more copies than her avant-garde debut. When she heard the producer's first pass at a mix, she was sorely disappointed, but she couldn't get him on the phone. Then she heard that he might have already skipped town, anxious to jumpstart his next project—some band, whatever they were called, some hicks from the sticks.

Frustrated, Patti went looking for Douglas at the most likely place, only to be rebuffed by the receptionist, who barely looked up to tell her that Jack wasn't there. Patti's blood boiled, and as she turned to leave she spied it there on the wall. A closer look confirmed her suspicions: it was an 8x10 of those bastards. That's what they were called! Now she remembered. Trick Baby. Cheap Trick. Whatever! She lunged for it.

BUN E. CARLOS *When we walked into the Record Plant they had all these pictures of bands on the wall, and the girl at the desk goes, 'We had your picture on the wall, but Patti Smith walked in here last week and tore it off the wall and tore it into about a million pieces.'*

Smith scattered the remnants and stormed out, to be swallowed again by the bustle of a city that was in dire straits. New York was a mess. A fiscal emergency had culminated in mobs of laid-off city workers marching through the streets in protest. Crime was so rampant that members of an organization calling itself the Council For Public Safety, purporting to represent eighty thousand police and corrections officers, distributed pamphlets to wide-eyed tourists, a skull-faced Grim Reaper staring out at them from beneath the title: *Welcome To Fear City*. The pamphlet counseled visitors to 'stay away from New York City if you possibly can.' The murder rate had doubled over the previous ten years, while the number of rapes and burglaries had tripled and robberies increased by tenfold. Films like *Death Wish* (1974), *Taxi Driver* (1976), and *The Warriors* (1979) starkly depicted the dystopian nightmare. Kevin Baker reflected on the harsh reality of those times for the *Guardian* in 2015:

There was a pervasive sense that the social order was breaking down. Most subway trains were filthy, covered in graffiti inside and out. Vandalism was incessant, with the expectation that anything not firmly bolted to the ground and covered in some protective coating would be stolen, broken, graffitied, spat on, pissed on, set on fire, used as a shelter, or tossed onto the subway tracks. Public mirrors (in reality, polished metal) were strategically placed by subway staircases so you could glimpse any lurking assailants.

Nineteen seventy-six was a doozy of a year, as detailed by the *New York Times* in March of 1977:

A total of 648,147 serious crimes were reported in New York City last year, making it the worst crime year for the city since the Police Department began compiling such data forty-five years ago. On average 1,798 serious crimes or felonies were committed, for a rate of seventy-five every hour. The city's crime rate rose six times higher than the national average last year.

The first shooting attributed to David Berkowitz, the self-christened 'Son Of Sam,' took place in the Bronx on July 29, 1976. Two young women, Jody Valenti and Donna Laurie, were sitting in a car talking when a man emerged from the shadows and fired three shots into the vehicle. Both women were struck. Valenti died and Laurie survived. Little more than a month later Cheap Trick and crew rolled into town.

BUN E. CARLOS *We drove in on a Sunday in our motorhome. Sid was driving.*

They checked into the Gramercy Park Hotel, or, as it had come to be known, the Glamercy, nicknamed as such after David Bowie and his entourage spent a raucous two weeks there in 1973. The rooms had been booked for September 6 through 28. Max Weissberg, grandson to the owner at the time, Herbert Weissberg, described the hotel for a *Rolling Stone* article in 2018:

Under my grandfather's proprietorship, little had changed since the hotel was built in 1925: Dim chandeliers. Blood-colored carpet. A feeling halfway between Casablanca and the Titanic. The guests found great comfort in its worn edges—the cigarette burns on the carpet, the television sets that were missing a knob or two, the out-of-tune baby grand piano in the lounge. For many, the Gramercy Park Hotel was an anchor in an ever-changing world, a place they wanted to celebrate—yet keep a secret.

Lou Reed, recently dumped by both record label and girlfriend, was ensconced there at the time, and one never knew who else might turn up.

KEN ADAMANY *My partner Charles Gottlieb and I represented Leslie West around that time. He was in and out of the Gramercy Park, but was doing a lot of touring for us.*

Leslie left a note for the band on his way out of town, scribbled on hotel stationary:

Dear Ken & Cheap Trick,
All the best luck in the world with your album—you will need it working with Jack. He is out of his mind! Only kidding.
Love, Leslie West

The Glamercy was five blocks east and twenty blocks south of the Record Plant, where Cheap Trick would record their first album with Jack 'out of his mind' Douglas.

Three days after Cheap Trick arrived at the hotel, punk pioneers the Ramones performed less than two miles away at CBGB. The next week, the Heartbreakers they had expected to see at B.Ginnings prowled the same stage. Rick Springfield opened for NRBQ on September 12 at Paul Colby's Other

End on Bleecker Street. The Band brought their farewell tour to the Palladium on September 18 and 19. Films like *King Kong, The Omen,* and *Monty Python And The Holy Grail* screened in local theaters.

At the Record Plant, Cheap Trick recorded more than twenty songs in just three weeks. There were plenty of songs to choose from—nearly three times as many as were recorded. Douglas whittled them down from the tapes Adamany sent him, tapes Bun E. had given him at the Sunset Bowl, and whatever else the band presented to him at Full Compass in Madison during pre-production. The impressive cache of material was mostly thanks to Rick Nielsen, going all the way back to the Sick Man Of Europe days:

'Ain't Got You'

'I'm A Surprise'

'Bean' (aka 'Song Of China')

'Ultramental'

'Mandocello'

'Tom's Blues'

A few songs from the Xeno era:

'Hot Tomato'

'Daddy Should Have Stayed In High School'

'Lovin' Money'

And then, of course, the treasure trove of originals the band had stockpiled since Robin Zander came on board:

'Number One'

'Down Down Down'

'The Ballad Of Richard Speck'

'I Want You To Want Me'

'He's A Whore'

'Blow Me Away'

'Son Of A Gun'

'Go Go Girls'

'High Roller'

'I Was A Fool'
'Disco Paradise'
'Oh Candy'
'Need A Little Girl'
'Tonight'
'Punch Ya'
'You're All Talk'
'You Talk Too Much'
'Hello There'
'Auf Wiedersehen'
'Come On Come On'
'Taxman Mr. Thief'
'Southern Girls'
'Fan Club'
'Good Girl'
'Can't Hold On'
'Arabesque'
'Loser'
'Pain Pain'
'Surrender'
'Hot Love'
'ELO Kiddies'
'Girls On Fire'
'I Need Love'
'Violins'
'Cry Cry'
'Lookout'
'Dream Police'

Not to mention the band's cache of road-worn cover tunes:

'Dealer Dealer'
'Please Mrs. Henry'
'Down On The Bay'
'Ain't That A Shame'
'Speak Now Or Forever Hold Your Peace'

BUN E. CARLOS *Jack kind of picked the song selection.*

KEN ADAMANY *When you are new you listen a lot and try to accommodate and fit in. It was the first record, and we didn't want to step on toes, we gave opinions but we weren't pushy.*

'We had enough songs where it was like, Whatever they say,' Nielsen remembered. 'We hoped to be making more records so if it didn't make it on this record, we'll do it on another record.'

BUN E. CARLOS *The obvious candidates, as you're recording, kind of rise to the surface.*

'I wanted the first album to be a sociopolitical album, and that's what it is,' Jack Douglas explained. 'All of the statements in that album are either about drug addiction, male prostitution, serial killers. It all sounds like fun but when you delve into what the subject matter is of each song on there, they're sociopolitical statements.'

Robin Zander observed that Douglas 'tried to pick songs that were controversial.' There were plenty to choose from. As Rick Nielsen put it: 'Our songs are not just about the typical and topical subjects.' Still, Douglas framed his approach as: 'How we can move this record forward. Let's see how we can expand our artistic horizons. Let's talk about what this record is about.' That would come down to Rick's lyrics.

'I was just wanting to comment about things that I'd observed,' Nielsen explained. 'That's all it's ever been for me as a lyricist. It's never been writing from a totally autobiographical place. My lyrics weren't all boy loves girl, girl loves boy, happy, happy, happy or boy misses girl, girl misses boy, sad, sad, sad. There's more to life than that and that's what I tried to write about in my songs.' According to Rick, 'A song that's gooey all the way through is disgusting; on the other hand, if you're just, Kill your mother, kill your father, kill your dog! the whole time, that's too extreme the other way.' Writing for *Triad*, Cary Baker would reference Rick's 'bizarre, often turgid lyrical fantasyland,' and 'lyrical obsession with the boundless folly of mankind.' Ira Robbins would note, with either frustration or admiration, that the 'bizarre thoughts behind the words' were 'too obscure to figure out … there's always a certain bit he's not telling.'

Rolling Stone staffer Charles M. Young later declared Rick's lyrics to 'run the gamut of lust, confusion, and misogyny, growing out of rejection and antiauthoritarian sentiments.' D. Lawless from *Bay Area Reporter* would reduce Rick's lyrics to 'a delirious stream of infantilism with just a teensy bitch streak for color.' That 'bitch streak' might be what Daisann McLane later called 'lyrical nose-thumbings.' Tom Wheeler from *Guitar Player* later sensed 'a ticking parcel, a satirical bomb' and deemed Rick's 'psycho humor' to be 'a combination of method and madness.'

'It's not planned out that much,' Nielsen countered. 'Life doesn't have to have deep hidden meanings at every turn.' He later explained to *Circus* that he was 'not into that peace/love/dove crap' but into 'real life.'

Given the breadth of material available, most of the songs selected by Douglas do bear out those 'sociopolitical' intentions, be it the psycho glam of 'ELO Kiddies,' where 'money rules and everybody steals it'; the punky ode to cougar bait 'He's A Whore,' whose narrator would do 'anything for money'; the similarly themed 'Lovin' Money'; the bluntly titled 'Taxman Mr. Thief,' where THE MAN 'steals your shit and thinks that it's funny'; the deceptively pretty 'Oh Candy,' a plaintive reflection on the aftermath of suicide; the insane redneck cosplay of 'Go-Go Girls'; the dumb-on-purpose parody of 'Disco Paradise.' According to Bun E. Carlos, there was 'no fucking way' 'Disco Paradise' would have made the album, but they recorded it at the Record Plant, as per Douglas's request. Douglas also homed in on two of the band's oldest songs, somewhat similar in style and tone: the exceedingly abrasive 'The Ballad Of Richard Speck,' a disturbing detour into the psyche of a spree killer; and the *I feel dirty* creepiness of 'Daddy Should Have Stayed In High School.'

BUN E. CARLOS *We were all kinda like, Daddy!?*

It was one of the first two songs Nielsen wrote for the band. He figured Douglas must have thought it was 'weird enough and cool enough.' And yet, Douglas did not focus solely on Cheap Trick's serious (or seriously odd) material. He also selected the horny stomper 'Hot Love,' bitter groover 'Cry Cry,' lush and orchestral 'Mandocello' (performed with both Stewkey and Xeno but never with Zander), power-pop gem 'Lookout,' staccato screamer 'You're All Talk' (in some ways closer to disco than 'Disco Paradise'), obstinately upbeat 'I Want You To Want Me' (Robin McBride's favorite), and Cheap Trick's epic hard-rock reimagining of Terry Reid's 'Speak Now Or Forever Hold Your Peace' from his 1969 self-titled album.

BUN E. CARLOS *'Lovin' Money' and 'Lookout' were of quality—they could have easily gone on the record—but there was only room for ten.*

'Basically, it's a Who pop song,' Nielsen said of 'Lookout.' 'We never emulated The Who, but if we ever stole anything from them, at least we changed the key.' They also tackled a couple of Rick's more recent compositions in the studio: 'Surrender' and 'Dream Police.' Jay Messina's assistant engineer, Sam Ginsberg, still remembers the latter.

SAM GINSBERG *It was a different version but it was there, basically there.*

BUN E. CARLOS *Rick wrote 'Dream Police' back in 1976, and we played it in the bars a few times with a different arrangement.*

The song was mentioned in a *Lively Times* article in December of '76.

BUN E. CARLOS *The only basic part that ended up to be in 'Dream Police' was 'dream police they come to me in my head,' it had a slightly different melody, same chords, 'the dream police they're coming to arrest me, oh no.' Then it went into this thing, 'tonight tonight you're gonna hold me tight,' it went into a different part and a different ending. So just the 'dream police' part got kept and added to later by Rick.*

Cheap Trick recorded in Studio A at the Record Plant on a classic Spectra Sonics console, known for its unique 101 preamp, capable of higher gain with less noise.

It's difficult to imagine a band more primed and ready to record a debut album than Cheap Trick in late 1976. Each member had at least a decade of gigging under his belt, and as a unit they had been napalming the Midwest club circuit for three solid years. Here was a band brimming with confidence and loaded for bear—or as Orville Davis, whose band Rex was recording at the same time across the hall, succinctly puts it, 'Tight as a cat's ass. The sound was tremendous.'

SAM GINSBERG *They were so solid and tight and so together. They obviously were playing a lot of clubs. It was very easy to lay down tracks with them because they were so polished.*

JAY MESSINA *They were really tight, that's why it went so fast.*

'We did it really fast. There was no reason to mess with what they were,' Jack Douglas remembered. Rick Nielsen agreed: 'It was really exciting and we were ready. We did it in a hurry. We did basic tracks so fast, but we knew them backwards and forwards.'

Douglas was impressed with the band's work ethic: 'When you get in a room with them, there's no lollygagging. Get to work.' Cheap Trick hammered out the basic tracks in little more than a week, full band, live in the studio, just caustic and raw. According to Nielsen, 'That's key to capturing the feel, especially trying to get a good basic track.'

SAM GINSBERG *Rick was almost, like, performing in the studio, which was amazing because he's such a great guitar player, he's just phenomenal, and he does sing, and he's got that peculiar kind of voice that blends in with Robin. Just great.*

'I like records that sound like the band are having fun,' was Nielsen's philosophy. As Douglas explained, 'I wanted them to sound on the record like they did live, raw and crazy. We did most of the instruments and some of the vocals live in the studio.'

BUN E. CARLOS *He didn't try to clone our live sound, he kind of blended it in with his production.*

'Back then when we did a record we looked at it like a jazz record, we wanted the instruments to sound like the instruments,' Douglas told Mitch Gallagher. He 'wanted a very realistic sound. I didn't want what was the popular sound.' As Rick put it, 'We used a brand new technique: no overdubs. That album was just done in one or two takes.' Jack Douglas once explained his ideal approach as 'rehearse so we're in the ballpark when we go into the studio, but let's leave enough room for improvisation.' Cheap Trick were beyond ready and willing.

Douglas also contended that 'you can't have a great album without people playing and singing the hell out of a tune.' No wonder he liked Cheap Trick so much.

Rick Nielsen laid down most of his guitar parts with his favorite six-string, a '58 Sunburst Les Paul affectionately referred to as 'the loud one,' plugged directly into an Orange amp. According to Rick, 'I never use any pedals, except for in my car.' In 2012, the '58 Les Paul was on display at the Rick's Picks exhibit in Rockford, along with this description:

> The volume it is capable of producing is partially due to its early PAF pickups: both sets had their covers removed to increase overall volume. The bridge pickup is known as a 'zebra' due to its black and white coils.

Rick did use one non-car pedal on the album: an MXR Phase 90, on 'The Ballad Of Richard Speck.' According to Carlos, it was 'a prototype' and 'sounded great' but 'got stolen out of the Record Plant.' Robin Zander played a '52 white Telecaster, a Blackguard procured from Rick, who bought it in 1967. Zander traded him a 'weird-looking guitar' for it. 'I think it was made by Olympic, we called it the Iranian banjo,' he remembered.

Tom Petersson recorded his bass parts with his trusty '64 Gibson Thunderbird II run through Sound City guitar amps. 'It's the only bass I owned for our first two albums,' he explained. 'There's something about the resonance of a one-pickup model that seems better than the two-pickup. Those '63–64 models were the greatest.'

Bun E. Carlos laid down his drum tracks with his 1967 Rogers set, a small kit with a big sound. 'When I saw Mitch Mitchell had a Rogers Swiv-O-Matic, I went out and bought two of them in 1967,' he remembered. 'If it was good enough for Hendrix, it was good enough for me. I didn't know any better, and I probably still don't.' He retired the Rogers kit from the stage in 1973, switching to a WMP Super Classic Ludwig set until 1975, when he started using a pre-war Slingerland Radio King set, which he played until 1978. With each of these kits Carlos used a vintage Ludwig Super Sensitive Snare (until he switched to a Supraphonic). But when it came time to record the first two albums, Bun E. busted out the trusty Rogers kit. They gated and compressed the snare and used an oscillator on the kick, 'to get the real low end,' according to Jay Messina.

BUN E. CARLOS *We worked about four hours on the rack tom for 'ELO Kiddies,' to get the perfect rack-tom sound.*

* * *

While Cheap Trick were hunkered down at the Record Plant crafting a hard-rock masterpiece, it just so happened that fifteen miles away, in a seven-story apartment building called Pine Hill Towers in Yonkers, a part-time taxi driver named David Berkowitz was pacing back and forth beside a bare mattress on the cluttered floor of his studio apartment, 7E, down at the end of a shadowy hall. Oblivious to the nice view of the Hudson from his window, Berkowitz was busy arguing with the demons in his head (and perhaps his neighbor's dog).

Cheap Trick recorded their first album in between the first two Son Of Sam shootings. The second attack in the year-long crime spree took place on October 23 in Flushing, when someone fired upon a man and woman, again seated in a parked car. Both survived. The Son Of Sam shot twelve more people, killing five, before Berkowitz's shocking arrest the following August.

* * *

The Record Plant facility was home to three different studios.

ORVILLE DAVIS *They had two studios on the main floor and then up on, I believe it was on the tenth floor, they had another studio, as well as the mastering facility up there.*

KEN ADAMANY *After you walked in, you took a left down a hallway to the doors of Studio A. There were a lot of people in the studio complex at the time, so I placed Jolly and Sid Wingfield, our six-foot-six road manager, at the door when they were recording the basic tracks.*

ORVILLE DAVIS *You'd go in the front doors at West 45th Street and you'd walk down a hallway and there was this door and nothing else, and you'd walk in the door and all of a sudden you were standing in this little cubbyhole. They'd ask who you were and what you were there for and you'd tell them, and then you'd walk through another door and all of a sudden it was incredible-looking. Hallways with carpeted walls and a sitting area and then you'd walk down a hallway and*

to your left was studio A and to your right was Studio B and you just kind of
stood there looking at each one of them going, Holy shit, this is the most amazing
place I've ever scene.

'It was the coolest place to be, and this is even before you get in the studios. This is just the vibe of the place,' Jay Messina remembered. 'So it was like the coolest club in town.'

At the same time Cheap Trick were making magic in Studio A, Rex Smith's band Rex were recording their second album, *Where Do We Go From Here*, across the hall in Studio B, with Jack Douglas's childhood friend and bandmate from Privilege, Eddie Leonetti, producing. Rex consisted of Rex Smith, Lars Hanson, Mike Ratti, Lou Vandora, and Orville Davis.

BUN E. CARLOS *He had a girl singer come in to sing with him, and she was sitting out in the hall having a cigarette, and Robin goes 'What do you do?' And she goes, 'I'm a session singer,' and he goes, 'Oh, what would we know you from?' And she goes [sings], 'Life savers …' She was the Life Savers girl. We thought that was the coolest thing.*

That was Linda Lawley, a veteran Broadway performer who also contributed background vocals to the unreleased Wicked Lester (pre-KISS) album. Lawley was Rex Smith's sister-in-law at the time, married to his brother Michael Lee Smith, the singer from Starz. Lawley later had a band called Thieves who released one album with Arista, produced by Mike Chapman.

BUN E. CARLOS *We had extra gear they let us store in a room in the basement. Me and Tom went down there one day to get something out, and it was the John Lennon tape storage room. They let me and Tom go in there—it was always locked. There's the 'Cold Turkey' tapes. There's a tape of Lennon and Mick Jagger jamming at the Record Plant. There's 'Whatever Gets You Thru The Night.' There's the multi-tracks for the* Imagine *album. All his tapes. We were taking boxes out, touching them and putting them back. We were in awe that we were in a room with such greatness.*

At some point they took a break from recording long enough to head over to a photography studio at 253 Fifth Avenue, a few blocks from the Empire

State Building. Steinbecker/Houghton specialized in fashion photography but were branching out into the world of album covers, having recently taken the pictures for Ted Nugent's second album, *Free For All*. The studio occupied the entire fifth floor of the building, where they had been for almost ten years. Steinbicker described the layout in detail for his *Life's Little Adventures* blog:

> The rear of the studio area, marked 'Client Area' on the diagram, was all black: ceiling, walls, and floor. There was a pool table, director's chairs, and a powerful stereo system with massive speakers and dozens of the latest rock records, along with my beloved classics. The rest of the studio area, marked 'Shooting Area,' was again pure white, with a neutral grey floor for color balance. Here sets were built, shot, and taken down. Modular wall units could be assembled many different ways. There was a huge Mole-Richardson wind machine on wheels, the type used in Hollywood studios. And overhead scaffolding for those high-level shots. Cameras and lenses were kept in a safe, and film in a refrigerator. Finally, a large electric service panel allowed us to plug in a dozen or more heavy studio strobe lights, which drew thousands of watts of juice.

Jim Houghton manned the camera. He darkened the room and shone a spotlight on the band, as if caught red-handed. He also shot each member individually, which included asking them to jump up and down. They thought it was goofy but went along for the ride.

The photo shoot was quick and easy and yielded worthwhile results, although Zander asked that a different shot of himself be cropped into the image that was ultimately selected for the cover. Also of note: Rick Nielsen showed up to the photoshoot toting his framed print of Rich Kwasniewski's accordion photo.

RICH KWASNIEWSKI *Rick did say, 'Hey, I got your picture on the cover at least!' I'm like, 'Cool! Thank you!'*

Jim Houghton was up for anything. Not long after photographing Cheap Trick, his lens captured the gory images of Angus Young impaled by his own guitar for AC/DC's *If You Want Blood ... You Got It*.

Speaking to *Circus* in May of 1977, Jack Douglas described Cheap Trick as 'different than anything I've ever worked with as a band.'

SAM GINSBERG *It was one of the most fun albums that I did with Jack and Jay. Cheap Trick does stand out in my mind as one of my favorite sessions of all time.*

Douglas has also cited *Cheap Trick* as one of his favorite albums to have ever worked on. He and Rick Nielsen definitely hit it off. While the others were at the Glamercy, Rick stayed with Jack at his house in Montclair, New Jersey. 'Yogi Berra lived next door and there was a White Castle down the street,' Rick remembered, 'so it had everything going for it.'

BUN E. CARLOS *We went over to Jack's after basics were done on a Sunday for a little picnic in Montclair, and we shot some hoops in the driveway. Jack had the twenty basics on tape and put 'em on in the living room, and we all sat down and listened to 'em, and after about ten songs I was the only guy in there—they all went out and played basketball.*

Carlos eventually joined his bandmates for a game of horse. And won.

* * *

With basic tracks complete, it was time for Zander to record the vocals. Cheap Trick had not performed live in weeks, far and away the longest they had gone without wrecking a club since Robin had joined the band two years earlier. It seemed that a visit to the legendary Max's Kansas City, just four blocks from the Glamercy, was in order.

BUN E. CARLOS *The guy said, 'Well, we only do original material at Max's.' And we said, 'Yeah, we've got original material, three sets worth.' And the guy said, 'Holy cow! None of the bands around here have more than forty minutes worth of stuff.' And we're like, 'Well, we're not from around here.'*

Adamany booked two nights at the historic venue, mostly so Robin could fire up his engines.

BUN E. CARLOS *Scream and yell and get his voice back into shape.*

Epic Records seized the opportunity and distributed invitations to the local rock intelligentsia that threatened, 'The show begins promptly at 9pm, at which time you may expect to have your brain boiled.'

If there was one song in the repertoire Robin needed to get his voice into proper shape to record, it was the cataclysmic 'The Ballad Of Richard Speck.' Coincidentally, Richard Speck's first parole hearing took place on September 15, thus it was reported in newspapers across the country on September 16 that Speck's parole, of course, had been denied. That night, Cheap Trick performed at Max's Kansas City for a small crowd, including a contingent of Epic staffers (Jim Charne, Dan Beck, VP of national promotion Jim Jeffries, VP of marketing Jim Tyrell, Alan Ostroff, Sam Lederman, etc). Photographer Jim Houghton was there, as was Jack Douglas, along with his engineering team, Jay Messina and Sam Ginsberg. Chip Rachlin and Ralph Mann from ICM came, as did Hank Ransome, who drove up from Philadelphia. Also present: a cluster of prominent NYC scenesters like Paul and Miki Zone from The Fast, David Johansen, Wayne County, and Gene Simmons and Paul Stanley.

BUN E. CARLOS *They were at one of the long tables right at center stage.*

The KISS Spirit Of '76 tour ended four nights earlier in Springfield, Massachusetts, with another of Jack Douglas's pet projects, Artful Dodger, opening. Peter Crowley, who'd been the booker at Max's Kansas City since it reopened in 1975 ('the guy' Bun E. was referring to), remembered Cheap Trick performing 'as if they were at Madison Square Garden in front of twenty thousand people.'

They delivered three blistering, hour-long sets. The floor at Max's Kansas City was lined with long wooden tables, and at some point Rick Nielsen stepped off the stage and onto the nearest one. He stalked from table to table until he loomed over the unmasked Demon and Starchild. 'Literally, I was smitten,' Gene Simmons remembered. 'The image of the band was so great,' Paul Stanley agreed.

I can see it now: Nielsen striking a nerdgod pose and copping Simmons's patented move, sticking out his tongue. Gene Simmons laughed, fished a twenty from his pocket and held it out to Rick. A gratuity. Rick snatched the bill, pressed it to his still wagging tongue, and slapped it against his forehead, where it stayed, thanks to a gluey mixture of bodily fluids. 'Smashes it to his forehead, which is full of sweat, and continues playing,' Gene Simmons recalled.

BUN E. CARLOS *Then he took it off and acted like he ate it.*

Nielsen does not know whether he spat or swallowed. 'That's one detail I can't remember.' The performance at Max's served its purpose. So well, in fact, that a second engagement booked for Sunday the 19th was canceled.

KEN ADAMANY *There were two nights booked, but we only did one.*

BUN E. CARLOS *We did the one and Robin was ready to sing.*

Zander laid down his vocals in a matter of days, careening through the schizophrenic selection of songs like an actor making a demo reel. 'I always thought of singing as sort of what an actor would do in a movie,' he once said. Nielsen appreciated that: 'I always wanted to have that voice. I worked with some great people but Robin was the guy who could do it all, he could sing the ballads, he could be Mr. Nasty, he could be Mr. Sweet.'

'The great actors weren't pigeon-holed into one type of character,' Zander elaborated. Nielsen made great use of Zander's versatility: 'He works more by instinct when it comes to the more subtle aspects. His voice has so many modulations, it's the perfect instrument for my songs, that he can utilize his pitching to convey the basic emotions required with ease.'

Zander has compared himself to a certain lizard. 'That's my personality in the band,' he said. 'Rick is the crazy one, and I'm the chameleon.'

MATTHEW PERRIN *Once he went to work with Jack Douglas, he really changed the way he sang. Jack got him to scream more and abuse his voice more, an added rawness. When he was in the clubs, he was singing a lot smoother, a lot cleaner. It was a drastic change after the first album.*

* * *

In the end, three years of hard work culminated in three weeks of easy work. Ira Robbins put it plainly in *Trouser Press*: 'Epic got a good deal—a band that required neither guidance nor rehearsal.'

While Cheap Trick were off gallivanting in the big city, back home they were rewarded with a cover story in *Midwest* magazine, the Sunday supplement to the *Chicago Sun Times*. Author Cynthia Dagnal summarized her article as an 'inside look at the trials and tribulations of a struggling Chicago rock band.'

'Cheap Trick is hardly considered a major rock'n'roll band,' she noted. 'But their management was already grooming them for their eventual stardom.' She pointed out that 'Cheap Trick rarely plays inside the city limits. Yet they have a large cult, and pull down an even larger salary, the highest for a local band. They even have their own T-shirt, a sure sign of success.' Dagnal's prediction: the band were 'highly regarded musically' and as such, 'not long for the storage room circuit. They simply know how good they are.'

Dagnal attended a performance at Camel's Hump, 'a club in Hanover Park located in what used to be the loading dock of some sort of warehouse or factory, in a tiny industrial mall.' The venue exuded a 'dank, smoky smell' and was 'very dark.' A shirtless Hank Ransome features prominently in one backstage photo. Rick Nielsen informed Dagnal that the letters RN on his ring stood for 'registered nut' and boasted about his huge collection of pornography, 'rivalled only by that of Raymond Burr.' Someone gave Dagnal the impression that Bun E. Carlos was thirty-nine years old. He was barely twenty-six.

'We all like what we're doing,' Nielsen told Dagnal. 'It's not a flake, it's not a fluke. It's not a mathematical formula. I mean, since we're good, the rest'll just happen.'

And it was happening, but with the album in the can they went straight back to work, Sunday and Monday night, September 26 and 27, at Haymakers in Wheeling, with Chicago legends The Shadows Of Knight (although the only remaining original member was singer Jim Sohns) opening, followed by a hometown gig at Flight of the Phoenix on Tuesday, back to the Sunset Bowl on Wednesday, and Electric Ballroom in Milwaukee on Thursday. They kicked off the month of October at Huey's in Chicago, with locals Horace Monster, known for their 'dueling double neck guitars,' opening, but then Rick and Robin had to fly to New York for a few days of overdubs at the Record Plant with Jack Douglas.

The second weekend of October found them back at Night Gallery in Waukegan. On Saturday the 9th, filmographer Chuck Lishon and his crew arrived from Chicago to shoot footage for five prospective promotional videos. Lishon and his partner, Hans Wurman, founded Sonart Productions and dB Studios in early 1972. A former employee described their business operations in a discussion thread at the 'Professional Recording Workshop' forum:

The studio did TV commercials for national distribution and had several 35mm machines that looked more like movie projectors than tape machines. The machines, including the actual projectors, were all synchronized. The format was standard 35mm film that had three stripes of magnetic media; all of the dialog, sound effects and music were on individual tracks of the three-stripe. When more than three tracks were used there were multiple rolls of film that had to be threaded onto the machines. They might have done more than just commercials, but that was the bread and butter at this particular place.

Cheap Trick play-acted performances of five songs for the cameras: 'Oh Candy,' 'ELO Kiddies,' 'Hot Love,' 'He's A Whore,' and 'The Ballad Of Richard Speck.' No costume changes or set decoration, just the same four dudes on the same cramped stage. They mimed along to rough mixes sent over by Douglas.

BUN E. CARLOS *The album wasn't finished being mixed yet. When it came time to do the show that night, we were just knackered—we had been there onstage for four or five hours, up there lip-synching these things, playing like we were really playing. Boy did that wear us out.*

Sonart pieced together five promotional video clips from the footage, rife with choppy edits and primitive effects.

* * *

And so it went for the rest of 1976, while the album was being prepared for proper release, Cheap Trick did what they did, night after night, on stage after stage throughout the Midwest: Second Chance in Ann Arbor; the White House in Niles, Michigan; Harlow's in Chicago; the Mars Theatre in Lafayette, Indiana. On November 7, they played for the first time at a place called Mother's in Chicago. Crystal K. Wiebe described the bar for *Northwest Indiana Times* as 'a hip, no frills rock'n'roll joint, where bands practically played in the crowd's lap.'

On November 13, Cheap Trick opened for Rush at Rockford Armory.

BUN E. CARLOS *They gave us about six feet of stage.*

Less than a year later, Cheap Trick would headline the same venue. Also booked to appear with Rush was Paris, Bob Welch's post–Fleetwood Mac band, of which Thom Mooney had been a founding member, but Paris were a no-show.

KEN ADAMANY *We booked a string of dates for Paris, but the band ended up canceling all of them.*

Paul Carrack's band Ace (two years removed from their one hit, 'How Long') played instead. Photographer Rich Kwasniewski reunited with the Cheap Trick backstage, and an image he captured of all four standing in a shower stall at the Armory would grace the cover of *Triad* magazine the next September, but printed upside down.

After entertaining a private party in Madison on November 19, Cheap Trick drove deep into the frozen tundra of Wisconsin for an appearance at a tavern in Portage (population 7,800) called the Roost; then ninety miles east for a gig in Port Washington (population 8,700, right on Lake Michigan) at Weiler's Ballroom, 'initially a single log building made from tamarack trees salvaged from a nearby swamp, the facility soon grew to become a world class dance hall,' according to *Historic Ozaukee County-Then And Now.*

DEONE JAHNKE *One of the most memorable Cheap Trick shows I attended was at a crazy old ballroom called Weiler's. We drove the forty or so miles to the show and found about thirty-five people in the house. This at a time when Cheap Trick were packing clubs in the city. And the band came out and did a show fit for a crowd of five hundred. We were so impressed that they cared to play their hearts out for so few people and that they brought professionalism with them whether the crowd was tiny or huge. I think that's really when it struck us that they were going to be big.*

Cheap Trick finished off November with performances at familiar haunts like Flight Of The Phoenix, Night Gallery, Waverly Beach, and Haymakers, plus excursions to Chicago for shows at the Holiday Ballroom and Thirsty Whale.

December 1 marked the infamous appearance of the Sex Pistols on the *Today* program, hosted (not for much longer) by Bill Grundy. The controversy-courting punks were a last-minute replacement for Queen, who blamed Freddie Mercury's dental surgery for their cancelation. Grundy intentionally antagonized the Pistols and their entourage, until finally Steve Jones called him a 'dirty fucker' and 'fucking rotter' on live television. That night, Cheap Trick performed at the Red Lion Inn in Champaign. And the next night? The other Red Lion in Bloomington (an ad in the *Argus* named them 'Chicago's Number 1 band,' while an ad in the *Vidette* named them 'Chicago's Favorite Band').

Cheap Trick headed to Milwaukee for the weekend, performing at the Electric Ballroom, a movie theater that was converted to a dancehall in the fifties, at 26th & State. Within a couple years the club had changed its name to the Palms. Wendy O. Williams was arrested there in 1981. On December 5, Cheap Trick were back at Stone Hearth, where Wally Bryson from The Raspberries' new band Tattoo opened. Thom Mooney was the drummer.

On December 14, Cheap Trick found themselves on the same bill as similarly monikered British hard rockers Dirty Tricks, made up of Kenny Stewart, Terry Horbury, Andy Beirne, and Johnny Fraser-Binnie. Dirty Tricks were supporting the release of their second album, *Night Man*, on Polydor. A friendly rivalry developed based around the similar names, and the evening was playfully dubbed the 'Battle Of The Tricks.'

BUN E. CARLOS *Ken booked them with us at the Stardust in Rockford.*

KEN ADAMANY *I didn't book them! Somebody else—*

BUN E. CARLOS *Somebody booked it! And it was like, We'll see who gets the name Trick …*

KEN ADAMANY *Oh wait a minute, that was at the Stone Hearth, I did book that date.*

Ken still has the Western Union Mailgram he received from Gemini Artists Management in New York on December 10:

```
DIRTY TRICKS CONFIRMS DECEMBER 13 STONE
HEARTH SCALE VERSUS 80 PERCENT OVER 1000
DOLLARS AND DECEMBER 14 TO OPEN FOR CHEAP
TRICKS DECEMBER 14 CONTRACTS TO BE SENT
IMMEDIATELY THANK YOU KEN
```

The 'Battle Of The Tricks' went down at Flight Of The Phoenix, formerly the Stardust Lounge. Dirty Tricks guitarist Johnny Fraser-Binnie (later a member of Rogue Male) recalls the experience less for the rivalry than for the camaraderie.

JOHNNY FRASER-BINNIE *I do remember when we arrived in town getting a message from Rick Nielsen, 'Did we want to meet up?' Of course we did, so he picked us up at our hotel in a GMC motorhome like the racing car teams used to use. Certainly beat our station wagon. He was an absolute gent. He took us to his house to look at his guitar collection. He was obviously proud of it and rightly so. For me, it was like Santa's grotto.*

The gig was well received, the two bands different in style. Cheap Trick had a good following, and I was impressed by their performance and delivery. Obviously watching Rick throughout.

BUN E. CARLOS *We ran into one of those guys in England, years later, and he was like, 'You guys killed us.'*

December 17 and 18 were spent at a place called Luigi's in the suburb of

Chicago Heights. One newspaper ad declared, 'They're Here. The Group You've Been Waiting For.' Another branded the band 'ROCK AT ITS BEST.' And on and on: Quincy, Kenosha, Twin Lakes, Waukesha, and Beloit, for an appearance highlighted by *Lively Times*:

> Cheap Trick will bring their sensational sound and antics to Waverly Beach Wednesday, December 29th. The last show Cheap Trick did at Waverly was definitely a sellout performance. Their sound and show just keep getting better and better. This will be an excellent opportunity to see this great band. Their first album will be out soon and local performances will probably be less frequent as they hit the road to tour.

Cheap Trick bid adieu to 1976 with a New Year's Eve celebration at B.Ginnings (calendars the club had printed for November asked, 'GUESS WHO'S COMING NEW YEARS EVE?' in block letters). A poster for the event called for 'Proper Attire.' The cover ($15 per couple, $8 for singles) included an Italian-style buffet and unlimited champagne, which, according to *Triad* writer Moira McCormick, was 'a bit flat from circulating through that diminutive fountain' and gone by ten o'clock.

> Everyone was in a festive mood, fortunately; they smiled patiently when you stepped on their feet or knocked their drinks to oblivion in your attempts to reach the restroom, but it wasn't long before you realized the conditions were approaching combat proportions. You made a game effort to mingle, but until the tables were cleared from the dance floor during Streetplayer's second set it was Sardinia from one end of the club to the other. Approximately quarter to 1977 the stage darkened. The dance floor filled with Trick fanatics (yourself included). And the excitement. It had to be felt to be believed—it was tangible, unbearable. The entire club was tuned to the point of frenzy like a great clenched fist. Cheap Trick was coming out one by one in the darkness, picking up their instruments, everyone cheering like demons, the stage lights flashing, and then they were exploding.

By now, Matthew Perrin had been added to the permanent road staff, and Rick Nielsen had a special request for his lighting coordinator that evening:

MATTHEW PERRIN *Rick wanted to have sparks flying out of his guitar speakers, and he wanted me to come up with a way that was not using fireworks, so I devised an auto-feeding grinding machine that had welding rods forced down onto it and shot out sparks, but it weighed a ton. We only used it for that night.*

* * *

Up next: two high-profile gigs opening for Queen. Adamany booked the dates with Randy McElrath, whose Daydream Productions brought the British glam phenoms to Wisconsin. Queen's fifth album, *A Day At The Races*, had been on the shelves for a month and just entered the *Billboard* charts at no.36. Both shows were sold out, first at the Mecca Auditorium in Milwaukee on January 13, then at the Dane County Coliseum in Madison on January 14. Thin Lizzy were supposed to open that leg of the tour, but guitarist Brian Robertson injured his hand in a brawl at the Speakeasy Club in London. He was defending his friend Frankie Miller, who'd climbed onstage to jam with a band called Gonzalez and, in his inebriated state, somehow mortally offended one of the band's members, who came at him with a broken bottle in the dressing room afterward. Robertson intervened and came away with arterial and nerve damage to his hand. Injured or not, the bloody Irishman broke the bottle-wielder's leg, and another man's collarbone for good measure. The dressing room brouhaha came to an abrupt conclusion when Robertson was hit over the head with a second bottle. Thin Lizzy drafted in Gary Moore as Robertson's replacement, but not in time for the Wisconsin shows.

Adamany caught wind of this and called McElrath.

KEN ADAMANY *I suggested Cheap Trick as the opener and pestered him with promotional materials. Randy probably forwarded it all to their agent in LA so they would sign off on us for the two dates.*

Brian May told Ira Robbins, 'We were always involved in those decisions.' And he remembered Cheap Trick. 'I personally watched everything they did on those nights, to the detriment of the finer points of my wardrobe … great melodic content set them above most of what was happening on that circuit at that time.'

KEN ADAMANY *Their then manager John Reid and their then booking agent were both there, wearing long camel-hair winter coats.*

Madison-based WIBA-FM spun an advance copy of Cheap Trick's soon-to-be-released debut in its entirety that day, according to a write-up in the *Madcity Music Sheet* on January 18:

Opening the concert, and only announced at the last minute, was Madison's own super heroes of destructo rock&roll CHEAP TRICK. On the eve of their Epic album release, they have secured many excellent concert dates, including dates with QUEEN in Milwaukee and Madison (due to THIN LIZZY cancelling the tour) and with the KINKS at the Auditorium in Chicago. The album is due Jan. 24th, but WIBA-FM was hot on an advance pressing and aired it the evening of the concert. Having to go on without a sound check ('… that's what happens to opening acts …' sez Jolly), CHEAP TRICK played a good sampling including the killer 'Ballad of Violet (sic) TV (Richard Speck).' It was good to see bassist Tom Petersson out there bouncing around the stage, giving Rick Nielsen someone to bounce off of … Bun E. Carlos, the drummer, ended the night in classic Keith Moon fashion with a pair of three foot drumsticks to nearly destroy his set.

Cheap Trick's set:

```
'Speak Now Or Forever Hold Your Peace'
'ELO Kiddies'
'Southern Girls'
'Hot Love'
'Tom's Blues'
'You're All Talk'
'He's A Whore'
'The Ballad Of Richard Speck'
'Goodnight Now'
```

'The Japanese press was there seeing Queen, of course, but really liked us,' Nielsen remembered. 'We didn't know anything about Japan. It might as well have been the moon.'

'After the show, they asked me to write an article, what's it like to tour with Queen,' Nielsen told *Uproxx*. 'I'm so full of crap, I'll write anything. What do I know? We used to make fun of every band, and Queen was one of them.

But we didn't on those two nights.' (On an episode of *In The Studio*, Rick and Robin did admit to making fun of Queen on those nights, in troubling terms.) 'After I wrote the article, it came out in Japan and we started getting fan mail. And there were caricatures of ourselves in the Japanese magazines. We were kind of easy to draw funny.'

Playing with Queen was an exciting opportunity, but Cheap Trick came away dissatisfied with how their crew had handled it.

BUN E CARLOS *For front-of-house sound, we had Jim Girling. We built our own PA and he ran it, and we were killing 'em in clubs, but we got up there with Queen for those two gigs and Jim was out of his league.*

David W. Chandler's review in the *Wisconsin State Journal* was not glowing. 'Openers Cheap Trick have been carefully nurtured from area favorites to the impending release of their first national label album,' he wrote, 'but still mix the stuff of stardom with an awkward lack of clear focus.'

Michael Oosten, who'd organized the Moon Valley concert in 1975, witnessed the Madison show and recalled the sound issues.

MICHAEL OOSTEN *When they came on they sounded like a toy radio at the far corner of a gym. What the heck! I thought. I did not want our biggest local band on their first big Madison gig to sound like crap, so I went to the guy running sound and complained. He explained to me it was Queen's PA and they had given him about a sixth of the board to use and less than half the total power.*

KEN ADAMANY *If memory serves, David Lewis mixed sound for us with an additional FOH guy from Chicago for the Queen shows [meaning Girling may have been replaced earlier]. The extra person did a separate mix with just Bun E.'s drums. Gerry Stickles [Queen's road manager] was none too pleased that we had two men at the soundboard. He questioned every name I presented for passes. He was difficult but accommodating in the end. The same Gerry who was road manager for Hendrix at the Factory shows, and for Steve Miller later on.*

At some point, either after the Queen show or before, soundman Jim Girling (who the band called 'Les Manly,' a nickname obliquely derived from his last name's similarity to 'girly') was unceremoniously dismissed, despite years of service, right when the whole shebang was about to go international, and replaced by Dave Lewis, who owned and operated a Madison PA company.

KEN ADAMANY *I stole Lewis from Ziggy & The Zeu. He was their road manager and sound man.*

Girling declined to speak with me for this book.

Just two weeks later, it was reported in the *Madcity Music Sheet* that Cheap Trick had also parted ways with longtime roadies Ampe and Jolly:

> Cheap Trick's roadies Jolly and Pat Ampe recently went on strike for more respect and money and were let go by the group's management. Both Jolly and Ampe believe their effort was worth more, on both counts, than they were receiving and Adamany's office had no comment. Probably Pat will go to work for a New York group called Starz, featuring former Madcity Bungi band member Richie Ranno. Jolly will be going with the next Kansas tour working for DB Sound out of Chicago.

The crew had tried to unionize, actually asking for a piece of the record deal. It was unprecedented, and Adamany balked. Nielsen had recently found himself a guitar tech named Dave Wilmer, and Wilmer recommended his friend John 'Muzzy' Muzzarell to fill one of the open spots on the crew.

MUZZY *I was working construction, and in the wintertime we got laid off because of the weather, and my buddy Dave Wilmer, who was Rick's guitar guy for twenty years, lived across the street from me and we knew each other, and he goes 'Hey, so what are you doing?' A couple guys he was working with quit the band and he needed some help, he wanted to know if I could drive a truck and if I could set up drums. I wasn't a player of any instrument. I said sure, I could help.*

On January 15, Cheap Trick performed at Rusty Springs (now a Jiffy Lube) in St. Louis, missing the debut of the immediately iconic Conehead characters on *Saturday Night Live*. Nielsen clearly developed an affinity for the Remulakians, so much so that he claimed proprietorship. 'We'd always screw around saying, *We are coneheads.* I know they'll never admit it, but we were sort of the inspiration behind that whole thing,' he told *Scene*.

The rest of January saw Cheap Trick grinding it out at all the old familiar places: Haymaker's, Red Lion, Electric Ballroom, the Brat Stop. Wherever they went, they left it all on the stage. The powers that be at Epic were feeling very optimistic indeed.

At the end of the month, Cheap Trick were summoned to Atlanta to entertain the suits at the annual CBS convention at the Omni Hotel, the timing of which happened to coincide with a slew of terrible winter storms throughout the northeast and Midwest, dangerously cold temperatures, and piles of snow. Carlos and Adamany shared conflicting accounts as to how they made it down to Atlanta.

BUN E. CARLOS *They closed the highway to St. Louis, the interstate. We got on it anyway, drove around the roadblocks, drove to St. Louis, because we had to fly out in the morning. We flew to Atlanta, barely got there.*

Adamany recollects an attempt to drive down in the band's motorhome. They ended up stranded overnight at a church somewhere in southern Illinois, with some sleeping on pews. He was able to communicate the delay to those expecting them in Atlanta via the state-of-the-art Motorola Pulsar mobile phone they had installed in the motorhome the past June.

Either way, they made it to Atlanta just in time.

JIM CHARNE *At the convention every night we had dinner shows where the whole company gets together for banquets, and then there's a show—three or four acts from the labels appear on the stage. There have been memorable, historic shows of talent, like Barbra Streisand coming out and doing a show, Earth, Wind & Fire, Santana. But we had a chance to put Cheap Trick on a show and just had to absolutely take advantage of it, because it was a chance to showcase what we thought was a fabulous band before the whole company. And one little detail about those shows is they were notorious for bands going on and on and on for, like, ninety minutes—two-hour sets, two-and-a-half-hour sets—and so these shows could be endless. They'd go on until the late hours of the night, and the guys from the company—you'd have to get up for early meetings, it's a work event, so sales meetings, production presentations, programming meetings, regional meetings, promotion meetings, and we're sort of thinking about what to do to showcase Cheap Trick in a way that's gonna get people talking. And actually I came up with* *an idea, which Ken completely bought into—we didn't tell anybody else in the company about it at all, it was me and Ken and the band—Cheap Trick went onstage, they did their opening number, they did two numbers, they did their closing number, and they said goodnight and they walked off stage. And we thought that everyone would think this band was so fantastic that this set went by so fast that they couldn't believe it. When in fact it did go by fast—they were offstage in fifteen minutes—and then we said there will be a clamoring for an encore, we know there will, and what they should do is come back and take a bow, no encore. Which they did. They came back, took a bow, standing ovation, raucous reception by the company, and that was it. We were done. Mission accomplished. So there was a huge buzz for that band in the company, and that really led to great support at every level of the field organization and our ability to break the band.*

RON ALEXENBURG *They blew the place away and that helped launch the album.*

Photographs from the event appeared in *Billboard* in February, with a caption that read:

CBS Meeting—Epic recording group Boston, above, is presented a platinum album for Boston at the beginning-of-the-year CBS Records marketing meeting in Atlanta. To the right of the group is Ron Alexenburg, vice president and general manager of Epic & Associated Labels. After a performance by the new Epic group Cheap Trick (below), the group is joined by Bruce Lundvall, president of Columbia Records Division (far left); Alexenburg (rear, center); and Walter Yetnikoff, president of CBS/Records Group (right).

The distinct personalities of all four members are very much on display in the photograph. Rick Nielsen and Bun E. Carlos kneel in front, Rick's mouth askew and his eyes rolled back in his head, just the whites visible. Bun E. smiles, clutching what at first glance appear to be two Louisville Sluggers (his patented giant drumsticks). Robin Zander and Tom Petersson stand behind them with the three executives (Lundvall, Alexenburg, and Yetnikoff). Robin looks like a kid (he was twenty-three). Mr. Tom, ever the charmer, has his arms draped around Alexenburg and Yetnikoff's shoulders. As for Boston, 'These guys eat bands like Boston for breakfast' would be Steve Zepeda's verdict when he reviewed *Cheap Trick* for the *Daily Forty-Niner* in March.

Newly elected US president Jimmy Carter had recently issued a blanket pardon for all Vietnam era draft dodgers. More than fifty-eight thousand young Americans lost their lives in the war, and countless others saw their lives upended. For many, a nightmare was finally over. For Cheap Trick, a dream was coming true. The band's first, self-titled album was about to be released by Epic Records.

KEN ADAMANY *We turned down the first master—we didn't like the way it sounded, and they went back and remastered it. It was done at the Cutting Room then, not at Sterling.*

'To me, a record or a song or whatever is like a movie,' Jack Douglas once pontificated, 'so there are things that are in the forefront and in the rear, but you see all those things when you're watching a movie, and the idea for me is to give a record the depth so that you discover things in a mix, not to flatten out everything and bring it all to the forefront so you hear everything all the time.'

BUN E. CARLOS *We would say what we liked and didn't like, but I remember not having much say in the sequencing.*

Ah, the sequencing …

No sympathy for your symphony...

Which song is the first song on the first Cheap Trick album?

In 1977, the vinyl record was the dominant format—the only format that mattered, really. Sales of long players peaked that year with 344 million sold. Each of those albums had two sides, thus two first songs—the first song on Side One and the first song on Side Two—but the first song on Side One was the first first song, given that an album was a collection of songs arranged in a specific order, i.e. sequenced. Side One (or Side A) was intended to be played first, thus the first song on Side One opened the album and the last song on Side Two (or Side B) closed the album. When done right, an album was meant to be listened to in its entirety, and in the proper order, taking the listener for a ride.

Here's the rub: *Cheap Trick* did not have a Side Two. *Cheap Trick*'s sides were labeled 'Side One' and 'Side A.' It was a prank or a joke, and not even the band's idea. Someone at the label, empowered by the satirical nature of the band, wanted in on the fun. As the label put it, 'The band just hasn't any "B" material.'

So, with a Side One and a Side A, which side was the first side? The back cover clearly answered that question. It all came down to the layout, which, according to graphic designer Paula Scher, was subject to band approval. The list of five songs beginning with 'Hot Love,' labeled 'Side A,' was positioned to the left of and slightly higher than the list of five songs beginning with 'ELO Kiddies,' labeled 'Side One.' That positioning, in and of itself, communicated that the 'Hot Love' side was the first side, the side meant to be played first, making 'Hot Love' the first song on the album. Further proof: upon sliding the record from the sleeve, one discovered that the 'Hot Love' side, Side A, was numbered AL-34400, and the 'ELO Kiddies' side, Side One, BL-34400, indicating that Side One was the B-side. White label promo copies of the album listed Side A on the left (stage right) side of the label and Side One on the right (stage left), also clearly indicating that Side A was the first side and 'Hot Love' the first song.

The compact cassette incarnation, also issued in 1977, left no room for confusion, with 'Side One' printed on the 'Hot Love' side and 'Side Two' on the 'ELO Kiddies' side. Apparently, no one at Epic had the foresight to ensure that the 'no "B" material' concept was carried over to this format. Also, when the brand new cassette was unwrapped and popped into a tape deck, the 'Hot Love' side was cued up to play first. Epic also issued the album on eight-track tape in 1977, and, you guessed it, 'Hot Love' was the first song on the tape. And then, wait for it: when the album came out on compact disc in 1990, 'Hot Love' was track one, 'ELO Kiddies' track six.

But then, in the late nineties, producer Bruce Dickinson was tasked with overseeing a reissue of the album, and he made a shocking discovery. The boxes in which the master tapes had been stored told a different story. It was standard in 1977 for a master tape to be generated for each side of an album. The box for the master tape beginning with 'Hello Kiddies' (how it was spelled on the box) was labeled 'Reel 1 of 2.' The box for the master tape beginning with 'Hot Love,' 'Reel 2 of 2.' The songs were also numbered sequentially; on the 'Hello Kiddies' box the songs were numbered 1–5, and on the 'Hot Love' box they were numbered 6–10. Evidence continued to mount: AL-34400 was written on the 'Hello Kiddies' box, but a ballpoint pen had been used to scribble a B over the A. Even more tellingly, on the 'Hot Love' box the BL was crossed out, with AL written above it. And then, as a final wrinkle, someone wrote at the top of the 'Hello Kiddies' box: 'Called Side 1 on label instead of Side B.' Thanks for muddying the waters!

Clearly, 'ELO Kiddies' was a perfect album opener and 'The Ballad Of Richard Speck' a perfect climax, ending with a gunshot that was supposed to end the album. As Bun E. explained, 'At the end, everyone dies.' A cursory examination of the master tape boxes made it clear that this was the original intention. Dickinson took this to heart and, in consultation with Carlos, made the controversial decision to correct the error. Thus, when the album was reissued on CD with bonus tracks in 1998, 'ELO Kiddies' was made track one, 'Hot Love' track six.

It was then, and only then, that any debate ensued. Before 1998, all evidence available to the public, rightly or wrongly, indicated that 'Hot Love' was the first song on the album. No record buyer would have had any reason to think otherwise. I certainly always thought of 'Hot Love' as the first song. The back cover of the album told me it was.

'Hot Love' also served as a perfect introduction to the band, as JD Morgenstern described it in his review for the *Eagle* in March 1977: 'The album opens [see?] with the kick-tusch rocker "Hot Love." It sets the tone for the rest of the album: emitting an animal-like energy while simultaneously exhibiting a sophisticated musical institution.'

And then there's Doug Pollen's assessment in the *Lubbock Avalanche Journal*: '"Hot Love" opens [again!] this slightly ambivalent disc with the power of a Mack truck going full speed.'

Rick Nielsen's handwritten lyrics, seen on display at Rick's Picks, revealed that at some point he entertained the idea of replacing the line 'hot love will burn your heart' with 'hot love will burn your palms.' As he has admitted, 'Being an only child, you had to learn how to play with yourself.'

The second song on the album was Cheap Trick's brilliant interpretation of 'Speak Now Or Forever Hold Your Peace' by British songsmith Terry Reid. Named for an entreaty from the traditional Christian wedding vow, the phrase does not appear in the song's lyrics.

'We tried to learn that number for about two years,' Bun E. Carlos told *Trouser Press*. 'We had about fifty different ways of doing it. It evolved.' They nailed it, and as a matter of fact the song as heard on the album was laid down entirely live in the studio, with Bun E.'s drums set up in the hallway for a better live sound. A band called Christopher Milk had released their own version of the song on their 1972 album *Some People Will Drink Anything*, but Cheap Trick's version is far superior—and in fact many, including myself, might argue that Cheap Trick's version is superior even to the original.

Up next on the album came a fan favorite, 'He's A Whore.' 'It's always been kind of, not underground, but it's always been kind of like hipsters who liked it,' Nielsen told *AV Club*. He told *Guitar Player*, 'I liked the idea, just the title, so I built it around that.' 'He's A Whore' opens with an instantly recognizable and infectious beat from Carlos. Punky and punchy, it's the kind of song that set Cheap Trick apart from their hard rock contemporaries. 'It's a reversal of roles,' Nielsen told *Nuggets*. 'But you don't have to listen to a Cheap Trick album with a dictionary.'

'I was writing that before *American Gigolo* ever came out,' Nielsen bragged. Paul Schrader's film came out in 1980. Nielsen crowned himself 'the Richard Gere non-lookalike in Illinois.' Jack Douglas seems to have liked recurring themes, and the 'whore' in 'He's A Whore' might have been the same character from 'Hot Love,' wherein the narrator professed to be 'selling this hot love,' even if he was selling it to support his girlfriend, whom he gave it to. Nielsen told *Nuggets* the song 'refers to all sorts of things. Radio station people, etc. Doing things for money. People are whores for money.'

Douglas selected a deep cut for the next song, 'Mandocello.'

BUN E. CARLOS *He heard that and said, 'That should go on the record.' I don't know if Rick played it for him, or maybe I made him a tape: 'Here's all the songs we have.'*

'I think we said, Take a listen to this,' Nielsen remembered. 'You know, we used to do this song, and we probably sat down and goofed around with it. Because I don't think Robin ever worked on that.' It might even have been that Paul Prestopino—an employee at the Record Plant and associate of Jack Douglas's who played 'slide banjo' on 'Last Child' by Aerosmith—just happened to have left his mandocello lying around and Nielsen said, 'Check this out.' Nielsen used Prestopino's mandocello for the recording, having left his own behind in Rockford. The song dates back to the Sick Man Of Europe days, but it was also performed during the new band's very first live set at the Top Deck in Lake Geneva.

BUN E. CARLOS *We learned it with Xeno. I remember we made a tape when we were practicing in the basement of Carlson Roofing. It used to be a minor seventh, and then when we did it on the first album it ends up to be a major seventh, so a bit of the melody got rewritten to sweeten it up a little.*

Rick named the song for the instrument he wrote it on, an oddity he was first exposed to at his parents' store and fiddled around with (pun intended). ('Like fiddling while Rome burns. Hey, one person's having a good time!'—Rick Nielsen). 'I really didn't know the instrument that well and it helped me write the song,' he told Ken Sharp. 'There are a lot of weird and wacky changes in that one.'

The mandocello is an eight-stringed instrument, double-strung like a mandolin but tuned like a cello. 'I've always liked stuff that's tuned low,' Nielsen told Craig Gieck for *Night Sites & Sounds*. He told *Guitar Player* that he liked the way 'the strings vibrate at a different rate than tighter strings. They warble back and forth and make it almost sound like a voice, or an eerie sound.'

PAUL HAMER *In the early days of the twentieth century there was a big mandolin revival, and Orville Gibson took the idea of the violin family and translated it into the mandolin family. So there were different scale lengths, similar to a violin, a viola, a cello, and a stand-up bass, and people started creating these mandolin orchestras where there would only be instruments built for the mandolin family. And they were wildly popular, so there's a lot of photos of mandolin orchestra where collectors go, 'Oh, where could I find that one,' because the photos show all the different instruments that were built. The mandocello has a string length— the easiest way to describe it would be it sits between a guitar string and a bass string, and sits astride that tonal range. So the strings are longer, they're heavier, and they're tuned in duplicate—they're not tuned an octave apart. So it's the same string, same note, twice on each group of four strings, two strings each, so eight strings. And it has a really beautiful, rich sound.*

'They weren't a very popular instrument, so there weren't a lot of them around,' Nielsen told Ira Robbins. 'But it just had such a neat sound. And I never was an acoustic guitar player. I did learn some stuff. I used to be able to play okay, finger-picking kind of stuff. But it was never what I wanted to do. It didn't have enough impact. But when I first played that instrument, it had such a beautiful ... you know, the mandolin has kind of a whiny sound, but this had like that rich sound. And I've always liked orchestra stuff. So then I just wrote a song around it.'

JOL DANTZIG *Gibson had an entire mandolin orchestra. You could get the mandolin, which is the highest pitched one, then the mandola, which was a little bit larger, then the mandocello and then the mandobass. Around the early teens, around the first World War, they would have these mandolin orchestras with all the different sizes and of course Rick knew about that stuff, being his father had the old music store and he was into old instruments.*

Dantzig eventually built Rick an electric mandocello, and Hamer sold another to Daryl Hall (who in July 1977 told Robert Hilburn that 'the groups I'm most into now are new rock bands like Television and Cheap Trick').

JOL DANTZIG *We measured it and copied the scale length and just fabricated one from scratch. I used the same bridge on it that I [eventually] used on the twelve-string bass. The mandocello and the ten-string bass were finished at the exact same time.*

Side A closes with 'The Ballad Of Richard Speck,' the title of which was changed at the record label's request (or demand).

BUN E. CARLOS *They said Richard Speck's victims would sue if we called it 'The Ballad Of Richard Speck,' and they didn't want the album to get injuncted and they didn't want legal fees, and they said if we call it 'Richard Speck' they won't back us. So it really wasn't much of a question. The title had to go.*

KEN ADAMANY *The Lawyers got involved. CBS lawyers.*

Adamany asked the band's own attorney Richard Shelton for an opinion. His response:

Dear Ken,
I have received the memo from CBS' attorney and researched the law in connection with same.
In my opinion, their objection is well taken which leaves two alternatives. First of all, you could attempt to secure a release from Speck, or in the alternative, perhaps you could change the title so that the reference to Speck would not be as specific.

Speck was incarcerated at Stateville Correctional Center in Crest Hill, Illinois, a less than two hour drive from Rockford, but no one volunteered to go visit him and ask for his permission. Instead, they changed the title to 'The Ballad Of TV Violence,' a more timely reference. Searching for an explanation (or excuse) for the dramatic spike in urban violence in the sixties and seventies, Congress conducted hearings and funded research about a phenomenon dubbed 'TV violence.' Studies purported to link real-world aggression to the aggressors having seen similar behavior portrayed on television. In 1972, the Surgeon General officially declared 'TV violence' to be a 'public health problem.' Television was a convenient scapegoat, as described by Tom Shales in a 1979 article for the *Washington Post*:

TV was blamed for much in the 1970s, especially violence in American society. It was claimed (but rejected in court) that an incident depicted in the NBC movie Born Innocent led to an attack on a teen-age girl. It was contended that ABC's telecast of the movie Fuzz inspired juvenile delinquents in Boston to imitate the immolation of winos—just as they had seen it done in the film. And in a landmark Florida trial, a defense attorney argued that his client, a shy teen-age boy, murdered an elderly neighbor because, while robbing her house with friends, he found a gun in a drawer and, conditioned by years of exposure to violent TV cops shows, proceeded to use it. A jury found the boy guilty nevertheless.

The specter of 'TV Violence' still haunted the zeitgeist in 1977, making the change a solid one, even if 'TV violence' was not what the song was supposed to be about. Rather, the song seems to have been written as a sort of empathic attempt at understanding whatever the hell was going on between the ears of a ghoul like Richard Speck, hence Nielsen's assertion more than once from the concert stage that he did not 'condone or condemn' the man. When talking to Ken Sharp, Nielsen philosophized that 'not all bad guys are one hundred percent bad and not all good guys are one hundred percent good.' Okay, maybe Speck was 99.9 percent bad.

Writing for *Phonograph Record* magazine, Cynthia Dagnal described the song as the 'piercing, primal sociopathic screams of a mind unhinged.' She went into even more detail in her article for *Midwest*:

The song was spellbinding: a strange, serious departure. In his trance again, Robin sang the grisly words with an odd detachment. But the climax was electrifying. 'I was a lonely boy!' he cried incessantly until it became a menacing chant of frustration and rage. Then came an ominous warning: 'I'm not the only boy!' The crowd grew still with the grim realization that he had captured something important in his portrayal of this tormented soul, intensified by a macabre twist: those animalistic screams and moans were executed with a stone cold gaze. It was a chilling coup. A touch of the sociopath.

'Of course I'm not saying, *Go out and kill people*,' Nielsen retorted. 'I'm just telling a story like people write books. They write books about murder. They write books about cooking.' For the song, Zander engaged in some Alice Cooper–level role-play. The song depicts an escalation. It builds and builds until it breaks, at which point Zander is howling like a maniac. *Nuggets* described the song's coda as 'acid chaos.'

* * *

'Side One' kicks off with a Junk Shop Glam behemoth called 'ELO Kiddies.' Gary Glitter and Slade in a blender with 'roids and lube. Rodney Bingenheimer reportedly loved the song, spinning it regularly on KROQ before the album even came out. 'I wrote that song with two meanings behind it: one has to do with plagiarism and the group ELO and stuff that people have stolen from them and stuff they've stolen and stuff we steal, and the other meaning is just an introduction,' Nielsen told *I Wanna Be Your Dog*.

BUN E. CARLOS *It wasn't ELO, although we liked The Move and we liked ELO, but it was 'elo. There should have been an apostrophe.*

These kiddies 'lead a life of crime,' which is how they unwind. Not another song about Richard Speck! But wait: 'Hope you didn't get it off the television.' Recurring themes! *Nuggets* described the song as 'fiercely defiant,' with its 'neck-grabbing approach.'

The narrator of 'ELO Kiddies' declares that school is for fools, but the title of the very next song contradicts that edict. 'Daddy Should Have Stayed In High School' opens with Petersson battering his bass, the sounds of children playing in the background. One shouts 'touchdown!' The antihero of the song lurks lecherously outside a school, leering and jeering at the young girls. 'I might even know your daddy' escalates to 'I might even be your daddy.' Nielsen's original handwritten lyrics had 'I might even be' before 'I might even know.' The obvious comedic choice was to swap the lines, which Zander delivers with perfect emphasis on the word be. Wanting 'more than a kiss' means whipping, spanking, and grabbing. Who is doing what in these scenarios, and how old

February 11, 1976

Mr. Jack Douglas
c/o Copley Plaza Hotel #529
Copley Square
Boston, MA

RE: CHEAP TRICK

Dear Jack!

The group and I are most enthused over the possibility
of your being involved in our project. We look forward
to meeting with you on March 14 in Waukesha, Wisconsin,
and will make arrangements from this office to have
you flown in and driven to the club.

As we discussed earlier today, I will speak with you
by telephone late next week.

Thank youuffery mueh for your interest.

Yours truly,

Ken Adamany

KA/jn
ATW/76

DANCE
TONITE 8-12
"FRIENDS"
SAT. "EL REY and the NIGHT BEATS"
SUN. "CHEAP TRICK"
COMING
WED.   "CIMMERON SHOW REVUE"

^ FREE BEER 7-8
SUNSET BOWL

TOP LEFT A carbon copy of the original
letter that was sent to Jack Douglas.
Courtesy of Ken Adamany.

TOP RIGHT Rick at Night Gallery—note
the wrecked ceiling tile above him.
Courtesy of Kim Schlater.

ABOVE An advertisement from the
Waukesha Freeman for the band's
appearance at Sunset Bowl on the
Sunday night Jack Douglas attended.

LEFT The band posing offstage at Flight
Of The Phoenix, with Hank Ransome
behind Rick, July 1976. *Photo by
Sharon (Prochaska) Milway.*

ABOVE Double drummers! Summer 1976. *Both photos by Rich Kwasniewski.*

RIGHT Ads for five shows around Wisconsin, at Wonder Bar, Twin Lakes, opening for Freddie King, July 1975 (note that Silver Fox, featuring Craig Myers, Joe Sundberg, and Chip Greenman from Grim Reapers/Fuse, along with Rick Pemberton, performed at the same venue just a few days earlier); Sammy G's Circus, Kenosha, Christmas 1975; Humpin' Hanna's, Milwaukee, April 1975; the Horny Bull, Appleton, June 1976; and JD's White Elephant, Monroe, February 1976.

OPPOSITE A set of advertisements featured in the March 12, 1977 issue of *Record World* magazine.

MEET A CHEAP TRICKSTER.

He's Rick Nielsen. Rick has always wanted to be a cartoon character He abandoned his plans to fulfill this lifelong ambition, however, to play guitar in a compelling new American rock band called Cheap Trick. We're all grateful he did. Producer Jack Douglas described Rick as the best writer he's ever worked with.

**CHEAP TRICK.
ONLY ROCK AND ROLL
COULD BRING THEM TOGETHER.
ON EPIC RECORDS
AND TAPES.**

MEET A CHEAP TRICKSTER.

He's Bunezuela Carlos. Bun E. to his family. Bun E. is the drummer in a compelling new American rock band called Cheap Trick. Bun E. ignored his mother's plans to "See Venezuela first" and left hearth and home to journey with the group on their tour of America's clubs, bars and bowling alleys.

**CHEAP TRICK.
ONLY ROCK AND ROLL.
COULD BRING THEM TOGETHER.
ON EPIC RECORDS
AND TAPES.**

MEET A CHEAP TRICKSTER.

He's Robin Zander. He's impeccable and he has a nice smile. Robin is the lead singer of a compelling new American rock band called Cheap Trick. He and his fellow Cheap Tricksters spent countless days and nights on the road—slamming Rock and Roll in bars, bowling alleys and warehouses—in preparation for this, their first album.

**CHEAP TRICK.
ONLY ROCK AND ROLL
COULD BRING THEM TOGETHER.
ON EPIC RECORDS
AND TAPES.**

MEET A CHEAP TRICKSTER.

He's Tom Petersson. Wide-eyed and otherworldly, he creates auras wherever he goes. Tom plays the bass guitar in a compelling new American rock band called Cheap Trick.

**CHEAP TRICK.
ONLY ROCK AND ROLL
COULD BRING THEM TOGETHER.
ON EPIC RECORDS
AND TAPES.**

RIGHT AND BELOW Opening for Peter Frampton at the Summerfest grounds, Milwaukee, Wisconsin, August 21, 1976. Roadie Patrick Ampe can be seen squatting at the far side of the stage.

OPPOSITE Backstage at Frampton show with Ken Adamany (top, Rick Nielsen walking away in the background). *All photos by Rich Kwasniewski.*

OPPOSITE AND ABOVE In the shower at Rockford Armory before opening for Rush, November 13, 1976.

LEFT Tom and Wheel posing 'backstage' at Grant Field in Atlanta, before Cheap Trick went on as surprise guests at the Dog Day Rock Fest, which also featured Foreigner, Heart, Atlanta Rhythm Section, and Bob Seger, September 3, 1977. *All photos by Rich Kwasniewski.*

ABOVE AND LEFT Rick and his babies.
Both photos by Rich Kwasniewski.

are they? Crazily enough, this is one of the very first songs Rick Nielsen wrote for this new, post–Sick Man Of Europe project.

Up next came the only song from the Ardent demos to pass the Jack Douglas smell test: 'Taxman,' now called 'Taxman Mr. Thief.' Tom Petersson told *Relix* magazine in 1980 that the song was inspired by 'Dancing With Mr. D,' the first song on The Rolling Stones' 1973 album *Goats Head Soup*. And yet, it's The Beatles who are referenced. 'The line was he's got no feelings, he ain't human,' Nielsen told *Melody Maker*. 'And [Tom] always thought it was like the Beatles, he ain't human. So I thought, That sounds better, we'll use it.'

Writing for the *Eagle*, J.D. Morgenstern doled out some low praise, categorizing the song as 'intelligible social commentary.' Obviously it was, at least in part, an homage to George Harrison's 'Taxman,' the opening track from The Beatles' 1966 album *Revolver*. The month before The Beatles recorded 'Taxman,' Harold Wilson, whose Labour government levied a 95 percent 'supertax' on the wealthy, was re-elected.

Britain's tax rate for its top earners peaked at 99.25 percent during World War II, before dropping to around 90 percent during the fifties and sixties; then, in 1971, Ted Heath's conservative regime lowered it to 75 percent. In 1974, the year that Rick Nielsen wrote his song, that top rate rose to 83 percent. When Harrsion wrote his song, Ted Heath was the leader of the Conservative opposition to Harold Wilson. By the time Nielsen wrote his song, Heath was Prime Minister. Nielsen lifted the word 'Heath' from The Beatles' song, presumably as a symbol of 'government.' 'Thief' basically rhymed with 'Heath,' so that worked. Ted Heath was actually a talented musician who had attended Oxford on a music scholarship. After serving as an artillery commander during World War II, he was elected to parliament in 1950, then Prime Minister in 1970. Monty Python's Flying Circus lampooned Heath's peculiar way of speaking in a sketch called 'Teach Yourself Heath,' a recording of which was distributed as a flexi-disc with a December 1972 issue of *Zig Zag* magazine.

It was John Lennon's idea to namecheck Wilson and Heath in the song. Harrison's original lyric was 'Anybody got a bit of money?' That was replaced with the Wilson/Heath chant. Paul McCartney played the guitar solo. *Rolling Stone* described the song as 'skeleton funk,' citing 'Harrison's choppy fuzz-toned guitar chords moving against an R&B dance beat.'

If Harrison's song was snotty, Nielsen's was aggressive. The taxman in Rick's song is looking for a 'run-in,' or, according to Merriam-Webster, an altercation. J.D. Morgenstern pointed out that 'the band's obsession with moola may be wishful thinking.' Cheeky bastard. 'I got in trouble with "Taxman,"' Nielsen told the *Illinois Entertainer*. 'The only people that really listened to the lyrics were the people at the IRS because I got audited every year for about five years. They didn't like that song.'

'Cry Cry' is the only original song on *Cheap Trick* not written solely by Rick Nielsen. Zander and Petersson are also credited. The song is a slow groove with an amazing hook on the chorus. The band nailed the basic track on the very first take, a moment Nielsen cited as his favorite in the studio.

Side A closes with 'Oh Candy,' Nielsen's tribute to photographer Marshall Mintz, whose nickname was derived from his initials. 'Here was a guy who committed suicide, and I was asking him why,' Nielsen explained. It is a skillfully written song. Nielsen explores his own very personal feelings about what happened to his friend, while at the same time leaving the song open to interpretation. Many probably assumed, if they were not listening too closely, that the song was about a girl named Candy. 'Nobody wants to hear about some older guy that I knew. I just tried to tell the story in such a way that as many people as possible could identify with it,' Nielsen explained.

In April of 1977, less than two years after Mintz took his own life, Epic released an alternate version of 'Oh Candy' (with a different vocal take from Robin Zander) as Cheap Trick's very first single, an understandable choice in terms of melody and production. As *Cashbox* magazine stated, 'Jack Douglas's 1977 "wall of sound" production lends character to the endlessly reverberating harmonies.'

Tom Petersson had mixed feelings about the recording. Douglas convinced him to use a borrowed Precision for the track instead of his trusty Thunderbird ('it was too rough'), and plugged directly into the board. Tom deemed the results 'kind of weak.' Regardless of those reservations, it was a catchy song, at least on the surface, even if a darkness lurked beneath. Alas, the single was not destined for the pop charts, especially with 'Daddy Should Have Stayed In High School' on the B-side.

In the end, Douglas's 'sociopolitical' intentions yielded an album about death, sex, and money, populated by gigolos, perverts, and criminals. An additional album's worth of material was recorded, to varying degrees of completion. 'Go Go Girls' and 'Disco Paradise' cannot have been seriously considered for inclusion on the album. The former was a character study, but of the worst kind of character.

BUN E. CARLOS *'Here's a song with a redneck singing it.' But you couldn't explain that on the record.*

It is important to note that all three of what would become Cheap Trick's signature songs and concert staples—'I Want You To Want Me,' 'Surrender,' and 'Dream Police'—were attempted at the Record Plant. It is not surprising that 'I Want You To Want Me' did not make the final cut. It would not have fit on the album. For some reason, neither 'Surrender' nor 'Dream Police' even made it past basic tracks. The songs were held over for future use, as were 'You're All Talk' and 'Lookout.' Again, Douglas had a certain kind of album in mind.

'Jack Douglas is great,' Tom Petersson told Ken Sharp. 'He'd put little touches on things. Little stuff you'd hear in headphone mixes like a triangle on there and what's that over in the corner? You know, he loved all that sort of stuff. And he was a bass player himself, so he loves bass, and that was a big part of our sound. We're a small four-piece group. He just liked the way we played and the way we sounded and he just brought out the best in us.'

JOHN MASINO *I think they really recreated the raw sound and energy of the band.*

SAM GINSBERG *It's just a killer album. I have it on my iPhone. I listen to it when I'm on the elliptical machine. It's just a great album. It really is. Some bizarre lyrics. He's a bizarre guy. He sent me a Christmas card they all signed and it said, 'I don't care what Jack says, you're the tits. Mentally yours, Rick.'*

20

More than a hundred juicy poses...

'Here is a witty, musically impressive, heavy metal foursome that Epic and ICM believe in enough to put substantial resources behind ... CBS, through its subsidiary, Epic Records, has anointed them for stardom. A reported $300,000 has been spent in promotion alone.'

Something was brewing, as Dave Zimmerman noted in his article for Rockford's *Sunday* magazine on April 10, 1977 (excerpted above). The powers that be had greenlit a generous marketing budget for Cheap Trick, as predicted by *Billboard* in March: 'You can expect major merchandising and touring support on this release.'

JIM CHARNE *There was a lot of enthusiasm for the band at the label. The Epic promotion department was just behind this band 500 percent.*

Billboard highlighted the hype machine again in May: 'Tom Genetta [sic] worked with a local record retailer near the campus of the Univ. of Wisconsin at Madison to plug the group Cheap Trick. His plan, which drew crowds, was to put performing jugglers and magicians in the record store window. Alongside was a sign asking, *Is this a Cheap Trick?*'

TOM GENETTI *This was* my band. *My favorite band. So it was easy for me to blow it up big and I tried to do everything I could.*

Genetti, who did local marketing for Epic, was present at the Stone Hearth on June 29, 1976, the night Steve Popovich agreed to sign Cheap Trick.

JIM CHARNE *There was a huge buzz for that band in the company and that led to great support at every level of the field organization. They were completely original, a breath of fresh air. They were not a genre band, believe me, we had plenty of genre bands.*

RON ALEXENBURG *They were fun. They were different. When you look at Cheap Trick and you look at the personality of the band, the fun that my people were having with them, the promotion department loved them.*

The team at Epic naturally tapped into the humor and absurdity Cheap Trick projected. 'Tongue, meet cheek' was the prevailing dynamic, including when staff writer Eric Van Lustbader was tasked with writing a band biography for the album's inner sleeve.

ERIC VAN LUSTBADER *The band and I sat down together and sketched out the fake bios for all of them, then I sat down and wrote.*

According to Van Lustbader, Rick Nielsen was 'born in Chicago, but certainly spent little time there,' and Tom Petersson was born in Sweden and grew up 'somewhere in the hinterlands of America, under somewhat mysterious circumstances.' Rick and Tom's supposed first meeting took place in Europe, after which they commenced 'wandering through Germany, Italy, England, and Spain, blowing amps and minds with astonishing frequency.' It was supposedly not until Rick and Tom finally settled in the south of France, 'amidst a warm sunny clime, nubile bodies, and a plethora of expatriot [sic] American musicians,' that they finally met Robin Zander, 'the thin man with a thousand voices—some say he is related to Lon Chaney—was born in either Boston or Kansas City, depending on which day you approach him,' and Bun, 'short for Bunezuela,' who hailed from Venezuela.

It was a barrage of hyperbole.

When asked about his contemporaneous reaction to this curious rewriting of history, founding member Xeno remarks that 'there were a few spilled coffees.' Hamer's Jol Dantzig describes the sculpting of mystery as 'rock'n'roll propaganda.' Robin Zander's former partner Brian Beebe observes that 'they invented a mystique.' Cary Baker described it as 'blatant subterfuge' in *Lively Times*. Many of the fans back home were bewildered and confused by what fan Deone Jahnke calls 'the ridiculous background stories printed on the dust jacket.'

DEONE JAHNKE *Having seen them for years scrabbling up the club circuit, like regular hardworking Midwesterners, we thought it was kind of foolish.*

But when it came to rock'n'roll's place in the popular music landscape, much had changed between 1974 and 1977. In many ways, Cheap Trick were suddenly a square peg (glam rock/hard rock) for a round hole (punk/new wave). The band's oddball image, more than anything, helped bridge the gap. Stunts like the fake bio played a role.

BUN E. CARLOS *Eric Van Lustbader's bio created this mass confusion. For years we had to go along with it.*

When asked about Van Lustbader by *Sounds*, Nielsen equivocated. 'He had dark hair as I remember, and a funny name,' he said, 'so I'm not sure how real he actually was, if you know what I mean.' When challenged over such obfuscation by *Rolling Stone*, he bristled. 'That bio was written by a writer, you know,' he said. 'We didn't have our names at the bottom of the thing.' Rick later claimed on *In The Studio* that they 'told him the truth but nobody believed it, so we had to go back a second time and do a bio and then of course we lied and now that's history. It's a better story.'

The manufactured intrigue dovetailed nicely with the confounding visuals, a dynamic Daisann McLane from *Rolling Stone* acknowledged:

'Isn't it much more interesting this way?' Rick asked me last year, after I'd interviewed him for a half-hour and gotten a half-hour of quick quips, fantastic fibs, and not-so-serious stories. I had to agree. As every performer knows, the best way to keep them entertained is to keep them guessing.

In terms of serving up ballyhoo to the press, Cheap Trick exhibited minimal hesitation. Tom told interviewer Dierdre Wilson that he was a magician who loved chemistry. 'Tom used to be a great ballroom dancer,' Rick added. Cynthia Dagnal was told that Bun E. Carlos's hobbies included 'ballroom dancing and shallow relationships.' Nielsen cryptically remarked to the *Van*

Nuys Valley News that 'some of the group could be said to have sordid pasts.' *Rolling Stone* was somehow given the impression that Robin Zander was born in Fairbanks, Alaska (Van Lustbader's bio claimed 'Boston or Kansas City'), and Elizabeth Reich reported in the *Register* that Bun E. Carlos was 'a veteran of twenty years or more of drumming.' So he turned professional when he was six?

Epic promotional materials oscillated between playful and sardonic. Consider the script for a radio commercial the label produced, wherein a coed arrives home for a weekend visit with the entire band in tow:

> Mom, Dad, meet Cheap Trick. Robin's the lead singer, isn't he adorable? Tom Petersson plays the bass guitar and creates auras. And Rick was a cartoon character before he joined the group. And this is Bunezuela. He was named after a country in South America I think. They've played in bars and bowling alleys and even warehouses and they've got an album out!

An elaborate 'popup' promo pamphlet tagged the band as 'highly unconventional, to couch it in a euphemism.' An advertisement in the *Chicago Tribune* in February was more to the point, declaring Cheap Trick's music to be 'explosive, driving, unpredictable hard rock,' which they slammed out with a vengeance. An ad in the *Village Voice* in March proclaimed that 'together they spent countless days and nights on the road, slamming rock'n'roll in bars, bowling alleys and warehouses, preparing for this, their first album.'

That same month, an elaborate series of ads in *Record World*—including four individual ads, one for each member—called Cheap Trick a 'compelling new rock band.' The hype was a lot to live up to: unconventional and compelling, while simultaneously explosive and slamming? Another page in the same issue of *Record World* folded open to reveal the entire Cheap Trick album cover with an effusive write-up on the flap:

> It's never happened like this! It could only happen to them because there's nothing else like them. In Columbus, Ohio, 'Cheap Trick' was reported high up in the Top Ten salesmakers solely as a result of in store play. In Los Angeles, disc jockey, impresario, and tastemaker Rodney Bingenheimer reports that he has never received so many phone calls for an album. As a

result of Rodney's enthusiasm, LA sales are building, building, building. And in Indianapolis, no two of the six hundred patrons who witnessed Cheap Trick's in-store appearance/performance were able to agree on what they saw. But they all agreed that whatever it was, it was great. These are not merely isolated, unrelated incidents. They are indicative, in their own peculiar way, of the unusual but highly favorable reaction that is meeting the unusual but highly remarkable Cheap Trick.

Another set of four ads (again, one for each member) was interspersed throughout an April issue of *Circus*, proclaiming, 'Only rock'n'roll could bring them together.' Robin Zander was described as 'impeccable and he has a nice smile,' while Tom Petersson was 'wide-eyed and other-worldly.' Rick Nielsen 'met a lot of pen-pals during the group's cross-country odyssey,' and Bun E. Carlos's 'forebears' were 'instrumental in building the Panama Canal.'

The marketers at Epic were far from the only creative types to be seduced by the Cheap Trick muse. Over the course of the late seventies, journalists and critics from across the country and around the world employed a boundless plethora of adjectives to describe Cheap Trick's music:

'… deliciously unsettling.' *Lively Times*
'… calculated weirdness.' *Green Bay Press Gazette*
'… anglometallic neurosis.' *Sacramento Bee*
'… madcap fantasy.' *Triad*
'… sheer unorthodoxy.' *Triad*
'… elusively unorthodox.' *Lively Times*
'… self-consciously cute.' *Minneapolis Star*
'… dynamically zany.' *Grooves*
'… aggressively snide.' *Circus*
'… smug sassiness.' *Circus*
'… controlled violence.' *Daily Collegian*
'… disciplined aggression.' *Daily Collegian*
'… rebellious chop-chop.' *Arizona Republic*
'… rip-roaring energy.' *Berkeley Gazette*
'… barely controlled schizophrenia.' *Rolling Stone*
'… warped vagabond visions.' *Crawdaddy*
'… raw-edged snarl.' *LA Times*

'… subtle zone of disorientation.' *NME*

'… denizens of the absurd.' *Triad*

'… punky virtuosos.' *Eagle*

'… new wave extremism.' *Spectrum*

'… constant sense of imminent explosion.' *Daily Collegian*

'… evoking strange nightmarish worlds.' *Phonograph Record*

'… an uneasy assault.' *Arizona Republic*

'… brain damage music.' *Tempo Music*

'… a breath of fresh carbon monoxide.' *NME*

'… hard driving pulsations.' *Daily Collegian*

'… teen cataclysm rock.' *Billboard*

'… obnoxious metal-rock.' *Kansas City Star*

'… theatrical heavy pop-rock.' *Cash Box*

'… hard menacing rock that occasionally blows you a kiss.' *LMC Experience*

'… biff-boom-bam rock music.' *Buffalo Courier-Express*

'… upbeat rock powerhouse.' *Vancouver Sun*

'… zooming, frantic, gutsy, riff-laden rock.' *LA Times*

'… ear-buzzing, instinctive rock.' *George Burazer*

'… raw, unbridled rock.' *Fort Worth Star Telegram*

'… no-jive power rock.' *United Press International*

'… taut, compellingly powerful hard rock.' *NME*

'… exuberant, well-played rock.' *Detroit Free Press*

'… rip-snorting rock'n'roll laced with wit.' *Cincinnati Enquirer*

'… hard as nails rock'n'roll.' *Record Mirror*

'… mean kind of rock.' *Vancouver Sun*

'… energetic rock.' *Daily Breeze News-Pilot*

'… rollicky rock.' *Plain Dealer*

'… slapstick rock.' *Williamsburg Flat Hat*

'… highly invigorating rock'n'roll.' *LA Times*

'… destructo rock&roll.' *Madcity Music Sheet*

'… monolithic destructo crotch-rockers.' *Lively Times*

'… chrome-searing.' *Melody Maker*

'… mold-shattering.' *Van Nuys Valley News*

'… fuzz tempered.' *Variety*

'… devastatingly talented.' *Winnipeg Free Press*

'… loud and crashing.' *Tempo Music*

'... frenzied and ferocious.' *LA Times*

'... musical skylarking.' *Morning Call*

'... heavy metal harmonizing.' *Des Moines Tribune*

'... heavy metal pop.' *Zig Zag*

'... hard-edged pop.' *Crawdaddy*

'... progressive pop.' *Capital Times*

'... minirock symphony.' *Chicago Daily News*

'... unadulterated rock hysteria.' *Circus*

'... quite intelligent heavy metal.' *Record Mirror*

'... planned professionalism and utter chaos.' *SunRise*

'... sometimes zany, but never boring.' *Performance*

'... fun, zany, musically powerful.' *Miami Herald*

'... the rock is raunchy, the sound is greasy.' *Star News Pasadena*

'... a delirious commitment to rock's raunchiest traditions.' *Chicago Daily News*

'... a cruncher yet crystalline in melodic delivery.' *Prodigal Sun*

'... melodic to menacing to melodic again.' *Phonograph Record*

'... slams hard and intriguingly at the visceral midsection.' *Daily Independent Journal*

'... unsubtle, but good gut music.' *Nuggets*

'... a bit outlandish.' *Rock Spectacular*

'... devil-may-care tunes.' *Cincinnati Enquirer*

'... sarcastic, smart, nasty, powerful, tight, casual.' *Trouser Press*

'... sharp punch and wit.' *Los Angeles Times*

'... amusingly entertaining.' *Los Angeles Free Press*

'... adolescent slant.' *Berkeley Gazette*

'... zany four-man aggregation.' *Star Tribune*

'... a formidable aggregation of playing talent.' *Winnipeg Free Press*

'... hard rock candy for sweet-toothed schoolkids.' *Bay Area Reporter*

'... truly crazy, but such nice sounds.' *Daily Tribune*

The critical reaction was almost universally enthusiastic and well-articulated. Charles M. Young, who championed punk rock at *Rolling Stone*, observed in his review that 'these guys play rock'n'roll like Vince Lombardi coached football: heavy emphasis on the basics with a strain of demented violence.' As for the members themselves, 'Cheap Trick not only sounds like their attendant forgot to lock their cages, they look like it, too.' Young's conclusion: 'Catch them before Nurse Ratched slices open their frontal lobes.' Writing for *Rolling Stone* two years later, Daisann McLane described *Cheap Trick* succinctly as 'a tour de force of heavy metal rock'n'roll; raw, loud guitar tones offset by witty songs and arrangements.'

Tom Butch from the *Daily Collegian* hailed *Cheap Trick* as 'a brilliant first album from a band with a bright future and it is a bright spot within the void into which pure, unblemished rock has fallen. ... The energy level seems to build throughout and each song offers slight theme and melody variations, or twists that keep the listener in constant anticipation of songs to come and in the end they leave you at once satiated and thirsting for more.'

Steve Buress declared in *Dark Star* that the album was 'the product of a raw band stoned senseless on their own electricity, energy and life.' The *Winnipeg Free Press* proclaimed *Cheap Trick* to be 'one of these all too rare instant hard rock classics. ... It's the kind of record which sounds even better the 200th time you hear it.'

Writing for *Phonograph Record*, Cynthia Dagnal branded the band 'Beatles with balls ... a brash young hybrid of American punk sass and British inventiveness.'

'People compare us to The Beatles, which is flattering, since they were the best,' Rick Nielsen reflected to the *Associated Press* in 1979, 'but you can't sit around and listen to old Beatles records if you want to know what's going on today. Because as neat as it was, it's old news. Good songs or bad songs, they're old songs.'

Ira Robbins referenced The Beatles within his *Creem* review, but put forth that *Cheap Trick* betrayed 'a sinister streak that seems to be more anti-Beatles than anything.' When he reviewed the album for *Trouser Press*, Robbins predicted that the band was 'destined for something great.'

Gerry Barker from the *Fort Worth Star Telegram* agreed, and he explained why:

'Fresh' is a term seldom applied to a hard rock group, since most of the ground in the medium has been explored and re-explored countless times. But there is a fresh quality to Cheap Trick. It may be their enthusiasm or their avant-garde appearance, but whatever the reason, fresh is something hard rock fans are hungry for.

Cheap Trick sold about 150,000 copies, a respectable number for such an unapologetic collection of unrelenting hard rock. Mainstream appeal proved elusive even with far less alienating material. When the European arm of CBS declined to release the album in the UK, Stiff Records, a defiantly successful independent label steeped in punk and new wave, offered to put it out. I guess it was 'worth a fuck.' The offer was rebuked, but a thumbs-up from the likes of Stiff seems to have been what Jack Douglas, who admitted he 'was hoping that it would hit the college circuit and they would get it,' had in mind. When asked about the album's lackluster sales by *Trouser Press*, Tom Werman surmised that *Cheap Trick* 'was too harsh for most people.'

Writing for *Lively Times*, Cary Baker diagnosed the album as a 'showcase of the extremes' but noted that 'critics of the uneven presentation detected acumen beneath the novelty.' Reflecting on the fate of the album in 1980, *Relix* magazine concluded that it was 'so raw and ragged that the subtleties and hidden meanings, to say nothing of the melodies, were too subtle and too hidden.' Richard Riegel put forward a similar hypothesis in *Creem*, noting that 'the band's unflinching logic was just a bit too logical for some unfortunately large segments of the rock public.' According to Daisann McLane, 'Critics liked *Cheap Trick*'s intelligent rock'n'roll, but the album never found its audience.'

The album did find its audience, just not a wide audience. Why not? One might argue that it was *too good*. As Bruce Meyer asserted, the band stood 'prominently apart from the current run of technically excellent but utterly unimaginative groups.' Unfortunately, in terms of record sales, standing apart rarely trumped being unimaginative. Cheap Trick (and *Cheap Trick*) proved impossible to pigeonhole. Case in point: a pair of references published exactly one week apart in the *Ottawa Journal* described them as 'a punk rock band' on July 8 and 'heavy metal specialists' on July 15. Similarly, Malcolm Dome referenced both a 'heavy metal bite' and a 'melodic inventiveness.' *Melody Maker* simply gave up: 'File under heavy metal or was it aberrant pop amped up to a studio-stun level with a strange strain of demented irony? They can be hot and nasty as well as gentle and perceptive.'

Renowned curmudgeon Lester Bangs missed the point entirely, dismissing the band as 'packaged.' Packaged by who? The label? Ha! Bangs skewed cynical, but he was way off. His crabby verdict: 'They couldn't write a song to save themselves from being buggered by a moose.' Did he even listen to the album? At least Grumpy McGrumpster's semi-scathing review culminated with a self-aware mea culpa: 'Maybe I'm getting bitter. Somebody, somewhere, is bound to write a story claiming that this crew is the best rock group to slop down the pike since Cream waved goodbye. Not me.'

Cream broke up in 1968.

* * *

Cheap Trick's image, like their music, was overt and memorable, if not confusing. Ira Robbins remarked that, 'visually they look as related as a police lineup.' J.D. Morgenstern claimed in the *Eagle* that 'by their looks alone, Cheap Trick appears to be just another wild bunch of post-adolescent, anti-social, pizzanos and portnoys.' That clears it up. Writing for the *Los Medanos College* student newspaper, Art Taylor declared Cheap Trick 'a bizarre collection of bizarre people. They ain't punk. They ain't normal. And they ain't wholesome.' The disparate presentation telegraphed to the listener that they were likely to discover a bit of chaos between the grooves. As veteran scribe Robert Hilburn put it, the band's 'off-center personnel' refused to hold to 'a single, dog-eared stance.'

Writing for *Circus*, Salley Rand offered an example of the kind of reaction the band could elicit from the uninitiated. 'Pulling up to the Arizona Biltmore after a successful Phoenix gig, the Tricksters hopped out fast and smiling. The bellman took one offhand look and slurped, What's that? Two guys look like rock stars, but the other two look like wrecked trucks.'

Considering the uninhibited verbosity writers and critics unleashed while describing the band's music, it's hard to believe they had even more fun describing Rick Nielsen:

'… unashamed jester.' *Zig Zag*
'… unabashed loon.' *Triad*
'… consummate lunatic.' *Trouser Press*
'… quintessential klutz.' *Lexington Leader*
'… screwball mastermind.' *Galveston Daily News*
'… indescribably bizarre.' *Omaha World Herald*
'… craftily wacky.' *Miami Herald*
'… extremely irritating.' *Record Mirror*
'… zany self-advertisement.' *LA Weekly*

'… ludicrous walking advert.' *NME*

'… textbook nerd.' *Tallahassee Democrat*

'… semi-sane.' *Trouser Press*

'… live-wire goof.' *Melody Maker*

'… goof in a beanie.' *Decatur Daily Review*

'… wiry, short-haired kook.' *Plain Dealer*

'… bent creator.' *Detroit Free Press*

'… aging batboy.' *The Province*

'… costume engineer.' *Creem*

'… inmate of Bedlam.' *Lebanon Daily News*

'… character out of Dostoevsky.' *Howie Klein*

'… Dr. Demento reject.' *Neil K. Citrin*

'… Mr. Personality Personified.' *Circus*

'… cute in a perverse sort of way.' *Rock Spectacular*

'… crazed character like Curly from *The Three Stooges* or Phil Silvers from *Sgt Bilko*.' *NME*

'… a schizoid, twelve-year-old Art Carney.' *News Journal*

'… resembling Ed Norton of the Honeymooners.' *Journal-Star*

'… resembles Dizzy Dean and Gomer Pyle.' *Oshkosh Advance Titan*

'… a real jerk in hardcore ways that Steve Martin never dreamed of.' *Lexington Leader*

'… abandoned his plans to become a cartoon character to join the group.' *Village Voice*

'… a twin homage to Bing Crosby and Bugs Bunny.' *Dark Star*

'… does more ridiculous things than Beppo the trained seal.' *Trouser Press*

'… Moose lifted from the pages of the Archie comics.' *Berkeley Gazette*

'… Jughead look-alike.' *Triad*

'… hyperthyroid hybrid of comic book Archie, the Deadest Dead End Kid and Bill Haley.' *Triad*

'… hyperthyroid Donald Sutherland.' Epic promo

'… over-amphetamined reject from *Our Gang*, a Spanky gone shanky.' *Drummer*

'… making demented, Eddie Cantor eyes at the adoring crowd.' *Midwest*

'… darts about the stage as the late Groucho Marx used to do.' *Plain Dealer*

'… Tony Randall after rock'n'roll shock treatment.' *Sounds*

'… an image reminiscent of Leo Durocher.' *Ballroom Blitz*

'… Laurel and Hardy antics.' *Record Mirror*

'… looks like a cross between Stan Laurel and Bill Haley.' *Lively Times*

'… moves like Jack Benny.' *Rolling Stone*

'… moves his eyes like old Ben Turpin.' *Plain Dealer*

'… looks like Eddie Haskel.' *Daily Breeze/News Pilot*

'… dressed like a cast member of *Leave It To Beaver*.' *San Francisco Chronicle*

'… dresses like a refugee from *Howdy Doody*.' *Daily Breeze/News Pilot*

'… dresses like a high school drop-out.' *Fort Worth Star Telegram*

'… delicate lack of fashion.' *Creem*

'… seems to have stopped buying clothes in 1955.' *Rockford Morning Star*

'… someone we would have all made fun of in the fourth grade.' *Buffalo Courier Express*

'… dopey look, dopey mugging and dopey movements.' *Variety*

'… weirdo expressions.' *Nuggets*

'… left field calisthenics.' *NME*

'… tripping merrily across the stage.' *SunRise*

'… bobs and jiggles like the hula doll in a cabby's rear window.' *Rolling Stone*

'… throwing himself around the stage like a hooked Marlin.' *Sunday Magazine*

'… aping with manic glee the moves of every narcissistic guitarist.' *Rockford Morning Star*

'… so energetic he could kick himself repeatedly in the head.' *Austin Daily Texan*

'… looks and acts like a complete nut.' *News-Pilot*

'… almost-humorous, obnoxious.' *Journal-Star*

'… spiderlike-fingers and wild-eyed leers.' *Michigan Daily*

'… windmill in a hurricane.' *Music Beat*

'… architect of the lunacy.' *Berkshire Sampler*

'… frantic stage antics.' *Crawdaddy*

'… could have passed for a circus clown.' *Scottsdale Daily Progress*

'… shoulders locked in a perpetual shrug.' *Rolling Stone*

'… the group's saving grace from total boredom.' *Oshkosh Advance Titan*

'… one of the funniest guitarists alive.' Ira Robbins

'… give Rick Nielsen back his Ritalin real quick-like.' *Back Door Man*

'… contrary to the image he projects he is neither retarded nor stupid.' *Berkeley Gazette*

Many respected the method to Rick's madness, like Moira McCormick writing for *Lively Times*: 'There's a certain integrity in Mr. Nielsen's buffoonery, a spontaneous quality to his antics that assures you that even he probably doesn't know what he's going to do next.'

But some, like Gary Huoy from the *Scottsdale Daily Progress*, misinterpreted Rick's rise as a fall. 'The unfortunate side is that Nielson (sic), a truly talented songwriter and musician, has to act like a clown to make it in the rock music business.'

Rick had little patience for those who failed to 'get it.'

'I can't go to everyone's house and try to explain it,' Rick spat. 'That's ridiculous.' Yet even his own father admitted to having had to 'adjust my thinking and philosophy to a different spectrum of entertainment.' No matter: Rick was all-in. As Joe Perry once remarked, 'He's got Cheap Trick written on his fucking eyelids.'

'There's lots of bands that have zero identity,' Nielsen opined. 'Who's who? No one knows. Foreigner? Boston? Except for maybe one guy you don't know what's going on. Our personalities are strong enough, I think. We wouldn't settle for that lack of personality and because of that, image is important.'

Speaking of image, Bun E. Carlos had a distinct one, so much so that he inspired his own slew of obtuse descriptions from journalists:

'… Nebraskan assistant minister whose church was just foreclosed.' *Rolling Stone*

'… H.L. Mencken working on updates for the Scopes' Monkey Trial.' *Performance*

'… bank teller in a thirties gangster film.' *Detroit Free Press*

'… time-warped from a Dutch Schultz gangland killing.' *Illinois Entertainer*

'… commuter running for the 7:52 from Huntington.' *Trouser Press*

'… missed the 7:14 from Stamford to Grand Central Station.' *Berkshire Sampler*

'… nervous accountant.' *Tallahassee Democrat*

'… chain-smoking accountant with a robust appetite.' *Miami Herald*

'… escaped Nazi war criminal turned accountant.' *Omaha World Herald*

'… wouldn't look out of place on a plantation run by deported Mafia.' *LA Weekly*

'… could double for any overweight bureaucrat in Washington.' *The Eagle*

'… should be managing a Safeway.' *Berkeley Gazette*

'… wire service operator on a late deadline.' *New York Times*

'… the kid at school you called professor.' *Record Mirror*

'… bored musician in a burlesque show orchestra pit.' *Los Angeles Times*

'… overweight detective, cub reporter, or possibly professional gambler.' *Deversions*

'… a cross between an overweight Mr. Whipple and a Times Square Pimp.' *Triad*

'… somewhat less bombastic-looking Oliver Hardy.' *NME*

'… extra from a Bogart movie.' *Dark Star*

'… down at heel Sidney Greenstreet.' *NME*

'… Tom Bosley with a moustache and wirerims.' *Journal-Star*

'… lovable rotund uncle.' *Plain Dealer*

'… very normal.' *Madcity Music Sheet*

Writers had a lot less to work with when it came to Robin Zander and Tom Petersson, but they tried. The *Los Angeles Times* noted Robin's 'classic teen idol looks' and Tom's 'accessibility,' concluding that 'you'd think they were picked by a faultless rock computer.' As for Rick and Bun, 'The other two members look like they were picked as a practical joke.' Rob Patterson, writing for the *Salisbury Daily Times*, described Tom as a 'version of Warren Beatty,' while bemoaning Robin's 'wispy blondness.' Evan Hosie from the *Berkeley Gazette* worried that Robin was 'almost too fragile-looking.' Moira McCormick pointed out in *Lively Times* that 'Petersson seems to be unaware that everyone around him is having a Halloween party.' Cary Baker called Tom a 'bramble-tressed mystagogue.'

In the post-glam era of 'new wave,' Cheap Trick's incidental gimmicks were definitely a bonus. 'The image mocks an era of rock'n'roll that takes itself all too seriously,' Graham Kicks wrote for the *Brandon Sun*. 'It's a thoroughly refreshing laugh, long overdue in popular music.' Mike Duffy from *Detroit Free Press* agreed, asserting that 'the rise of mediocre mojo in the form of sterile studio pop' made Cheap Trick 'all the more impressive.' The *Star Phoenix* praised them for lacking 'the pretentiousness of Hollywood' and the *Des Moines Tribune* declared them 'much needed idols for weird looking guys everywhere.'

MIC FABUS *The way they captured character and caricature was brilliant.*

Terry Atkinson put forth in the *LA Times* that 'many skeptics refuse to believe this stunningly polar combination wasn't planned.'

Define planned. What mattered was, it worked.

Cary Baker pondered why it worked for *Triad* magazine, and concluded thusly: 'In the current fragmented epoch of rock, it's possible to be anyone you choose, given the right devices.'

Cheap Trick had the right devices.

21

Go to the end of the world...

SUPPORT ACT. STARWOOD. WHISKY.
TOM WERMAN.

With the album in stores, ICM's strategy became to put Cheap Trick in front of as many rock fans as possible. Most of February was spent on the road supporting established acts like The Kinks, Santana, Journey, and Kansas. Ironically, the strategy meant a pay cut, as Rick Nielsen explained to *Guitar Player*. 'When our first album came out we lost a lot of money, because you go out as an opening act. You can't go in the clubs anymore—you go in the concerts, and they're gonna pay $250. Who's Cheap Trick?'

Tom Petersson concurred, telling the *Augusta Chronicle*, 'We had become a hit in places like Milwaukee and Chicago and were doing really well for a bar band. Then we got our deal and started making less money.' I suppose ICM's thinking was: less money now, more money later. In a February article for *Lively Times* titled 'Tricksters Of The Western World,' author Moira McCormick pondered the band's prospects:

> You've heard about this bunch, no doubt. The rock group that ate Rockford, the foursome that charmed Jack Douglas away from Aerosmith and Starz long enough to produce their first album, the nutcases with notoriety in their stars. The Next Big Thing. The hype abounds, but the fact is Cheap Trick actually do have a sizable shot at the big time. Consider a fanatical coterie of admirers all around the Midwest, a recording contract with Epic Records. Extensive and favorable press, and most important, a carefully nurtured, distinctive image—not a bad start at all. Now the question is, can the Trick pull it off on a national scale?

They were going to try.

On March 5, Cheap Trick opened for The Runaways at the Music Theatre in Royal Oak, Michigan, twenty miles north of Detroit. The *Windsor Star* proclaimed, 'The punks are at the Royal Oak tonight.' Also on the bill were Tom Petty & The Heartbreakers (misspelled 'Tom Pety' on the marquee out front). The Heartbreakers opened their set with a song called 'Surrender,' unreleased until the year 2000. Cheap Trick neglected to perform their own song of the same name, but the Royal Oak crowd still demanded an encore.

Bassist Jackie Fox remembered the 'kick-ass bill' as her favorite show with The Runaways: 'Hours of great music and great performances in front of a crowd in one of the best rock'n'roll cities in the world.' Cherie Currie also remembered it being a great show: 'That was just the very beginning for everyone.' Lita Ford tweeted about the show on its anniversary: 'Admission was $4. The good ole days.'

Evelyn McDonnell spoke with Bun E. Carlos about that period for her 2013 book *Queens Of Noise: The Real Story Of The Runaways*.

Cheap Trick drummer Bun E. Carlos had met the Runaways in Beloit, Wisconsin, on their previous tour; they all signed his copy of The Runaways suggestively, except the down-to-earth West. A year later, the band seemed hardened and demoralized. They were driving a rental car that they had failed to return and were 'living on nothing, on peanuts and stuff,' he says. 'The gild was off the lily for the band ... We knew they were being taken advantage of ... They were out there paying their dues and suffering. Their attitude was, We're getting fucked over by our manager, but we're out there.'

The manager responsible for the fucking over was Kim Fowley, with whom Cheap Trick were intimately familiar.

Royal Oak was less than an hour from Ann Arbor, so Cheap Trick swung through for a weekend engagement at Second Chance. An advertisement in the *Michigan Daily* billed them as 'The Next Supergroup.' The visit was covered by a local 'zine called *Ballroom Blitz*, which reported, 'Boston's Cheap Trick brought a lot of Britain's spirit of '67 with them to Ann Arbor's Second Chance this month, indicating the next British invasion may not necessarily come from Liverpool.'

The author erroneously reported that Tom was born in Sweden and Bun

E. in Venezuela, and that the four had originally joined forces in Boston. That same month, an article in the *Daily Independent Journal* out of San Rafael, California, also claimed that 'members come from places like Boston, Venezuela, and Sweden.'

Ballroom Blitz scribe Mike McDowell compared Zander to the two Keiths, Relf and Partridge. Keith Relf, the former frontman for The Yardbirds, died tragically two months later, electrocuted by his own guitar. *The Partridge Family* had been canceled two years earlier, and David Cassidy was pursuing a solo career, but he looked a lot more like Paul Williams than Robin Zander on the cover of his 1976 album *Home Is Where The Heart Is*.

When asked about the band's unique set of influences, Bun E. Carlos explained, 'The collector perspective adds a lot of influence into both our original material and whatever cover versions we do onstage. We like to incorporate a lot of obscure British things into our stage show.'

The *Ballroom Blitz* article concluded thusly:

Originals like 'He's A Whore' and 'Surrender' reflect some of the most fascinating rock around today, with the obvious British influences providing the essential vitality that prevents the artist from falling victim to typical '70s mediocrity. Collectors with a burning desire to perform your favorite obscurities onstage take notice—Cheap Trick is proving it can be done.

So Cheap Trick did not play 'Surrender' in Royal Oak but did play it in Ann Arbor. They then continued east where they performed at the Agora Ballroom in Columbus on March 9, and joined Rush and Max Webster for a March 11 show at the Tower Theatre in Upper Darby, Pennsylvania. Next on the agenda was a trip to New York City and a performance at Yorkville Palace, where there was a pre-show incident involving Richie Ranno from Bungi and Starz. He was on the guest list, his plus one being his wife, who 'looked like Bo Derek.' Their arrival caused a bit of commotion just as Susan Blonde from Epic was attempting to corral the band for some pictures.

RICHIE RANNO *She rudely asked us to move from where we were standing. I said, 'I was here first.' We had a discussion which ended with me telling her to fuck off. A short time later, [Sid Wingfield] told us [Susan Blonde] wanted us thrown out. I just thought she was an employee of the venue.*

Next up, three shows in Pennsylvania: two with Kansas, then one with Rush and Max Webster in Pittsburgh on March 14, reviewed by Pete Bishop for the *Pittsburgh Press*. Bishop felt Cheap Trick 'didn't do badly' but relied 'heavily on the antics of goofy guitarist Rick Nielsen, who dressed like a frat pledge of the 50s,' adding, 'Nielsen can play when he feels like it (and he's not too busy jumping on the monitors).'

Next on the band's itinerary: a return trip to Los Angeles for three more nights at the Starwood, March 17–19. Also on the bill was former Velvet Undergrounder John Cale, who was in between record deals, and his new solo band: Richie Fliegler on guitar, Bruce Brody on keys, Joe Stefko on drums, and on bass Michael Visceglia, who remembered the walls at the Starwood 'being covered with the jackets from their first album.'

MICHAEL VISCEGLIA *We played, but the energy in the room was all about the Cheap Trick release.*

Rumor has it that an inebriated John Cale tossed an egg at Cheap Trick while they were onstage, but he was unable to put much heat on it.

BUN E. CARLOS *It didn't get very far because he was literally falling down drunk. Cale wasn't having a good time that year.*

Definitely not. Before long, Cale's entire band quit after he hacked a chicken to death onstage with a meat cleaver. Al Stewart, whose single 'Year Of The Cat' had just that week entered the Top 10 on *Billboard*, came out to the Starwood one night. Rodney Bingenheimer made an appearance and invited Cheap Trick to appear on his radio show the next day. The band also spent an afternoon at Greg Shaw's BOMP record store at 5320½ Laurel Canyon Boulevard, signing autographs.

Later that year, Shaw made an interesting claim in *BOMP* magazine:

> The album that never was, recorded live at BOMP Records, and canceled by legal problems. All that survives is the cover idea, taken from Debbie Shaw's photo of Rick Nielsen outside the BOMP store. The few test pressings that got out are already changing hands for hundreds of dollars among rabid collectors …

It seems to have been wishful thinking or a joke. The supposed cover photo showed Rick Nielsen straddling a motorbike, a shopping bag containing a copy of the first Cheap Trick album dangling from its handlebars.

The Starwood engagement was reviewed by Franc Gavin for the April 15 issue of *Performance* magazine, which featured Rich Kwasniewski's accordion photo on the cover:

The group opened with 'Speak Now Or Forever Hold Your Peace' from their debut Epic LP, intensifying the dense textures that were producer Jack Douglas's handiwork on that just-released outing. Lead guitarist Rick Nielsen's stage antics might qualify him as prime candidate for World's Only Living Cartoon Award, but his playing is no joke—while he's busy hamming it up in true idiot fashion, he's simultaneously spraying out some of the most interesting attempts at metallic flash-and-die heard in years, as he aptly demonstrated on 'Oh Candy' and 'Cry, Cry.' His instrumental passages act as perfect punch-counterpoint to vocalist Robin Zander's confident stage manner, as Zander struts with a low key brazenness and Nielsen spits guitar picks out into the audience.

Gavin did not forget the rhythm section, declaring Carlos 'a joy to watch as he chain smokes his life away' and Petersson 'more than adequate, providing a firm and sinewy central shaft.' (That's what she said.)

Cheap Trick performed at the legendary Golden Bear nightclub on the Pacific Coast Highway in Huntington Beach on Monday, March 21, then headed north to San Francisco for a two-night stand at the Old Waldorf on Battery Street. One patron remembered Nielsen making a game out of landing flicked picks in the pitchers of beer on the tables.

The boys must have been homesick, because they squeezed in a gig at the Brat Stop in Kenosha on the 25th before heading to Minnesota for shows supporting Kansas in Minneapolis and St. Cloud.

On March 29, Cheap Trick returned to Madison for a homecoming bash at the Stone Hearth, written up by the *Madcity Music Sheet*:

Tues. March 29th found Epic Recording Artists CHEAP TRICK dropping in for a long evening of high energy music at the Stone Hearth. They have been touring consistently with groups like KANSAS, the KINKS and KISS and record sales are picking up cross country on their first LP released in January. CHEAP TRICK has always had a strong cult of fans in their business 'hometown' and this night drew 1,000+ people to the Hearth. It was crowded from the edge of the stage to the front door as the crowd pushed forward to catch every bit of nonsense guitarist Rick Nielsen threw out. Nielsen's moves have become classic in Madcity with 'thumbs up' flying through the audience in response to Rick's questioning looks and guitar picks in constant barrage at the first few rows of rockers.

On the very last day of March, a Thursday, Cheap Trick performed three sets at the Electric Ballroom in Milwaukee. Second set:

'Hot Love'
'Oh Caroline' (a recent addition to the Nielsen oeuvre)
'Oh Boy'
'Please Mrs. Henry'
'Down Down Down'
'Oh Candy'
'Southern Girls'
'Tom's Blues'

Third set:

'You Talk Too Much'
'Ain't That A Shame'
'Cry Cry'
'Girls On Fire'
'Big Eyes'
'He's A Whore'
'The Ballad Of TV Violence'
'Goodnight Now'
'Down On The Bay'

On April Fool's Day they made a return flight to California to open for The Runaways at the Santa Monica Civic Center—a performance shoddily preserved on a vinyl bootleg called *Perfect Female Body*, named for the R.

Crumb drawing used as a 'cover' (a photocopy included with a plain sleeve). Cary Baker asked the band about the bootleg when he interviewed them for *Triad* magazine. Robin lamented that 'the recording was terrible. They made my voice sound stupid.' Bun E. theorized that the offender 'took a $75 cassette machine in the fiftieth row or something with no EQ added.' Rick chose to accentuate the positive: 'Though I must say, the performance was brilliant!'

They took no time to relax on a California beach, but instead headed straight back to the airport, as they had reluctantly pledged to perform at a fundraising event the very next evening in Rockford. Dave Zimmerman described the scene for *Sunday Magazine* as 'chilly if not downright cold last Saturday night in the dressing room at the Riverview Ice House as Cheap Trick changed into its costumes in front of space heaters.' Rick Nielsen told Zimmerman that the band had originally (and wisely) declined the request. 'But this woman! She kept calling and calling us so we decided we would do it.'

That woman was Becky Fransden, who represented the Figure Skating Club of Rockford. She was clearly persuasive, as the Rockford Park District allowed her to use the rink at no charge for the event, called 'Rock-Skate,' and she reeled in WROK-Radio as a sponsor. Attendees could bring their own ice skates or rent them on site. Some skated while the band played, others sat in the stands and watched. Fransden hoped to cash in on the popularity of the band even though she admitted to not being a fan herself, citing the 'pornographic aspects' of the group's material.

Dave Zimmerman described the surreal scene that unfolded at Riverview Ice House:

The Rock-Skate participants began zipping around the ice, occasionally colliding in the semi-darkness. The hard rock sound skimmed out across the ice beautifully until it reached the stands. Then, the plastic wall which shields hockey crowds bounced the sound up into the metal gridworks of the ceiling, from where it fell in shatters. Some of the kids in the stands weren't happy, especially those who laid out $5 of their McDonald's-scale wages for a ticket. The police were on the job, urging kids to sit down and not block the entrances. They were also keeping their eyes out for certain numbered tickets that had been reported stolen from the Silver Dollar Jeans store. Finally, one was spotted. Its young possessor was whisked away while telling police he had bought his ticket from 'some guy.' There also were other legal incidents. Two youths were caught smoking marijuana. Police called their parents. 'Wouldn't that just be the most embarrassing thing that could happen to parents,' exclaimed one of the figure skating mothers at the entrance. While counting the tickets, club members found that they had allowed at least four people in with counterfeit tickets. It was a good likeness, except the purple number on each stub had not been printed by the copy machine. The skating club needed to sell seven hundred tickets to break even. The final tally was around eight hundred.

Having survived Rock-Skate, the next item on the Cheap Trick agenda was a string of nine dates with The Kinks. They joined the tour in Texas, where the *Fort Worth Star Telegram* misidentified a photo of Robin Zander as 'Bun E. Carlos,' even though the accompanying article described Bun E. as looking 'like your typical accountant' while Robin was appraised as 'boyishly handsome.' The tour swung through Oklahoma City and Omaha before heading to Minneapolis where the show was reviewed by Michael Anthony for the *Minneapolis Star Tribune*. Anthony enjoyed The Kinks' 'exuberant music,' but his reaction to Cheap Trick was mixed: 'A pick is used for a minute or two, then thrown into the audience. The zaniness seems forced and rather grotesque, but the music is quite well done, though the tunes on this occasion tended to end rather sloppily.'

All was not kosher in the Kinks camp. Dave Davies was consistently overserved, while drummer Mick Avory was furious with Dave's brother Ray for some reason. Nielsen told the *Irish Independent* that 'The Kinks were one of my favorite bands until I met 'em. Everybody was great, but Ray was difficult. He was the maddest multi-millionaire I ever met. I remember Ray pushed Dave over an amp one night and knocked him down.'

Cheap Trick dropped off The Kinks tour after a show at the Riverside Theatre in Milwaukee and spent the rest of April opening for the likes of Kansas, Boston, and Nazareth. An April 30 gig with Boston in Ottawa caused a bit of controversy in local rag the *Citizen*. On May 2, writer Neil Macdonald feted 'Cheap Tricks' with a glowing review:

Cheap Tricks did a number of things right. They started on time, used a number of neat gimmicks to build up their audience, spoke to people instead of at them and generally put everything they had into their 40 minutes. Effective simple costumes, great lead vocals (surprisingly mellow for their screaming intensity), relentless guitar-playing and good timing were their pluses. The one big minus of the group, and probably why they're still openers, is their rawness: they need a good deal more polish. Anyway, an obviously appreciative audience gave them an encore and a veritable forest-fire of lit matches.

A 'letter to the editor' published five days later begged to differ:

Editor, Citizen: Before Neil Macdonald reviews another Civic Centre concert, he should be instructed not to fall asleep at the show or perhaps not even be present. He gave good reviews to one of the top 10 worst bands ever to hit the Civic Centre; Cheap Tricks. There were more 'Boos' and 'Go Homes' for Cheap Tricks than for any other band I've witnessed. Neil also seems to be quite confused about encores and the lit-match fad. When Cheap Tricks left the stage, next to nobody applauded (let alone stood and applauded). As for the 'veritable forest-fire of lit matches' (by the way, is this Neil's first concert?) Neil should be made aware of several things: A fair portion of Civic Centre concert crowds are young teenagers who go there not only for the music but for a safe place to meet friends, 'hang out,' and smoke up. This is all well and good except they have a tendency to welcome every band with lit matches. It's 'cool' and 'in' (to use 50s phrases with which I am sure Neil is familiar) to do so.

Cheap Trick returned to Second Chance in Ann Arbor on May 1, a night made all the more memorable by the arrival of Fred 'Sonic' Smith from the MC5. The band urged Fred to jam with them, and while he was reluctant at first, he finally acquiesced and joined the band onstage for chaotic renditions of 'Let It Rock' and 'Route 66.' Bun E. remembered Smith and Nielsen writhing on their backs, playing their guitars behind their heads. A photo of the odd couple trading licks appeared in *NME* in December with the caption, 'Well, kick out the jams ... Cheap Trick comes to town and Fred "Sonic" Smith lets them know he's a master magician.'

Next up: four consecutive nights opening for Ted 'Fred' Nugent and more dates with Rush and Max Webster, after which ICM paired Cheap Trick with

Procol Harum for a short jaunt across Ontario. 'They were like, Yeah, we've got three dates booked with Procol Harum,' Bun E. remembered. 'And we're like What!? Procol Harum!? It was like, we're selling more records than they are, and we're hardly selling any records.' Tellingly, the dates were canceled 'due to lack of ticket sales,' according to Anthony Rowat at procolharum.com.

Star Wars premiered in theaters on May 25, and Cheap Trick actually had the night off! Meanwhile, in a galaxy not far away, as Carlos noted, copies of *Cheap Trick* were not flying off the shelves at light speed, meaning Epic was already inquiring about the next album. As Rick complained to Andrew Magnotta at Q105.3, 'We did one record, it had just come out and the guy from the record company says, Just wait till the next one! *The next one*!?'

Tom Petersson shared a similar recollection with *Rock Cellar* magazine. 'People would say to us, OK, get ready for the ride, and we were like, OK. Yeah, right. And then a couple of weeks later, they'd be like, Well, the next one's the one. (laughs) And we'd be like, Wait a minute, what do you mean?'

* * *

As it turned out, Jack Douglas was otherwise engaged, as Aerosmith's *Draw The Line* took over a year to complete. 'That's when the drugs weren't working,' Douglas admitted. He claims to have recommended Rick Derringer as his replacement with Cheap Trick for the second album.

KEN ADAMANY *Jack's contract was just for the first album. I don't think Derringer was ever considered.*

Tom Werman jumped at the chance.

TOM WERMAN *I was scheduled to produce Eddie Money for Columbia, and then the Cheap Trick thing came up. Bruce Lundvall, the president of [CBS] at the time, intervened on my behalf, because I told him I would rather do Cheap Trick.*

Werman was born in Boston and attended Columbia University. As he told *Tape Op*, 'Music was always the main thing in my life. I just couldn't ignore it, and I knew that I had the capability for it in some way. I wrote a letter to Clive Davis; the fact that I had an MBA made me appear more serious. I presented myself as a musician who was a student of rock'n'roll, who also had two degrees and a job. Instead of saying, Give me a job. I need a job, I said, I'd much rather work in music because, honestly, I don't like what I'm doing. I think I saw three or four other people and the last one said, I want you to see Mr. Davis. Mr. Davis gave me a job and that was it.'

Clive Davis was the president of CBS at the time (1970). Werman worked his way up in the A&R department and finally hit paydirt in 1975, when he signed Ted Nugent. His first choice to produce Nugent's Epic debut was Pete Townshend, but Townshend's manager reportedly burst out laughing at the mere suggestion. Lew Futterman was eventually hired, but Werman was hands-on and gradually became more involved. As he told *Tape Op*, 'Lew was a reasonably creative guy, but he didn't know much about rock'n'roll and he was nice enough to give me co-production credit. There I was, a producer. I also remixed the whole record.'

By the time Werman signed on to produce Cheap Trick, he had two more albums with Nugent under his belt, and two with Mother's Finest. It was Cheap Trick's idea to record their second album in California.

TOM WERMAN *I think we all stayed at the Sunset Marquis.*

BUN E. CARLOS *We did one day of pre-production at a rehearsal hall, just to get the arrangements tweaked and stuff.*

TOM WERMAN *They had a lot of songs and they had sections or portions of songs, there would be an idea and they would demo that. They had a lot of demos.*

BUN E. CARLOS *There was a batch of tunes including 'Clock' and 'Oh Caroline' that got written around Thanksgiving or Christmastime and we made a tape for Werman in January. 'Violins' was on there. I have some rehearsals from around then, we were working on songs that ended up to be 'Need Your Love' (working title 'Last Night I Had A Dream') and 'World's Greatest Lover.'*

TOM WERMAN *The songs were there. Definitely. He was a unique songwriter.*

Cheap Trick warmed up with back-to-back nights at the legendary Whisky A Go-Go, June 3 and 4. Werman had Wally Heider Studios send down their mobile unit from San Francisco to record the shows. A New York band called

The Mumps, who had just done three nights at the Whisky with Van Halen (who had signed to Warner Bros but not yet recorded their first album) a week earlier, opened. Writer Steve Rosen recounts meeting Eddie Van Halen for the first time at Cheap Trick's Friday night performance at the Whisky. 'He was there to see Cheap Trick,' Rosen told *Dave & Dave Unchained*. 'He was a huge Cheap Trick and Rick Nielsen fan.'

Mumps frontman Lance Loud had a bit of notoriety thanks to his involvement with the PBS documentary series *An American Family*. The other three Mumps were Jay Dee Daugherty, Rob Duprey, and Kristian Hoffman, who, like Eddie Van Halen, was a big Cheap Trick fan, having seen them at Max's Kansas City the previous September.

KRISTIAN HOFFMAN *Paul Zone took me to see Cheap Trick at Max's. A life-changing experience. Rock/pop suddenly seemed not only possible, but fun!*

Hoffman purchased the first album as soon as it came out and was beyond excited to be on the same bill with them. He remembers Cheap Trick having 'ten foot fake Marshall amps that took up most of the stage that we had to set up in front of!' He still has the autographs he procured from all four.

KRISTIAN HOFFMAN *They had a lot of empty record sleeves stapled to the walls so I just ripped one off the wall and had them autograph it.*

Zander wrote, 'Chrissy of The Mumps. Goin Wild at the Whiskey [sic].' Taking Kristian's name literally, Rick Nielsen wrote, 'Dear Jesus, I really love you!'

Rodney Bingenheimer turned up both nights to introduce the band. He told Ken Sharp that 'the Whisky was packed for every show. A lot of girls showed up. It was like the new Beatles had arrived.' Rodney featured the band on his radio show on June 5.

The Brothers Mael had recently returned the Sparks operation to California, and they too turned up at the Whisky, along with the rest of their band, including bassist Sal Maida, formerly a member of New York glamsters Milk N' Cookies.

SAL MAIDA *The Big Beat band was together, sort of, I wouldn't say in limbo, but in LA just waiting around to see what the next move was gonna be.*

Maida was blown away by Cheap Trick.

SAL MAIDA *It was one of the greatest things I've ever seen. One song after another, rapid fire. Just blazing, bone crunching rock'n'roll. Let me put it this way, there were no clunkers in that set.*

Just a few months earlier, according to Bun E. Carlos, the Mael brothers had floated the idea of a collaboration.

BUN E. CARLOS *The two brothers proposed we join up together for a six man band. They had a song for us, 'Fact Or Fiction.'*

Nothing came of it. Now that the brothers had moved to Los Angeles, they were in transition mode again, and they re-set their sights on Rick Nielsen.

SAL MAIDA *They were always trying to think of interesting guitar players for their records. Mick Ronson was supposed to do Big Beat. They had gotten rid of the touring guitar player [Jeff Salen], so that's why maybe they approached Rick. I remember going to a diner, me and Ron and Russel, and we're supposed to meet up with Rick and Rick brings along Tom (laughs) who's a bass player and I already have the gig so it was a little awkward.*

I don't think it was too serious of a thing. I think it was just an idea that didn't happen. I spoke to Russell, and it never went past a dinner meeting.

In the end, the Maels ditched the entire band and used studio mercenaries for their next album, *Introducing Sparks*.

* * *

After laying waste to the Whisky, Cheap Trick hunkered down at Cherokee Studios in Hollywood, where they had booked three weeks to record their second album. Issues arose immediately. Apparently, improvements were being made to the facility. The band would be in the middle of a take when the hammering or drilling would begin. People would wander in and out while they were recording, including an unwelcome cameo from Art Garfunkel. The unprofessional atmosphere proved untenable, and with just four basic tracks in the can, the decision was made to pull the plug and regroup elsewhere.

They landed at Kendun Recorders in Burbank, where the process went much more smoothly.

TOM WERMAN *We just jumped from song to song to song. We got stuff done so quickly. I was spoiled by them. The favorite band I ever produced, far and away. Just a great, productive, funny, smart group.*

Everybody in Cheap Trick was brilliant. Robin Zander was the best vocalist I ever worked with, Bun E. Carlos was the best drummer, and Tom Petersson was the best bass player. They were great!

As great as they were, Werman was feeling the pressure to produce a more commercial record—one that would sell more copies than the first one had. As Bun E. Carlos remembered for *Classic Rock Revisited*, 'The basic blowback from the label we got was, Look, the first record didn't get on the radio. This guy's gonna get you on the radio. And that's why we're gonna tame ya down a little bit.' Tom Werman elaborated on his intentions for *Trouser Press*: 'I wanted to make the band more palatable; more, I hate to use the word, commercially acceptable, without forcing them to compromise their artistic integrity.'

'Werman wanted us to be like The Who,' said Nielsen.

'More like The Guess Who,' said Petersson.

Werman explained his approach to Greg Brodsky: whereas Jack Douglas had 'captured the band pretty much as they were,' Werman 'used the studio technology to a greater degree,' including 'more instruments and more layered guitars and things' so 'it came out with more space.'

'I think you could hear everything a little better than on the first LP,' Werman added. 'There are ways to treat buzzing guitars in a studio so that they don't take up as much frequency range and don't compete with the other instruments.'

TOM WERMAN *We did some overdubs at Westlake Audio because I remember that's where we put the piano on 'I Want You To Want Me.'*

Werman heard the song as a 'dancehall tune.' He rented a tack piano and brought in a session guy named Jai Winding.

JAI WINDING *What I remember about recording the piano was Tom Werman was adamant about not having any overdubs stick out, especially from a session* *musician keyboard player. Tom wanted the focus to be just on the band and not having their Midwestern rock band cred tainted by the addition of session players. So I tucked the piano part tightly into Rick's rhythm guitar part and Tom's pulsing quarter note bass part with no extra movement or notes to make the listener wonder if there was a piano part. Feathering the piano just far enough behind the rhythm guitar, with my left hand doubling Tom's driving bass line.*

Werman enlisted the services of another session guy, the legendary Jay Graydon, to lay down some genre-appropriate lead guitar on 'I Want You To Want Me.'

TOM WERMAN *Rick wasn't putting the song across the way I heard it, the way I thought it should be, and I wanted a more club, jazz, thirties sound.*

Nielsen claimed that he 'wasn't there when it was going on. It was not like any lacking on my part.' Graydon described what he did for the song as 'wire choir.'

JAY GRAYDON *Harmonizing guitar parts. Play a single line and then work out the harmony to it. Sometimes one harmony part, sometimes two. That's a big part of the studio musician's job. I'm supposed to come up with a memorable hook. If the producer wants me to play a line in the beginning of the song, my job is to come up with a simple, memorable lick.*

'I Want You To Want Me' was the only time Graydon ever 'ghosted' on a record—otherwise, he was always credited. How did Nielsen feel about having a stunt guitarist? He told *Ultimate Guitar* that he 'told them what I was looking for, and yet, it really got taken away from what I was thinking and had in mind.'

TOM WERMAN *He probably didn't enjoy having that done, but he didn't complain at the time. He was very agreeable to everything in the studio.*

Werman's approach to the song certainly represented a departure for the band, yet it made sense as an interpretation, given the inherent vibe of the piece. Considering the misgivings that the members of Cheap Trick have expressed about the direction that was taken with the song in hindsight, Werman harkens back to a specific moment in the studio when he felt like he was given the thumbs up.

TOM WERMAN *They were on the couch, we were doing an overdub, and I turned to them and I asked them a question. 'Do you like this, or should we do that?' And [Rick] said, 'You're the producer.' And I remember that. And I thought that was,* You're doing a good job, just keep going, I'm cool.

Robin Zander has been more forgiving of the song's 'real boppy' production. 'I didn't hate it,' he told *Sentinel Daily*. 'It just wasn't us.' It might have seemed, at the time, as if all was for naught, as the single did not become a hit. And yet, Cheap Trick undeniably assimilated elements of the Werman arrangement into the way they performed 'I Want You To Want Me' moving forward, including on *Cheap Trick At Budokan*.

TOM WERMAN *It was a live version of the studio version.*

The new approach imbued the song with a swing and a bounce. Prior to *In Color*, Cheap Trick's performances of 'I Want You To Want Me' could be choppy, even clumsy; 'Yardbirds-ish,' is how Zander described it. Yet the ditty clearly had potential. Robin McBride and Jack Douglas both heard it. Werman made it what it kind of wanted to be, a genre piece or a novelty tune. All I'm saying is, it was not an unjustified approach.

In 1978, Rick Nielsen told *Nuggets* that 'working with Tom's been good, he's easy to work with.' Werman felt the same. 'We had a really good time in the studio,' he told Chuck Harrell. 'The vibes were great, there was a lot of laughter.' As for the net result, Nielsen conceded to *Ultimate Guitar* that Werman 'did a good job and the record got released and the songs are good,' then added a caveat: 'but it's like he made a heavy band sound wimpy.' Werman begged to differ. 'I never mixed a record without running it past the group,' he insisted. 'I always gave it to the group for approval. You know, it's just common courtesy.'

'*In Color*, no matter what you thought of it, was a time and place, and that's where we were,' Zander reflected for *The Jeremy White Podcast*. 'And we allowed all that to happen and some people like that record best of all of our records.'

* * *

With the second album in the can, Cheap Trick went straight back to work: DeKalb, Peoria, Bloomington, Champaign, Highland Park, Madison,

Schaumburg, Milwaukee, and Decatur. On June 24, while Cheap Trick were in Bloomington, Elvis Presley performed in Des Moines, Iowa, and, right after, flew to Madison, where he was picked up at the airport by a limousine rented from Ken Adamany Associates. It was very early in the morning on June 25, while Cheap Trick were still bashing it out at the Red Lion, that Presley witnessed an altercation and opted to intervene, as described by the *Wisconsin State Journal*:

> Only minutes after flying into the Dane County Regional Airport, Presley halted his limousine along E. Washington Ave. to break up a fight involving a seventeen-year-old service station attendant and two other youths. 'Alright, I'll take you on,' challenged Presley, who left his heavily guarded entourage shortly after 1am to quell the brief fist fight at Skyline Standard Service, 1506 N. Stoughton Rd.

Keith Lowry, the gas station attendant and son of the owner, had been outnumbered until Elvis, still clad in the blue jumpsuit he had just worn onstage in Des Moine, leapt from the limo to even the odds.

According to the *Capital Times*, 'Elvis's high-powered, high-paid, heavy-duty presence stopped the fight cold.' According to Lowry, 'The two other guys turned around and were shocked. They didn't move.' At which point Elvis asked, 'Is everything settled now?' The King shook hands with all three combatants and some onlookers and was heard saying 'Did you see those guys' faces?' as he climbed back into the limo. A review of that night's show in Des Moines mentioned Presley's voice slurring when he spoke, the writer adding that 'the cause of the slur remains a mystery.' Presley had less than two months to live.

On June 26, Cheap Trick performed during the day at Centennial Park in Highland Park, Illinois, set up at the bottom of a small hill. People sat on the hill to watch. They finished off June with appearances at the Stone Hearth, B. Ginnings, Electric Ballroom, and a place called Times Square in Decatur. They played one last show in the Midwest, at the Brat Stop in Kenosha on July 3, before heading east: first to Port Clinton, Ohio, for a Fourth of July performance at the Surf Place; then on to Cleveland for an 'if I had a time machine' night at the Agora Ballroom, where Cheap Trick took the stage in between The Dead Boys and The Dictators. At the time, The Dictators were a six-piece band with Mark 'The Animal' Mendoza on bass. The Dead Boys had yet to sign with Sire Records.

Jane Scott described the vibe at the Agora for the *Plain Dealer*:

Punk flunked here this week. The punk audience scene, that is. Not a torn T-shirt, ripped out jean, heavy chain necklace or razor blade pendant at the Agora. Three New Wave bands—the Dead Boys of Cleveland, Cheap Trick and the Dictators—played here for the first time. But the audience looked about like it does any time. Jeans, T-shirts, tennis shoes.

Cheap Trick next headed to Manhattan for a photoshoot at the loft of photographer Benno Friedman on July 6. 'We wanted to call the album *In Color*, and we go to do the photoshoot and the guy showed up with only black-and-white film,' Rick Nielsen told Redbeard. According to Benno, 'I only shot black and white for years. All of my early work, commercial and not, was black-and-white. It stayed black-and-white for my noncommercial work much longer than my commercial work.'

Benno's assistant procured some color film, and they rendezvoused in the parking lot at Shea Stadium in Queens. 'It was raining out,' Robin Zander remembered. 'Nobody expected that.' It was a blessing in disguise, as wet pavement can be very photogenic. Robin and Tom mounted motorcycles, and Benno shot them in color; then Rick and Bun E. mounted scooters, and Benno shot them in his trusty black-and-white. You can see the Pavilion observation towers that were constructed for the 1964 World's Fair at Corona Park in the distance behind them.

The next morning, Cheap Trick boarded Air Canada flight 698 from New York to Halifax, with an ETA of 12:35pm. Hal Sherburne, who had replaced Sid Wingfield as road manager, picked them up at the airport in their brand new GMC Beachcomber Motorhome, purchased to replace the old one that finally gave out while the band were in Los Angeles recording *In Color*.

KEN ADAMANY *The rest of the crew left to go back to the Midwest in the old one with some of the not-needed stage gear when it broke down. I had the old one towed to the GMC dealership, where I traded it for the new one.*

Hal Sherburne had begun working for Adamany in the mid-sixties.

KEN ADAMANY *I had him at the door, or doing security, on almost every big show we were involved in, starting in maybe 1966. Hal was one hundred percent reliable and a wonderful person to have around. When he went out with Cheap Trick I thought it would be a perfect fit, and it was.*

The crew hauled all of the band's gear to the Great White North behind a brand new, thirty-eight-foot GMC Model H1 green diesel truck purchased by Hilaria Music Incorporated, another of Ken Adamany's companies, for $30,450 (plus $7,000 for the box trailer).

Adamany had recently taken a call from Bill Elson, the newly appointed Executive Vice President at ATI (American Talent International). Ken and Bill's business relationship dated back a decade or more, and Bill was calling to offer Cheap Trick the opening slot on an upcoming tour—a big one—but only if they could get out of their contract with ICM to sign with ATI.

KEN ADAMANY *Chip, Shelly, and the ICM agents on both coasts were a pleasure to work with. They were supportive of Cheap Trick and produced many opportunities for us.*

And yet, it was an offer they could not refuse. Adamany was able to extricate them from the ICM deal, telling Doug Brod 'we did have to pay something.'

They hoped it would be worth it.

MATTHEW PERRIN *I remember going up the highway from Maine up to Halifax, Nova Scotia. The highway wasn't even paved, it was a gravel one-lane road. We caravanned the whole tour up there, all the KISS tour buses, all the black and silver trucks.*

22

I'm thinkin' more than a KISS...

On June 22, Gallup declared KISS the most popular band in America. A week later, Marvel Comics issued a forty-page *KISS Super Special* wherein the not-of-this-earth band duked it out with the likes of Dr. Doom. The comic was supposed to have been printed with actual blood from all four members of KISS mixed into the red ink, but confusion at the printing plant resulted in the bloody ink most likely staining the pages of an issue of *Sports Illustrated* instead. Blood or no blood, the KISS comic was a hit, selling at least half a million copies.

In the first week of July, the new KISS album, *Love Gun*, debuted in the Top 10 on *Billboard*. The subsequent tour, officially dubbed the Can-Am Tour, would be the band's biggest yet, with $200,000 spent on new costumes, instruments, and stage production. Hydraulic balconies lowered KISS to the stage and hydraulic platforms lifted them out over the audience. They had matching stages constructed so one could be ready and waiting in the next city when KISS arrived via private jet (it was leased). Cheap Trick drove.

MATTHEW PERRIN *We went coast to coast up there. Played every hockey arena in Canada I think. It would be raining under the stage, the humidity would be so high. The condensation from the ice under that stage.*

Halifax. Moncton. Montreal. Ottawa. Toronto. Kitchener. London. Greater Sudbury. Winnipeg.

BUN E. CARLOS *Took a couple weeks for us to get soundchecks. No smoking onstage because of the explosives.*

That's like telling Gene Simmons to keep his tongue tucked away! And what about that fire-breathing act of his?

When the tour hit Vancouver on July 24, Cheap Trick were declared 'too loud, painfully loud, to enjoy' by Vaughn Palmer of the *Vancouver Sun*. Joe Sornberger from the *Edmonton Journal* agreed, dismissing Cheap Trick as a 'too-loud rock band.' Writing for the *Calgary Herald*, Peter Morton mislabeled Cheap Trick as an 'LA metal band' but conceded that their 'hard-driving rock' was performed 'fairly well.'

The final Canadian stop was at the Agridome in Regina, Saskatchewan. Ken Culbertson reviewed the show for the *Leader Post*. His assessment seemed positive at first, then took a turn: 'The lead-in act was a driving, foot-stomping group called Cheap Trick. They had all the talent and intensity of the fluorescent plastic tubing the hawkers were peddling to the audience.'

The next show was a thousand miles away in Salt Lake City, and Charles M. Young was there waiting, sent to report on the spectacle by *Rolling Stone*:

> A roadie soon clears the dressing room of outsiders, and I venture into the audience. In my New York provincialism, I have anticipated wide-eyed Donny and Marie types; they do appear healthier than the average Madison Square Garden crowd, but they quickly reveal themselves as typical KISS worshippers, out for a night of good fun and human sacrifice when the firecrackers and smoke bombs start exploding. Such crowds are known for destroying (physically) opening acts, and Cheap Trick seems headed for this fate when they hit the stage to lukewarm response, except for a few kids down front who (I am told) have been following them along the tour. Nielsen announces a song 'from our first album' and the traditionalist sitting next to me comments, 'These turkeys have an album?' But by the end of the forty-minute set, Cheap Trick has received two standing ovations and wrenched an encore from the KISS faithful.

Also waiting for Cheap Trick in Salt Lake City was a new recruit to the road crew named Kirk 'Wheel' Dyer.

KEN ADAMANY *I hired him right off of Oscar Mayer. He was shoveling brains there. As soon as he gets to Salt Lake, Hal Sherburne says, 'Change the tire on the motor home.' That was his first job.*

After all, his nickname was 'Wheel.' Speaking of wheels …

BUN E. CARLOS *We had a rolling card game going, and Wheel lost his T-bird to Tom in two weeks. Tom took the car and turned around and gave it to his brother.*

There was plenty of fun to be had on the KISS tour, but not necessarily with one Mr. Simmons. As Nielsen later put it, 'Who is Gene going to hang out with, the guy who does his merchandise? He can't just hang out. He doesn't do that. At least, back then he didn't.' Carlos summed up Gene's idea of small talk: 'Why are you wearing that shirt? Get a newer shirt.' Zander referred to Simmons as 'Uncle Gene.' Gene was twenty-seven.

After conquering Salt Lake City, the tour headed north to Montana, where a cluster of protesters convened outside the venue, the Yellowstone Metra. A letter from some kook named Thomas A. Rhodes, published by the local newspaper that July, might shed some light:

Within a month, the rock band KISS shall be performing a concert in Billings. This fact meant little to me until I met some of their hard-core followers. I was stunned by some of the hideous stories regarding the group, and I noted several nauseating parallels. The name KISS stands for 'Kings In Satan's Service' and that is only the beginning. Their costumes and actions led me to review my knowledge of the occult. What I discovered was that several pieces started to create a picture. The following are supposedly done by KISS and in direct association to the black arts: the drinking and spitting of human blood; the killing of certain animals; the mixing of one's blood with ink; the breathing of fire; the wearing of costumes resembling supernatural beings, and the involvement of vulnerable children.

Paul Stanley responded to the accusations mid-show, as reported by Patrick Dawson in the *Billings Gazette*. 'I know what you been reading in the papers,' Stanley screamed from the stage. 'You can tell 'em we don't kill no chickens, but we do play some good rock'n'roll!'

The tour hit Spokane a few nights later and the *Spokesman-Review* made light of the controversy. 'Their acronym might mean Keep It Simple, Stupid, because that's exactly what they do.' The paper was more generous to Cheap Trick:

Overshadowed by the electric scenery was the back-up group, Cheap Trick, an up-and-thundering hard rock band. The group out-shocked KISS by their sheer understatement. With a drummer who looks like a GU law student, complete with short-cropped hair, necktie and wire-rimmed glasses, and a guitarist who wears a baseball cap, a two-sizes-too-small sweater and 'slacks,' coupled with two other members who look like our run of the mill rock stars, the group is a truly strange assemblage. And they can play, with a sound fondly reminiscent of early Who.

The tour swung through Seattle on August 12th, prompting a review from Patrick MacDonald for the *Seattle Times*. 'The last time KISS was in town in February of 1976 at Paramount Northwest, I dumped on them unmercifully, calling them "dumb" and "weirdos," among other things.' He amended his verdict after witnessing the spectacle at the Seattle Coliseum. 'I still think the band is weird but they aren't so dumb.'

As for the Cheap Trick, 'The show was opened by a band that looked pretty weird, too,' he began, but he came away impressed:

After their show, in the obligatory meeting with radio personnel and the press new bands have to go through, they came off as quite real. Their clothes weren't costumes, that's what they always wear (you could tell from the fact that the clothes were in bad shape—obviously this band hasn't made any money yet). Surprisingly the unlikely characters could play and put on quite a show.

Next stop Portland, where *Cash Box* reported on an incident that occurred during Cheap Trick's set:

When panties flew through the air at recent Cheap Trick concerts, the Epic promotion staff followed up on the idea of distributing sets of pastel-colored panties with the Cheap Trick name emblazoned over the crotch. Meanwhile, up in Portland a feminine fan got so excited that she tore off her shirt and threw it on the stage, baring her breasts and almost ensuring the band's return for a hasty encore.

That same night, an error made by the KISS crew resulted in 'Magical Mystery

Tour' starting to play instead of the backing track for 'Beth.' Peter Criss, alone onstage, tossed roses at the crowd while the tapes were switched. The next gig was at the Cow Palace in Daly City on August 16, reviewed by Joel Selvin for *San Francisco Chronicle*:

Onstage, the warm-up act was blasting off. The vibrations were thick and nearly tactile. They rattled the glass of the phone booths in the lobby and made the steel guard rails quiver. 'We're Cheap Tricks,' yelled one of the Tricks. 'Can you hear us back there?'

Elvis Presley's lifeless body had been discovered on his bathroom floor that afternoon, Codeine, Quaaludes, Valium, Valmid, Placidyl, and Phenobarbital in his system, some at toxic levels, and KISS dedicated 'Rock 'N' Roll All Nite' to The King.

Next stop Fresno and then San Diego, a show reviewed by Frank Green for the *San Diego Union*. Frank dismissed KISS as 'strictly cro-magnon' but Nielsen made a more lasting impression:

Lead guitarist Rick Nielsen injected a dubious new art form, rock ballet, into the proceedings. He was an unlikely figure for the setting. Dressed in short pants and tennis shoes with a crew cut topped with a baseball cap, Nielsen pranced around the stage like a demented karate ace, taking high kicks and chops at the air.

A release party and record signing for their new album, *In Color*, was held in Los Angeles the next day, as described by Chuck Comstock for *Cash Box*: 'A circus atmosphere will prevail when Epic throws a giant party for Cheap Trick at Tower Records on the 20th, featuring fire-eaters, snake charmers, stilt-walkers, organ grinders and a motorbike giveaway.' The event began at 8:30pm on the back lot at Tower on Sunset. Invitations urged potential attendees to *Be there or be square!*

The Can-Am Tour next descended upon Arizona, where the Tucson show garnered a review from John S. Long for the *Arizona Daily Star*, who wrote, 'KISS was preceded by Cheap Tricks. The group received two ovations, something almost unheard of for a group opening a concert for someone as popular as KISS.'

It was in Tucson that someone caught wind of a local band calling themselves Cheap Trix.

BUN E. CARLOS *We pulled up to the bar when we were leaving town in our motorhome and Ken ran in to check 'em out.*

Someone snapped a photo of the marquee with the impinging name on display. The joint was called Smiley's Again, and the marquee read:

THE BEST IS BACK
CHEAP TRIX

The info was forwarded to the band's lawyer, Richard Shelton, and he promptly dispatched a cease-and-desist letter to Cheap Trix, whose members were Lee Schwarz, John Markovitch, Mike Holloway, Jay Quiros, and Tony Kishman.

TONY KISHMAN *We were doing four sets a night, six days a week, singing our hearts out, and that was it. We didn't have the game plan down. We were young. We were playing clubs all around the Tucson area and then we finally got a really good agent, and we started booking our band in Southern California.*
We got to be a pretty popular local band. Cheap Trix was a fun group—we would do a lot of different crazy stuff onstage and we would play songs by The Tubes and different cool bands at the time. We would play songs by Frank Zappa, and we'd have a dummy onstage and spotlight the dummy.

At some point, Tony heard a Cheap Trick song on the radio.

TONY KISHMAN *I was kind of impressed but then kind of upset.*

Then came the communique from Richard Shelton.

BUN E. CARLOS *We got a record out, it's time for you guys to change your name now.*

TONY KISHMAN *We couldn't believe that we were getting a letter from Cheap Trick. We were so young and silly, young and stupid, as they say. We didn't realize* *anything, we just said, 'Oh my gosh, we're getting a letter from Cheap Trick. Wow, we're so famous.'*

Tony soon caught wind of another opportunity and auditioned for the touring version of a Broadway tribute to The Beatles called Beatlemania.

TONY KISHMAN *I flew into LA and went to SIR studios, where there were several Pauls dressed up as Ed Sullivan McCartney. The musical director was there, Jack Carone, and Bunk 4: David Leon, Rob Laufer, Ralph Castelli, and Jim Odem. They asked me to sit in with their group to audition me, so my first audition was with David Leon. We did 'Can't Buy Me Love.' I was very nervous, sang almost all of the song but stopped and couldn't sing anymore. I was very dry and nervous. So they all said, 'Don't worry just take it slow.' I was then asked to do 'Yesterday.' I was a little more comfortable with that one. I sang it pretty well. I then sang 'Hey Jude' on the piano, and I remember doing the ending just like the record. All the scat screams were really close to Paul's. I remember being very excited and really wanting to be in the show.*

Tony nailed it and was cast as Paul. He toured with Beatlemania for the next five years and still mounts a McCartney tribute to this day. As for Cheap Trix …

TONY KISHMAN *I don't think the band would have stayed together much longer anyway. When I left the band they changed the name to Freestyle.*

The next stop on the KISS tour was Phoenix. That same night, back home in Rockford, the members of Cheap Trick were publicly chastised by the musician's union, as reported by *Trouser Press*:

At a meeting of Local 240 of the Rockford Musical Association, American Federation of Musicians, Bun E. Carlos, Richard A. Nielsen, Thomas J. Petersson, and Robin W. Zander (along with a stack of local talent) are suspended for 'failure to pay Union Dues. Work Dues and/or other indebtedness.' The Local's Secretary warns, 'Do not work with these former members until their reinstatement is valid.'

KEN ADAMANY *Typical of the Musicians' Union, then and probably now.*

Cheap Trick's time with KISS was almost over, with just three nights remaining at the Forum in Los Angeles, August 26, 27, and 28. It was on the second night that Bun E. almost had to spackle on the Catman makeup. Peter Criss was 'under the weather,' telling tour manager Fritz Postlethwaite that 'he just wasn't feeling good,' but Postlethwaite found it 'obvious that there was something else going on; everyone could tell.' Lydia Criss told Doug Brod, 'I don't think Peter was familiar with the drug he took.' Peter's speech was slurred, and he was nodding off. Meanwhile twenty thousand rock fans clamored for KISS. Gene Simmons gave Bun E. a heads up: 'You'd better get some makeup on, Bun E. We might need you to play tonight.' Bun E.'s reaction: 'Yeah, whatever.' He 'could have stumbled through it.'

A doctor administered an injection, and Peter regained consciousness, if not lucidity. A couple of roadies carried him onstage and propped him up behind the kit, his drum tech positioned behind him for the entire show to keep him upright. It was an unfortunate turn of events, as Peter had held it together for most of the tour. Carlos remembered that 'he was really drumming good on that tour, like up in Canada. He had taken some lessons from Jim Chapin and stuff. He was a good swing drummer. So he was playing good up in Canada and then we hit the States and he sort of regressed.' Gene Simmons's hair caught fire that night as well. When it rains it pours, right people!? Let me hear ya!

Studio legend Eddie Kramer was present at the Forum to track recordings for possible release as *KISS Alive II*, and he became an instant fan of Cheap Trick. Adamany gave him some tapes.

William White Wing wrote a glowing review of the Cheap Trick's last hurrah with KISS for *Record World*, calling it 'a fast-paced set that opened up a few thousand old ears at the Forum made just as many new fans. Possibly the hottest performance by a non-headliner at the Forum in the past year.'

Chuck Comstock also raved about the opening band for *Cash Box*:

Epic's hot-as-a-pistol Cheap Trick warmed up the crowd for the KISS entree with another in their series of A-1 openings. They've played to steadily increasing multitudes of mostly astonished rock fans since they burst on the scene earlier this year with their cheerily melodic material that is performed with verve and polished professionalism. It's just about time for this well-balanced band of mixed and distinct personalities to take their rightful place at the top of the bill for an extended set of their infectiously entertaining material. The sooner the better.

KISS headed to Texas for four more shows in the first week of September, but Styx opened. Cheap Trick traveled across the country for shows in Jacksonville and Atlanta, then north to Delaware, North Carolina, and Virginia. After a stop in Columbus to play the Agora on September 12, they headed to Detroit, where they jumped on a bill with Spirit and Styx. Some curmudgeon named Mark Beyer was not impressed. He reviewed the show for the *Michigan Daily* and dismissed Cheap Trick as 'rockers of the Volume School' who exhibited 'little delicacy' when it came to 'cheap circus buffoonery.' Beyer did credit the band with inventing a new genre: 'Glunk.' A glam-punk stew? Sounds good to me.

The KISS tour was an amazing opportunity. Rick Nielsen called it 'a very good break.' Cheap Trick were able to perform in front of more than two hundred thousand of the KISS faithful, many of whom were more than on board with Glunk. As Bun E. Carlos told Doug Brod, 'It was where a lot of the audience for *In Color* and *Heaven Tonight* first saw us.' Cheap Trick were not your average rock band. They proved capable of impressing the scenesters on either coast (the Starwood and Max's Kansas City), the in-crowd at Stiff (who offered to release the first record in the UK) and BOMP (who dreamt of releasing a live album), the erudite anglophiles at *Trouser Press*, and now, in a shocking twist, the meatheads and metalheads at a KISS concert.

As the seventies careened toward the eighties and the varied scenes diverged, it became increasingly rare for a single band to equally wow both the new-wavers and headbangers, the intelligentsia and the proletariat. Cheap Trick did it their way, and it worked in every way. As Rick Nielsen explained to the *Province* in 1979, 'I think our music brings the mainstream to us rather than we go towards the mainstream.'

* * *

In Color came out in September and was met with glowing reviews. The first album was recorded in a dystopian New York City and fittingly exuded a dark, noirish vibe (black and white). The second album was recorded in sunny California, and the results were much brighter and lighter (color). Jim Green noted in *Sounds* that 'with the production guidance of Tom Werman, the group has largely traded blast for deftness' and that 'Werman gave the group a subtlety.' Nick Kent remarked in *NME* that Werman 'hit upon a sound that had greater clarity and more verve.' Dave Marsh declared Cheap Trick to have 'won the war punk rock tries to fight,' branding the second album 'rock'n'roll at its best.' In the *Detroit Free Press*, Mike Duffy floridly opined that 'the record does not confuse pastel rainbows for palatability—it devastates in the deceitful pallor of light humor' and that 'Rick Nielsen's guitar work cracks the endless boogie into sonic submission, resurrecting epitaphs of accentuated tenderness.'

Max Bell observed in *NME* that 'Cheap Trick has nothing standing in its way to full acceptance, massive popularity, and the formula to fleece the entire universe stone dry.' Jim Green lauded the album as 'a masterpiece of 70s hard rock.' Robert Hilburn declared, 'If this band were on the Rock Stock Exchange, I'd mortgage the house and get on the bandwagon.' Writing for *Record Review*, Boni Johnson observed that 'Cheap Trick's music is not really a new wave at all; it's a throwback to when bands crammed treatises on being a teenager into three minutes.' Douglas R. Weil declared the album to be 'one of the purest in years' in the *Daily Nebraskan*. 'Standing out in a business such as music is indeed an accomplishment.'

In Color opened with a Tom Werman favorite, 'Hello There,' a song inspired at least in part by the intro to *Elmer Gantry's Velvet Opera* from 1968.

BUN E. CARLOS *Rick might have lifted that. We used to do 'I Was Cool' from that record, the Oscar Brown tune.*

Nielsen hijacked the spotlight for those performances of 'But I Was Cool,' accompanying himself on an expendable instrument plucked from his parents' store.

BUN E. CARLOS *Anything his dad had at the store that he wanted to get rid of, and then it would get smashed at the end of the song. That was the one song Xeno would play guitar on.*

At one point, Ralph Nielsen purchased an entire inventory of electric violins from a company that was going out of business, so Rick had quite a stash. He capped each rendition of 'But I Was Cool' with an atonal solo, and then smashed the instrument. 'This was on our big nights,' he said.

Rick wrote 'Big Eyes,' the second song on *In Color*, at the Record Plant in New York while the band were recording the first album, building the song around a riff he bashed out on the studio's piano, admitting he 'tried to take a Fleetwood Mac riff that I liked and turn it around.' He also acknowledged that 'the chorus is pretty reminiscent of our being influenced by Alex Harvey.'

A few of Nielsen's earliest Cheap Trick compositions finally found a home on *In Color*: 'Down Down Down' (shortened to 'Downed'), 'I Want You To Want Me,' 'Southern Girls,' and 'Come On Come On.' Going even further back, a Sick Man Of Europe song called 'I'm A Surprise' became the last song on the album, 'So Good To See You.' It was also the last song they recorded.

Nielsen had reportedly already returned home when he somehow heard a tape of Zander's vocal for the song. Something was off. Robin had never really sung the song before (they dropped it from the set after Xeno left). So Nielsen flew back to Los Angeles to help Robin fix it, but fixing it meant: sing it the way Stewkey did. According to Zander, 'I learned it from Stewkey over the telephone.'

As has already been established, Zander was a talented mimic. When Stewkey heard the completed recording, he was stunned. 'He was so shocked because he thought it was himself, and he couldn't figure out how the hell we got his voice onto this,' Tom Petersson remembered.

'You're All Talk,' a chaotic version of which had been recorded during the first album sessions, finally made the cut alongside more recent compositions 'Clock Strikes Ten' and 'Oh Caroline.' Rick once said of the latter, 'One person's Caroline is another's heroine. Meaning a vice or vices people have.'

When 'I Want You To Want Me' was released as the first single, an instrumental track for 'Oh Boy' was included on the B-side. The song had lyrics, but a proper vocal had not been recorded (it would be later, with Jack Douglas). It was a fun song, riff-laden power pop. Nielsen wrote it not long after the first album was finished, at the end of 1976.

The single failed to chart.

* * *

The September 30 issue of Chicago-based *Triad* magazine contained an interesting exchange between interviewer Cary Baker and Rick Nielsen and Tom Petersson:

BAKER: I heard you recorded a live album in LA.

NIELSEN: We did record live at the Whisky in the middle of recording *In Color*, but it probably won't come out.

PETERSSON: Who wants a boring live album?

NIELSEN: We've got other subjects we're more concerned with.

At the end of September, Cheap Trick embarked on a string of dates supporting prog/glam Brits Be Bop Deluxe.

BUN E. CARLOS *We were doing six nights with them, ending in Buffalo.*

An advertisement for the first show at Cleveland Music Hall billed them as 'The Bizarre Cheap Trick.' Jane Scott called them a 'madcap band' in her review for the *Plain Dealer* and accused Rick Nielsen of wearing 'wrestler's shoes.'

KEN ADAMANY *He did. I remember when we purchased them.*

Scott described Rick's Hamer guitar, modeled after a Gibson Explorer, as 'kind of a funny shape, like an italic rectangle. He calls it obtuse.' She added, 'This band had a loose kind of fun show. It didn't even bother them when a man strolled out onstage during its third number. Road manager Kirk Dyer, once a pro hockey player, just reached in and pulled him off.'

The tour next swung through Chicago, where both bands jumped on a bill with REO Speedwagon at the International Amphitheatre. Eddie Kramer, whom they met on the KISS tour, happened to be in town and caught Cheap Trick's soundcheck.

BUN E. CARLOS *We did 'Fan Club,' and he came up to the stage in tears, and he was like, 'I've gotta do that song, I've gotta do your record.'*

Unfortunately, it didn't happen. Kramer was an incredibly accomplished engineer but rarely produced more than a record or two per year.

After Chicago, the tour headed to St. Paul, where trouble that had been slowly brewing finally came to a boil.

BUN E. CARLOS *They didn't give us a soundcheck, but that wasn't unusual. Then we* *walk out onstage and all the cords are next to the monitor boxes, unplugged. The house lights go on in the first song. All this shit happens to sabotage our show.*

MATTHEW PERRIN *They started turning breakers on and off. The lights were going on and off, they'd start a song and the monitors would go off.*

BUN E. CARLOS *So we do about five songs and stomp off stage.*

As Tom Petersson recalled, headliners could be ruthless. 'They'll do anything to make you sound bad. If you're going over good, all of a sudden the PA goes out and you don't realize it.' But Cheap Trick were still able to upstage the saboteurs, as reported by Tim Carr for the *Star Tribune*: 'Cheap Trick, an Illinois-based comic-rock quartet, opened the evening with a forty-minute set that was less pretentious, visually more exciting and about ten times louder than the headliners.'

The band reigned victorious from the stage, but the crew still hungered for revenge.

BUN E. CARLOS *We had this batch of these stickers that wouldn't come off.*

Be Bop Deluxe's departure from St. Paul might have been delayed, as the windshield of their station wagon somehow became plastered with said stickers.

Cheap Trick took a break from fighting with the headliners long enough to swing by Toronto for an *In Color* release party, as detailed by Robert Charles-Dunne in *Record World*:

CBS certainly did it right for a recent Cheap Trick appearance at the El Mocambo. During the band's stay, CBS promo reps used handshake buzzers, trick candy and numerous other 'cheap trick' novelty items. The best (and probably also the worst) trick came when CHUM-FM was due to simulcast the band's set one evening. Announcer Larry Wilson took to the stage to perform MC duties, accompanied by a young lady clad only in a pair of panties and a Cheap Trick T-shirt. Just as Wilson announced the band, the lady peeled off the shirt, bringing catcalls from the half-tanked audience which sounded to radio listeners like an overwhelming response for the band. Wilson kept his cool, delivering the intro without a stutter.

There was one last show booked with Be Bop Deluxe, at the Century Theatre in Buffalo, an event promoted by Harvey & Corky Productions, as in Harvey Weinstein (along with brother Bob) and Horace 'Corky' Burger. The trio also owned the venue, which would be forced to close within a matter of months 'after a balcony inside began swaying during a Lynyrd Skynyrd concert and housing inspectors warned that another such show could turn deadly,' according to Steve Cichon at the *Buffalo News*.

Nineteen year-old actress Linda Blair was at the show. *The Exorcist II* had recently set an opening weekend record. A different kind of exorcism was about to be performed at the Century Theatre, as Be Bop Deluxe were to be expelled from the Cheap Trick calendar.

BUN E. CARLOS *All the managers and booking agents and label guys showed up in Buffalo because people were fighting, roadies were fighting.*

Cheap Trick stole the show again, as reported by Tim Switels in the *Spectrum*:

These boys from Chicago come across with one of the best rocking stage performances of the seventies. They are truly entertainers, performers as opposed to being total musicians. The notion of Cheap Trick stands on its own two feet ... even as Be Bop performed what would be considered an incredibly tight set, it was evident that most of the people here are leaving with visions of Cheap Trick that dance in their heads.

* * *

Cheap Trick made the leap to headlining status at the Rockford Armory on October 8—a milestone they had little time to celebrate, as they immediately headed out on tour with Blue Öyster Cult and Black Oak Arkansas for a couple of weeks, squeezing in a gig with Foreigner at Cobo Hall on October 23. Reviewer Tim Yagle called Cheap Trick 'one of the best warm up acts I have seen.'

Cheap Trick excited the sold-out arena with some good, scorching music from their first and second albums. The energetic lead guitarist stole the show, running back and forth across the stage, making wild gestures at the audience, jumping offbeat and soliciting applause during his crunching.

With the additional aid of a frenzied drum solo, Cheap Trick did the job and then some in warming up the fans for the featured act.

On October 29, Cheap Trick headlined the ancient Riviera Theatre in Uptown Chicago. Opening was a labelmate from Epic, Meat Loaf, whose bombastic album *Bat Out Of Hell* (produced by Todd Rundgren) had just come out. 'I remember pulling up to the theater and it says, *Tonight! Cheap Trick, with Meat Loaf,*' the stout singer told Redbeard on *In the Studio*. 'And I said to myself, *These people think we're serving dinner.*'

It was the very first show of the *Bat Out Of Hell* tour, and the debut performance by Meat Loaf's band, The Neverland Express, composed of his partner in crime Jim Steinman on keyboards, brothers Bob and Bruce Kulick on guitar, Karla Devito on vocals, and drummer Joe Stefko, who was with John Cale's band when Cheap Trick played with them at the Starwood in March.

'We were all dressed in weird outfits,' Stefko remembered. 'They started the show off with speeches, not music, and that was wrong.' It was worthy experiment, injecting a rock show with a Broadway vibe, but an unruly crowd of Chicago riff raff made for a terrible focus group. Meat Loaf and friends toughed it out for two or three songs before, under fire from an oppressive volley of boos and jeers, they beat a hasty retreat. Stefko remembered Meat Loaf freaking out backstage. 'Chairs were going—Meat just throwing shit all over the place.'

BUN E. CARLOS *He was in there yelling and screaming at management, label guys, etc. after his short set. There really wasn't much dressing room to trash at that venue.*

That same month, Adamany sent a package to Steve Paul at Blue Sky Records, along with a letter that read:

Dear Steve:
Pursuant to Jim Charne's request, I am pleased to enclose a cassette tape of ten compositions by the members of CHEAP TRICK, complete with lyric sheets (seven only), for the possibility of the inclusion of some on the next Rick Derringer project.

We hope both you and Rick will find them to your liking and we look forward to working together. There is much more material available should you request more.

Thank you for your consideration.

Derringer ended up recording a pair of Rick Nielsen compositions, 'Need A Little Girl' and 'It Must Be Love,' for his 1979 album *Guitars & Women*, co-produced by Todd Rundgren.

Cheap Trick next headed to Los Angeles to tape an episode of *Don Kirshner's Rock Concert*. According to *Trouser Press*, the show's production staff objected to 'He's A Whore' and 'some of Rick's gestures,' but 'after much haggling, set is recorded for posterity.'

The episode aired on November 10. Cheap Trick commandeered the stage with a rough-hewn confidence, treating the cameras like half-in-the-bag Sunset Bowlers. I cannot imagine watching that episode and not becoming a lifelong fan. Cheap Trick crushed it. A November 13 article in the *Rockford Morning Star* referenced the television appearance and also remarked on the success of the new album ... especially in Japan.

The group's second album, *In Color*, has been ranked in the low 70s in sales by *Billboard* magazine for the past several weeks. The album currently is number 17 in Japan and has just been released in Venezuela and Australia.

That night, Cheap Trick opened for UFO and Rush at the Civic Center in Baltimore. *The Baltimore Sun*'s review focused almost entirely on Cheap Trick:

He stands frozen in the spotlight, his eyes bugging out the left side of his face while his mouth is sliding off the right. He looks like the opening shot in a Looney Tune. Except for one thing. He is wearing a killer electric guitar slung across his left hip and his right hand is pumping rapidly across the strings. Sound waves are running amok. Rick Nielsen snaps out of his self-induced trance. He kicks his left leg high in the air and mauls his guitar. For the next half hour, he will fling himself around the stage like the crazed child of Peter Townsend and the Bride of Frankenstein.

Cheap Trick remained out east for the rest of November, including a performance at the legendary Stone Pony in Asbury Park on November 16, reviewed by Jim Green for *Sounds*:

> Robin's gorgeous face and impeccable dress at first seem to clash with his vocal antics, a broad burlesque of the McCartney voice of 'Kansas City' and 'Beware My Love'—Paulie on an STD trip, cajoling, crooning, growling, begging, leering. But you can almost believe his characterisation in 'He's A Whore,' and by the time the band slam into Dylan's 'Please Mrs. Henry,' reclothed in heavy metal knickers, you're shouting along with him, 'DOWN on mah knee-HEES, I ain't got a di-HIIIIME'—and all the while Rick's flicking his personalised guitar picks at the audience with a marksman's aplomb, 'twixt scrubbing thunderous chords from his axe, leaping in the air with cheeks and eyes abulge, and tearing off arrogantly dexterous runs. Between sets, Rick mingles with the regulars and is approached by a coy young thing wearing a black T-shirt depicting white tennis balls over her ample frontage. 'Will you sign my balls?' 'Of course, my dear,' smiles the ever-suave Rick, dotting the 'i' smackdab on the nipple. And in the second set he continues the mischief in a musical vein, his axe spitting fire (and his mouth spitting guitar picks) as the Cheaps lent a new slant to Fats Domino's 'Ain't That a Shame,' romping through 'I Want You to Want Me,' and ripping all hell loose with 'Southern Girls.' It's over all too soon, even if it is nearly 4am, but we float out of Asbury Pisshole in a state of bliss, as if in a dream.

They played a couple of shows with The Motors in Pennsylvania, then with Crack The Sky in New Jersey, Bob Seger in Upper Darby, Crawler in Boston, and Utopia (featuring Todd Rundgren) in Commack, New York. Next came more dates with Rush, including the Capitol Theatre in Passaic, where Rick Nielsen endured a Rush fan 'giving me the finger like for twenty minutes.'

BUN E. CARLOS *[Rush] fans yelled insults, made rude gestures, threw shit at us, booed us, at every gig we did with them as I recall.*

Cheap Trick closed out November with a triumphant homecoming to their home away from home in Madison, where they were booked to headline the massive Dane County Coliseum. The night before, Rick Nielsen made a surprise appearance at Bunky's on the corner of Park and Regent (capacity about two hundred), where he delivered a 'comic introduction' (according to the *Madcity Music Sheet*) for Elvis Costello & The Attractions, who were on their first US tour.

BUN E. CARLOS *He introduced them as 'Elvis Costello and his band' because we didn't know the band had a name.*

Costello remembered them making their way 'through the snow and wind to Madison' only to find Rick Nielsen there to greet them and 'make an evangelical announcement to ease us over with the hometown crowd,' who Costello pictured as 'poised with pitchforks and flaming torches at that point.' Rick 'said that we were people he recommended personally.' It just so happened that *In Color* had been in heavy rotation on the Costello tour bus. 'Cheap Trick would become the missing piece in our private hit parade, the one that nobody really suspected,' Costello revealed. He even tried to write his own Cheap Trick song, which turned into 'Clean Money,' a song he conceded was 'a direct imitation of their style.'

Jake Riviera, co-founder of Stiff Records and Costello's manager, was also present at Bunky's, along with his fashion designer girlfriend Antoinette Sales, who Nielsen had recently tasked with tailoring some checkerboard pants (soon to be featured prominently in *Rolling Stone*). Riviera was still disappointed that his label's offer to release the first Cheap Trick album in Europe had been rejected by Epic—an extremely lamentable missed opportunity. *Cheap Trick* would have been the second long player released by Stiff, in between *Damned Damned Damned* (February 1977) and *My Aim Is True* (July 1977).

Cheap Trick's ascension to the Dane County Coliseum stage the next night was a big deal, as evidenced by a letter they received from the venue manager, Roy Gumtow:

It's our pleasure to welcome you as the headliner for tonight's performance. We've watched you climb the ladder of success during this past year as you've entertained Madison area people in January when you appeared with Queen, and again in April when you worked with Ted Nugent and Head East. We offer you congratulations as well as this token gift of Wisconsin's favorite cheeses. Perhaps you'll have time for a cup of hot coffee before going on stage.

The event was covered by Jean Davison for the *Madcity Music Sheet*:

> It was their first appearance as 'stars of the show' at the Coliseum. The
> 'coming' of CHEAP TRICK was witnessed by approximately four thousand
> ['more than that,' according to Ken Adamany]. CHEAP TRICK's longtime
> fans and followers were upset by the fact that now they were expected to
> pay $6.50 to see them perform in a huge building when they were used to
> experiencing CHEAP TRICK up close for $3.00.

December of 1977, like any month, was a busy one for Cheap Trick, but
significantly included no club dates: the smallest venue they visited was a
theater. There were a couple of shows with UFO and one with AC/DC.

Toward the end of December, Cheap Trick jumped on tour with Kansas,
whose *Point Of Know Return* was climbing the charts. After shows in San
Diego and Tucson, they bid adieu to 1977 with a New Year's Eve concert at
Long Beach Arena, reviewed by Terry Atkinson for the *Los Angeles Times*:

> The ringing in of the New Year Saturday night at the Long Beach Arena
> might have been more festive and satisfying if the order of the acts had been
> reversed. As it was, the packed house greeted 1978 with Kansas, one of the
> most ponderously pretentious groups around these days, which followed
> a set by one of 1977's most exciting newcomers, the rollicking quartet
> Cheap Trick … compared to the headliner, Cheap Trick's elemental, fun-
> filled approach seemed far more in accordance with the merrymaking of the
> occasion.

The band was in top form. Following an epic performance of 'Downed,' Rick
Nielsen announced, 'These next few tunes we're gonna do are some tunes
that may be on our next album. And we hope you like 'em. If you don't like
'em we'll give 'em to somebody else.' They launched into 'High Roller,' soon
to be recorded for the third album, followed by 'Ain't That A Shame,' yet to
be made famous by the live album. Following a blistering version of 'Clock
Strikes Ten,' Rick bellowed into the air, somewhere near to a microphone,
'Good night and a happy new year!' and the band launched into the decidedly
non-celebratory 'Auf Wiedersehen,' a song described by infamous stick-in-
the-mud Robert Christgau as 'a sarcastic ditty about suicide.' Cheap Trick

exited the stage to the throbbing echo of Robin howling that very word, over and over. Happy new year, indeed! The crowd was thrilled enough to call them back for an encore and duly treated to a wildly energetic rendition of 'He's A Whore.'

In the car after the show, the band heard themselves on the radio. 'We came on KLOS,' Rick Nielsen recalled.

KEN ADAMANY *We were driving to a party in Woodland Hills, thrown by friends of the band originally from Lake Geneva.*

The DJ spun a block of three songs from the most recent album: 'Hello There,' 'Clock Strikes Ten,' and 'Southern Girls.' As Rick remembered, 'It was like, *All right!* We're in LA, we just played a big gig, and we're on the radio! That was the start of something big.'

* * *

The Kansas tour reconvened on January 3 in Seattle and swung through Salt Lake City and Wichita on the way to Tulsa, Oklahoma.

BUN E. CARLOS *We had a day off, so Rick got out the phone book and looked up Twilley. There were about six Twilleys in there, so he just started calling Twilleys asking for Dwight.*

Dwight's mother answered the second number Rick dialed. 'Dwight has his own place now,' she told Rick, and he jotted down the number, then cold called Dwight and introduced himself. Rick told him about the band, and that they were fans. Dwight said, 'Come on over.'

Dwight Twilley and Phil Seymour met as teenagers, at a matinee screening of *A Hard Day's Night*, and immediately formed a band they called Oister. Like The Grim Reapers, when they signed a record deal the label made them change the name. 'Denny Cordell thought my name was so wacky that it had to be the name of the band,' Twilley remembered.

The Dwight Twilley Band cracked the Top 20 with their very first single, 'I'm On Fire,' which came out in August of 1975. They swiftly recorded a very similar follow-up called 'Shark,' but the release was inexplicably shelved when the label got cold feet, convinced the song would be derided as a novelty tune concocted to cash in on the recent success of Steven Spielberg's *Jaws*. After releasing two quality albums to a tepid response, The Dwight Twilley Band, which was just Dwight and Phil, called it a day, and Phil chased his dreams to Los Angeles.

Dwight stayed behind in Tulsa, where he was woodshedding songs for his first solo album when his phone rang.

BUN E. CARLOS *Rick was like, 'Here's the address where Dwight's at, if you guys wanna go over there.' Someone was driving us around or something. I don't think Wheel took us in the motor home, although he might have.*

There was this two-car garage that had a studio built on the second floor of it and he was up there working on some tunes. Dwight had keyboards, guitar, and scratch vocals down, and me and Tom put bass and drums on this track.

The song, called 'Out Of My Hands,' ended up being the first song on Dwight's excellent solo debut, *Twilley*, released by Arista in 1979. Jim Lewis played bass and drums on the record, but Bun E. still has a recording of the demo with the Cheap Trick rhythm section.

BUN E. CARLOS *It sounds really fucking good.*

* * *

After performing at the Tulsa Fairgrounds Pavilion (capacity ten thousand) they had two whole days off, followed by three consecutive dates in Texas (Houston, San Antonio, and Fort Worth). On January 9, Bun E. and Tom jammed with Dwight Twilley, then on the 10th they headed for Texas, where the Sex Pistols were scheduled to perform that night at the Longhorn Ballroom in Dallas, halfway between Tulsa and Houston. 'We were driving, hellbent to get there,' Rick told *Guitar Player*. But they missed the exit.

BUN E. CARLOS *Wheel went the wrong way and drove for an hour before he figured it out.*

Dallas was the fifth stop on the Sex Pistols' controversial (by design) two-week tour of the southern United States. The Longhorn Ballroom became so tightly packed that rubberneckers could lift both feet from the floor and remain suspended by the crushed bodies. A drunken Sid Vicious unwittingly 'played' a portion of the concert with his bass unplugged (probably for the best) and later employed a slimy fish as an unwieldy pick. By the end of the night, Sid was a bloody mess. The whole band was a mess and broke up after just two more shows.

'That was our one chance to go see those guys and we blew it!' Nielsen groaned. Johnny Rotten ditched the rest of the Pistols after a disastrous show in San Francisco on January 14, when he asked the crowd, 'Ever get the feeling you've been cheated?'

Following the three shows in Texas, the Kansas tour headed for Denver to play McNichols Arena on January 15, then down to Las Vegas for a show at the Aladdin Hotel on January 17. A less than cordial greeting awaited Cheap Trick in Sin City. An Epic memo described the incident:

> Upon arrival in Las Vegas for a show at the Aladdin Hotel with Kansas, Epic Recording group Cheap Trick found no mention of their appearance on the marquee in front of the hotel. After inquiring about the absence of billing, Cheap Trick was informed that the owner of the hotel had passed the word down to the manager of the Aladdin, who in turn, informed the promoter of the show that the two words Cheap Trick, could not appear together on the marquee in front of his hotel.

The incident was also reported on by *Cash Box* magazine:

> On the last leg of the Kansas/Cheap Trick tour, the latter group ran into some difficulty because of its name. The owner of the hall Cheap Trick played apparently refused to have the name appear on the marquee, perhaps fearing a negative reaction on the part of the people who would read it. The group would not have been as surprised had the event taken place in a small midwestern town, or some other city known to be of a conservative nature, but the venue in question happened to be the Aladdin Hotel in Las Vegas, and those in charge would not allow the words 'Cheap Trick' to appear outside the hotel.

Bill Elson from ATI fired off an exasperated letter to the uptight Las Vegas promoter, James Tamer:

Mr. Tamer:

It has come to my attention that on the CHEAP TRICK show of last night, that in spite of signing our contract and rider you neglected to fulfill Paragraph #2 concerning billing and advertising. I would like to take this opportunity to inform you that I find your conduct in this matter high-handed, arrogant, and un-professional. For the information of yourself and staff, CHEAP TRICK has already headlined a significant number of cities: they sold out the International Amphitheatre (capacity: 12,000) in Chicago last month. It seems likely they will become a National headline act very shortly. It also seems likely that in the event that they could sell out the Aladdin Theatre and chose to play there, that the same question of 'aesthetics' would be more suitably resolved.

'Expensive Trick' might have gone over better, considering it was Nevada. Columnist Joan Beck similarly misconstrued the band's name in an article for the *Columbus Daily Enquirer* in August of 1978, beneath the smug headline 'Culture Gone From College Studies':

It's no wonder parents are troubled when they suspect the level of great thoughts their offspring acquire at college is reflected in the philosophy they flaunt on the T shirts they wear home from school. One father, for example, is hoping the 'Cheap Trick' message his daughter wears across her chest advertises a rock group and not her budding interests in going into the business.

23

Don't get paid to take vacations...

HEAVEN TONIGHT. 12-STRING BASS. EUROPE.

Less than a week after the Sex Pistols imploded in San Francisco, Tom Werman arrived in Los Angeles to commence work on Cheap Trick's third album. For a brief moment it had looked as if Jeff Lynne might produce it.

KEN ADAMANY *The band brought up Jeff's name from time to time and asked that I contact his management about the possibility of their working together. On that subject, the producers for the earlier albums—Jack Douglas, Tom Werman, George Martin, Roy Thomas Baker, Todd Rundgren, Richie Zito, and Ted Templeman—are, in my opinion, all the very best!*

Adamany had recently been in touch with David Arden, son to ELO manager Don Arden (and brother to Sharon Osbourne), and subsequently sent Lynne some tapes. He sent Arden a package on December 6, 1977, along with a note that read, 'RE: CHEAP TRICK / Jeff Lynne. Enclosed find some of the latest on CHEAP TRICK. CBS International will be sending records over to your office shortly. It was a pleasure speaking to you today; I look forward to meeting you.'

Unfortunately, the interesting pairing did not come to pass. Time was tight, as the plan was for Cheap Trick to accompany Kansas on a brief tour of Europe with a departure date of March 5, and recording needed to be completed before then.

'We had three days of rehearsal and a little less than four weeks to record the entire album,' Werman told *Trouser Press*. The band had some new songs to learn during those three days: 'On Top Of The World,' 'Takin' Me Back,' 'On The Radio,' 'Heaven Tonight,' and 'How Are You.' None had been played live. They also rehearsed 'Need Your Love.'

The album was recorded at both the Record Plant and Sound City. Things got off to a rocky start at the latter, beginning with the drum sound, which took four days to nail down. 'We ended up calling Bobby Colomby, the drummer in Blood, Sweat & Tears, who was now working at Epic,' Bun E. Carlos explained to *Blender*. 'I went over to his house, got his kit that he'd used on "Spinning Wheel," and it still had the original heads on it. I took those off and put on new ones. Didn't want to wreck his historical drumheads. We finally got the sound we wanted by setting the kit up out in the hallway.' They also met Colomby's girlfriend, actress Pam Grier.

Lurkers from the live set like 'Surrender,' 'High Roller,' and 'Auf Wiedersehen' were finally given proper studio treatment. Tribute was paid to a major influence with a cover of The Move's 'California Man' (even though 'Down On The Bay' seems to have spent more time in the set list). Inspired by the results of a photo shoot in a bathroom with veteran photographer Reid Miles, Epic floated *American Standard* as a possible album title—a rare plumbing joke. The band said thanks but no thanks and eventually settled upon *Heaven Tonight*, which (presumably) failed to reference the location of the cover shot.

The title track boasted the recorded debuts of a pair of fantastical instruments Cheap Trick had commissioned from Hamer: the electric mandocello and, more significantly, the twelve-string bass.

* * *

As the story goes, Tom Petersson's quest to achieve a fuller bass sound dated back to the Sick Man Of Europe days, when he experimented with plugging an old Fender 12-string electric guitar into an Octave Divider he purchased at 8th Street Music in Philadelphia. The distortion pedal, manufactured by Mu-Tron, paired the note played with the note an octave below it, 'matching tone color and dynamics over an exceptionally wide range,' according to the company's website. Tom quantified his mission as 'getting the low end' but discovered that the Octave Divider 'didn't track well unless you played really slowly.'

Tom's bass of choice for his first few years with Cheap Trick was a standard four string Gibson Thunderbird II strung with Rotosounds (a la John Entwistle), channeled through a Moog Taurus pedal.

JOL DANTZIG *He used a lot of distortion on his bass when he used a four-string.*

'Musicians often came up to me and asked how we could make something so simple sound so good,' Petersson told the *Minneapolis Star*. 'I used little amps with high watts and full blast.'

At some point, Tom got his hands on an experimental Hagström eight-string bass, most famous for its association with the Jimi Hendrix Experience. Karl-Erik Hagström first constructed his prototype in Sweden in 1966 and put them on sale the next year. About 2,200 were sold before the H8 was withdrawn in 1969. Petersson deemed the Hagströms 'lousy instruments.'

JOL DANTZIG *Initially, Tom wanted to know if we could do something to the Hagström to make it more robust, stay in tune, and sound better. He liked the concept, but he didn't like the execution and it grew from that. They only had four bridge saddles and each group of two strings, even though they're an octave apart, were on the same saddle so you couldn't intonate the two different strings because the bridge needs to be in a different position for each string but you couldn't do it, so he wanted to know if we could fix that so I went about drawing up a plan for a bridge that could fix the Hagström and then before that even happened Tom had the idea for the twelve-string bass so we just kind of scrapped the bridge for the Hagström and went on to building the twelve-string bass.*

Further inspiration came from the Tiple, a triple-strung South American instrument that definitely passed through Ralph Nielsen's Music—the same place Rick Nielsen discovered the mandocello. On the *Silver* DVD, Nielsen declares the Tiple to be 'the world's smallest twelve-string bass' (Tiples are smaller than the average guitar). Jol Dantzig has also credited the twelve-string nature of the Tiple as an influence.

The basic idea was to have one instrument that could sound like several instruments playing at once, creating a thick sound that plugged holes. 'We just wanted our sound to be as big as possible,' Tom told Orangeamps.com, 'so I thought, *Why don't I just get a bass with a whole bunch of strings, so it'll sound kind of like a guitar player just playing along with the bass player?*'

JOL DANTZIG *We were going to make him an eight-string bass as we thought there would be too much tension on the neck with a twelve-string and it would be difficult to control.*

'They thought the neck wouldn't be able to handle all that tension,' Tom remembered, which had been an issue with the Hagströms: the necks bowed, and they would not stay in tune. Dantzig feared encountering the same problem with his creation.

JOL DANTZIG *I think I may have come up with the compromise, saying, 'Why don't we just triple the D and G strings,' and we can get away with that tension as a halfway measure. Tom agreed, and we built a ten-string for him. It was a solid maple bass with a double cutaway style, and it had a cool color: Pepto Bismol pink! The ten-string bass worked so well, and the neck was so easy to adjust that we thought maybe the neck could stand two more octave strings.*

'After I had the bass for some time, the guys from Hamer heard me play, and they conceded that I was right all along and that the bass sounded great,' Tom told *12-String Bass Encyclopedia*. According to Jol Dantzig, 'When that worked, then we realized, Okay, well this is really manageable, let's put twelve strings on it and see what happens.' Still wary, Jol went with a medium scale to minimize the tension exerted on the neck.

'I wanted the piano sound you get from the long-scale basses,' Tom told *Bass Player*. 'But I couldn't dissuade them from making short-scale basses.' He 'wanted it to sound like a Gibson Thunderbird with two guitar players playing along.' According to Dantzig, 'I think we had already used the split V headstock on a twelve-string guitar by then, we just carried it over to the bass. It was a nod to the Gibson Futura prototypes that preceded the Explorer model. I just trimmed it down a bit to make it a little more sleek. As far as the design decisions are concerned, much of it was collaboration and some of it was dictated by what was available or possible with the materials that we had at the time.'

JOL DANTZIG *I have to say that I cannot remember how long it took, but it was probably a long time. Months, that is. We weren't set up for anything with tooling, it was all chisels and drills. Besides, we were making it up as we went along. We just kind of did it by trial and error.*

'The longer the scale, the higher the tension has to be to achieve the same pitch,' Jol told *Music Mart*. 'Essentially, you're making your scale longer so you need to pull the string tighter to maintain the same note so this tends to accentuate the upper harmonics so you get more high end out of a longer scale.' Dantzig engineered a rounder, deeper neck and pre-emptive back bow. Next came 'the mechanics of figuring out where everything goes.'

JOL DANTZIG *Where's the neck gonna join the body, where does that put the bridge, where are all the components gonna go, how are you gonna stick twelve tuners on the headstock? Luckily, Schaller in Germany made three different sizes of tuners, so each group of three strings had three different size tuners.*

Petersson saw no limits. Why not have four separate pickups—one for each grouping of three strings? Of course, that meant four different outputs with four different volume and tone controls. Dantzig asked Seymour Duncan to build him something.

JOL DANTZIG *Each group of strings had its own pickup, volume, treble boost and cut, bass boost and cut, and a switch to select the frequency the EQ worked at. I had to find a circuit board that we could put inside the guitar that would have four channels on it. I had a friend [Rex Bogue] who did electronics, and I asked him to make a custom board that would fit inside.*

Rex Bogue 'had this preamp he called Balz Deluxe, and we just had him make those for bass with four channels,' Dantzig told *12-String Bass Encyclopedia*. 'We specified bass and treble frequencies and it had a switch that selected the peaks. Each one of those channels had a separate output. A little bit extreme, but it was fun.'

JOL DANTZIG *I asked him if he could build these little miniature coils—it's like a half a Stratocaster pickup turned sideways with three pole pieces on it so there's an individual coil under each group of strings. Each group of strings has its own pickup, and each one of those pickups is then routed to one channel and what effectively is a four-channel mixer on the front of the guitar.*

I had to build a box, too. At the other end of the cable, you have to have a box that takes the four signals and splits them into four separate outputs that you can plug into the amplifiers, so it had to have a little converter box at the other end. All that stuff had to be made, it all had to be fabricated, I had to get a box and drill the holes and put the thing in it and wire it. But it was worth it. It was fun.

And then I had to figure out how to make a cable that would carry all four of those signals.

Dantzig christened his Frankenstein's monster the Quad. But in addition to the four individual outputs, Jol also included a universal option, just in case: a fifth pickup, responsible for all twelve strings at once.

JOL DANTZIG *I had no idea what it was gonna sound like or if it would even work, and we're starting to build the bass and I was like, 'You know what, I'm just gonna put a second pickup on it that's just a regular bass pickup with its own output that you can just plug into a regular guitar amp so if the whole thing doesn't work, we got a back up plan.'*

For that fifth coil, Dantzig used a 'blade pickup' from Bill Lawrence.

JOL DANTZIG *So it actually had five outputs: it had the four separate, which we called the Quad outputs, and then it had a separate output that was just a regular guitar jack, and as it turned out he really only used that single jack output most of the time. The rest of it was kind of for show.*

As for the strings:

JOL DANTZIG *We actually had the guitar string company that we worked with— GHS, which was up in Michigan—make special sets for us. We actually had to determine what would work. I started with what would go on the Hagström and talking it over with Tom—should these be lighter, should these be heavier—and then you just try different strings, the different gauges, until you find the one that had the right tension for the note that it was being tuned to.*

The octave strings lay above the main strings, just like on any twelve-string guitar. Each string had its own adjustable bridge. The body of the first Quad was a double cutaway, top half maple and back half mahogany. They also used Mahogany for the neck, with a single truss rod. Hamer produced just nine Quad basses before reevaluating the design and switching to single cutaway and double truss rod. 'The twelve-string bass isn't just a gag, it truly answers a question and serves a need,' Dantzig told *Bass Player*. 'It filled out Cheap Trick and put a unique stamp on their sound.' The fuller sound 'allowed Rick to do a lot of different stuff.'

'It really adds dimension,' Nielsen told *Guitar Player*. Petersson told Ken Sharp in 2021, 'It just ended up where it's kind of an orchestrated thing, just naturally. I mean, I want to sound like a cello that's going through a Marshall and a grand piano and a B3. (laughs) Can we get all those things at once?'

As Tom explained to *Bass Player*, 'It's supposed to sound really big ... we used to be accused of playing tapes, because when Rick would stop playing for a second, people couldn't figure out where the sound was coming from.'

When *Circus* writer Lou O'Neill Jr. leveled such an accusation at the band, he earned himself a strongly worded letter:

Dear Lou,

In view of your libelous statement regarding Cheap Trick in the July 10 issue of *Circus* magazine, please be advised that not only do the band most certainly not use any prerecorded tapes of any kind during their live performance, but when Ira Mayer printed his doubts in a review of their May 24 Palladium show in the *NY Post*, both myself and Ken Adamany, Cheap Trick's manager, phoned him to personally invite him backstage while the band performed the following evening. This he declined to do, owing, he said, to other commitments. Then Mr. Adamany extended the invitation to include travelling with the sound crew, inspecting the equipment and coming backstage during any Cheap Trick concert in the future to prove the non-existence of the so-called tapes he conjectured about in his review. When he was told that a crew member played the synthesizer part in 'Surrender' offstage, that seemed to satisfy him.

I would suggest you check your sources before you print such statements in the future, or do you always believe what you read?

Best regards,

Lois Marino

Manager

East Coast Publicity

Epic/Portrait/CBS Associated Labels

As for Tom's playing style and setup: 'I always use a pick, and sometimes I'm more riff-oriented with the twelve,' he told Britt Strickland. He told Jon D'Auria that he uses 'a lot of palm-muting.' According to Tom, 'If you want a heavier sound, mute with your right hand. You'll notice that the bottom end leaps out. You also want to use your left hand to mute strings so they don't create overtones.' Also, 'Downstrokes sound better and are more consistent.' He also loved the 'string noise within the tone.' According to Tom, 'It isn't possible to get the 12-string bass sound that you want out of one speaker cabinet. Get your distortion and highs out of one amp and the low end out of another. The more amps, the better.'

'The idea is to play through both guitar and bass amps, simultaneously. That provides a glassy kind of guitar sound with great low end at the same time—sort of like Duane Eddy on bass. I want my tone to sound like a grand piano, cello, guitar, and bass all at once, through a big stack of amps.'

The twelve-string transformed Cheap Trick's live sound, but the instrument was almost never used in the studio.

BUN E. CARLOS *He didn't use it on the records because the engineers would say, 'We don't know how to record this. We can't handle that. Put that thing away. Get a four string out. Plug it into the board. Play another guitar along with it later, just overdub another guitar to make it sound like that.'*

As Tom admitted to Ira Robbins, 'It's certainly easier to play a regular bass. It's more fun to play a regular bass.'

* * *

The European tour kicked off on March 8 with shows in Holland and Sweden before they headed to Germany for seven shows, then on to Zurich. *Melody Maker* mentioned the impending arrival in February, calling Cheap Trick 'one of the most highly-rated new American bands.'

BUN E. CARLOS *We almost didn't even get to Europe. We didn't even have enough money to send our gear over.*

KEN ADAMANY *We barely broke even on the first tour of Europe with Kansas even though we received tour support from CBS Records International.*

Next up was a show at the Pavillon de Paris on March 23. The bus ride to the venue was an interesting one.

BUN E. CARLOS *The posters, which were four feet tall and two feet wide and plastered everywhere, had Cheap Trick above Kansas. And we all rode over to the gig together and we went by some of these posters and the Kansas guys looked out the window, and their faces just dropped.*

KEN ADAMANY *The promoter definitely screwed up.*

In light of the poster snafu, Cheap Trick took their exclusion from the next date, at the Hammersmith Odeon, personally, but Jim Capaldi from Traffic had been booked to open for Kansas in London instead. Cheap Trick were back on the bill for the March 27 show at the Apollo in Manchester. March 28 was a busy day, with a photoshoot at 10am and luncheon with CBS International executives at 1pm, followed by a 3:30 visit to the BBC for a taping of *The Old Grey Whistle Test*. Cheap Trick performed 'I Want You To Want Me' and 'Clock Strikes Ten' (even though an Epic memo suggested 'Southern Girls') for the cameras.

They learned the hard way how host 'Whispering Bob' Harris came by his nickname. The band was meant to start on cue. His cue.

BUN E. CARLOS *How am I supposed to hear him introduce us? He's like thirty feet away with his back to us talking to the camera, and you can't hear him when you're in his face.*

After four more shows with Kansas in Plymouth, Birmingham, Newcastle, and Northampton, Cheap Trick returned to London to headline a punk rock show at the Roundhouse on April 2, with The Stukas and Johnny Moped opening.

BUN E. CARLOS *People were spitting at us onstage. Rick yelled at them and it let up a bit.*

Executives from CBS/Epic, including Jim Charne and Lennie Petze from America, were there, along with representatives from EMI publishing and members of the Japanese press. Jake Riviera from Stiff came, along with Dave Edmunds, who declared Cheap Trick 'the best band I've seen since I can't remember when.' Nick Lowe was a fan as well, similarly declaring Cheap Trick 'the best group I've seen in years.'

'They're great cus they've got a sense of humor,' Lowe told *BOMP.* 'There's so many people who take themselves seriously. Cheap Trick are tight. They got it all covered. They've got two pretty boys and two bozos. It works perfectly ... I'd really like to work with them.'

Also found on the guest list for the Roundhouse: 'Dagmar +1.'

* * *

On April 1, a fortuitous blurb appeared in *Cash Box*: 'In addition to the Kansas tour dates, Cheap Trick has added 5 concert dates in Japan.'

The dates in Japan had been booked thanks to the persistent efforts of a Japanese promoter who, after calling around, was eventually put in touch with ATI. Considering the rate at which Cheap Trick records were selling in Japan, paired with the volume of press coverage the band had garnered there, the concerts seemed guaranteed to be well-attended. Dates were booked for the last week of April in the cities of Fukuoka, Nagoya, Osaka, Tokyo (two nights), and Shizuoka.

It was a thirteen-hour flight, direct from Chicago.

* * *

Rick Nielsen asked George Faber to join Cheap Trick not once but twice. George shot him down both times. Cut to: George Faber's phone ringing, and guess who's calling ...

Long distance.

GEORGE FABER *You know, from Japan, and he said, 'We're in Japan! Eat your heart out!'*

Epilogue...

Post-WWII, Japan faced an occupation by Allied forces, the mission being to rebuild and reshape the war-torn nation. Consequently, the Japanese people were exposed to and subsequently adopted various elements of Western culture, for example: consumerism. As prosperity returned, the nation's youth developed a keen interest in the latest trends from overseas.

In 1966, The Beatles arrived, booked to perform at Nippon Budokan, an arena constructed for the 1964 Summer Olympics. The Fab Four hammered out five half-hour sets in three days, each performance witnessed by ten thousand awestruck fans surrounded by three thousand stone-faced police.

Many in Japan, including the prime minister, objected to this new kind of invasion from the West, but there was no stopping it. Led Zeppelin performed at Budokan in 1971 and Deep Purple in 1972 (released as *Made In Japan*). Next came the flamboyance of Queen in 1975 and 1976, and KISS in 1977. The stage was set for Cheap Trick.

'We were like cartoon characters ... the Japanese, they got a kick out of it,' Tom Petersson told Dan Rather. Robin Zander added, 'It had a lot to do with the caricatures of ourselves, but the music had to be there too.'

Cheap Trick were greeted at the airport by a throng of thousands. 'We left Chicago a local band and when we arrived five thousand fans were screaming for us,' Zander told *Northwest Indiana Times*. 'None of us were ready for that kind of response.' The hotel became a prison from which they warily ventured only to be whisked to and from the venue by a security team. 'There was cab after cab after cab chasing us down the street,' Nielsen told *Goldmine*. 'They would try to pass us and be hanging out the window yelling at us. It was very dangerous, but it was also pretty darn cool.'

'About fifteen minutes before we were going to go on, our manager came up to us and said the Japanese production guy said we needed another song, because our set's not long enough,' Zander told the *St. Pete Catalyst*. 'He suggested putting "I Want You To Want Me" in the set, so we did.'

'It hadn't caught on anywhere else,' Petersson told the Library of Congress. 'Our Japanese tour promoter told us it was very popular in Japan and couldn't believe we weren't playing it, so we threw it back in the set at the last minute.'

'The girls started shouting out the crying, crying, crying part. It took us by such surprise that we almost stopped playing,' Zander reflected for *Northwest Indiana Times*.

It was a surreal experience. A different world.

BUN E. CARLOS *I remember playing a room tape from Budokan for my mom and commenting to her,* Check out all the screaming girls, just like The Beatles!

Adamany played that same tape for Jonathan Little, a program director at WISM in Madison, and Jim Charne from Epic, who was in Madison around that time. Both predicted that 'I Want You To Want Me' would become a huge hit.

JONATHAN LITTLE *I told Ken it was without question a hit and WISM would begin playing it as soon as it was released.*

It helped that the concerts in Osaka and Tokyo had been professionally recorded for potential release by Epic in Japan.

Cheap Trick returned to America and re-assumed the role of supporting act, opening that summer for the likes of REO Speedwagon, Foghat, Sweet, Uriah Heep, Blue Öyster Cult, and Rainbow. They sold out four headlining shows at the Bottom Line in New York for June 12 and 13, two sets per night; a band called The Heaters, which included sisters Missy and Maggie Connell, opened.

MAGGIE CONNELL *Apart from the general excitement, I remember Robin Zander thought our lead singer, Mercy Bermudez had a 'great ass' or the like—according to our manager.*

MELISSA CONNELL *Robin asked our manager which one of the three girls was the wild one, wink, wink, wink. I guess he was ready to party! We were very shy and didn't have any further exchange with them.*

Almost everyone from CBS/Epic was there. Susan Blonde brought Andy Warhol. Jack Douglas brought Steven Tyler, who anointed the band's dressing room by puking in the toilet. Warhol ventured backstage as well. 'He liked some of the weird stuff we had,' Nielsen told Mark Agnesi. Someone snapped some pictures of Warhol grinning while holding Rick's original 1958 Korina Flying V (today worth $250,000).

Robert Palmer (the simply resistible one) penned a mixed review of the show at the Bottom Line for the *New York Times.*

Cheap Trick, a hard-rock quartet from Chicago that fills stadiums in the Midwest and in Japan but has not yet become a household word here, cut short its second set at the Bottom Line on Monday night. Robin Zander, the lead singer, complained that he was losing his voice. One was scarcely surprised. The group was pumping out enough decibels to fill Shea Stadium, and one stumbled out of the Bottom Line with whole frequency bands of one's hearing rendered inoperable. Even though he was singing through a beefed-up public address system, Mr. Zander had to bellow just to be heard.

Palmer deemed the performance 'less than satisfying' but conceded that a 'club full of rabid fans' disagreed. He did enjoy the 'wonderfully zany' Rick Nielsen, with his 'goggle-eyed looks' and 'calculated clumsy stage moves.' He even acknowledged having heard some 'catchy hooks.'

Cheap Trick had to cancel the second set that night because, as Palmer mentioned, Robin was losing his voice. They requested a soundcheck for the next day, in order to reassess Robin's situation, but Allan Pepper, co-owner of the venue, demanded a fee for the 'service,' to which Adamany objected.

KEN ADAMANY *I was there waiting for the band to arrive when I was hit with having to pay for the soundcheck. We were having enough problems, and Tom Petersson was correct in his criticism after the first show, in that the band was playing too many consecutive dates. We wanted to perform that second night but* *didn't want to pay to find out if we could. I instructed the crew to pack up and head for Toronto, and then: all hell broke loose!*

Cheap Trick were booked to play Massey Hall in Toronto on June 15. A couple of days off would benefit Zander greatly, so they skipped town. Pepper and his partner were irate—remember, the shows were sold out—and Adamany became persona non grata at the Bottom Line, banned from the premises for years to come.

At the end of June, Rick Nielsen flew to Los Angeles to make a cameo appearance on the Gene Simmons solo album. He arrived at Cherokee Studios decked out in his full regalia: hat, bowtie, and a black cardigan heavy with buttons. During a break, Rick and Mitch Weissman—from the original cast of *Beatlemania*, there to sing background vocals—played ping-pong using Rick's guitar picks instead of balls. Pick-pong.

When Rick laid down his solo for 'See You In Your Dreams' he snuck in a few notes from the melody of the Disney standard 'When You Wish Upon A Star,' a tune Simmons had inexplicably recorded for the album. Did Rick find a way to bust Gene's balls on his own album? I like to think so. Simmons was not present when the solo was recorded. Maybe producer Sean Delaney played some of Gene's crooning for Rick, like 'You gotta hear this …'

Rick's compensation from Casablanca Records: $944 ($4,000 today).

In July, Cheap Trick headlined the Royal Oak Music Theatre and Santa Monica Civic Center, two venues where they'd opened for The Runways the previous year. Ken Wilson's review of the Civic Center show remarked upon the range in age of the Cheap Trick fan. He noted 'the youthful horde in black T-shirts' but also:

> Commingling with the kids in Cheap trick T-shirts are the less vocal, but just as animated, concertgoers in blazers, gabardines and gold jewelry— they're the over-thirty crowd whose numbers make up a healthy third of the audience. Is the over-the-hill-gang at the concert part of a music therapy program from an LA rest home? 'Hell no,' says one thirty-four-year-old. 'I just think Cheap Trick plays rock'n'roll the way it's meant to be played.'

In August, Cheap Trick embarked upon a series of co-headlining dates with an up-and-coming band from Down Under called AC/DC. 'Harvey Leeds from Epic had a brother who worked for Atlantic and said this group they had just signed from Australia had a guitarist that ran around a lot like me,' Rick Nielsen remembered.

HARVEY LEEDS *I was like, Hey, Rick, there's this guy that's a cartoon character just like you.*

'Harvey gave me a copy of the album and, from the first notes that I heard, I've loved these guys ever since,' Nielsen recalled. 'The best rock band, bar none, that I've ever heard. When we toured together, I watched every show from the side of the stage. Nothing fancy, just great playing and great songs. No ballads.'

Each band had developed a distinct personality and sound, infectious and biting. They complemented and complimented each other, but Cheap Trick aspired to be more than just a band's band, admired by their more successful peers. All the same, the respect was well-earned.

Also in August, Hall & Oates's seventh album, *Along The Red Ledge*, was released by RCA, featuring Rick Nielsen tearing it up on a track called 'Alley Katz.' The song's riffage and arrangement are reminiscent of Cheap Trick but, dare I say, Rick would have written a better chorus. Nielsen also performed on Alice Cooper's *From The Inside* during this period. Both records were produced by David Foster.

* * *

That fall in Colorado, a low-budget film was shot in about three weeks, helmed by a thirty-year-old French director named Jonathan Kaplan. To be called *Over The Edge*, it chronicled a violent uprising staged by a group of disaffected suburban youth, led by a fourteen-year-old Matt Dillon in his theatrical debut. Cheap Trick songs provided a soundtrack to much of the action. According to Kaplan, it was teen actress Pamela Ludwig who turned him on to the band. 'Pamela was practically the music supervisor for the movie,' he remembered. 'I just listened to what she played me and paid attention. The movie is better for it. I think the soundtrack was ahead of its time. Not many movies used rock scores then.' Cameron Crowe agreed, remarking in 2006 that *Over The Edge* 'was the first time I'd seen contemporary rock used in this way.'

Ludwig was made hip to the band by her older boyfriend, who, as she recalled, 'worked as a roadie for a few different bands, and he introduced me to all of the music around that time. He took me to see Cheap Trick, and I fell in love with them.' Ludwig remembered rocking out in the van on the way to the set every day. 'We would blast "Surrender" and all sing, "Surrender! Surrender!"' *Heaven Tonight* had only been out for a few months. In one of her more memorable scenes, which was improvised, Ludwig pretends that a gun is a guitar as she mimes along to the song.

Rick Nielsen was asked about the film by the *Boston Globe* in May 1979. 'I saw a rough of it and it was real interesting and funny and serious and neat and cool,' he meandered. 'It had all kinds of good qualities and some crummy qualities that help boost the good qualities, know what I mean?' Nielsen also discussed turning down an offer to appear in Roger Corman's *Rock 'n' Roll High School*: 'It didn't work because we wanted to write ourselves into it and make it something that would benefit us, too, instead of just being *the band in the movie*.'

* * *

Cary Baker became a Cheap Trick devotee while attending Northern Illinois University in DeKalb.

CARY BAKER *I was living in a dorm and I had a rock'n'roll roommate, played in a band, who I'd actually known since high school, and he went out to see music one night and I didn't. I was asleep. And he came in about midnight and said, 'Dude, I saw this band called Cheap Trick and they're like a cross between The Kinks, The Move, and The Who and Mott The Hoople. You need to see them.' And I said, 'Well, you've touched on all my food groups there.' So I made it a point to see them the next time they played and sure enough, even better than described. I just freaked out. How does this unsigned bar band from Rockford have this look, the sound, these songs, that logo, this truck, that road crew? I was mesmerized.*

In 1978 there came an exciting opportunity. Baker had already made a name for himself as a rock writer (quoted multiple times in this book). Now, Armand Chianti, program director at WYFE-FM (Y95) in Rockford, was offering Baker a shot at radio.

CARY BAKER *I had an on-air audition for an interview show, a rock'n'roll interview show on Y95, and my first interview subject was Rick Nielsen, and I hadn't even calculated or suspected or let my mind entertain the possibility that Rick might be playing with me or making this difficult for me, but he certainly did. I was just basically an innately shy, Midwest college student. I had a really good opportunity here. I thought I might even have a future in radio.*

Rick Nielsen decided to be uncooperative.

CARY BAKER *He was real cynical and gave kind of cynical answers and that was that. I didn't hate him for it. I don't know what got into him that day or why he decided to do that, but, needless to say, I didn't get the job.*

The on-air segment opens with Cary stiltedly reading a press release from Epic Records:

CARY: Rick Nielsen, Robin Zander, Tom Petersson, and Bun E. Carlos, collectively known as Cheap Trick, are back in the USA following tours of Europe and Japan. The continent of Europe has long been a market for the band. ELO Kiddies was a hit single and their first two LPs sold pretty well, but more recently Japanese fans welcomed the band as if they were aristocracy. They landed in Tokyo on April 22nd to the flash of press photographers. They were whisked away from the cheering crowds through the back exits and when they arrived at their hotel the scene was more fans and more cameras still. While in Japan Cheap Trick was interviewed by Japan's two leading music magazines, *Music Life* and … [hesitates]
RICK: *Ongaku Senka!*
CARY: Thank you, Rick.
RICK: *Ongaku Senka*, Cary. Come on, get with it.
CARY: … both of which plan to feature the band on the covers of their May editions. Guitarist Rick Nielsen received an award from *Player* magazine, a custom-built one-of-a-kind special Rick Nielsen Ibazez guitar. *Music Life* magazine chose Cheap Trick as the brightest hope of the year, topping the category with almost forty thousand votes. Their Japanese single, 'Clock Strikes Ten,' from the *In Color* album, is no.4 in Tokyo with sales of *In Color* exceeding forty-seven thousand copies [double platinum]. Their third album,

Heaven Tonight, was released in Japan before anywhere else in the world. Americans are still waiting. In one Japanese city, six hundred screaming fans mobbed the airport as the band landed, having to be physically restrained by police. The hysteria level at the concert was so high that the local promoter warned them that if Rick threw any of his guitar picks into the audience the promoter would shut down the show in fear of a riot. Naturally the band refused to oblige. 'Clock Strikes Ten' has ...

Cary forces a laugh as Rick peppers him with picks.

CARY: Quit throwing the picks.

He keeps reading ...

CARY: 'Clock Strikes Ten' has been the number one single in the area for six consecutive weeks. The new single, the title track from *Heaven Tonight*, sold more than four thousand copies in one day.

The papers rustle as Cary sets them aside.

CARY: That's quite a success story. How do you account for your success across the Pacific?
RICK: Gee Cary, you do that so smooth. [laughter from Robin] That was terrible! You're supposed to be a writer, you're supposed to be able to read stuff. [more laughter from Robin] That was written by Susan Blonde in New York, and she sent that to you, Cary, and I thought you could pronounce those big words. What was your question? I'm sorry.
CARY: How do you account for your success in Japan?
RICK: Well, uh, they like our music, just like they do in Rockford, and just like they do in Madison and it's just ... it was our first tour there and, uh, it was a lot of fun.
CARY: Do they have an active promoting staff?
RICK: Hey look, who's gonna get technical, y'know? Who knows about that? Nah, they like the way Bun E. plays the drums and Robin sings and the way I play guitar and Tom plays the bass. That's it. Who knows about all that other stuff. They like our records. I already said that.

CARY: What's Japanese radio like? Is it anything like we have in the States?

RICK: Yeah, except you can't understand it unless you know Japanese.

Late in the interview, Cary poses an interesting question.

CARY: Have you thought about album number four?

RICK: Of course. And five, and six …

CARY: … and seven.

RICK: Well, as a matter of fact, when we were in Japan we recorded three nights there. We recorded two nights in Tokyo and one night in Osaka. So there will be a live album in Japan …

CARY: Released just in Japan?

RICK: I believe just released in Japan. Maybe it'll become an import.

* * *

While the live album was readied for an October release in Japan, Cheap Trick carried on, performing multiple dates supporting Ted 'Fred' Nugent, Eddie Money, and Foreigner, and also headlining the Palladium in New York City on September 28, with an up-and-coming band from Boston called The Cars opening. In November, seven songs from the Palladium set were broadcast on the nationally syndicated *King Biscuit Flower Hour* radio program, including a ten-minute version of the at that point unreleased 'Need Your Love.'

Post-Palladium, Epic threw a well-lubricated after-party, which was filmed for a potential broadcast on local television, hosted by Epic publicist Susan Blonde. Blonde interviewed various attendees, including singer-songwriter Elliott Murphy (also signed to Epic), former Modern Lovers bassist Ernie Brooks (who had a new band called The Necessaries, not signed to Epic), former New York Doll David Johansen, actress Linda Blair (hello again), an unegged (as opposed to unarmed) John Cale, and Ramones manager Danny Fields.

Introducing members of Cheap Trick for the camera, Blonde says, 'They're number one in Japan, they're still gonna be number one here, they're real big but they're not number one yet.' Bun E. Carlos, standing beside her, says, 'Susan, I know you and Epic Records are gonna do it for us.' Then Rick Nielsen chimes in: 'Susan, I have more pimples this year, but I'm trying to keep that youthful image.' Rick brags about owning seventy-two guitars, then quips, 'Tom is so modest, but I'm not!' Susan also interviews an enthusiastic Ira Robbins, the head honcho at *Trouser Press*, who declares, 'This magazine usually only writes about English people and to get on the cover of this magazine if you're American is really a rarity, and Cheap Trick did it.' He adds, 'I think Cheap Trick have more going for them than any American band, except for maybe the Ramones.'

That same month, word came down that 'I Want You To Want Me' had finally cracked the Top 40, as reported by the *Capital Times*:

> Sense of humor is the overriding theme both onstage and off. As the audience waited for the band's entrance, Cheap Trick tricked 'em by playing a tape they'd just received—a recording of 'I Want You To Want Me' by France's Nicol Flynn, that country's answer to Frank Sinatra. 'Believe it or not, it's no.39 on the French charts,' says a grinning Rick. 'And we think it's hilarious. It's doing better there than we are here.'

That would be Niko Flynn, who was hardly the French Frank Sinatra, considering that the 'I Want You To Want Me' single seems to have been his only release. Flynn's spacey version, translated as 'J'attends toutes les nuits,' was heavy on the bass yet devoid of guitar.

Cheap Trick's own recording of 'I Want You To Want Me,' as produced by Tom Werman, was actually a big hit in parts of Japan. In fact, an alternate version of the song was about to be released there—the live recording from April.

On October 22, the band began recording their fourth album at the Record Plant in Los Angeles, again with Tom Werman.

In November, they were featured on an episode of NBC's *The Midnight Special*, hosted by Ted Nugent. Spirited performances of 'California Man' and 'Surrender' were aired, Nielsen wielding his brand new checkerboard Hamer, which, when seen on display at Rick's Picks, bore this description: 'To achieve the checkerboard pattern, the guitar was first painted all white. Special tape was then cut into squares and meticulously hand fitted onto the guitar. It was then painted black. When the tape was removed, the famous pattern was revealed.'

The fourth album was mixed and ready by December, but Epic placed it in a holding pattern while they pondered giving the Japanese live album, which had become quite popular as an import, a domestic release. Maybe they would issue *Cheap Trick At Budokan* stateside in February, to prime the pump for *Dream Police* in March …

* * *

'We fought against releasing it here,' Tom Petersson told James Simon for the *Associated Press*. 'We had already recorded *Dream Police* and it would throw off our schedule.' As it turned out, *Dream Police* was shelved for ten months while the live album scaled the charts, climbing to no.4 on *Billboard*. It was eventually certified triple platinum. Forty years later, *Cheap Trick At Budokan* was added to the National Recording Registry at the Library of Congress, selected from more than eight hundred recordings nominated that year as 'culturally, historically, or aesthetically significant.'

The live album's roaring success was the happiest of accidents. 'We didn't like the recording, we didn't like the cover, we didn't like anything about it, really,' Robin Zander told *Elliot In The Morning*. 'So we were arguing with our manager about it, saying, We don't want this thing to come out, and he said, Don't worry, it'll be fine, only the Japanese audience will hear it, and they deserve it because they brought us over here.'

'After *Heaven Tonight* we were so far in debt we didn't know what to do with ourselves,' Zander told Martin Popoff. Tom Petersson concurred: 'By the time *Budokan* came along, we were so far in the hole it was ridiculous.' Rick Nielsen told *Guitar Player*, 'The longer that it takes you to get successful, the longer it is to pay off everything.' According to Bun E. Carlos, they 'were about a million bucks in the hole.' Zander put it bluntly: 'If it weren't for *Budokan* it might have been the end for us.' He acknowledged that the live album 'saved us from probable obscurity.'

KEN ADAMANY *Records show a different scenario regarding financials at that time, but no matter. Without a doubt, the Budokan album changed everything for the band and the future of all involved in a very positive way. They are to be congratulated for their great performances in Japan, and in the making of this fantastic-sounding, best-selling live recording. Simply stated, Cheap Trick is one of the very best and most talented bands to have ever performed and recorded.*

* * *

On April 1, 2007, the Illinois State Legislature unanimously passed a resolution that concluded thusly:

> ... be it RESOLVED, BY THE SENATE OF THE NINETY-FIFTH GENERAL ASSEMBLY OF THE STATE OF ILLINOIS, that we designate April 1 of every year as Cheap Trick Day in the State of Illinois; and be it further RESOLVED, that suitable copies of this resolution be presented to Rick Nielsen, Robin Zander, Bun E. Carlos, and Tom Petersson as a symbol of our esteem and respect.

Aaron Chamber penned an entertaining article for the *Rockford Register-Star* that chronicled Rick Nielsen's visit to Springfield to accept the honor:

> Rick Nielsen entered the Capitol like the rock star he is: a flashy man in a zebra-stripe jacket, trademark ball cap and dark sunglasses—but he had to remove his jewelry to clear a metal detector at the front door. Then the Cheap Trick guitarist and Rockford native was off with a bang. For the next two hours, he shook Illinois government free from its traditional decorum with a never-ending stream of wisecracks about sex, drugs, rock'n'roll, and criminal activity. The rocker charmed state officials, lawmakers, legislative staff, and bystanders during his first visit to the Capitol.
>
> Nielsen said he picked April 1 to be the band's official day because it's April Fools' Day ...

Nine years later, Cheap Trick were finally inducted into the Rock and Roll Hall of Fame. They became eligible in 2002—the same year that the Ramones and Tom Petty were inducted—but Cheap Trick had to wait until 2016 to even be nominated. Thankfully, they made it in on the first go round, a triumph of perseverance.

'Music has always been my savior,' Robin Zander remarked during his acceptance speech. 'It found me at an early age. It's all I've ever done for my living. You can write *retirement* on my tombstone.'

Notes and sources...

Acknowledgments

Thank you ... to my parents for everything ... to Ken Adamany for your kindness, wisdom, generosity, time, and effort, hopefully this book makes clear that the role you played in this story cannot be overstated ... to Jim Charne for making the introduction and conducting the audition, and for sharing your invaluable recollections ... to Bun E. Carlos for being Bun E. Carlos, and for your patience and benevolence ... to Steven Roth for being a great advocate ... to Tom Seabrook for your crucial assistance and advice ... to Rich Kwasniewski for so kindly sharing your treasures ... to Ken Mills for your friendship and kind heart (You plucked me from obscurity!) ... to Clive Palmer for your indispensable help and encouragement ... to Greg Renoff for much guidance and inspiration ... to Dean Falcone and Derek Brown for cheering me on ... to Dan Riches for being there since kindergarten ... to Craig Gieck for going to see Cheap Trick with me at least twenty times ... to Chris Standish for having great taste in music and friends ... to Dan Plovnick for bailing me out more than once ... and to Ducky and Lydia Kramp, wherever would I be ...

And to:

Alex Adamany, Ron Alexenburg, Ashley Alhadeff, Michael Alhadeff, Jeff Ament, Ross Anderson, Stewkey Antoni, Terry Arbegust, Holly Ayers, Cary Baker, Jimmy Barnes, Dan Beck, Brian Beebe, Joseph Bergamini, Mimi Betinis, Johnny Fraser-Binnie, Rachel O'Donoghue Binnie, Brian Blockinger, Susan

Blonde, Boris Boden, Jim Bonfanti, Donna Boyce, Steve Boyce, Doug Brod, Michael Butler, Dan Buyck, John Calacci, Aaron Camaro, David Carroll, Eric Carmen, Sparkling Joe Chamberlain, Clark Colborn, Jenn Collins, Pete Comita, Maggie Connell, Melissa Connell, Al Craven, Bob Creagan, Cameron Crowe, Chris Crowe, Chris Czynszak, Mark Dahlgren, Jol Dantzig, Orville Davis, Bruce Dickinson, Joe X. Dube, Timothy Eaton, Walter Egan, William J. Eib, Brad Elvis, George Faber, Paul Faber, Mic Fabus, Pat Fenelon, DX Ferris, Terrence Flamm, Darrell Fornell, Pat Francis, Rick Freiman, Russ Freiman, Dave Frey, John Furland, Dave Galluzzo, Gary Gand, Tom Genetti, Christian Gerolmo, Sammy Gerolmo, Julian Gill, Sam Ginsberg, Kim Gisborne, Jay Graydon, Steve Grimm, Joe Guarino, Mark Hallberg, Paul Hamer, Lars Hanson, Brendan Harkin, Shayne Harris, Mike Hayes, Joey Haynie, Rich Hazdra, Loren Heinzeroth, Jackie Hendricks, Kristian Hoffman, Randy 'Xeno' Hogan, Bernie Hogya, Keith Hollis, Todd Houston, Tod Howarth, Steven Hufsteter, Deone Jahnke, Cliff Johnson, Dave Kawczinski, Scott Kawczinski, Mike Kelley, David Kenney Jr, Ted Kenney, Heather Kerr, Tony Kishman, Gary Klebe, David Konow, Walter Kornbluth, Timmy K. Kramp, Martin Krohne, Mark Krueger, Scott Krueger, Rich Kwasniewski, Kenn Kweder, Jon Lamoreaux, Justin Langenberg, Robert Langenberg, Robert Lawson, Harvey Leeds, Yvonne Lewicki, Jonathan Lipp, Jonathan Little, Bill Lloyd, Sal Maida, Cynthy Mandl, Handsome Dick Manitoba, Roman Maroni, Greg Mariotti, John Masino, Susan Masino, Robin McBride, Lee McCormack, Jim McInnes, Ryan McKay, Timothy McKeage, Chris McLernon, Richard Menning, Jay Messina, Hilly Michaels, Eric Miller, Sharon Milway, Dale Mincey, Helene Mintz, Thom Mooney, Jessica Morales, John Muzzarelli, Craig Myers, Ed Myers, John Myers, Lori Myers, Mike Myers, Bill Natale, John Nelson-Horn, Daxx Nielsen, Rick Nielsen, Janie Norby, Jim Nowack, Michael Oosten, Jordan Orleans, Denny Orsinger, Brad Page, Jon Parrot, John Pazdan, Rick Pemberton, Victor Penalosa, Matthew Perrin, Tom Peterson, Tom Petersson, Lennie Petze, Chip Rachlin, Richie Ranno, Hank Ransome, Heather Ransome, Kathi Ransome, Roger C. Reale, Sarah Riches, Ira Robbins, 'Count Floyd' Robertson, Marty Ross, Mark Rowe, Joe Royland, Bill Rude, Danny Sage, Paula Scher, Kim Schlater, Scott Schoenbeck, Jay Schwartz, Sarah Seiler, Denny Seiwell, Ken Sharp, Madeline Shirley, Todd Shuster, Patrick Skinner, Craig Smith, Gary Sohmers, Mark Spector, Bobby Startup, David Steffen, Joe Stefko, Jody Stephens, Butch Stone, Joe Sundberg, Mark Swanberg, Richard

Swanson, Chuck Sweeny, Brian Sword, Michael Tafoya, Timi Tanzania, Bobby Tanzilo, Jack Thibault, Danielle Thompson, Adam Thompson, Chuck Toler, Paul Trap, Katie Tromello, Dwight Twilley, Chris Utley, Eric Van Lustbader, Mike Vanderbilt, Melvin Verhein, Michael Visceglia, Carolyn Vogel, Ken Voss, James Wald, Jeff Waluch, Tom Werman, Dan Wielgus, Byron Wiemann, James Willbanks, Jai Winding, Curtis R. Wright, Cassidy Yazzie, Tracy Yeshulas, Robin Zander, Vern Zech, Paul Zone, Jim Zubiena. And a heartfelt thanks to Nigel and Jawbone Press for rolling the dice!

And to anyone I missed, I am sorry, and thank you as well.

Bibliography

Aerosmith with Stephen Davis. *Walk This Way: The Autobiography Of Aerosmith.* New York: HarperEntertainment, 1997.

Jack Altman with Marvin Ziporyn, M.D. *Born To Raise Hell: The Untold Story Of Richard Speck.* New York: Grove Press, 1967.

Lawrence M. Baskir and William A. Strauss. *Chance And Circumstance: The Draft, The War, And The Vietnam Generation.* New York: Alfred A. Knopf, 1978.

Tom Bates. *RADS: The 1970 Bombing Of The Army Math Research Center At The University Of Wisconsin And Its Aftermath.* New York: Harper Collins, 1992.

Tom Beaujour with Richard Bienstock. *Nothin' But A Good Time: The Uncensored History Of The '80s Hard Rock Explosion.* New York: St. Martin's Press, 2021.

Dennis L. Breo with William J. Martin. *The Crime Of The Century.* New York: Bantam Books, 1993.

Doug Brod. *They Just Seem A Little Weird.* New York: Hachette Books, 2020.

Elvis Costello. *Unfaithful Music & Disappearing Ink.* New York: Blue Rider Press, 2016.

Kent Crowley. *Surf Beat: Rock 'N' Roll's Forgotten Revolution.* New York: Backbeat Books, 2011.

Pat Cunningham. *Rockford: Big Town/Little City.* Rockford: Rockford Newspapers Inc, 2001.

Mary E. Donnelly with Moira McCormick. *Boys Don't Lie: A History Of Shoes.* Vestal, NY: PurePopPress, 2013.

Murray Engleheart with Arnold Durieux. *AC/DC: Maximum Rock & Roll: The Ultimate Story Of The World's Greatest Rock And Roll Band.* Sidney: Harper Entertainment, 2006.

Michael S. Foley. *Confronting The War Machine: Draft Resistance During The Vietnam War.* Chapel Hill: The University of North Carolina Press, 2003.

Sherry Gershon Gottlieb. *Hell No We Won't Go: Resisting The Draft During The Vietnam War.* New York: Viking, 1991.

Curt Gooch with Jeff Suhs. *KISS Alive Forever: The Complete Touring History.* New York: Billboard Books, 2002.

Mike Hayes with Ken Sharp. *Reputation Is A Fragile Thing: The Story of Cheap Trick.* Willow Grove: Poptastic Books, 1998.

Landon Y. Jones. *Great Expectations: America And The Baby Boom Generation.* New York: Coward, McCann & Geoghegan, 1980.

Lawrence D. Klausner. *Son Of Sam.* New York: McGraw-Hill Book Company, 1981.

Robert Lawson. *Still Competition: The Listener's Guide To Cheap Trick.* Victoria, BC: FriesenPress, 2017.

Jon W. Lundin. *Rockford: An Illustrated History.* Tarzana: American Historical Press, 1996.

James H. Madison. *Heart Land: Comparative Histories Of The Midwestern States.* Indianapolis: Indiana University Press, 1988.

Steve Matthes and Joe Moffett. *The Ultimate: An Illustrated History Of Hamer Guitars.* Atglen: Schiffer Publishing, 2013.

Barry Miles. *The British Invasion.* London: Sterling Publishing, 2009.

Steve Miller. *Detroit Rock City: The Uncensored History Of Rock 'N' Roll In America's Loudest City.* Boston: Da Capo Press, 2013.

Rick Nielsen. *Rick Nielsen's Cheap Licks.* London: Hal Leonard, 2019.

Keith W. Nolan. *Ripcord: Screaming Eagles Under Siege, Vietnam 1970.* Novato: Presidio Press, 2000.

Simon Philo. *British Invasion: The Crosscurrents Of Musical Influence.* New York: Rowman & Littlefield, 2015.

Ian S. Port. *The Birth Of Loud: Leo Fender, Les Paul, And The Guitar-Pioneering Rivalry That Shaped Rock 'N' Roll.* New York: Scribner, 2019.

Mark Ribowsky. *Dreams To Remember: Otis Redding, Stax Records And The Transformation Of Southern Soul.* New York: Liveright Publishing Corporation, 2015

Ira A. Robbins. *Music In A Word Volume 2: Fandom And Fascinations.* New York: Trouser Press Books, 2021.

Bruce J. Schulman. *The Seventies: The Great Shift In American Culture, Society, And Politics.* Cambridge: De Capo Press, 2001.

Ken Sharp. *Play On! Power Pop Heroes Volume 2.* Encino: Jetfighter, 2015.

Jon C. Teaford. *Cities Of The Heartland: The Rise And Fall Of The Industrial Midwest.* Indianapolis: Indiana University Press, 1993.

Dave Thompson. *Better To Burn Out: The Cult Of Death In Rock 'N' Roll.* New York: Thunder's Mouth Press, 1999.

Dave Thompson. *Sparks—No.1 Songs In Heaven.* London: Cherry Red Books, 2009.

Brad Tolinski and Alan Di Perna. *Play It Loud.* New York: Anchor Books, 2016.

John Van Der Kiste. *Roy Wood: The Move, Wizzard And Beyond.* Seattle: Amazon, 2012.

Steve Waksman. *Instruments Of Desire: The Electric Guitar And The Shaping Of The Musical Experience.* Cambridge: Harvard University Press, 1999.

Mick Wall. *Like A Bat Out Of Hell.* London: Trapeze, 2017.

Ed Ward. *The History Of Rock & Roll Volume One 1920–1963.* New York: Flatiron Books, 2016.

Warren Zanes. *Petty: The Biography.* New York: Henry Holt and Co, 2015.

Endnotes

CHAPTER ONE

'You need to do something else ...' Brassneck, *Illinois Entertainer*, April 2021

'He talked my dad into ...' / 'feast or famine ...' / 'long, long hours ...' / 'realize being in retail ...' *Guitar Aficionado: The Collections*

'Maybe five times in my life ...' DannyWimmerPresents.com, 2020

'You sucked up America as energy ...' Simon Philo, *British Invasion: The Crosscurrents Of Musical Influence*

'Some of my best friends ...' Tom Wheeler, *Guitar Player*, November 1979

'People started laughing ...' / 'I played drums until ...' *Rock Scene* YouTube channel, September 27, 2018

'I'd never have admitted ...' Mark Blake, *Planet Rock*, December 2018

'I'd play the melody ...' *Rock Scene* YouTube channel, September 27, 2018

'I'd say the sax player ...' Jim Sistril, *IMAGINE*, Nov/Dec 1978

'It was on a payment plan ...' *Gretsch News*, July 6, 2016

'I plunked around and taught myself ...' *Legendary Rock Interviews*, November 5, 2012

'I'm a fourth-generation drummer ...'
Robin Tolleson, *Modern Drummer*
'My mother went to Sears ...' / 'My dad was a
musician ...' Dan Rather, *The Big Interview*
'When The Beatles and The Kinks ...' Mark Blake,
Planet Rock, December 2018
'When I first heard The Who ...' Patrick Goldstein,
Chicago Daily News, October 27, 1977
'I remember driving home ...' Mick Burgess, *Metal
Express Radio*, April 9, 2021
'That was our whole life ...' Ken Sharp, *Rock Cellar*,
June 14, 2021
'The whole British Invasion ...' *Gretsch News*,
July 6, 2016
'I was more of a fan ...' *In The Studio With
Redbeard*, April 4, 2021
'It was that sort of secondary ...' Rob Hughes,
Classic Rock, May 11, 2021

CHAPTER TWO
'After two years of piano ...' *It's Psychedelic Baby*,
June 30, 2015
'They did two sets ...' Bun E. Carlos comment at
www.drumforum.com
'because he came up with ...' Amit Sharma, *Total
Guitar*, November 10, 2017
'He was always the most ...' Michael Hann, *The
Quietus*, August 7, 2017
'I've played on stuff ...' Roger The Engineer, YouTube,
July 5, 2014
'We always had them in ...' Daisann McLane,
Rolling Stone, June 14, 1979
'they were playing almost day ...' Jim Lenahan,
Rockford Register Star, December 21, 1990
'We had a local hit in Rockford ...' Daisann
McLane, *Rolling Stone*, June 14, 1979
'All of the Dads drove us ...' Todd Houston, *Rock
River Times*, Nov 12–18, 2014
'Rick had a strobe light flashing ...' Mark Blake,
Planet Rock, December 2018
'I didn't want to be one of ...' BrainyQuote.com

CHAPTER THREE
'funny spinning sensation ...' Mark Ribowsky,
Dreams To Remember
'we had been told they were coming ...' Dave
Tianen, *Milwaukee Journal Sentinel*, December
10, 1997

'People were walking around ...' *Wisconsin State
Journal*, April 6, 2003
'We got on with our lives ...' Kristian Knutsen,
Isthmus, December 10, 2007
'Hendrix had it all ...' Michael Hann, *The Quietus*,
August 7, 2017
'Jimi Hendrix really drove me crazy ...' Patrick
Goldstein, *Chicago Daily News*, October 27,
1977
'I was a rhythm guitarist ...' / 'When I started ...' Jon
D'Auria, *Bass Player*, January 8, 2020
'I never liked it ...' Willie G. Mosley, *Vintage Guitar*,
April 2007
'There were eight people there ...' *Gibson TV*,
September 16, 2021
'Ken had been booking bands ...' Lynn Van Matre,
Chicago Tribune, December 14, 1980
'We got $80 to $100 a night ...' Natasha Kassulke,
Wisconsin State Journal, April 22, 1999
'Ken could still get bookings ...' Lynn Van Matre,
Chicago Tribune, December 14, 1980
'He sat his guitar on the top ...' Amit Sharma, *Total
Guitar*, November 10, 2017
'I said, You don't know me ...' *Rockin' The Suburbs*,
episode 1000, December 3, 2020
'Some Juniors and some Standards ...' Amit Sharma,
Total Guitar, November 10, 2017
'Rick: Grim Reapers was my band ...' Ira A. Robbins,
Music In A Word Volume 2
'My Dad had asthma ...' / 'I wouldn't go one more
minute ...' Brassneck, *Illinois Entertainer*, April
2021
'We got off the plane ...' Rob Hughes, *Classic Rock*,
May 11, 2021
'Halfway through their set ...' Rick Nielsen, *Cheap
Licks* bonus video
'At that time, The Beatles' *White Album* ...' *Gretsch
News*, July 6, 2016
'We walked about a block away ...' Kylie Olsson,
uDiscover Music, August 21, 2017
'Listened to them on acid ...' Michael Hann, *The
Quietus*, August 7, 2017
'It was the dual keyboard Mellotron ...' Jason Roth,
Daily Swarm, September 4, 2009
'He was telling us all about ...' Ella Stormack,
Orangeamps.com, July 4, 2017
'Rick was leading the band ...' *It's Psychedelic Baby*,
June 30, 2015

CHAPTER FOUR

'Epic were going to be there ...' *Rockford Register Republic*, November 24, 1969

'too dark ...' *It's Psychedelic Baby*, June 30, 2015

'Those guys pulled up ...' / 'I really liked your band ...' Ira A. Robbins, *Music In A Word Volume 2*

'It was something we did ...' James E. Sullivan, *Rockford Register Republic*, September 25, 1969

'the guys that were working ...' *Hit Parader*, April 1980

'The band was much better than ...' Ira Robbins, *Trouser Press*, February 1978

'The whole thing turned out to be ...' *Hit Parader*, April 1980

'They were fearless ...' Steve Matthes and Joe Moffett, *The Ultimate*

CHAPTER FIVE

'I saw a naked lady ...' djtees.com

'We waited all night ...' / 'We were to be the first band ...' *It's Psychedelic Baby*, June 30, 2015

'People used to go to college ...' Natasha Kassulke, *Wisconsin State Journal*, April 10, 1997

'So there we were ...' *It's Psychedelic Baby*, June 30, 2015

CHAPTER SIX

'He was there with ...' / 'I talked to him then ...' Steve Gett, *Guitar Heroes*, July 1983

'I really couldn't afford it ...' Dan Hyman, *Noisey*, April 5, 2016

'We were never too serious ...' Ira Robbins, *Trouser Press*, February 1978

'I tried to emigrate to Australia ...' Rod Yates, *Sydney Morning Herald*, July 5, 2018

'I couldn't go there because ...' Gwen Ihnat, *AV Club*, March 10, 2016

'I actually lived with her ...' Brassneck, *Illinois Entertainer*, April 2021

'I went there with the idea ...' Dave Zimmerman, *Rockford Morning Star*, January 16, 1972

'I saw him at a club ...' Ira A. Robbins, *Music In A Word Volume 2*

'It was a big place ...' / 'They had a huge sound ...' Brian Beebe Facebook post

'Everything seems crazy now ...' *The Pop Culture Show*, April 14, 2021

'I look bad with a beard ...' Christopher Borrelli, *Chicago Tribune*, August 16, 2012

CHAPTER SEVEN

'Rizzo kidnapped the fucking city ...' Jake Blumgart, Vice.com, October 22, 2015

'They turned us down ...' Dennis Getto, *Milwaukee Sentinel*, June 16, 1978

'We did the audition ...' / 'Rick said he got this thing ...' Ira A. Robbins, *Music in a Word Volume 2*

'the world's worst band name ...' Jason Roth, *Daily Swarm*, September 4, 2009

'They blew my mind ...' Joe Bosso, *Music Radar*

'I was living in Philly ...' *Talk Is Jericho*, episode 315

'I got a call from Paul Hamer ...' Bob Cianci, *Premier Guitar*, May 20, 2009

'I always bought used guitars ...' Dan Hyman, *Noisey*, April 5, 2016

'Ken Adamany, who'd been ...' Lynn Van Matre, *Lexington Leader*, April 17, 1980

'He was steamed ...' Tim Steagall, *Ugly Things*, Winter 2020

CHAPTER EIGHT

'I'd already had a taste ...' *Chris Demakes A Podcast*, episode 15

'we played as a trio until ...' Todd Houston, *Rock River Times*, Nov 12–18, 2014

'We got together in Rick's ...' / 'My wife at the time asked ...' Stew Erickson interview courtesy of Mike Hayes

'We're laughing it up ...' Temple Ray, *Gig For Working Musicians*, February/March 1989

'reaction to art rock goofballs ...' Natasha Kassulke, *Wisconsin State Journal*, April 10, 1997

'Where did you get your name?' *Super Rock*, December 1978

'They were telling us to ...' *Chris Demakes A Podcast*, episode 15

'Oh, you're actually working ...' Ira A. Robbins, *Music In A Word Volume 2*

'After Bo Diddley drank ...' Daisann McLane, *Rolling Stone*, June 14, 1979

'It was just a lot of rhythm ...' Rick Nielsen, *Cheap Licks* bonus video

'He said, I don't need …' John Rzeznick, *Chorus & Verse*, Sirius XM, May 2018

'never tell you what key it's in …' Rick Nielsen, *Cheap Licks* bonus video

'Chuck Berry let Rick do more …' / 'I learned more about the feel …' Salley Rayl, *Austin Daily Texan*, October 31, 1977

CHAPTER NINE

'We would almost never stop …' Ira A. Robbins, *Music In A Word Volume 2*

'Back then, people used to …' Willie G. Moseley, *Vintage Guitar*, June 10, 2020

'which turned into a drunk fest …' Rob Hughes, *Classic Rock*, May 11, 2021

'kinda mutual …' Andy Gannon, 23WIFR, April 1, 2016

'I remember going to a battle …' Simon Glickman, *Hits Daily Double*, December 11, 2015

CHAPTER TEN

'Trick needed a singer …' Michael Seymour, *Illinois Entertainer*, December 1977

CHAPTER ELEVEN

'It was young artists in hell …' Scott Starr, cheaptrick.com

'It was handmade when given …' Tim Steagall, *Ugly Things*, Winter 2020

'Tom immediately thought …' / 'a stroke of luck …' / 'I wish I could take some credit …' / 'I've thought to myself …' Scott Starr, cheaptrick.com

'It was like, Ahh …' Ed Symkus, *Savannah Morning News*, July 23, 2019

'When we got Robin …' *In The Studio With Redbeard*, February 29, 2019

'Early on, I was into …' Daisann McLane, *Rolling Stone*, June 14, 1979

'too antsy to sit …' Mike Vanderbilt, *Chicago Reader*, April 7, 2016

'little podunk towns …' Sheryl DeVore, *Lake County News-Sun*, February 23, 2017

'There'd be seven people …' Bill Locey, *Los Angeles Times*, January 3, 1994

'You can play for a week …' Temple Ray, *Gig For Working Musicians*, February/March 1989

'We weren't like anything else …' Thomas Wictor, *Bass Player*, July 1997

'setting progressively higher goals …' Richard Riegel, *Creem*, July 1979

'I'd start up a little shuffle …' Daisann McLane, *Rolling Stone*, June 14, 1979

'We usually played on these …' Dennis Getto, *Milwaukee Sentinel*, June 16, 1978

'All four of us in the band …' Robin Tolleson, *Modern Drummer*

'always waited until the end …' / 'I drank more beer …' Mike Vanderbilt, *Chicago Reader*, April 7, 2016

'Before you knew it …' Temple Ray, *Gig For Working Musicians*, February/March 1989

CHAPTER TWELVE

'completely depraved pervert …' R.C. Baker, *Village Voice*, August 22, 2017

'I remember that I could still …' Brad Elvis Facebook comment

''jumping around …' / 'thought the band was interesting …' Doug Brod, *They Just Seem A Little Weird*

'We said, Thanks for letting us play …' Michael Hann, *The Quietus*, August 7, 2017

'Who wanted new? …' John Rzeznick, *Chorus & Verse*, Sirius XM, May 2018

'I wouldn't give it back …' / 'bug races …' Mark Agnessi, Gibson TV, December 23, 2021

'really didn't hone stuff …' *Chris Demakes A Podcast*, episode 15

'We try to flush the idea out …' *The Underground Garage*, April 2021

'unpredictability …' / 'a mash of cool stuff …' / 'irreverence …' / 'couldn't be constrained …' Michael Hann, *The Quietus*, August 7, 2017

'Cheap Trick has absorbed …' Andy Mellen, *Winnipeg Free Press*, April 9, 1977

'Cheap Trick's British rocker sound …' Lawrence Keenan, *Illinois Entertainer*, January 1976

'Obviously we're influenced …' Temple Ray, *Gig For Working Musicians*, February/March 1989

'We experimented, tried all kinds …' Ira Robbins, *Trouser Press*, August 1978

'I thought it was Kentucky Jelly …' Mark Agnessi, Gibson TV, December 23, 2021

'When a band's music starts …' Lynn Van Matre, *Chicago Tribune*, March 2, 1980

CHAPTER THIRTEEN

'It was intense ...' Tom Beaujour with Richard Bienstock, *Nothin' But A Good Time*

'Lose $10,000 and go home ...' Jimmy Leslie, *GIG*, April 2003

'The first night there ...' Temple Ray, *Gig For Working Musicians*, February/March 1989

'Kim Fowley wanted to sign us ...' Ira A. Robbins, *Music In A Word Volume 2*

'He goes over to Rick ...' *In The Studio With Redbeard*, April 4, 2021

'He came up to us ...' Bill Kopp, *Tangents*, May 12, 2017

'He wanted to give us ...' John Rzeznick, *Chorus & Verse*, Sirius XM, May 2018

'Pezband lost a limb ...' Brad Elvis Facebook post

'We just kept going ...' Ken Sharp, *Rock Cellar*, June 14, 2021

CHAPTER FOURTEEN

'things would always ...' / 'He knew I liked my grandmother's piano ...' Corey Folta, *Tape Op* #90, July/August 2012

'I was playing anywhere I could ...' John Bard Manulis, *Ageist*, May 8, 2019

'They brought in girl background singers ...' Rod Harmon, *Houston Chronicle*, April 12, 2003

'We had sixteen-track machines ...' Joe Bosso, *Milwaukee Magazine*, December 19, 2012

'was totally obsessed with ...' Richard Buskin, *Sound On Sound*, December 2009

'it was a bit of a mismatch ...' Michael Summers, *Fort Wayne Reader*

'Todd made great records ...' Ben Yakas, *Gothamist*, July 20, 2016

'The sessions involved politics ...' Peter Makowski, *Classic Rock*, October 18, 2016

'He got in over his head ...' Corey Folta, *Tape Op* #90, July/August 2012

'Jack essentially did the grunt work ...' Rod Harmon, *Houston Chronicle*, April 12, 2003

'They were totally disorganised ...' / 'sounds like it was made ...' Richard Buskin, *Sound On Sound*, December 2009

'My reward for recording ...' Corey Folta, *Tape Op* #90, July/August 2012

'When I started producing ...' Jonathan Widran, *Close Up*, July 31, 2020

'Doing the record ...' Joe Bosso, *Milwaukee Magazine*, December 19, 2012

'By the time I finished ...' Corey Folta, *Tape Op* #90, July/August 2012

'They had a lounge ...' Bryan Wawzenek, *Ultimate Classic Rock*, February 11, 2017

'They had a show ...' Warren Huart, *Produce Like A Pro*, YouTube

'a combination of a carnival ...' / 'couldn't believe how good ...' / 'just knocked out by ...' / 'It was really loud ...' *Consequence Of Sound*, May 13, 2021

'Everything about them was tremendous ...' Joe Bosso, *Milwaukee Magazine*, December 19, 2012

CHAPTER FIFTEEN

'I called up Tom Werman ...' Joe Bosso, *Milwaukee Magazine*, December 19, 2012

'We were looking for talent ...' Greg Brodsky, *Best Classic Bands*, January 2018

'Get this—it didn't break ...' *Guitar Aficionado: The Collections*

'I've seen bands come out ...' BrainyQuote.com

'very extreme experience ...' Ira Robbins, *Trouser Press*, August 1978

'It was a long night ...' Sheryl Devore, *News–Sun*, February 23, 2017

'They had wooden shutters ...' / 'We always had a larger pool ...' / 'It seemed like the bigger clubs ...' Mike Vanderbilt, *Chicago Reader*, April 7, 2016

'We sat down at practice ...' *Cheap Trick: The Epic Archives Vol. 1* liner notes

'We had two sets of drums on stage ...' Ira Robbins, *Trouser Press*, August 1978

'We had a drummer and a half ...' Doug Brod, *They Just Seem A Little Weird*

'It was so good that I immediately ...' Ira Robbins, *Trouser Press*, August 1978

CHAPTER SIXTEEN

'came from playing clubs ...' Steve Morse, *Boston Globe*, May 24, 1979

'When you see Cheap Trick ...' Jeffrey Peisch, *Record World*, October 20, 1979

'I've always liked to ...' Ryan Roxie, *In The Trenches*, August 5, 2020

'I wrote it at home ...' Joe Bosso, *Guitar Player*, October 14, 2020

'You can lose a lot ...' Adrian Thrills, *Zig Zag*, June 1978

'We were kind of the perfect band ...' Brassneck, *Illinois Entertainer*, April 2021

'It's my business card ...' George Manno, *Vintage Guitar*, September 1997

'For the first couple of years ...' Brassneck, *Illinois Entertainer*, April 2021

'I wasn't a sex-god ...' David Burke, *Quad City Times*, Jul 26, 2014

'Do you know what people say ...' Todd Markel, NAMM 2019 interview, YouTube

'We were standing backstage ...' Brett Christensen, *Wisconsin Music*, October 15, 2018

'One of our last shows before ...' Tom Beaujour, *Guitar Aficionado*, October 1, 2012

'B.Ginnings was really good ...' Mike Vanderbilt, *Chicago Reader*, April 7, 2016

'Before we even made ...' Ken Sharp, *Goldmine*, July 5, 2016

'I'll tell you another band ...' Warren Zanes, *Petty*

'They were good, but ...' Tim Steagall, *Ugly Things*, Winter 2020

'So I'm talking with this guy ...' / 'They hit the stage ...' Warren Zanes, *Petty*

CHAPTER SEVENTEEN

'We had enough songs where ...' Chris Demakes A Podcast, episode 15

'I wanted the first album ...' Warren Huart, *Produce Like A Pro*, YouTube

'tried to pick songs that ...' Mike Hayes with Ken Sharp. *Reputation Is A Fragile Thing*

'Our songs are not just ...' *Madcity Music Sheet* #37

'How we can move this ...' Corey Folta, *Tape Op* #90, July/August 2012

'I was just wanting to comment ...' Ken Sharp, *Goldmine*, November 9, 2017

'A song that's gooey ...' Joe Bosso, *Music Radar*, April 12, 2012

'It's not planned out that much ...' Mike Davies, *Nuggets* issue #10, University of Birmingham

'We're not into that ...' Jim Farber, *Circus*, July 6 1978

'weird enough and cool enough ...' *Chris Demakes A Podcast*, episode 15

'"Lookout" is fun ...' Joe Bosso, *Music Radar*, April 12, 2012

'We did it really fast ...' Joe Bosso, *Milwaukee Magazine*, December 19, 2012

'I like records that sound ...' Michael Hann, *The Quietus*, August 7, 2017

'Back then, when we did ...' Mitch Gallagher, *The Sweetwater Minute* Vol. 205

'We used a brand new technique ...' Tom Wheeler, *Guitar Player*, November 1979

'Rehearse so we're in the ballpark ...' Corey Folta, *Tape Op* #90, July/August 2012

'you can't have a great album ...' Joe Bosso, *Music Radar*, December 19, 2012

'I never use any pedals ...' BrainyQuote.com

'Prototype ...' / 'sounded great ...' / 'got stolen ...' Tim Stegall, *Ugly Things*, Spring 2021

'weird-looking guitar ...' / 'I think it was made by Olympic ...' Shawn Hammond, *Premier Guitar*, May 17, 2016

'It's the only bass ...' Willie G. Moseley, *Vintage Guitar*, June 10, 2020

'When I saw Mitch Mitchell ...' Robin Tolleson, *Modern Drummer*

'It was the coolest place ...' Max McAllister, producelikeapro.com, June 9, 2020

'different than anything ...' *Circus*, May 26, 1977

'Yogi Berra lived next door ...' Mitch Gallagher, *The Sweetwater Minute* Vol. 205

'Literally, I was smitten ...' / 'Smashes it to his forehead ...' / 'That's one detail I can't remember ...' Doug Brod, *They Just Seem A Little Weird*

'I always wanted to have that voice ...' Ryan Roxie, *In The Trenches*, August 5, 2020

'He works more by instinct ...' Nick Kent, *NME*, September 8, 1979

'That's my personality ...' Daisann McLane, *Rolling Stone*, June 14, 1979

'go from a loverboy ...' Adrian Thrills, *Zig Zag*, June 1978

'Epic got a good deal ...' Ira Robbins, *Creem*, August 1977

CHAPTER EIGHTEEN

'Thin Lizzy wasn't gonna show up ...' Joe Bonamassa, *Live from Nerdville*, episode 19

'We were always involved ...' Ira A. Robbins, *Music In A Word Volume 2*

'The Japanese press was there ...' Dan Hyman, *Noisey*, April 5, 2016

'After the show ...' Steve Hyden, *Uproxx*, March 26, 2021

'To me a record or a song ...' *Consequence Of Sound*, May 13, 2021

CHAPTER NINETEEN

'Being an only child ...' Ryan Roxie, *In The Trenches*, August 5, 2020

'We tried to learn that number ...' Ira Robbins, *Trouser Press*, February 1978

'It's always been kind of ...' Gwen Ihnat, *AV Club*, March 10, 2016

'It's a reversal of roles ...' Mike Davies, *Nuggets* issue #10, University of Birmingham

'I was writing that before ...' Gwen Inhat, *AV Club*, March 10, 2016

'the Richard Gere non-lookalike ...' BrainyQuote. com

'refers to all sorts of things ...' Mike Davies, *Nuggets* issue #10, University of Birmingham

'I think we said ...' Ira A. Robbins, *Music In A Word Volume 2*

'Like fiddling while Rome burns ...' Brassneck, *Illinois Entertainer*, April 2021

'I really didn't know the instrument ...' Ken Sharp, *Play On!*

'I've always liked stuff ...' Craig Gieck, *Night Sites & Sounds*, January 19–February 1, 1995

'the strings vibrate at a different rate ...' Tom Wheeler, *Guitar Player*, November 1979

'They weren't a very popular ...' Ira A. Robbins, *Music In A Word Volume 2*

'the groups I'm most into ...' Robert Hilburn, *Los Angeles Times*, July 10, 1977

'not all bad guys are ...' / 'Of course I'm not saying ...' Ken Sharp, *Play On!*

'I wrote that song with two meanings ...' Philippe, *I Wanna Be Your Dog*, issue #7, November 1977

'The line was ...' *Melody Maker*, February 11, 1978

'The only people that really listened ...' Brassneck, *Illinois Entertainer*, April 2021

'Here was a guy who committed suicide ...' Mike Hayes with Ken Sharp, *Reputation Is A Fragile Thing*

'it was too rough ...' Ira A. Robbins, *Music In A Word Volume 2*

'Jack Douglas is great ...' Ken Sharp, *Rock Cellar*, June 14, 2021

CHAPTER TWENTY

'He had dark hair ...' Sandy Robertson, *Sounds*, February 10, 1979

'That bio was written by ...' Daisann McLane, *Rolling Stone*, June 14, 1979

'told him the truth but ...' *In The Studio With Redbeard*, February 29, 2019

'Tom used to be a great ...' Dierdre Wilson, YouTube interview

'some of the group could be said ...' Cristofer Gross, *Van Nuys Valley News*, April 1, 1977

'People compare us to The Beatles ...' James Simon, *Associated Press*, December 28, 1979

'was hoping that it would hit ...' *Consequence Of Sound*, May 13, 2021

'too harsh for most people ...' Ira Robbins, *Trouser Press*, August 1978

'If people don't get it ...' Allan Campbell, *Hot Wacks* #18, 1979

'adjust my thinking and philosophy ...' Dave Zimmerman, *Sunday Magazine*, April 10, 1977

'written on his fucking eyelids ...' Doug Brod, *They Just Seem A Little Weird*

'There's lots of bands ...' Allan Campbell, *Hot Wacks* #18, 1979

CHAPTER TWENTY-ONE

'When our first album came out ...' Tom Wheeler, *Guitar Player*, November 1979

'We had become a hit ...' Steven Uhles, *Augusta Chronicle*, October 10, 2019

'Hours of great music ...' Tracy Sirotti, 'An Interview with Jackie Fox,' March 12, 1998

'That was just the very beginning ...' Dirk Belligerent, *Motor City Blog*

'the recording was terrible ...' / 'took a $75 cassette machine ...' / 'the performance was brilliant ...' Cary Baker, *Triad*, September 30, 1977

'But this woman ...' Dave Zimmerman, *Rockford Morning Star*, April 10, 1977

'The Kinks were one of my ...' N. Kelly, *Independent.ie*, May 28 2011

'The booking agency we were using ...' Martin Popoff, *Classic Rock Revisited*, June 30, 2016

'We did one record ...' Andrew Magnotta, Q104.3, April 13, 2021

'People would say to us ...' Ken Sharp, *Rock Cellar*, June 14, 2021

'That's when the drugs weren't working ...' Warren Huart, *Produce Like A Pro*

'Music was always the main thing ...' / 'Lew was a reasonably creative guy ...' Tom Beaujour, *Tape Op* #102, July/August 2014

'Paul Zone took me to see ...' Kristian Hoffman, Facebook comment

'The Whisky was packed ...' Ken Sharp, *Out Ta Get You* liner notes

'The basic blowback from the label ...' Martin Popoff, *Classic Rock Revisited*, June 30, 2016

'captured the band pretty much ...' Greg Brodsky, *Best Classic Bands*, January 8, 2018

'wasn't there when it was going on ...' / 'told them what I was looking for ...' / 'He did a good job ...' Joe Matera, ultimateguitar.com, August 19, 2009

'real boppy ...' / 'I didn't hate it ...' / 'Yardbirds-ish ...' Leeno Dee, *Sentinel Daily*, March 12, 2022

'We had a really good time ...' / 'I never mixed a record ...' Chuck Harrell, KUTV, July 14, 2009

'*In Color*, no matter what ...' *The Jeremy White Podcast*, episode 30

'Presley's voice was slurred ...' Jim Haley, *Des Moines Register*, June 24, 1977

'We wanted to call the album ...' *In The Studio With Redbeard*, April 4, 2021

'I only shot black and white ...' Charles Giuliano, *Rolling Stone*, August 25, 2014

'It was raining out ...' *In The Studio With Redbeard*, April 4, 2021

'I had to extricate us ...' Doug Brod, *They Just Seem A Little Weird*

CHAPTER TWENTY-TWO

'Who is Gene going to ...' / 'Why are you wearing that ...' Doug Brod, *They Just Seem A Little Weird*

'Uncle Gene ...' michaelcavacini.com, February 7, 2015

'under the weather ...' / 'he just wasn't feeling good ...' / ''obvious that there was something else ...' Curt Gooch with Jeff Suhs, *KISS Alive Forever*

'I don't think Peter was familiar ...' / 'could have stumbled through it ...' Doug Brod, *They Just Seem A Little Weird*

'he was really drumming good ...' *CMJ New Music Report*, 1998

'I flew into LA ...' beatlemaniaalumni.com/ TonyKishman.htm

'a very good break ...' Doug Brod, *They Just Seem A Little Weird*

'This was on our big nights ...' Temple Ray, *Gig For Working Musicians*, February/March 1989

'tried to take a Fleetwood Mac riff ...' *In The Studio With Redbeard*, April 4, 2021

'I learned it from Stewkey ...' / 'He was so shocked ...' Ira A. Robbins, *Music In A Word Volume 2*

'One person's Caroline ...' Salley Rand, *Circus*, October 27, 1977

'They'll do anything to make ...' Elizabeth Reich, *Fun Times*

'We were all dressed in weird outfits ...' / 'Chairs were going ...' Mick Wall, *Like A Bat Out Of Hell*

'giving me the finger ...' Ira A. Robbins, *Music In A Word Volume 2*

'through the snow and wind ...' Jim Bessman, jimbessman.com, November 9, 2015

'make an evangelical announcement ...' Elvis Costello, *Unfaithful Music & Disappearing Ink*

'poised with pitchforks ...' Jim Bessman, jimbessman. com, November 9, 2015

'Cheap Trick would become ...' Elvis Costello, *Unfaithful Music & Disappearing Ink*

'We came on KLOS ...' / 'It was like ...' Richard Bienstock, *Billboard*, April 8, 2016

'That was our one chance ...' Tom Beaujour, *Guitar Player*, August 23, 2021

CHAPTER TWENTY-THREE

'We had three days of rehearsal ...' / 'with mixing ...' Ira Robbins, *Trouser Press*, August 1978

'I went over to his house ...' Johnny Black, *Blender*, June 2003

'getting the low end ...' / 'didn't track well ...' Britt Strickland, *Bass Player*, July 2006

'Musicians often came up ...' Jon Bream, *Minneapolis Star*, July 20, 1979

'sound to be as big as possible ...' orangeamps.com

'They thought the neck ...' Britt Strickland, *Bass Player*, July 2006

'After I had the bass ...' Christopher Buttner, *12 String Bass Encyclopedia*

'When that worked ...' / 'I wanted the piano sound ...' Britt Strickland, *Bass Player*, July 2006

'I think we had already ...' Mark Rowe, *12 String Bass Encyclopedia*

'The longer the scale ...' Petra Jones, *Music Mart*, March 2006

'had this preamp he called ...' Mark Rowe, *12 String Bass Encyclopedia*

'The twelve-string bass isn't ...' Britt Strickland, *Bass Player*, July 2006

'It really adds dimension ...' Tom Wheeler, *Guitar Player*, November 1979

'It's supposed to sound ...' Thomas Victor, *Bass Player*, July 1997

'I always use a pick ...' Britt Strickland, *Bass Player*, July 2006

'a lot of palm-muting ...' Jon D'Auria, *Bass Player*, January 8, 2020

'If you want a heavier sound ...' / 'It isn't possible to get ...' Britt Strickland, *Bass Player*, July 2006

'The idea is to play through ...' Jon D'Auria, *Bass Player*, January 8, 2020

'It's certainly easier to play ...' Ira A. Robbins, *Music In A Word Volume 2*

'the best band I've seen since ...' Ira Robbins, *Trouser Press*, August 1978

'They're great cus ...' *BOMP*, January 1979

EPILOGUE

'We were like cartoon characters ...' / It had a lot to do with ...' Dan Rather, *The Big Interview*

'We left Chicago a local band ...' Tom Lounges, *Northwest Indiana Times*, May 1, 1998

'There was cab after cab ...' *Goldmine*, December 23, 2008

'About fifteen minutes before ...' Bill DeYoung, April 4, 2020

'It hadn't caught on anywhere else ...' Library of Congress, March 30, 2020

'The girls started shouting out ...' Tom Lounges, *Northwest Indiana Times*, May 1, 1998

'He liked some of the weird stuff ...' Mark Agnessi, Gibson TV, December 23, 2021

'Harvey Leeds from Epic ...' / 'Harvey gave me a copy ...' Murray Engleheart with Arnold Durieux, *AC/DC: Maximum Rock & Roll*

'Pamela was practically ...' / 'worked as a roadie ...' We would blast ...' Mike Sacks, *Vice*, August 31, 2009

'We didn't like the recording ...' *Elliot In The Morning*

'After *Heaven Tonight* ...' Martin Popoff, *Goldmine*, June 25, 2018

'By the time *Budokan* came along ...' Steven Uhles, *Augusta Chronicle*, October 10, 2019

'about a million bucks in the hole ...' *Legendary Rock Interviews*, November 5, 2012

'If it weren't for *Budokan* ...' Ken Sharp, *Classic Rock*, October 15, 2008

ALSO AVAILABLE FROM JAWBONE PRESS